MONEY MANAGEMENT

CREATIVE PERSON

BOOKS BY LEE SILBER

NONFICTION

Money Management for the Creative Person
Self-Promotion for the Creative Person
Career Management for the Creative Person
Time Management for the Creative Person
Aim First!
Notes, Quotes & Advice
Successful San Diegans
The Guide to Dating in San Diego

FICTION

Summer Stories
Tales from America's Finest City

MONEY MANAGEMENT

FOR THE

CREATIVE PERSON

RIGHT-BRAIN STRATEGIES TO BUILD YOUR BANK ACCOUNT AND FIND THE FINANCIAL FREEDOM TO CREATE

LEE SILBER

THREE RIVERS PRESS • NEW YORK

Published by Three Rivers Press, New York, New York.
Member of the Crown Publishing Group,
a division of Random House, Inc.

www.randomhouse.com

THREE RIVERS PRESS and the Tugboat design are registered
trademarks of Random House, Inc.

Printed in the United States of America

Design by Rhea Braunstein

Library of Congress Cataloging-in-Publication Data
Silber, Lee T.
Money management for the creative person : right-brain strategies to
build your bank account and find the financial freedom to create /
Lee Silber.
1. Finance, Personal—United States—Popular works.   2. Artists—
United States—Finance, Personal.   3. Financial security.   I. Title:
Right-brain strategies to build your bank account and find the
financial freedom to create.   II. Title.
HG179.S473   2002
322.024'01—dc21   2002018132

ISBN 0-609-80625-4

10   9   8   7   6   5   4   3   2   1

FIRST EDITION

This book is for creative people who want
the financial freedom to create what they want,
when they want, and how they want—
and get paid handsomely for their efforts.

CONTENTS

Acknowledgments   viii

Introduction   x

Money Myths and the Creative Person   xiii

1: The Creative Life   1

2: Be Careful What You Wish For   38

3: Get Out of Your Own Way   73

4: Give Yourself a Raise   124

5: Cover Your Ass-ets   181

6: It's What You Keep That Counts   221

7: Creative Ways to Save   274

Contact Information   317

Bonus Chapter: I Did It My Way   318

Bibliography   319

Index   323

ACKNOWLEDGMENTS

In the movie *The Muse,* Albert Brooks plays a writer who has lost his edge. His best friend, played by Jeff Bridges, sets up a meeting with a real live muse (Sharon Stone), who offers to help him get back on track—for a price. It seems that this muse has some very specific needs (and expensive taste) like a suite at the Four Seasons, a limousine, and gifts from Tiffany's. In my experience I have found it is much more efficient (and cheaper) just to say "Thanks" to those who have helped me, and what better place to do that than at the beginning of a book.

Just saying "thanks" doesn't seem like enough when it comes to my agent (and muse), Toni Lopopolo. As you will soon read in this book, a career in the creative arts is like a roller coaster with thrilling highs, unexpected twists and turns, and a few low points. It's helpful having someone seated next to you who is along for the ride and has also been there before. Toni has guided the career of many a writer, and I feel so fortunate to have her helping me now.

When a writer thanks his editor, many times he does it through clenched teeth. I can honestly say I am genuinely thankful for my editor, Becky Cabaza. I'm lucky enough to have one of the best in the business! She is equally adept at helping with the business side of a book as she is with the art of writing it. Like any good muse, she is just demanding enough to keep me on my toes and knows when to stand back and let the creative process work its magic.

It would seem that a muse's work is never done, and that's why

I'd like to thank Carrie Thornton. As a muse's assistant (she was Becky's right-hand woman), Carrie dealt with a lot of the dirty little details that go into making a book possible and did it both effectively and efficiently. She did them so well, in fact, she is now an editor in her own right—my editor!

Muses work in mysterious ways. Sometimes it can be a subtle thing and other times they hit you over the head to get you to pay attention. This next muse is more the latter than the former. My mom has taken over the role of grammarian and fact-checker for my books, and she takes this job very seriously. Not much gets by my mom. I tend to write fast and furious and don't worry too much about "little" things like spelling and punctuation. Thankfully, my mom is there to save me (again) from making a fool out of myself.

In mythology there are nine total muses. I've already told you about four of mine so far. Let me now thank the other four, including my assistant Susan Guzzetta, my mentors Joseph Oppenheimer and Mary-Ellen Drummond, and my biggest inspiration of all, my wife, Andrea.

I realize that is only eight muses. There is one more I haven't thanked yet—you, the reader! You are the real "without whom" I need to thank. Over the past few years (and three books in this series) you have provided me with inspiration, ideas, and insights on the creative life that have proven invaluable to these books. In this book you will learn that money isn't everything and that couldn't be more true than when it comes to writing these books. The best part of the process isn't cashing the advance check or seeing the sales numbers; it's when someone takes the time to write to me and say that one of my books made a difference in their life. The warm fuzzy feeling a letter like that leaves me with is priceless.

Without ruining the suspense of the movie *The Muse,* let's just say it has a happy ending. I want to thank everyone who has been a part of the process of writing this book. It's been a pleasure working with you, my muses, and I owe you all big-time. (Fade to black.)

INTRODUCTION

*"I used to think that letting others handle my finances gave me
more creative freedom. I have discovered that you can
actually have more creative freedom when you control your
own financial and business matters."*
—David Bowie

A recent study showed that women think more about money than
sex. Hmmmm. I would never try to guess what women want. That
would be foolish. However, when it comes to creative people and
their money, I think I have a good grasp of what we are after. We
want some sense of financial security and *total* creative freedom. We
want to be able to concentrate on our art (and lives) without constantly having to worry about money. We want to make money without having to compromise our artistic integrity or take on projects
and jobs we loathe. We want to be able to do what we want, when we
want, and how we want. In short, we want *freedom*. The freedom to
do something meaningful or to try new things. The freedom to take
risks with our art and to be able to concentrate on our artistic endeavors full-time and maybe even work for ourselves if we want to. In our
personal lives we would like the financial freedom to travel or take
time off. We would also like freedom from our debt and other financial burdens. Want to know something? It's all possible.

There are plenty of creative people who have achieved this kind
of financial freedom, so we know it can be done. This book will show
you how to do it. (Isn't that reassuring?) Everything you need to
know about how to survive and thrive as a creative person is here in
your hand (presented in a fun and easy-to-read format, I might add).
You are about to get an education about how money works so that
you can gain power over it, get a handle on it, and make it work for

you. You will learn how to earn more money so you can attain financial and creative freedom and how to handle it once you get it.

This book contains real-world, streetwise financial advice from someone who has made it, lost it, and made it back again. It's a hands-on, how-to book. Reading and applying what you learn will produce lasting change in you and how you manage your money no matter how desperate your situation or how delinquent you've been in dealing with your finances. There is no need to punish yourself for your previous problems with money. We will be working on your financial *future,* and this book will serve as a coach, counselor, consultant, and, above all, a supportive companion offering sound advice and encouragement concerning all areas of your finances. So relax and enjoy the ride as we transform your finances from chaos and crisis to control and calm. We will get rid of your debt and despair and replace them with your dreams and desires. Really!

To achieve this we'll take an appropriately unconventional approach to all aspects of money management. No matter how many left-brained (conventional and boring) books you may have (tried to) read about finance, this book is different. Where other books attempt to use a one-size-fits-all approach, we will take a fresh look at a subject that many artists (of all kinds) struggle with. That's why we will take existing financial advice and mold it to fit the unorthodox lifestyle and challenges of creative people. We will delve into the basics of financial management, but then quickly veer off into new territory that is unique to creative people and their special circumstances and challenges. Instead of trying to cram a square peg into a round hole, we will take a decidedly different approach that matches up with, and makes use of your strengths. In fact, we will work with rather than against, your right-brain tendencies. This book shows you how to put your financial life in order in a way that you can both understand and embrace. It solves the mystery of making (and keeping) money with a very creative approach that feels natural and comfortable.

Before we begin, let me tell you a little about the structure of this book. It is written so readers can jump around (something the right brain loves to do) and find the information they need when they need it. You may notice that certain concepts and creative solutions are repeated. This was necessary for those who choose not to read the book cover to cover (sigh) but still need to know what to do. This book is like a buffet doled out in bite-sized morsels, so you won't choke on it. You can read in small helpings or gorge yourself: It's up to you. I suggest reading this book with an index card for a bookmark. When you find something that makes sense to you, write it down on your card and compile a list of action items you will apply in your life.

MONEY MYTHS AND THE CREATIVE PERSON

"I'm not overdrawn. I'm simply under-deposited."
—Mary Hunt

Myth: Once I hit it big, I am set for life.
REALITY: The creative life is a series of ups and downs. It pays to save for the down times.

Myth: Financial management is boring.
REALITY: True enough. But when we are talking about *your* money, doesn't it suddenly become more titillating? Thought so. Plus, dealing with the business side of the arts gives you a productive break from creating.

Myth: If I had more money, I could do what I want.
REALITY: You can do what you want now. It is about your choices. You could choose to cut back on your overhead and spend more time on your art right now.

Myth: When it comes to money, better safe than sorry.
REALITY: You shouldn't risk it all, but you must take a risk— on yourself. That is the best investment of all.

Myth: Everything in my life will be better when I have money.
REALITY: Having some money is better than no money at all, but as the saying goes, "Wherever you go, there you are." If you're not happy now, you won't be because you have more money.

Myth: My goal should be to do whatever I have to so I'll have enough money to retire early.

REALITY: If you love what you do, why retire? Your goal should be to find a better way to earn your money, something you enjoy doing so much you won't ever want to quit.

Myth: You have to be famous to make a fortune.

REALITY: Fame doesn't pay the bills, and it's fleeting. There are many more enjoyable, creative, and respectable jobs behind the scenes than there are glamorous jobs. Doing good work (that you enjoy) is more important.

Myth: If I make money at my art, I will lose my creative edge.

REALITY: Not having enough money to live on makes you desperate, angry, and can get in the way of your creativity.

Myth: Highly educated people get rich.

REALITY: Ha! It takes common sense—street smarts as well as book smarts—to make and manage money. Anyone can learn how.

Myth: If I made more money, I would save more.

REALITY: The more you make, the more you spend. You can save at any income.

Myth: I don't have to plan for my future. I plan to die young.

REALITY: The average life span is increasing every decade. It really is better to plan a little now and avoid suffering later.

Myth: There isn't enough money to support all the arts.

REALITY: You only have to worry about money for *your* art.

Myth: Artists have to work as waiters or cabbies just to get by.

REALITY: You may have to take a "day job," but it does *not* have to be drudgery. The best day job is in the field you are trying to break into. That way, you can gain experience, make contacts, and take on something you enjoy.

Myth: The only real artists are starving artists.

REALITY: Some art forms simply do not pay well, no matter how many dues you pay. But making money at your art does not mean you are a sellout. It means you are smart enough to find a market for what you love to do.

Myth: Because I work for someone else, I am an employee.

REALITY: We are all freelancers. When you work for someone else, he is your client. He may be your *only* client, but you still are a freelancer. Besides, the most likely way to get great wealth is from working for yourself.

Myth: Show me the money.

REALITY: Give me the money. You must demand to be paid and feel as if you deserve it.

Myth: I am an artist, so conventional financial management doesn't apply to me.

REALITY: There are some sound (and simple) things that you can do to get ahead.

Myth: Do what you love, and the money will follow.

REALITY: You must market yourself and your creations, and there needs to be a market to market to.

Myth: I'm in such bad financial shape, I'll never get out of it.

REALITY: You are resourceful and resilient. You can bounce back.

Myth: Those people pitching get-rich-quick schemes sound sincere.

REALITY: Uh, no. They usually are not money experts. They are scam artists.

Myth: I need to hit home runs with every project and score big.

REALITY: Little things add up.

Myth: Money comes from a salary. I have to work for it.

REALITY: Welcome to the "royalty" family. Royalties rule!

Myth: Hot stock tips are how people pick stocks.

REALITY: Bad idea. Do your due diligence. Then spread the wealth and the risk among several stocks or in a mutual fund.

Myth: I don't have to worry about the future, because something or someone will come along and save me or bail me out.

REALITY: What if they don't? You should be self-sufficient and solvent on your own.

1

THE CREATIVE LIFE

"People say I'm a millionaire, but that's not true—
I only spent millions."
—Robert Plant of Led Zeppelin

Most books about money management should include the disclaimer "This book may cause drowsiness and severe boredom." Oh my gawd, are some of these books dry (and mostly irrelevant for the creative person). I can't tell you how many times I have found myself facedown asleep in a book about financial management: I think I have finally found a cure for my insomnia. What I didn't find was a lot of useful information in preparation for writing this book. When I awoke from my "naps" inside yet another boring book on finances for left-brainers, I would first wipe the drool from my chin and then write little notes to myself like, "Whatever you do, don't write a boring book," and "Remember, right-brain!" and "Write outside the lines." I did my best to make this book interesting, relevant, and reader-friendly.

For some strange reason, left-brainers who write about the financial world tend to complicate things by using stupid formulas, silly terminology, and some really ridiculous ideas about what to do with your money. Why? My guess is, to make themselves feel important and useful (and to make us feel like idiots and incapable of dealing with this stuff on our own). You are NOT stupid, and you CAN do this without the help of a money chaperone. Just because you don't understand their lame lingo doesn't mean you don't know anything about money. Some of your best assets as a creative, right-brain person can be used to your advantage when it comes to making and managing money. When it comes to finances, thinking outside the box can actually be a good thing (within reason), and I believe the creative person has a lot of advantages over others in this area. All we lack is the knowledge about how money works so we can make educated (if not impulsive) decisions about what to do with our dollars. This book helps to demystify money so you can manage it (effectively) yourself.

It's a simple truth that the more you learn (about money), the more you earn. I will show you a simple, straightforward, and creative approach to money management. You don't have to deal with the details, but you at least need to know a little something about how finances work so you can make informed decisions. Many creative people are clueless about financial matters. Yet money is an integral part of the creative life whether you are aware of that fact or not. Having it can create a feeling of abundance, confidence, joy, validation, security, satisfaction, and freedom. The goal of this book is for you to experience freedom. Freedom from financial ruin. Freedom from debt. Freedom from stress. Freedom from horrible work. To free your mind from money hassles so that you can do what you do best—create. To go from being financially dependent (on others, your day job, and even your work) to being financially independent through a brand-new (healthy) mind-set about money, along with proven techniques blended with some unorthodox (to non-artists) ideas about how to earn, spend, invest, and save your hard-earned greenbacks without the worry or guilt that can sometimes accompany doing things that don't feel natural or are out of alignment with your beliefs. (Translation: You won't lose any sleep by doing what this book recommends, and you won't need to take a shower to wash away the dirt of doing something sleazy or selling out.)

This book is designed to help you make money with your creativity. (Make that a lot of money.) And why not? You deserve it. If not you, then who should be reaping the benefits of your ideas, talents, and hard work? Someone is going to be paid big bucks, and in my opinion it should be you. Then we will tackle how to manage all that money they lavish on you without letting it slip through your fingers.

Maybe you aren't aware of the importance of money in your life as an artist. That's a problem right there. No matter how hard you try, I will never be convinced that money isn't a major concern in your life. Maybe you aren't motivated by dollars and sense—oops, cents—but it is exactly that same thinking that kills so many creative people's careers. What's wrong with profiting from your art just like any other business? I was once in a band that was run like a Third World country (complete with its own benevolent dictator), and I knew it could never be a superpower because we spent all of our earnings on beer. Then we had to dip into our own pockets for demos, flyers, equipment, and other expenses.

The answer is to take a businesslike approach to running the business side of your artistic endeavors. If you don't, for whatever reason—lack of interest, lack of knowledge, or just plain neglect—the dream dies. How can we be creative with unpaid bills, little or no savings, debt, and a myriad of other potential pitfalls hanging over our heads? The answer is: We can't. Living a creative life is a unique challenge that is made more difficult because we must balance our need for money with sacrificing our artistic integrity. It is done with dignity all the time, and you can do it, too.

To me, making money at my art is insurance against having to live a boring, normal, uncreative (and thus unfulfilled) life. Somewhere along the line, artists pick up the attitude that being disinterested in money is noble. It is NOT easy to make money at art—it's almost impossible when you aren't even trying. I was never quite that bad, but making money was at the *bottom* of my top-ten list. I think that once I learned a little about the energy that surrounds money and how to harness it, I found it to be fun (yes, fun) to try to improve my financial situation. (And once I woke up my left brain and introduced it to my right brain, the two are happily managing my money quite nicely, thank you.) Then, once my finances were under control, I was able to focus and improve other areas of my life. This is what I want for you, too.

We need to counteract some of the negative things we're always hearing about how hard it is to make money in the creative arts. I keep profiles of people who either "didn't get the memo" or made it anyway by saying, "The hell with it, this is what I want to do—money or no money," and made it. This book is packed with positive stories of other creative people who have persevered and profited!

You don't even need a lot of money to benefit from this book. When we have nothing (and know very little about how to have more), it seems impossible to imagine ourselves with wealth and financial health. But don't write off your chances because you have no formal education in this area, aren't good with math, lack the ability to focus, and have done some dumb things in the past. Most of all, don't accept the labels others may have put on you (flake, dreamer, starving artist). No matter how much or how little you make now, we can help you make more or, at least, better manage what you have. No matter where you are, you can either get out of it or improve upon the situation.

We will look at small, simple steps you can take right away that will make an immediate impact on your finances. Managing money can be an enjoyable (doable) experience (surprise), and anyone can do it. People with wealth are not always the sharpest tools in the shed. Financial advisers are not gurus—they are people who got the special decoder cards in college so they can decipher all that money-related mumbo jumbo—but most don't have what you have: innovative, creative, right-brained thinking. So if you take it one step at a time, it's not complicated, and you can get your mind around it without much effort. Above all, it isn't as boring as it sounds (at least I am trying to make it as much fun as possible). Think of this as you would approach a blank canvas. You can dream up what you want to see and then start applying the processes in this book, along with your own ideas and insights, to create a masterpiece that you can be proud of. I promise.

💰 FAST FACT

According to a survey by Unity Marketing, spending in the United States on fine art and reproductions in 1999 was over $33 billion. Wow, there is money in the arts, after all!

It'll Work If You Work It

"My goal was riches in the uppermost strata."

—Harry Nilsson

This book will change your life. I know that is quite a claim, but I assure you that it isn't false advertising and there is no bait-and-switch. This is the real deal. Most books you have read on this subject were probably okay. Maybe you read them and said, "That's nice," and went back to your old ways. I *promise* this book is different—better. No matter where you are—swimming in money or drowning in debt—you will learn a lot about what it takes to achieve financial and creative freedom. You will also learn how to protect what you have, because as Adlai Stevenson said, "There was a time when a fool and his money were soon parted, but now it happens to everybody." Why is that?

• Many creative people (and I will put myself in this category, too) have ignored this important area of our lives for far too long and have picked up some bad habits that have hindered our ability to get a handle on our finances. Savings? Ha! "I don't need no stinkin' savings. I could die tomorrow. Let's party." "Record checks as I write them? Puh-leeze, who has the time? Besides, it's great not knowing what I don't have. I feel filthy rich." "Investing? That's for those pencil-neck, tie-wearing, regular folks. Not me. No way."

Let me ask you something: Where has this thinking gotten us? By ignoring this important part of our lives, it has atrophied. It's okay, it can be rehabilitated with some financial therapy, and we can gain that (financial) flexibility again. Call it freedom of movement. If you can stretch your thinking, you will have the ability to do what you want, when you want, how you want. Like all therapy (mental and otherwise), it takes time, and there may be some physical pain as well as some emotional baggage to work through, but in the end we are soooooo much better off for having gone through it. You will shout, "It's a miracle!"

• Maybe we don't have the same skills that left-brainers do that makes managing money seem like second nature to them. Our makeup is certainly different, and better, and we may never come to like bookkeeping, billing, and budgeting, but like any business (and we artists are in business, like it or not), letting these things go leads to chaos. When it comes to managing money, chaos is bad. So we can work with our strengths, overcome our weaknesses, and become better money managers. It's not only possible, it's gonna happen (if you continue to read this book and apply the principles in it).

• It's hard to watch others make millions, buy new homes, take exotic vacations, and live their dreams while we are barely making $20,000 a year from our art (and that is a good year!). We resign ourselves to the fact that our parents were right—becoming an artist is a hard way to make a living, we are destined to be destitute for the rest of our sorry-lives, only a fortunate few ever make a living from their art, and the rest of us have to struggle to support ourselves. We wallow in self-pity, feeling helpless and frustrated. We scream, "I'm having an out-of-money experience, here!" *Or* we see ourselves as that freakish exception to the rule, the one that fights through and uses that frustration to get fired up and focus on our finances until we break through and make it. Tired of being a charity case, we decide, "I'm going to run my life like a for-profit enterprise, and I'll show them!" You become the chief financial officer of your highly successful corporation called YOU, Inc. You start to pay attention to costs. You know that no business (and no individual) can survive for long without making money and making a profit on that money. So you seek out ways to make more, spend less, and invest the rest (even if it's just putting it back into your business). You start to see your balance sheet shift from red to black. "Well, I'll be—I actually have some money left over this month." Then you can quit your dreaded day job and pursue your art full-time. Once that happens, I doubt you'll want to go back to being bankrupt. You'll see that anyone with half a brain (even if it's the right brain) can become successful with money.

• You aren't screwed up after all. Yes, you'll have to work through feelings of fear (fear of making money and being a sellout and fear of what to do with the money you made so you don't lose it), but I know you can do it. If you don't, you will forever be controlled by a lack of money, and your creative career will never really get off the ground. Because rich or poor, there are some powerful forces that try to pull you away from making and managing money correctly. That's why this book shows you how to get in touch with your dreams and desires, because they are even more powerful. They can keep you from getting sidetracked and screwing up. I look at this book not as a book about finances so much as a book about having a dream and then figuring out a way to finance it. We need to find comfortable (and maybe even a little uncomfortable) ways to get it so we can have what we want, which isn't really money per se but, rather, what money can buy. Am I right? Don't you want peace of stress, some sense of security, less work and more time, a creative freedom? To earn your living (and a good one) at some that you would do for free but don't have to because people want to pay you to do it—and pay you well? A life where you are happy and living in harmony with your entire being. A life you are proud of. A sense of contentment and a permanent grin on your face.

• Having some money and being able to manage it (and save some) does produce freedom of the mind, spirit, and creative soul. Money is also power. It allows you the time you need to create great work AND promote it. The struggle of the starving artist is no way to live. Being desperate and on the brink of financial disaster all the time takes a toll on you, whether you believe it or not. I'm not saying you have to be a money-grubber. Just that you decide what level of comfort you want to live at and then find ways to maintain that lifestyle. Everyone's definition of fame and fortune is different. For some, selling a painting for $100,000 is success. For others, $10,000 would be a major milestone. What price are you willing to pay for what you want? That's the question. Do you want to make a million dollars and be miserable because you hate yourself for what you have to do to get it? Or would you prefer to live on less and do what you want? No matter what your aim, your target will be out of range unless you manage your money effectively. When you get a handle on your finances, your dream goes from fuzzy to clear, and you realize you can hit it. If it's to make millions or just be comfortable, you can do it.

• The first step is to acquire a money mind-set. A belief that there is enough money to go around and that some of it is earmarked just for you. That it's yours for the taking and that you aren't stealing it—no guilt. You must believe that opportunities to make money will present themselves. I have noticed that people with money don't worry about having enough money. They believe they are entitled, and somehow it comes to them. It's really mind over money. Once you harness and focus your talent, energy, and creativity and set your mind to something, it can be done. You don't need a degree (in fact, that can be a hindrance), and you already have most of the skills necessary. It's just a matter of making it more of a priority. After reading this book, you'll be able to just that.

MICHELANGELO

One of the world's all-time great artists was inspired by faith and not money. Ah, but he did make money, and like most artists, he had his share of money problems. Michelangelo signed a contract (yes, even then a handshake wasn't enough) to do the Sistine Chapel. His patron, Pope Julius II, was extremely demanding (and didn't pay him for a year for his work) and demeaned him (and even struck him once). The pope apologized for hitting him and, as an act of good faith, paid him as well. It was a good thing he got paid, because his dad was a deadbeat who always bothered him for money, which the dutiful son sent. Michelangelo's brother also asked for and received a handout. It was a good thing that business was thriving for the great artist—otherwise he would have gone broke. Michelangelo was a wealthy man and lived like a king in a large estate because he had a mind for business and a passion for his work. He had all the money he needed and ignored the backlog of commissions to pursue art that challenged and interested him—even if it wasn't what paid the most money. He kept learning, growing, and expanding as an artist and did some of his best work in his later years. (He sculpted until eight days before his death at age eighty-nine.)

What This Book WON'T Do for You

"Riches are not from an abundance of worldly goods but from a contented mind."

—Mohammed

Money is like air—it's not important until you don't have any. I can't force financial management on you any more than you could make a child take a nap when she doesn't want to. This book will tell you what to do to make and manage money (spend less than you earn, invest the difference, reinvest the returns, blah, blah, blah). You know what to do, but until you are ready to put these ideas into action, you'll continue to flounder. Some creative people will be perennially poor because they simply will not let money into their lives, and if it somehow sneaks in, they will find unique ways to get rid of it. If you don't feel like you deserve money in your life,

you simply will not have it. This book goes out of its way t
you how to change your attitude (for the better), but maki
change is really an inside job. Start where you are with wh
have (or don't have). You can't fix finances in one shot (usually),
so start small.

You have to make a commitment to be prosperous. This book
points the way and even holds your hand down the path, but you have
to follow and put one foot in front of the other. Success is just around
the bend if you'll just stay on the path to prosperity. Just keep hack-
ing away. It's your responsibility to make money and then protect it.
Not dealing with money can be hazardous to your health. Every area
of your life suffers. Some people are unwilling or unable to change
even if what they have done up to this point with their money has
been nothing but bad. They are afraid of change. Stubborn. Proud.
Indifferent. Mostly, they are in denial. Managing your money is a
habit—a good one. It eventually becomes second nature.

This is not a book about economics. We also won't cover the
nitty-gritty details about how to invest. This is a book about how to
create wealth, happiness, and above all, freedom. It's about improving the quality of your life. About being financially secure so you
can free up your time and your mind to pursue things more worthy
than fretting about finances. This book won't turn you into an Alex
P. Keaton (from *Family Ties*) and make you "all about money."

There are too many different types of artists (and art forms)
and just as many paths to prosperity for me to say which one will
work best. It's a personal choice you will have to make based on
what your vision is, your tolerance for dealing with the details of
the business side of the arts, how marketable your art form is, and
how hard you are willing to work at it. My role is to show you that,
one, it's possible to make and manage money and, two, to show
you how to do it. There is no magic to making and managing
money (it seems that way until you know what others have done,
and a light goes on in your head and you say, "I could do that!").
There are people who have less money and more debt but were
able to turn their financial life around, so there are no legitimate
excuses you can use to say "I can't do it." You can. You will. The
time to start is now.

Get Your Head in the Game

"The best part of my job is that you can create time and have the finances to see things you've never seen."
—Steve Stifler (Seann William Scott), American Pie

Finances are both boring and confusing, so we avoid dealing with them like we would a root canal. Both will get worse and be more painful in the long run if neglected. So I did my damndest to make this book relevant and real. You will "get it." You will never be made to feel like an idiot or be intimidated. You will learn that making money and making what you made grow is an art. This book will teach you how to get what you want, and how to avoid costly mistakes. It takes different skills to make money and then manage it. Creative people may be lacking in the latter, and come to think of it, we could also use some help in the earning department, too. That's why this book is so important.

Do as They Say, Not as They Did. When James Taylor was asked for his advice about how to make it in the creative arts, he said, "Avoid a major drug habit; don't have kids before you're ready to raise a family; and stay out of debt." Good advice. In this book we will look at what others in the arts have done and said to find clues about what works and what doesn't work. It's a much more interesting way to learn, don't you think? In what other book about finance will you read about ways to raise money that include stories like this: Actor Gary Coleman, like his co-stars from *Diff'rent Strokes,* fell on hard financial times after the show was canceled, but instead of robbing a video store, or posing nude, he came up with a creative way to raise capital. The "diminutive one" auctioned off "the shirt off Gary's back" for $31 and a night on the town, for which a six-foot-two-inch marketing analyst paid $4,000. Creative, no?

Oh, Yes, You Can! We will look at many myths about money, including the one that says being creative means you are automatically incompetent when it comes to financial matters. Renowned artist Robert Rauschenberg made a name for himself by sculpting and painting things using a haphazard, improvisational approach, but when it comes to his finances, he's much more methodical. He settled in Florida in the late '60s, choosing Captiva Island, an island off the Gulf Coast. When he first moved there he lived in a modest beach house with a tiny studio (so small he had to take his paintings outside and look out the kitchen window to get a good view of them). Today he owns a 17,000-square-foot studio overlooking a swimming pool and, through a series of smart moves, Rauschenberg is Captiva's biggest residential landowner, including nine houses and studios plus thirty-five acres of land (much of it beachfront).

R-E-S-P-E-C-T. When you have a healthy respect for money, money will respect you, too. You will learn how to earn it, then come to accept that you do deserve to be paid well so you don't piss it away and that this money has come into your life for a reason (or didn't come in for a reason). We have to break past unproductive patterns and form healthy new ones of financial freedom. We may be our own worst enemy when it comes to managing money (or is that mismanaging it?). We want financial independence (not having to worry about having enough money to do what we want, when we want), but by doing what we want, when we want before we can really afford to, we end up financially dependent (on others, to credit card companies, to jobs we hate). We'll look at a lot of issues that lead to us having to work more and end up with less and how to deal with them. Jimmy Iovine says, "Most people don't know how to get paid. That's an art." There's nothing wrong with wanting to get paid.

Make Yourself More Marketable. The truth of the matter is that the more you sell (and the more it sells for), the more you make. This is not new in the arts, but being bottom-line-oriented is now how the business side of the arts works. It's no big deal if your work sells and you don't mind actively marketing it. But if you don't have the temperament ("but I'm an *artiste*"), then there may be a problem. You can continue to create what you want and hope that it hits, or you can steer some of your creative energies into what sells. It is a tough pill to swallow for the serious artist. We will talk about how to get grants and internships, but when it comes to selling your talent and/or art, I want to point out that the person or company that puts up the money usually wants a return on that investment, and if one is unlikely, they may pass. It sucks, but it's a fact. As an author of niche books, I am what is known as a "mid-list" author. This is not a good thing. Just like any business, it seems that the rich get richer, and those in the "middle-class" are quickly disappearing. I was surprised to discover that many great authors did not sell a lot of books in their early careers (Henry David Thoreau sold only 2,000 copies of *Walden* in the first five years of publication), but publishers would nurse them along until they became bestselling authors. Not anymore. It has gotten so bad that there are some authors who publish under pseudonyms to separate themselves from their past sales record. Being a "good" writer is determined by the size of your sales (and potential future sales). Does this depress me? Not really. It motivates me. I know that to become a top-tier author, I have to find ways to have solid sales of my books. That's reality, baby.

Who, What, Why, When, Where, and How to Invest. Investing doesn't have to mean just stocks and bonds. Many musicians make money but end up broke. Others invest wisely. The Monroes had one hit, "What Do All the People Know." Keyboardist Eric Denton took the money he had and invested in and still owns the Guitar Trader music store in San Diego. It's still there. I know—I buy equipment from him from time to time. We will cover the major types of investments, as well, so you won't feel like an outsider. You may not choose to invest in a mutual fund or individual stock, but at least you'll know how. The fact is, creative people do make good investors once we combine our general curiosity, intuitive powers, and ability to color outside the lines with some general knowledge about investing. We'll balance our need to want to strike it rich quick and the truth about getting rich over time. Speculating and spending on investments we have no interest in and don't understand can be a disaster. Gambling and investing are two different things. We won't invest on long shots or on a whim but in assets that can make us rich. Some supersmart and talented people make some of the dumbest decisions when it comes to money. We'll look at why this is and then deal with them one by one. We'll also look at how to get out of debt so that instead of *paying* interest you can *earn* interest. Think about that for a moment.

Make Money While You Sleep? Yes! One of the beauties of being a creative person is that we can create something and then sell it. But wait. If we do it right, it can continue to generate income (royalties) each time it sells, while we are working on something else. Sometimes others with "real" jobs and steady income see us (creative types) as destined to be destitute. I know a guy who was a confirmed bachelor. When a woman (or her parents) would ask what he did for a living, he would be honest and tell them he was a painter. They would roll their eyes and say, "That's nice, but how do you support yourself?" He should have said, "Very well, thank you." See, he happens to be a very talented artist and a shrewd businessman. His wildlife paintings sell for tens of thousands of dollars. But the bulk of his money comes from the prints he sells worldwide. He paints for a couple of hours a day and then deals with the business of art. He doesn't necessarily enjoy the mundane chores that bring in the money, but he does it anyway. Dealing with printers, distributors, galleries, and doing promotion is the price he pays for his massive fortune. He has also found that he doesn't have to work as hard as he once did because his previous efforts greased the skids that got his career moving and the money flowing in.

Who Can You Trust? The sad truth is that creative people often have their money mismanaged because of a lack of interest, a general open-mindedness, and a burning desire to want to get rich quick. We are on autopilot and are about to crash into a mountain. We need to pay attention to take control, even if it's just as a co-pilot. We will start by learning about what good investments are and then who you can trust to help you with them. People will continue to take advantage of you as long as you let them. It may be that you are being used (enslaved) by bad decisions (poor negotiating, misunderstanding of the terms, not knowing your rights), so we'll also discuss how to get good deals and find trustworthy advisors to handle some of the detail work and decisions surrounding our finances.

That's the Plan, Man. Financial planning is a fundamental part of financial management, and contrary to what you might think, it can be flexible and fun. Planning can provide peace of mind and put an end to the feeling that you will wind up broke. Planning just means you are prepared for the future. It's deciding where you want to go and mapping out the best way to get there. You can still enjoy the journey, but you also have an eye on the road ahead, looking for any potential potholes. Planning is especially important for women. Statistics show that women make less money and take more time out to care for children, thus leaving them with less resources set aside for retirement. They have to work to save a higher percentage of their paychecks so they don't live longer than their money. So if you worry that you may end up a bag lady (and who doesn't), then the peace of mind that planning provides can tame that primal fear. A plan (plus common sense and consistent action) is better than a haphazard take-it-as-it-comes approach. We'll look at how to plan for the future (and still live for today).

When It Rains, It Pours. When we finally make some money after such a long drought, we will likely pay off our bills and, sadly, incur some new ones. If only we would set some aside. It's human nature to want to enjoy our good fortune. Instead, take a chunk and save it or invest it (wisely) and then, with what's left, go crazy, if you must. This classic pattern of the creative person being a starving artist, then gorging, then being hungry again, is also what happens to those who are lucky enough to have Ed McMahon knock on the door and give them an oversized check. Most lottery winners end up broke a few years later. If they had bought a home or started a business or just put some in a retirement account, they would be set for life. Instead, they buy boats or cars or take trips or give it away to others. This is certainly true of the people who "made" millions during the dot-com gold rush only to lose it (and then some) when the market went south. I saw people who invested everything they had (including their retirement money, equity in their homes, and more) trying to become dot-com zillionaires, only to end up with zilch. On the other hand, folk singer Jewel remembers what it was like growing up poor and then struggling to make it in music (even living in her van for a stint). "When I first got signed," she says, "I got $100,000. I put this in the bank and did not touch it." Bravo.

The Lean Years. This book is loaded with examples of people we see as successful and how they struggled to make it during their "salad days." In these stories we find comfort and hope that we can survive and then thrive. Singer Shana Morrison (daughter of supersuccessful recording artist Van Morrison) recalls that when she was growing up she envied other kids whose parents had normal jobs. Their parents didn't have to worry where the next paycheck would come from. She says there were times when growing up that she and her father would live in a mansion and buy a new car and stereo system one year and the next have to sell it all and move into an apartment. (And this is Van Morrison we are talking about!) That's why she didn't consider a career in music until later in life. Instead, she went to college and got a degree in business administration before giving in and following in their footsteps.

Who Wants to Be a Millionaire? You don't have to subject yourself to a game show to become a millionaire. You can become a millionaire if you *want*. I'm not kidding. This book will show you how you can have a net worth of one million dollars. It's not easy, and it does mean some sacrifices, but it's doable. I'll tell you right now how *not* to be a millionaire: Spend everything you make, go deep into debt on your credit card, and gamble everything you have on the biggest long shots you can find. For some creative people, making a million may *not* be the goal. We want people to see what we can do and have to say (and love it and praise us for our efforts). We want to be free to express ourselves. This kind of thinking can be dangerous. If you want to get your work out there at any cost, you are setting yourself up to potentially be taken advantage of. If you don't want to take care of your money, you may also be in danger of getting taken.

Dreams. Do you feel like your life is controlled by forces out of your control? You have more control over your financial circumstances than you think. It's your choices, actions, and beliefs that got you where you are now. Have you ever seen the actuarial tables that insurance companies create that tell you how long you can expect to live? It can be a wake-up call. Don't put your dreams on hold, because you don't have as much time as you may think. It's now or never. There are all kinds of ways to raise money (other than a day job) to live the dream of working on art full-time and ways to gain the exposure and recognition your art deserves.

Bestselling author Tami Hoag's success has allowed her to buy a seventy-acre Virginia horse farm, a Porsche Carrera Cabriolet convertible, and provided her with enough money for her husband to quit his job at IBM. Who would have thought that Hoag, who was working at a store called Bath Boutique, would achieve the dream of becoming a successful author? She did. She always wanted to be a writer but "just didn't know what to write." She was unable to finish anything and was floundering (and miserable). Then one day she was waiting for her truck to be repaired and reluctantly began reading a romance novel. By the time the truck was fixed she had decided to really go after her dream. She finished her first book, which didn't sell but got her an agent. Her second book, *The Trouble with J.J.*, sold, and her career took off from there, and today she writes murder mysteries and lives the life she dreamed of years ago.

Do What You Love and the Money May Follow. If the money doesn't follow right away, don't quit. Success is loving your life, and a lot of your life is spent trying to make money. So if you can enjoy the process of earning a living, you are a success. The secret of happy high achievers is that they had a talent of some sort, and they embraced, nurtured, and concentrated on it until it paid off. Yes, money was a motivator—but not the only thing that kept them going. What if I asked you, "If money weren't a factor and you had all you need, what would you want to do?" What would your answer be? We all have dreams. The obstacle (real or imagined) that gets in the way is the means to make it happen. Your right brain conjures up a scenario for your future, and before you can savor the moment, your left brain chimes in, "Oh yeah, well, how do you expect to make a living doing *that*?" All of a sudden the dream gets fuzzy and eventually disappears, and you are back to the drudgery that a life of compromises offers.

Since our left brain is hard to ignore (it's such a pain sometimes), let's put it to work. "Okay, logical (and annoying) brain, how can I make money by using my gifts and assets to get what I want? Who would pay? How much? How do I reach them?" Your left brain may just come up with a rational reason and link between what you want and the means to get it (or support yourself while you try). Opportunities are everywhere if you search long enough and look hard enough and are open to accepting them. You must believe that! The alternative is too bleak.

Julia Cameron, author of *The Artist's Way,* said it best. "Being an artist doesn't make you broke. Giving up your dreams makes you broke." George Parker invented his first game (which he produced himself) while still a teenager and managed to sell five hundred copies. His parents were unimpressed. So he went to college and got a degree, but what he really wanted to do was invent games. He finally gave in to his first love—game making. Together with his brother he took a Risk, got a Clue, and formed a Monopoly with his games (I just named them) and his business, Parker Brothers. When you make money doing something you truly enjoy, you feel energized, vibrant, alive, confident, in control, focused, excited, optimistic, and happy. Doesn't that sound like something you would be interested in?

"I Have a Head for Business and a Bod for Sin." I think Melanie Griffith utters those words in *Working Girl.* (Or was it just wishful thinking?) I just want to point out that as an artist it doesn't have to be a not-for-profit life. You can run your life like a business with an eye on the bottom line, and you can run your business like your life, have fun, and get things done. So what are we really talking about here? We are talking about living your life like an entrepreneur, really, where your product is your art and your asset is your talent. Start looking at where your money comes from and where it goes. Then look for ways to increase your income and cut costs, just like a business. You are the CEO of your own corporation. If you make decisions without emotion but based on a sound business strategy, you can turn a profit. You may have to lay off a few people (maid, gardener, personal trainer) and lower your inventory (sell off some of the junk in your garage), make profit-and-loss statements (bookkeeping and bill-paying), pay taxes (yuck), negotiate better deals (use coupons), increase productivity (wash your own car and mow the lawn), show some discipline (you eat in a little more), get to know the difference between needs and wants (we want a new car but we need transpo), budget (no new shoes *until* we pay the bills), plan (start saving for a vacation instead of charging it), reduce risk (get out of tech stocks), increase earnings (do a day job now and again), take advantage of benefits packages (we gladly accept everything an employer offers), and streamline paperwork (we enter checks as we write them). You will learn the basics of building a successful business in this book and you can apply this to your freelancing or your personal finances. Very few of us have ever learned about personal finance. That may be the reason for some of our past decisions and dilemmas concerning money, but it's not an excuse.

The Day Job. The dream, as I see it, is to have the freedom to do your art full-time, your way, and make a nice living. *Dilbert* creator Scott Adams spent seventeen years as a prisoner of a cubicle at a San Francisco bank and at Pacific Bell. While working at the bank he created *Dilbert* as a way to deal with the corporate stupidity that went on there. In 1989, the strip went into syndication, and a multimillion-dollar empire was born. In the early years, however, Adams didn't "quit his day job" and would get up at 5 A.M. to draw the *Dilbert* strips before heading off to work. The dead-end day job or terrible temp job can be a source for material we can use in our art. We will talk about how to survive the lean years by making money with dignity and pride while waiting for your big break.

We'll also look at how to scale back on both our lifestyles and dreams a little so that we can start small and build from there. Maybe you dream of making millions and touring in a private jet, when in reality, making a decent living (without compromises on your art) and flying commercial would still be fine. At least it's a start. Making it on a small scale can be nearly as rewarding as making it on a big scale. Most of the people you admire also struggled and started small just like you. So dream big, but start small.

Multiple Revenue Streams. If you can act, sing, and dance, you are called a "triple threat." This is a good thing. The more things you can do to bring in money, the better. Do you have untapped talent that could sustain you while you wait for other opportunities to open up? Can you teach what you know to others? Could you write freelance articles for money while your agent shops your manuscript around? Could you start a business based on your skills? There is always the day job, but it doesn't have to be as a waitress, cabbie, or office slave. How can you turn your talents into money-making ventures? Could you redirect your talent into another field? Maybe you could repackage your creations (or talents) and sell them to a new market? Maybe it isn't the dream job, but it's better than waiting tables. You will read about creative people who are diversified (without being spread too thin) and have money coming from several sources—which works for the right-brainer who enjoys variety. As long as you can come up with new and innovative ideas, you will always have a chance to make money.

Cashing In. Cashing in on our creativity is the difference between a dreamer who misses the boat and someone who makes money off his ideas. I met two guys who invented and now manufacture a beach chair for two or more. When people see these two and their chair, they often say, "Hey, I had this idea in 1983." Yes, but did you do anything with it?

Self-Help. More and more there are the "haves" and the "have-nots"— those who have book deals, record deals, lucrative contracts . . . and those who have nada. Those who haven't been lucky enough to land a deal can start their own record label, self-publish their own books, or be their own boss and have a chance to make big bucks. We will discuss how to make money by being an independent contractor, freelance artist, or small-business owner. How to put yourself in a position to create and market your own creations (which is harder but not impossible to do when you are deep in debt and have no savings). We will explore ways to raise money (with as few strings attached as possible) to fulfill our dream of owning our own business or get our creations out into the world. Many entrepreneurs turned their brainstorms into big bucks. When Kim Gosselin's six-year-old son was diagnosed with diabetes, she noticed a need for children's books that explained what diseases were. She lined up funding from pharmaceutical companies that make medicine for the diseases, and she was off and running. "I'm making a good living for my family, and I'm helping children live happier lives. It's the best feeling in the world."

Dumb Luck? Sometimes we see other creative people who are actually making a good living from their creativity, and naturally, we think they are lucky. But are they? Do they live a charmed life, or does it only appear that way? Luck is coming up with creative ways to increase your odds of catching a break, and when things don't go your way, taking it in stride and believing that things will soon go your way again. We will explore this further. We will also look at what creative people make, and you will be astonished at what is possible.

Risky Business. We will talk about taking risks (calculated risks) that can turn out to be rewarding. Jane Applegate took time off from her prestigious job at the *Los Angeles Times* to write a book. When she realized she liked the author's life, she put her money where her pen was and quit and has since built a business around her books and makes big bucks (more than she would have working her regular job).

Live Large on Less. You might think that if you could just make more money you would be better off. Statistics don't support this notion. Many families making major amounts of money are living close to the brink of a financial crisis with no money set aside for emergencies. According to a Census study, almost fifty million families had trouble paying an important bill. Increasing your income is one way to get ahead, but unless that is combined with a plan to cut back on expenses, you will never be secure and successful with money. Bestselling author Sebastian Junger hit it big with his book *The Perfect Storm* but didn't go nuts when he collected his windfall. He had always been frugal, and he remained frugal even after making millions. He invested the bulk of his earnings: "It's fun to have money, but the more money I get, the less interesting it becomes." We will look at why we spend and how to have fun and live a full life on less.

Always Carry Protection. Being risk-takers and "in the moment" people, we may not see value in being properly insured. We will explore some worst-case scenarios that may change your mind about protecting your assets from a variety of devastating destructive elements that can affect the creative person and his ability to create. We will look at different types of insurance (including hiring lawyers) to make sure we won't lose it all.

How to Get Out of Your Own Way. Since many of us get paid only when we produce, we must fight off our demons and do away with our artistic temperament that keeps us from finishing what we start. Singer-songwriter Randy Newman says, "The industry has created creativity by consuming a lot of it. People have assignments and do them. You have a job, so you have to come up with a story." He also admitted that he would "basically spend a lot of time watching television and worrying about not doing my work." The myth that we must wait for the muse to show up and then we can create is just that: a myth. We will also explore other "issues" that can get in the way of earning a good living and managing money.

Things Aren't as Bad as They Seem. If you were able to buy and read this book, you are better off than over a billion others in this world who have to survive on less than a dollar a day. Feel better? We will look at what led you to where you are and then see how to dig out from the hole you may be in. This book is about hope and positive thinking. What's the alternative? Years ago when I sold my surf shops to become a writer, my parents asked me if I had sold anything yet. I assured them I had—my home, car, and even my dog.

It's Never Too Late. No matter where you are or what you've done, there is hope (and help). One of the most read and successful financial gurus today is Suze Orman. Her books on financial management are bestsellers, and she is everywhere giving (good) financial advice. She's very open about her own financial missteps, and some were whoppers. Still, this is America and someone who was once deep in debt and a former waitress can now become a bestselling author telling others how to get out of debt and make millions in the process. Is this a great country or what?

Money Isn't Everything. Maybe you want to finish this last statement like you would a similar one for winning, "It's the only thing." But making money is not all it's cracked up to be. I know, you'd like to find out for yourself. You can still strive to be wealthy but also be happy along the way. To say "I'll be happy when I . . ."—and you fill in the blank with "own a home" or "land a book deal" or "make a million dollars"—would mean that you will be unhappy until you reach those goals, thus wasting months and even years of your life. Once you get all the money you want and deserve, it will not make your entire life better. All that improves is one aspect: your finances. You can be rich at any income if you feel rich. Jason Alexander says that spending lavishly to get people to pay attention to you and like you isn't real. What's real is when your soul is connected to your life and work—that's true happiness. He admits that he and his wife, Daena Title, were just as happy when they made $38,000 a year (between them) and lived in a one-bedroom apartment as they are today.

Money Makes the Art World Go Round

"The world has enough for everyone's need but not for everyone's greed."

—Mahatma Gandhi

Let me just say right now that for better or worse, the arts is a business. Big business. In fact, the arts is a $40 billion-a-year business! The art industry employs over one million people, some of whom make millions. That's right: You can become a multimillionaire by being an artist. I see you shaking your head and thinking, "Come on, the artist always gets screwed. Maybe the 'bidnessmen' make millions, but not the actual artists." Yes, many artists get ripped off and taken advantage of, but it doesn't have to be that way.

Artists have more power than they think. They provide income and opportunities for tens of thousands of non-artists. Yes, many of these non-artists make more money from art than the artists themselves, but again, that doesn't mean artists have to be helpless victims of the system that is set up to take advantage of them. Too many artists work too hard for too little. They feel they are being forced to give away their creations and services for next to nothing because they have no leverage. It seems that's just the way it is. Oh well. It's that attitude that allows non-artists to take advantage of us. They know we are more concerned about "the art" and getting it out there than we are about being paid, and they use it against us. That's their leverage over us.

We sometimes feel privileged that someone, anyone, would want to pay *anything* for our work. So we take the fast-food-like fees because we worry that if we don't accept their ridiculously low offer nobody else will come along with a better one, and our "patron" may find someone else to buy from. If we blame "them" and don't at least take a look at what we are doing to contribute to the problem, we'll never get anywhere.

It's true, the cards are stacked against us, so we need a better hand if we want to win. That means looking at ourselves to see if there is anything we can do to make ourselves more marketable, improve our talent level, align ourselves with the "right" people, and see if we are doing everything we possibly can to make sure we make money at our art form, whatever that may be, before we blame the agent, gallery, publisher, industry, and so on.

Billy Joel said it well, I think: "The [music] business is based on exploiting artists. Over the years musicians, who are not historically good businessmen—which is why we are musicians—give away pieces." If we don't take care of business, business will take advantage of us. Art is a business and like in any business, it is dog-eat-dog. More and more it is about the bottom line and other business-related agendas. It's sad but true. It's not worth your time to try to change it. You have only one choice: Deal with it. How? First, by being so good at what you do that people will fall all over themselves to pay you top dollar for what you do. Then, by being professional and by being profit-oriented yourself (without sacrificing your integrity or the integrity of your art).

Now, before you get too distressed, there are still many people in the arts who are not in it for the moolah. They are in it for the sake of art. Thank God! But these people are under pressure by the money people in the arts because, let's face it, if "investors" in art put their money in the stock market or real estate, they would get a better return than they do by investing in writers, musicians, painters, craftsmen, and so forth. The way it is supposed to work is if what we do makes money, we should make money, too. If we take the classic artist-versus-the-art-world attitude, we're not going to get anywhere. What can we do to make more money for us and them? If not money, what can we do to bring them recognition, respect, or some other residual benefit? This kind of talk may seem out of whack with what most business books for artists will say, but I believe that it is a losing battle for the creative person who has no idea about the business side of the creative arts.

It's not just the business world that's got this money thing going—it's everyone. Many times the first thing family, friends, and fellow writers want to know is, what kind of advance did I get? How many books have I sold? Has the whole world gotten greedy? I want to say, What about my positive reviews? How about the hundreds of fan letters I receive? What about the awards I win for my writing? Nope, they still want to know about the sales success. It seems that society measures success by monetary gain and not by the quality of the product. You aren't appreciated as an artist until you make money. I thought *Mission: Impossible* and the sequel sucked. But they made millions—so they are a success? Really, is this a good thing? My take on the whole situation is that money is a way for people to measure the worth of a project and thus the success of an artist. It shouldn't be this way, but alas, it is.

Maybe you read about writers who get six- and seven-figure advances and you think that's the norm. It's not. Many members of the Writers Guild don't make any money from their writing, and 20 percent of those who did made less than $4,000 a year. Does that mean they are bad writers? No. Does that mean they should quit writing? Of course not. It just means that by being consumed by reading about how much others in the top echelon make, it can either be discouraging or, taken another way, give you hope.

The fact is, being a creative person can be frustrating financially (and thus emotionally). It's not an easy life, and it is certainly not a career choice for the faint of heart. There are a great deal of sacrifices involved in making money at our art. We give up a lot and sometimes get so little in return. There are the compromises, the day job, the lack of stability, the parents pushing us in other directions, the spouses pressuring us to give it up and get a real job, the struggles to get good reviews and exposure—and that's just in the beginning stages! It can be terribly torturous and an uphill battle, even if you have achieved some level of success.

I don't think you ever really feel all that secure. There are so many potential pitfalls along the way that it leaves us in a constant state of peril. Financial insecurity is a result of potential dry spells or being dropped at any time (for no good reason) by a label, publisher, studio, or client. If you don't prepare for the droughts that are a part of almost every creative person's career, your whole financial world can come crashing down. We can create some sense of security by being smart with money, especially during the good times. This book will help you along those lines. For several reasons, having some money saved up is THE key to financial freedom. Nothing good comes from being desperate for dough. The creative life is a roller-coaster ride—a long uphill climb followed by several hair-raising dips and twists, all of which leave you a little wobbly in the knees. There is also the problem that it takes money to make money. Creative people have to do a lot of work that doesn't pay (either at all or right away). That includes training, promotion, practice, writing proposals, and doing work on spec. Even if you have a deal in place, it can take months and sometimes even years to get paid, but your landlord doesn't usually work on spec, so it pays to have some money set aside for this very common dilemma.

I share all this doom and gloom only because if you are still reading this, you probably have what it takes to make it. That, or you are delusional enough to keep at it. That's good. Being an artist isn't a rational decision. It's something that gets in your system and you just can't shake it. You are stricken with this virus that infects your thinking. You do it for the love and *then* the money. I just think it helps to go in with your eyes wide open. Some people romanticize the life of an artist. It isn't always as glamorous as it seems. For many writers, getting published is all they want, and their expectations of what that is like are a little out of sync with the reality. Getting a book deal is only the beginning. You somehow have to figure out how you are going to write the book while paying the rent (advances for first-time authors are relatively small), promote it like mad, hope that it sells and that someday you will experience the magic of fame and fortune. (Oprah loves your book, it becomes a bestseller, and you earn back your advance and start receiving big, fat royalty checks.)

This, of course, is the exception, not the rule. Same with Hollywood. You get that elusive meeting with a studio executive, and they tell you, "Love it, call me," but what they really mean is, "No way in hell are we gonna make your picture." Even if you get a contract, that still doesn't mean your film will see the light of day. Very frustrating. The same "moving meeting" happens in other businesses, too. There are some of us who still think it's a fair trade-off and wouldn't have it any other way. We are proud of who we are, what we do, and how hard we have had to work to get where we are. Some wear their lack of money like a badge of honor (on their thrift-shop jacket), and others find creative ways to get paid well for doing the kind of work they enjoy and do well. You are going to be in the latter group.

The Million-Dollar Question

"If you don't get the best grades, don't fret—I didn't do too well in school, and I'm a multimillionaire."

—Adam Sandler

What keeps some creative people from making money and achieving financial freedom from their creations? Whew, that's the million-dollar question, so to speak. Throughout this book we will revisit this question, but let's take a look at some of the potential problems that can hold us back.

• **Front End.** In Hollywood "front end" means money made before or during the production of a movie, as opposed to money from profits at the "back end." This is a lot like a creative person's life. We need to make money on the front end (to pay the bills) while we wait for the back end to kick in. In other words, we need a day job. Over 300,000 people in the United States consider themselves artists. Most also have to work a full-time job not related to the arts or take a day job to subsidize their artistic endeavors.

• **Cruise Control.** Sometimes we have to hit rock bottom before we say, "Okay, this is not working, I need to try something different." Other times we are stuck in a comfort zone that we are afraid to swim away from. It's a trap. You aren't happy where you are, yet you are afraid to let go of the side and swim to deeper water. If you have had some success it seems crazy to have to go back and start over again, but that may be just the ticket to more money and more fulfillment. Sometimes pride (or stubbornness) can get in the way of fixing our financial health.

• **Driving in Reverse.** Denial is a roadblock to getting our finances in order. You need to look at where you are and what got you there before you can fix the problem. One type of denial I see a lot is the creative person waiting for the "big fix" or the deal that will wipe away all past problems and set him free from financial worry.

Sometimes the big deal does come and wash away past sins (you can pay off all your debts), but what if it doesn't happen? Yikes! You end up deeper in trouble, and no deal can save you, not even bankruptcy.

• **Keep Your Eyes on the Road.** We worry about the minute details of our lack of money, which wastes time (time is money), and this worry gets in the way of our creativity and ruins otherwise perfectly fine days. Financial freedom, to me, is freedom from worry, and that can happen at any level of income. It's up to you. When your mind is locked in to a lack of money, resources, capital, supplies, and so on, it can drag you down and give you a built-in excuse not to do something creative, productive, enjoyable. Thinking about what is possible is a healthier mind-set. If your mind is so focused on your money problem, it will begin to affect other areas of your life and drag them down, too. You start to feel like a loser because you aren't making enough money (or make enough but seem to spend more), and the stress can lead to depression, which can lead to more spending and other problems. It's a sick cycle that must be broken.

• **The Timing Is Fine.** Saying you will work on your art when everything is just right isn't the answer. I have heard people say: "I'll start working on my book when I get a bigger house with a room I can turn into an office (costly and unrealistic)"; "I can't possibly write on this computer"; "When I get my degree, then I'll quit waitressing and get serious about my career." Do what you can with what you have—now. We all have different issues (whether we are rich or poor) that get in the way of our financial dreams, most of which we can control. We may be tempted to blame money for all of our problems in life. "As soon as I make a million dollars my life will be perfect" or "If only I . . ." It's not that way. Money helps, but it doesn't fix personal problems and sometimes even exacerbates them.

• **The Tank Is Full.** There is one more strange phenomenon that is rare but worth mentioning. Some people have enough money right now but don't realize it. They still stress out as if they are broke. They are proud of their povertylike ways and somehow feel like martyrs because they don't seek out money and that their art is more pure because they aren't paid. Neither of these situations is healthy. Why deprive yourself of basic needs if you don't have to? It's not good to treat yourself poorly by being too frugal. It's okay to live a little. It is also okay to want money. Those who are not making money use the argument that they are somehow better because of it for the simple reason they don't have any. If money were thrown at them, most would leap at it.

PUT YOURSELF IN THE PICTURE

Creative people like to flex their right brains when creating art, but when it comes to learning, a whole-brain approach is what is needed. When you read this book and put yourself in the picture, ask, "How does this affect me?" Look for connections to your situation. Try to picture the points visually. When I include or suggest exercises you can do, do them. You will learn deeper. Talk about what you have learned with others.

Being a Right-Brainer in the Left-Brain World of Finance

"Think left and think right and think low and think high. Oh, the THINKS you can think up if only you try."

—Dr. Seuss

Your personality is one of your assets, so draw on your strengths as a right-brainer to create income opportunities and handle the business side of your artistic endeavors. I know that not all creative people are dominated by right-brained thinking. Lisa Kudrow plays Phoebe, the ditzy blonde on *Friends,* but in real life she is described as logical, practical, and analytical. In fact, she almost didn't become an actress because "I thought all actors were idiots whose lives didn't work." Being creative and right-brained doesn't give you an excuse for being irresponsible and reckless with money. It may explain it, but it doesn't mean you are destined for a life of being destitute. Albert Einstein was a genius and had a mind for math, but when it came to his finances, the "oy"s have it. His second wife, Elsa, managed to get his annual salary at Princeton University increased from $3,000 to $16,000 annually for life. On the other hand, I loved Lucy and what she did with her money. Lucille Ball and Desi Arnaz were financial whizzes. They took a pay *cut* (hang on) for their roles in their hit television show in exchange for full rights. The couple sold the series to CBS for $4.3 million seven years later.

Always remember you are unique . . . just like everybody else.

Not all creative people are disorganized, distracted dreamers, guided by emotion and impulsiveness, making illogical and irrational decisions about money, and so allergic to detail they don't deal with things like balancing their checkbook or reading their contracts. Most creative people are very clever when it comes to managing money (this isn't always a good thing) and can come up with all kinds of creative ways to get what they want. This includes finding innovative ways to make money, unorthodox (but effective) strategies for managing that money, and definitely finding new and creative ways to spend money. Creative people are also very resourceful, using their craftiness to solve problems when they simply don't have the dough. Because we are a caring group, we are also generous and put people first (sometimes to a fault). So for every positive trait, I guess you could say there is a negative one, too. Thinking outside the box is good in many areas of the arts. It isn't always such a positive thing when it comes to dealing with our finances. That box I'm talking about is the structure that has proven to work. When we stay inside it and follow the path that has worked for years and years, we can almost be assured of wealth. All you have to do is follow the rules (not our strength), and without a lot of hassle, your money will grow. This allows you to be creative in other areas. By going outside of it, sometimes it pays off, and sometimes it is a disaster.

What I think we can all agree on is that we want an easy, quick, maintenance-free money-management system that will keep pumping money into our lives while we are free to work on what we want (or not work at all). We want no fuss, no muss. One author called it a "money-making machine." I like that term. You can leave it running, and it sort of prints money for you. There is such a thing, and it's called investing. When I say investing, I don't mean you buy a stack of lottery tickets and hope for the best. It means you invest in things that have a good chance of paying dividends, like the stock market or your own career. Yes, *you* are a good investment. A money-making machine could be a project that continues to pay off (long after the work is done) with royalties or residuals.

But because business and creativity reside in opposite sides of the brain, it makes for some interesting battles between good and evil. Some people are better at "show" than "business" because their creative brain rules. Others are able to make peace with their left brain and have a balance between business and art. "Taking care of business" is more than a line from a song. It's a way of life for the successful artist.

Creative people are known for being fun, childlike, and adventurous. Instant gratification can also be a trait of the right-brainer. Now give that person a credit card. Holy cow! We have to get a handle on, and reel in, our right brain when it wants to do things that can damage our finances. That certainly doesn't mean we have to stop the party—it just means we need a bouncer and curfew. It can work.

Now for the Good News

"Some people march to a different drummer—and some people polka."

—Unknown

Look at where you are right now and ask yourself how you got there. Even if you have never been good with money, you can change. We can retrain your brain and use your right-brain strengths to run your life and your business so that it shows a profit. Society frowns on our quirky and sometimes unorthodox ways. But many of these are essential in creating great works of art. They may seem unproductive to outsiders, but they help in the creative process. Being an idea person, risk-taker, dreamer, big-picture thinker, and believer in the impossible, curious, comfortable with change, passionate, emotional, and creative are not bad traits when it comes to dealing with financial matters. Know your strengths as well as admitting your weaknesses and see how to maximize one (your strengths) and minimize the other (weaknesses). That means breaking old habits and patterns of behavior that didn't bear fruit in the past. So even if you failed at everything you've tried before, that does not mean you will fail again! Stop describing yourself as being bad with money. You have a lot going for you if you can harness it. You may have a million money-making ideas, one of which is bound to hit it big. That means you always have hope. The key is to actualize some of them. Prioritize them into most doable or most sure thing, and do something about them.

Big-picture thinkers don't do well with details but are able to see several steps ahead, which can be even more important. That way you don't dwell on the small setbacks but, instead, you keep your eye on the larger goal. Then you are more relaxed and don't sweat the small stuff. This makes you a better artist, too. Instead of feeling fear, you are more assured of what to do and you're able to do it. You may even be willing to do some small stuff because you know how it will pay off later. We need to do the small steps that lead to big-time success. Otherwise, the dream will always be out there. The big picture is, well, big and overwhelming, but once we can break it down into a series of small micro-movements, it is doable. That just means putting one foot in front of the other while keeping our head up and looking where we are going so we don't trip and fall or get off track. Take saving money, for example. Start small. Open a savings account with the least they allow at the bank or credit union. Don't wait until there is a better time. Now is a good time.

Spontaneity is good. It's one of our strengths. But (you knew there had to be a "but") we can't just let the winds of fate blow us this way and that. Otherwise a strong gust of wind will put our little financial boat up on the rocks. Pick a destination or heading (your dream), and point yourself toward it. Total chaos (even though we are comfortable being uncomfortable) isn't a good thing when it comes to our money (or any area of our life, for that matter). We need a flexible plan. Not rigid, but one that will bend. Adjust, tack, trim, and so on. If there is a storm, you can ride right through it or haul in your sails, wait it out, and resume the journey.

We have addictive personalities. Sometimes that is good. You get it in your mind that you are going to get out of debt, and nothing will stop you. You may even become obsessed with saving and paying down that debt. It's a better habit than other costly vices, that's for sure. But being extremists can mean we go overboard with things. Don't go too far and try to punish yourself for past discretions by being a monk. Live a little. Spend money on important things like promotion, publicity, product, and so on.

We love to juggle and flit from thing to thing. Sometimes the best thing you can do is invest and leave the thing alone. Time is your ally. Also, don't spread yourself too thin with a multitude of investments (diversifying is fine, but don't take it too far). For one thing, it can get complicated trying to keep track of too many things going on at once. Being able to focus on one thing may be the best course of action.

The greater the risk, the greater the reward. We have no problem taking chances, but smart investors and entrepreneurs don't take *unnecessary* risks. There are smart, measured risks, and then there are foolhardy ones. (We are also open-minded, which can make us vulnerable to scams.) Protect what you have, and gamble only with what you can afford to lose. We love the thrill of living on the edge, the thrill of waiting until the last minute to make a decision or to act. This can cause problems. The adrenaline rush we love from living this way is a high, but the hangover can be a killer. There is still a thrill from investing and watching your money grow. We want to get rich quick, which causes us to go for some pretty crazy things to attain this unattainable goal.

Wealthy, successful, creative people have the same traits as you. They also have the same fears, hurdles, and worries that you do. They conquered their fears and demons and overcame obstacles to make money. If they can do it, so can you.

What's Wrong with the Right Brain?

"You can make a killing as a playwright in America, but you can't make a living."

—Sherwood Anderson

Yes, we can be quite neurotic about money (and the lack thereof), and there is some downside to being a creative, right-brained person, but it doesn't have to mean disaster for your finances.

• **Math Sucks.** Ten out of eight people have a problem with fractions. Math may not be your strongest subject if you are an artist, but it doesn't necessarily give you an excuse for why you can't manage money. Besides, there is a connection between musical ability and math skills. The real reason a lot of right-brainers don't do math and balance their checkbooks may be because they like the thrill of not knowing how much they really have. It's a little like living on the edge. There is a certain amount of excitement in not knowing exactly what you have. We say we aren't good with numbers and don't understand or want to deal with things like bookkeeping and billing, but the truth is, we just don't like doing it the left-brained way. So find a creative way that works for you. Being late in making payments or collecting payments from others costs you money. Some creative people don't open their bills because they think that what they don't know can't hurt them. They see money in their checking account and think they can spend it, but they haven't seen their bills yet. Once they do open them, uh-oh. So they have six new CDs but no power to play the stereo (it was turned off for nonpayment).

• **It's Here Somewhere.** Messiness, clutter, and disorganization can actually be helpful in the creative process, but they don't do any good when it comes to managing money. You don't know what's coming in and certainly don't have a clue about what's going out. Clutter can be a sign of other issues that may get in the way of making money. It makes sense to gain some control over clutter and chaos.

• **Fun and Games.** We like total freedom. We don't have time for all this boring business stuff. If we have to do it, we want it to be easy and quick. Sometimes that's possible, and sometimes that's the quickest way to go broke.

• **The Time Is Now.** We have no sense of time, and time and money are totally linked. We think we can do it all but are overwhelmed. We have to learn how to say "no." It may be that we are overly optimistic about what we can get done or just can't seem to prioritize. Maybe we like to risk and rush. But this can piss people off and blow deals, thus affecting your earning power.

• **The Devil Is in (*Not* Dealing with) the Details.** We prefer to wing it. It's more of a thrill and an adventure. Besides, safe and predictable is boring, and so is reliable, normal, and status quo. We want new, exciting, dangerous. Sounds like fun if it's a free-time activity, but not for finances. Haste makes waste. A little due diligence can save a lot of money and hassles. When we act without thinking, maybe going with the first vendor without getting additional quotes or not reading the fine print in a contract, we only later find out what a mistake we made.

• **Drama Queens.** They prefer to live on the edge financially by choice. They find it more comfortable to constantly be in a crisis mode. We call them "drama queens" because they seem to thrive on problems. They will even put themselves in a precarious position (again and again) because they are bored when things are going well. So they create a crisis, and that seems to be where they are most comfortable. It seems strange that someone would actually put herself in a precarious position over and over again—but it happens.

• **Live Fast, Die Young?** Legendary drummer Buddy Rich played like he lived—fast and furious. He was always in motion, racing around town in fast cars. Many people like to live life in the fast lane. Slow and predictable is boring. They prefer people who are unreliable and investments that are risky. Sometimes that comes from a feeling of being indestructible, omnipotent, powerful—we simply don't fathom failing, so it's not a risk. But when that wild, impulsive, crazy thing that seemed like such a sure thing goes south, we realize that maybe it wasn't such a good idea after all. They're looking for the perfect moment without any concern for the future. Smoking, drinking, gambling, unprotected sex, and other activities make people feel good when they are doing them and getting immediate gratification, but the dangers are real. It may be okay to do that with your hobbies, but not your money.

• **Emotionally Bankrupt.** We tend to be driven by emotions, and some of our biggest mistakes with money are emotional ones. It could be becoming a partner with someone we love or buying property that we fall in love with, and other decisions that are made with our hearts and not our heads. We may also suffer from M.S. (otherwise known as mood swings). Like a pendulum, we will swing from one mood to another. There is a cycle, in a sense. We are up, so we tend to go crazy and spend, spend, spend, which leads us to be bummed, and then we spend to try to make ourselves feel better. We may rally for a while, but eventually, when we get the bill, we are even more depressed than before. Then the pain passes (and we forget the "I'll never do it again" admonishment we made to ourselves), and we go on another bender. And so it goes. It seems that when we are doing well, we get a distorted view and lose sight of all reason. Why save, things are great! Cut back, not. The only problem is that nothing lasts forever (a good run and a bad run are both just cycles), so we need to keep our heads. I would recommend *not* making a big decision when you are at one or the other extreme. When we are in a down cycle, we can sometimes blow things way out of proportion, and everything feels hopeless. Not good. In general, when we are emotional (and when are we not?), we can make some whopping errors in judgment.

• **I Want It Now!** Unfortunately it takes discipline to make money. We can't give in to any whim and have whatever we want whenever we want it, or we will overindulge. I think it's great to be in the moment. As a creative person, this is one of our greatest strengths. There is magic in the moment, but after it passes we must face the future. By focusing on the future while paying attention to the present, you will be able to enjoy the here and now and have a healthy appreciation for what is coming next and what you'll need in the days, weeks, months, and years ahead. Since we aren't used to sacrificing for security and future success, this is a tough sell, but many creative careers take years to get off the ground, and during those lean years, what little money we have coming in must be funneled back into building the career. That means that instead of a luxury apartment, we live in a less-than-thrilling studio. Rather than driving a brand-new car, we have a quirky clunker. Maybe we don't do all the things we want, but we still manage to have fun without wasting money.

Back to being in the moment. This is a blessing rather than a curse, because we can find fun in just about anything, whether it costs a lot of money or not. But some creative people are so impulsive and have such a low threshold for patience that they expect everything to happen right away and if it doesn't, they overreact and muck things up. In the creative arts, deals and dealings take time. There is a lot of waiting, and patience is a virtue. When you try some of the tempting shortcuts, you end up on a road to nowhere or a dead end or worse. You have to do the little things like everyone else before you. Don't take unnecessary risks or always go for the big score when a lot of little successes are what you really need. Get real. You can lose it all by being impatient and impulsive, so don't just quit your day job and hope that things will work out. Without that support money you will fall fast. What if that risky big score doesn't pan out? You will not only feel like a fool, you'll likely owe a lot of money.

We all want to be stars, and we all want it to happen NOW. That's nothing new. Some of us take baby steps and learn to crawl before we walk, and we grow up to be healthy and wealthy creative people with careers built on a solid foundation.

• **The Big Fix.** There is a sort of White Knight or Big Fix mentality with a lot of creative people. It's almost a total disregard for money, because the thinking is that something or someone will come along and save them from ruin. Sometimes things do just work out somehow. Other times—well, time runs out and disaster strikes. It is far better to be independent than dependent on others or that one bankruptcy-saving deal to save the day. Take charge of your money (and your life), and if money does magically come to you, great. If it doesn't, that's okay, too. Don't romanticize about winning the lottery or getting a big inheritance. If you filter what you want through that mechanism called fantasy land where money will magically appear somehow, someday, it is sooooo easy to rationalize buying just about anything. Be careful.

• **Eight-Track Mind.** We are divergent thinkers (a nice way of saying our minds like to jump around). This is good in a way because we are NOT afraid of change, but despite the saying "Change is a good thing," change for change's sake isn't always good. New is definitely more exciting than status quo. There are problems with always seeking something new. For one, many times we aren't paid until we COMPLETE a project, and leaving a trail of unfinished projects just isn't profitable. Allowing (unpaid) distractions to get in the way of the paying work we should be doing can be dangerous. An inability to focus can be a form of self-sabotage. We want it all (now), and when we try to do it all but spread ourselves too thin or never quite finish anything, we become locked in perpetual potential and never quite reach the dream. We are busy, sure, but not with things that matter or make money.

Is this getting too psychological? Let me get back to basics. Jumping around can stunt your financial growth. For example, you have a great job but a better one comes along, so you jump over there. It takes months or years to qualify for a company's 401(k) plan, and you are never with one company long enough to qualify. Or you are always looking for new clients rather than building existing ones into bigger customers. It costs more to continually try to get new business than to turn existing clients into better ones. Or you reinvent yourself every year or so, which means training, new technology, and time to get up and running, all of which can be costly. There are other things related to an inability to focus, which can range from being bored so you spend on a new wardrobe, hairdo, and makeup, to picking up a new hobby each week. There is also the cost of people seeing you as flighty or flaky because you leave things unfinished, or you do a shoddy job so you can get on to the next new thing. Harsh, I know, but true for a great many right-brainers.

• **Dream On.** We live with our heads in the clouds, and that is okay for most areas of our lives. Being a visionary or abstract about things is what makes us great artists. With managing money, it can help us think about the future and all the possibilities, but we need to stop, look around, and take a reality check every once in a while. Part of it is, we don't want to grow up—ever. That means we don't accept responsibility, look to others to come to our rescue and bail us out, or reject authority and refuse to listen to others because we are rebellious. Many start-ups fail because the founder kept going in different directions without any regard to the cash-flow needs of the business.

 BRAIN POWER

With all this talk about being a right-brainer or a left-brainer, maybe you should see which half of your brain dominates your thinking when it comes to managing your money. Take a look at the two lists below and circle the traits that apply to you from each list.

A.) Planner, saver, conservative, organized, practical, logical, linear, focused, bottom-line, decisive, frugal, stable, reliable, detail-oriented, right-handed.

B.) Impulsive, big spender, risk-taker, disorganized, impractical, intuitive, distracted, chaotic, emotional, unstable, fun, dreamer, big-picture, left-handed.

Total "A" Answers:__ Total "B" Answers:__

If you have more "A" answers, you are a left-brainer. If you have more "B" answers, your right brain dominates your thinking. If you have an even amount from each list, you are a whole-brainer (or fully actualized, as the researchers like to say). Which is best? Well, each has its advantages and disadvantages, but I would say having some traits from both sides might be the most helpful when it comes to handling your finances.

2

BE CAREFUL WHAT YOU WISH FOR

"I'm so excited I can barely sit still or hold a thought in my head. I think it's the excitement only a free man can feel."
—Red, The Shawshank Redemption

Don't even try to deny it. You want it, need it, gotta have it. What is "it"? Money (and what money can buy—freedom). The only catch is, what are you willing to do to get it? Not many creative people like to discuss it, but we dream of what more money could mean to us. Just like many people don't remember their dreams, we may not be conscious of these deep desires for money and what it means in our lives and careers. Whether you know it or not, how you have handled money has affected your life and career.

Pamela York Klainer, a financial planner in New York, asks clients to write a "money biography" by looking at their life and writing their life story using money as the narrative theme. This will help you understand your relationship with money in a less threatening and yet enlightening way. It will help clarify where you went astray and give you clues about what to do next. Her advice is to start at the beginning. Look at your childhood and your exposure and experience with money. Then tell your story either chronologically or as you remember things. It doesn't have to be a literary masterpiece, just the process of thinking about money is what matters most.

Have you ever had money flow into your life easily and effortlessly? Has your creativity produced results people have paid for? Where it just felt right? Where you felt like you deserved it? All we need to do is re-create or (if you said "no") create it. For creative people, money is a product of our imaginations. We can create things that people will pay for. We must first feel we deserve to be paid for something that comes so easily to us and then come up with a figure of how much we deserve. That's why we must value our ideas and our time and decide what they're worth—and then convince others to believe it, too.

Step one to having everything you desire is to know exactly what you want and then pick your path and start down it. Once you begin moving in the direction of your dreams, unseen forces will help you along the way. Vision creates power, and so do decisiveness and determination. I know it sounds strange, but it has happened to too many people too many times to discount it. Once you set your sights on something and then commit to going after it, you are not alone anymore in your quest. You just have to define what you want and have the desire to go for it and the discipline to stay the course. You need to get in touch with the "feelings" these things will give you when you get them, because prosperity is a feeling, not a number. Then hang on to that feeling and go for the goal. We all wish we could make more money from our creativity or have more creative freedom. That's a given. What distinguishes the dreamers from the doers is that the doers are, well, doing something about their goals while the dreamers are wishing things would improve—someday, somehow.

I think that people fail to reach their dreams because they are nearsighted. What I mean is that they live too much in the moment and can't see more than a few days ahead. Sure, dreams are achieved through daily steps, but without an eye toward the future we can sabotage our long-term success by making poor choices in the present. Some short-term suffering may be needed for long-term gain. Maybe you skip that vacation this year or drive your clunker until you can truly afford a new car, and just maybe you don't buy a new computer just because it's a little faster than the one you have.

I think we need to look at how we spend our money and ask ourselves if our purchases are taking us further away from financial freedom or bringing us closer to our dreams. For example, you get a tax refund, and there are all kinds of things you want to buy. So you go on a shopping spree and get some summer clothes. By next summer they would be worth, what, a hundred bucks (if you could sell them at a thrift store)? If you took half that same money and invested it (wisely), you would have enough the following summer to take some time off and focus on your art.

It's easy to wander away from our dreams, and if we aren't careful we can get lost. Remember what it was like when you were a kid and you somehow became separated from your parents? You were frightened and frantic. When you found them you felt safe and secure, and everything was right in your little world. When you live your life out of whack with your dreams, there is an underlying unease. But when you are on track, you feel charged! You are excited, motivated, alive, calm, and creative, and generally you feel whole. If you take charge of your life by deciding what you want, how much money you'll need, and develop a flexible plan of how you'll get it, then you are in control of your fate. If you don't have a clue about where you want to go, how you will get there, or how much money you need, then your fate is left to others, and that is never a good thing.

Start by getting to know yourself and what turns you on. What makes you happy, or what do you think would make you happy? Olympic gold medalist Peggy Fleming knew early on what she wanted to do with her life: skate. She says in her book *The Long Program,* "I had found something that made me feel whole. Some people go a whole lifetime before they discover it. . . . You know when you find it: It's the thing that makes time pass differently so that you give all your hours to it and it still doesn't feel like too much." That's what *I'm* talkin' about.

I also think we should look at what we *don't* want as well. Many creative people do NOT want a traditional career. They see others working regular hours in regular jobs with regular lives, and they want to be different. They don't think it's risky to want to be freelancers or hop from job to job until they find what they are looking for. They are less likely to listen to those around them who tell them to take the road most traveled. They may have to be "starving artists" until they make it, but it sure beats giving up and giving in to the pressure to trade in a dream for a disappointing, depressing, and dreary existence of "settling down and getting a real job." Not gonna happen. That's not to say we can't support ourselves with "day jobs" to pay the bills until the advance money arrives or we get our big break, but to give up a chance to make money from our creativity for a nice home, fancy car, and a steady paycheck is not (usually) the way we want to go. (Despite what your parents say, it will not make you happy. Did it make *them* happy? Okay, then.) By the way, if you are reading this and asking, "But what if I am already trapped in a life I don't like and I can't possibly live on less or take a chance by going after what I really want?" that's okay. I don't think you should drop everything to pursue your passions—yet.

This chapter will help you uncover some of your unfulfilled expectations, and then once you know what they are, you can start chipping away at them little by little. There is always hope, and it's never too late. Stuntwoman Jennifer Lamb says, "If you find something you love doing as you're growing up, look hard to see if you can make a living at it instead of giving it up for something more sensible." There is always a way to change your life and get unstuck and get paid to do creative, challenging, inspiring, exciting, and fulfilling work. If all you get now is a paycheck and little else, there is a better way. It's scary to push away a steady paycheck. You think you will go hungry. You may have to go on a money diet (or budget), but you'll survive. It will be a dramatic change to have to find your own food (income), harvest clients (market), reap what you sow (collect money owed), and continue to plant seeds (network), but in the end it's a healthier lifestyle.

Let's do some soul-searching to see what it is you really want, then figure out how much you'll need to get it (and keep it) as well as how you'll go about getting it. By the way, you are not greedy just because you set a specific goal of how much money you want to make or have. It's actually a healthy thing to do. How much money do you want? Need? How much money would be enough? What will it take to make your dream come true? Once you can answer these questions, then you can go about getting it. Just like a business needs to plan, you need a financial plan. The dream will dictate what you need to do, but before you begin at least lay out a rough plan of what you think you will need to do. Or, if you have the discipline, figure out the exact amount of money you want and then work backward. How much will I need to generate every year, month, week, day, hour? Even if you don't do this exercise (do I know you, or what?), the fact that you have focused yourself on a money goal will open up your mind to possibilities and opportunities it may have otherwise missed and unleash your creativity and resourcefulness.

Making more money starts in your mind. You must be able to see it and focus on it. It becomes real. This doesn't mean that you will do anything to reach this magical money goal. You still do what you love, but maybe you do more of it or charge more for it. You stay aligned with your values and purpose, but because you now have that number, that North Star to guide you, you make better decisions with your money and become even more clever as your right brain looks for ways to help you get to it. Then, once you reach it you plot a new course (or stay on the one you were on), but you should never be without a dream to focus on. If a little doubt is creeping into your consciousness now, remember what *billionaire* Ted Turner said: "You don't have to be smart to make a lot of money." Just resourceful and resilient.

As much as we like to "let the chips fall where they may" and "cross that bridge when we come to it," there is something to be said for gaining some control over your finances, your future, and your life. You will be more disciplined, determined, and driven to reach a dream. Okay, let's delve deeper.

What Do YOU Want and How Much Do You Need?

"If you always do what interests you, at least one person is pleased."

—Katharine Hepburn

In the old television show *Run for Your Life,* Ben Gazarra, who plays a wealthy doctor, was told he had only six months to live. So what does he do? He buys a fancy sports car and tools around the country and visits exotic locales (loving a lot of the ladies and saving the day). For some, a life-threatening illness *is* a wake-up call. Others already know their calling. "I found my mission. Some people cure cancer; I help women find something to wear," says fashion designer Shoshanna Lonstein. Once you know what you want to do (whatever that may be), the next step is to figure out how to finance it. Sometimes if we can just get the car moving, we can "pop the clutch" and jump-start it. Don't believe me? Dennis Smith was a New York City firefighter who had written a few short stories and poems about this and that, but he had no luck getting them published. It was a letter to the editor that got him a call from a large publishing firm asking him if he would be interested in writing a book about his life. It was a dream come true, and his first book, *Report from Engine Co. 82,* went on to sell two million copies. Smith followed up with three more bestsellers. Amazing! The author surmises that the reason his writing was so well received was that he finally found a subject he was passionate about. A subject that burned within him as he wrote. Now when his children ask him for advice about what to do with their lives, his answer is always the same. He tells them to think about what they are feeling deep down in the pit of their stomach. To measure the heat of the fire there, because that is your passion. Your education and your experience will guide you toward making the right decision, but your passion will enable you to make a difference in whatever you do. Good advice, I'd say.

Once you decide what you want to do, the only thing left to figure out is how to support yourself while pursuing it. (Once people discover their calling, many would be willing to work for free, but you don't have to.) Put another way, we want to earn money doing something we love even if we don't make money right away. If the desire to do something is great enough, we will go for it against all odds because we simply can't let go. There are ways to support yourself while you are working on a dream, and we will explore those later in this book, but for now, deciding what we want our work to be is more important than how to make it work.

So let's go back to what we want in the way of a career and a life. Just like creative people are diverse, so are many dreams and desires (as well as tolerances for what one is willing to do to get those dreams), so it is impossible for me to know what you want. But I'll bet it involves earning enough money to pursue your passion, and that *is* possible. It may not be done the conventional way, but it can be done. This book is filled with examples of unconventional ways people have been paid to pursue their passions. Leave any baggage at the curb that contains phrases like "I can't" or "impossible" or even "But how will I . . ." Lighten your load and open your mind, because we are going to go on a journey to your future, where anything is possible and dreams do come true. Once we get to your deepest desires as well as your strengths, we will be able to find something that you want to do and can do for money that will make you happy, confident, and competent—all of which lead to success and fulfillment.

 **ACTION ITEM**

For the next few minutes, eliminate any limiting thoughts or beliefs and write, draw, doodle, talk into a recorder, discuss with a friend the following question: "If I didn't have to worry about money, what would I want?"

Life, Liberty and the Pursuit of Happiness

LIFE (STYLE)

Myrna Loy made this comment once: "They say the movies should be more like life. I think life should be more like the movies." What movie would you like your life to be like? What would the plot be? This is an important question, because you trade your life for the money to pay for the things you want. The good life, so to speak. You end up having to work, which means you can't spend that time (ever again) on something you want to do because you have already traded it for a paycheck. I just want to make sure that what you want is worth the price you have to pay.

1. Describe how you would live your life if you had all the money you wanted.

2. Looking back at your life, when were you happiest? Create a drawing or an essay based on your answers to that question.

3. Make two lists. The first list is everything you like about your life now and why. Then make a list of everything you don't like about your life and why.

4. Answer this, Do you want more money or more life? How much of your time are you willing to sacrifice for the pursuit of money (and things)? What are you NOT willing to do to make more money?

5. Who has what you want? What is it about their life that you admire? What did they have to do to get what they have? Are you willing to work that hard or pay that price?

ACTION ITEM

Draw a circle and divide it into a pie chart with each piece of the pie sectioned off to represent how you would like to spend your time if money weren't an issue.

LIBERTY (PASSION)

Liberty means freedom. Freedom to do what you want with your time and your life. Freedom to spend it on things that give you inner satisfaction and joy. In other words, we are talking about finding what pushes your buttons. When you know what you want without a doubt, you will be willing to sacrifice and work hard for it—but because you feel so strongly and intensely about it, you don't mind.

    1. What are a few of the activities where you feel focused or at peace? (Where it feels more like play than work.) Where you get absorbed and don't want to stop. What do you do that makes time fly? What are you doing when you get so excited you can physically feel it? What do you daydream about often?

    2. What is something you would do for a living even if you weren't paid?

ACTION ITEM

Make a list of your dreams, desires, missions, and must-haves, and then next to each one try to mind-map possible ways to make money at each.

THE PURSUIT

You have to make money to survive. It's best when you make money doing what you love and would do anyway. You are trading your (valuable) time for this money, so of course it is best when you are doing something enjoyable, something you are passionate about and do well (and are paid well for, too). Even if you aren't paid well, if you are happy with how you earn your living, then you are a success. Gwen Stefani of No Doubt said of her success, "The best thing about our success is that it affords us the lifestyle—I never have to wear a suit. I never have to wear nylons. I can do my hair pink [and she does]; I can do whatever I want." You don't want to be in conflict. Gwen's not!

1. What do you *not* like about how you make money now?

2. In your ideal job what would you be doing? Do you want to work for yourself or for someone else? What skills and talents would you use? What would you wear? Where would you work? (Indoors or outdoors?) When would you work? (What would your schedule be like?) What would you be paid? How would you be treated? What type of people do you like to work with? Write or draw what your ideal job/career would be like.

 **ACTION ITEM**

Name five things that would make you feel you "have it all."

The Pursuit of Happiness

Happiness is what you really want. You may think it's more money, but I'll bet it's peace, joy, contentment, respect, satisfaction, pride, and so on. These are things that will make you happy. A lack of money is no reason to be unhappy. It's your inner thoughts that prevent the feelings you are after and not a lack of money. Finish the following sentences. I am happiest when I am . . . • If I didn't have to work I would . . . • I am motivated by . . . • My mission in life is to . . . • My passion is . . . • All I want is . . . • I wish I could . . . • If I were lucky I would . . . • I would be willing to risk it all for . . . • I am great at . . . • The perfect job for me would be . . . • My top priorities are . . .

ACTION ITEMS

1. Begin with the question "What do I want/need more of in my life?" Then bounce a ball off the wall, and every time you catch it write down the first thing that pops into your mind.

2. Look at what your subconscious is telling you, and discover your deepest desires. What your heart and your head say. Grab some magazines and catalogs and rip out any picture that triggers something in you. Look for connections, patterns, ideas. Then make a collage.

3. Look around your home for clues about what you want, value, cherish, treasure. How do you decorate? What do you read? What hobbies do you enjoy? What photos do you have up and who is in them?

4. Make an inventory of talents, skills, and abilities that people would pay for. Include experiences you have had (travels, languages, classes). How can you capitalize on them? Who do you know? What kind of gear or tools do you have? What are your strengths? What do you have to offer the world? All these things may give you a clue as to ways to make money or point to a path to follow.

5. How would it *feel* to have the kind of freedom you have always wanted? What it would it be like to have all of your bills paid? To have money in the bank? Now let's get in touch with *why* you want the money. Next to each item on your wish list, write how much you need and *why* you want it.

💰 ACTION ITEM

I wish I could remember where I saw this exercise, because it is great! It opened my eyes, that's for sure. Step one is to write down what you make in a year. Go ahead, do it. Then multiply that number by two. (Example: $13,000 × 2 = $26,000.) Ask yourself, how would it feel to have that much money flowing into your life? What would it mean to you? How much would your life change? You repeat this step over and over until you feel you've gone too far. (Example: $26,000 × 2 = $52,000, followed by $52,000 × 2 = $104,000, and so on.) When you reach that magical number that you feel comfortable with, write it down in big bold letters. Then try to imagine where that money might come from and, using arrows from each source, draw it flowing into your magic money number. Then draw a picture of you, and use arrows to show that magic money flowing directly into you. Last, draw arrows showing where that money would flow to. What would that money buy? The reason I don't remember exactly how this originally worked is because I tweaked it to my liking. You should do the same. Get creative. Use words and phrases that explain how you would use this money. What would it mean to *your* lifestyle? What things could you do that you always felt you couldn't do before because you didn't have enough money? What would you work on? Where would you go? How and where would you live? Basically, what would your life be like if this was your annual salary? Spend some time on this.

THE PURSUIT OF PAY

According to the *Forbes* 400 the people on the list attained their wealth through real estate, the computer revolution, oil and gas, or acquired it through inheritance. I have to be honest: None of those methods for making millions really do it for me. How about you? Let's look at how much money you want and how you would handle it.

1. Describe in detail what you want your financial picture to look like. What areas do you need to improve in when it comes to managing money? How would you like to handle your money? What are some new habits you'd like to have regarding handling your money? What are some easy first steps you could take regarding your money?

2. What could you do/sell for money? Is there a demand? Name five people right now who could pay you for what you want to do. Can you? Are there any opportunities to make money with your idea? Is anyone else making money doing what you want to do? If so, how are they going about it?

_____

_____

ACTION ITEM

Make a list of everything you would like in your life. This includes *everything*. Next to each item write what it would cost you. Add up everything and total it.

_____

You Can Have Anything You Want, Just Not Everything

"Life is short and so is money."

—Bertolt Brecht

Since creative people are usually multitalented, it's easy to become overwhelmed with possibilities. So what we need to do next is cut down the number of goals to get to the "want tos" and eliminate the "could do" and "should do" items. We want the most meaningful ways to make money, and that means some things must go—for now. The first thing to do is eliminate things that are in conflict with your values. For example, if you want to be a super parent and a superstar musician, you may find that you can't do both, so which is more important?

1. Make a wish list that includes everything you want and then cut it down to your top ten dreams and desires. What matters most? Rank them like you would a movie. Five stars for a hit, down to a dog for something that really doesn't work for you. It's subjective and should be based entirely on your tastes and preferences. Ask yourself how much time you would like to spend on each one. Would it be worth the effort? What would be the benefits for reaching the goal?

2. Next to each item mark it with a heart if it's a heart's desire, put a cash sign if it is likely to make money, then put a check mark if it's doable, and finally add a star if it has already been done somewhere, by someone.

3. Now list your top ten desires and dreams, and look for any employment (or self-employment) opportunities to support yourself and get paid while pursuing these passions. Think outside of the box here. How could you make money off your idea?

4. Or, using index cards, write down your top ten desires. Now you have to make some tough choices. Prioritize them by arranging them into order with the most important one on top, and sort the rest so that you have them in order of importance.

5. Put a first step you will take today next to each item.

How to Stay On Purpose

"I had desires to be a rock star since the age of nine. I had all these pictures on my bedroom wall and dreamed that one day that would be me."

—Rick Parfitt of the band Status Quo

Seeing is believing. You want to be able to see it, feel it, believe it. Financial freedom begins by believing. The more you believe you will earn more money, deserve to have money, the more likely you will get it. You want a money mind and not one that is rooted in poverty. The way it works is, when you feel better about yourself and your money, you will worry less, make better decisions, and be more creative; basically, by feeling better, you bring good things to you and are better able to deal with bad things. That's why affirmations keep you focused and motivated. They will give you a sense of security and a sense of hope and keep your thoughts on the future. What you want is a result of how you think and feel. If you are burdened with negative thoughts all day, every day, you aren't operating at your best. You won't see solutions to your problems because they are buried under a mountain of negativity. You can't get rid of these thoughts, but affirmations and visual reminders of your goals are the antidote.

1. Put your goals where they are in plain view (to you), and make it a habit to look at them often. Plaster them all over your walls. Turn them into a screensaver. Set up a website where you can post all your dreams, and keep the address to yourself if you choose. Put your money goal in your purse, on Post-it Notes, in your planner. Make a coffee cup, sleep shirt, or postcards (or e-postcards) you send to yourself. Paint or draw a picture of you living your dream. Record your dreams on a tape and play it in your car or while you work. Turn them into a poem. Write a screenplay about your wishes. Score them on sheet music. Turn them into a song. The goal is to keep them at the forefront and remind you to focus on them and maybe even share them with others and ask for their help.

2. Take a bank deposit slip and write in the amount you would like to deposit each month. Create a bankbook and write in the balance that would "do it" for you. Anything visual is good. Create a mock-up of your new stationery for your dream company. Put your book atop the *New York Times* Best-Seller List. Make a mock-up album cover. Go ahead and record (no matter how crudely) some of your songs. Draw a blueprint of the studio you always wanted. Interview yourself as if you have already reached your dreams. Answer the question from the perspective of being where you want to be. Make it look real as if you were on the front page of *USA Today*. I did ALL of these things and still do.

3. Read success stories for clues about how the people who have what you want went about getting it. Don't compare yourself to them, but use their life story as a guide to what you should do or do next. Ask yourself, what do they have that I don't? What did they do that I'm not? Make a list of action steps they took, and now make one you can follow. Put your own life on a time line (age 15–20, 20–25, and so on). Go back if you want to see what got you where you are, but better still, put future years on this time line and start to write in what

you want to happen and when. It could look like a giant thermometer or a racetrack or just a line with the years on it. Who could you talk to that might be able to help you achieve your dreams? Find out how to get ahold of them and start making appointments to talk to them. Also ask yourself what you might need to make this dream come true (training, resources, time).

4. Turn your main goals into an affirmation you read to yourself over and over and that you write out ten times first thing every morning. This can be a sentence or two that states your purpose. Turn it into a poem if you want, or make it into a song you sing all day long. Make this an affirmation that causes you to stretch. Be specific about what you want. Do you want more money (one dollar is more money), or do you want one million dollars? Make the affirmation brief enough that you'll remember it. By writing and reading your affirmation you can overcome your fear and feel worthy of all the good things that will come. You will start to believe it as you retrain your brain. Create a mission statement for your goals for the next five years, such as "I want to make a difference through my art and make $110,000 a year." Use it as a guide for how to use your time and make decisions. Include what you want to own, earn, feel, do, have, experience. "I feel great because I spend my days writing books that touch people's lives and am paid over $100,000 a year."

5. Make a mind-map of your dreams. In the middle of the page put your main goal, a picture of what you want, or just simply your name. Then branch off into other sub-goals. Along with each sub-goal, branch off into what you need to make it happen.

6. Create a fake financial statement. This is your net worth (now), and this is your net worth on drugs. What I mean is, make it up. Go ahead, hallucinate a little. First, pick a date for this balance sheet (in the future). What are your (future) assets, including cash you have in the bank, investments, property, and anything else of value. This is what you (will) own. Then subtract what you owe (your liabilities). Subtract what you owe from what you own, and that is your net worth (in the future, the way you want it to be). Also, make a cash-flow analysis the way you want it to be. Where do you see your (future) wealth coming from? (Let your imagination loose.) What would you like your salary to be? Royalties? Endorsements?

Investments? Grants? Any other flow of dough. Make a fake bank statement with the balance you want. Create a make-believe investment portfolio.

7. Make a dream board. This is where you cut out pictures representing what you want and then paste them on a big board. I recommend adding a caption for each picture in the collage so you engage your left brain.

8. The logical brain helps you prioritize activities and can tell you what would kill a dream. Things like procrastination, self-doubt ("I can't") or perfections ("I'll never do it as good as . . ."). A deadline can cause you to get going. Keep you focused. It's not just out there anymore. Stop with the excuses and get going. Make a list of what you want to do by a certain age. By age thirty-five I will have . . . and so on. I want (fill in the blank). It will cost (find out and then fill in the blank). I'd like to have it by (fill in the date). I already have (how much?). Then do a little simple arithmetic. Divide the cost of what you want by the time you think it will take. Now it's not so "pie in the sky" and certainly more real. By breaking it down it brings it into focus.

The word "goals" sounds so left-brain, maybe a better word is "dreams." I have always had dreams. Always. That isn't to say I live in the future. Heck no. I live life as I go, but I know where I am going. I think this is the secret to my own success. When people first step into my office, one of the first things they notice is that my dreams are up where people can see them. I have a dream board with pictures of my goals. I have an affirmation on my desk (which I write out every single day). I made a mock-up of a *New York Times* Best-Seller List with my books ranked on it. I have a *People* magazine profile about me (in the future) that I read regularly. I put my goals in my planner, wallet, on the wall—everywhere. It sounds hokey, but believe me, it works.

With all this talk about the future and financial freedom, I don't want you to think I have forgotten that happiness is found in the moment—no matter what your financial situation. You can be happy right now. Don't waste your life waiting for your finances to be perfect. Pay attention to the present. This is where joy, happiness, and peace are found.

Goal for It

"Everyone has talent. What is rare is the courage to follow that talent to the dark place where it leads."

—Erica Jong

When I was in French Polynesia (on the island of Huahine), I wondered how I could make this my home. Impossible, I surmised. Then I met an American who not only lived there, he lived well. Peter Owens is a potter who fell in love with Huahine (and a Tahitian woman) and decided to move there. In addition to his art, he owns a pearl farm. His home is in the middle of the most beautiful lagoon on the most amazing island on earth. He did it! I have met people over the years who are able to earn a living and make their dreams come true doing the most unbelievable and unusual things. No matter how bizarre your dreams are, if there is a will there is usually a way. I don't have to look much further than my own life for proof that anything is possible. I grew up loving to surf and along with my brothers founded a chain of surf shops. Going surfing was part of my job description. Who would have thought? Then I decided to pursue another passion of mine, writing, and here I am. It's ten o'clock in the morning and I have been up for only half an hour. I went for a swim and then grabbed my laptop, stuffed it into the basket of my bike, and rode to my favorite coffeehouse by the beach so that I could finish this chapter. As soon as I am done I think I'll take the rest of the day off. I can't complain.

When we were kids we thought anything was possible. We need to get back to that limitless thinking. It's time to think big. Many creative people put limits on their dreams because of fear. Fear that they will screw up. They think that they always have so what's different now? What's different now is that you are going to knock off that self-defeating thinking. Even if you screw up, you'll survive. You will learn, grow, and try again. If you go for the impossible you just may surprise yourself and make it. When you are living on grilled-cheese sandwiches because that's all you can afford, it's hard to imagine having a million dollars in the bank. Don't let fear or your current circumstances hold you back from thinking big. Things will come to your life that you can't possibly foresee right now. Just point yourself in the right direction and watch what happens. It takes the same effort to think big as it takes to think small. There are no unrealistic dreams, just unrealistic time frames. So go ahead and acknowledge what you really want. Focus on the possibilities. You'll find a way.

"If I weren't afraid I would (fill in the blank)." Then ask yourself: What is holding you back? If another creative person is doing what you want to do and has the lifestyle or fame you crave, then it's possible. Maybe you need to write down all the reasons you think something can't be done and then systematically eliminate them by asking if anyone else has done it. Go down the line and add a "yes" next to each item on your list. Then in big letters make a sign that says "Yes!" and hang it where you'll see it every day. In your studio, office, car, bathroom, guitar case—wherever. This helps when everything goes to hell and you want to give up.

I have struggled at times, too. I also took some fairly risky steps on the way to reaching my financial goals. I quit working for a seminar company that provided steady income but was starting to get in the way of more lucrative opportunities. It was a bit sketchy at first, but now I work a lot less for *more* money. Thank God I had the courage to quit and resist the temptation to go back when things were tight, or it would have turned out a lot different—worse. The lesson I learned over the years is to have a dream or vision, then act on it and trust that things will eventually work out. I am not one of those people who says, "I'll pursue my dream as soon as I have . . ." Nope, I will not wait until the time is right. The time is right now to do it. If you say, "I'll become an author as soon as the kids are grown or as soon as I have more time," you may never get going. Go for it now, even if it's baby steps. Get moving in the direction of your dreams.

Actor John Mahoney, who plays Frasier's dad, Marty, on the hit TV show *Frasier,* worked a steady job as an editor of a medical journal until he was thirty-five. He was bored to death and felt trapped. He made good money, had a nice home, and even had a corner office. The most prudent thing would have been to keep the steady job and push the dream of acting aside. But he gambled and it paid off.

 **ACTION ITEM**

Look for ways your dreams overlap with your resources and opportunities. What experiences, skills, tools, training, education, talents, connections, and so on do you already have? Does the dream draw on your natural talent and skills? Find a connection to what you want to do and who will pay for it.

Finding Your Sweet Spot

"A writer? From this you make a living?"
—My grandfather, the businessman, to me, the writer

Have you ever had that pit-of-the-stomach feeling (no, not from spicy food) that is brought on by a deep desire to do something? I was reading an in-depth story about artist John Severson, who merged his love for surfing with art. He has had a long career painting surf scenes, photographing surfing, making films about surfing, starting and running *Surfer* magazine, and now living a quiet life on Maui. When I read his story, tears welled up in my eyes. I wanted what he had so bad, it hurt. This guy got it right. How he got it is equally inspiring. When he was first dating his wife, she asked him what he planned to do with his life. He said he had a five-year plan and a ten-year plan. The five-year plan was to get his surf films going and start a magazine about surfing. His ten-year plan was to sell the whole thing and support his life of art—painting, traveling, and surfing. Obviously, she liked what she heard because she married him. And he did what he said he would do. When I read this (and as I write it) it gives me goose bumps. Here is a *very* creative person with a purpose and a plan.

Robert Byrne once wrote that "The purpose of life is a life of purpose." Whatever that purpose is, it drives you. Don Henley once said the reason he became a rock musician was "money and girls." Okay, whatever pushes your buttons. Maybe it's the life around your work that matters most. Matt Groening, the creator of *The Simpsons,* said, "I never wanted to go to an office and carry a briefcase. I said, 'That's no fun. I want to play. I want to make up stories.'" In his career he has done just that, unlike Homer Simpson, the character he created, who says, "I used to rock and roll all night and party every day. Then it was every other day. Now I'm lucky if I can find half an hour a week in which to get funky." Find your passion and pursue it.

The difference between difficult and doable is passion. Jack

Lemmon once said, "Anything that is truly worthwhile, passion is a part of it." When there is something to strive for and you want it badly, you can endure the setbacks and struggles and sacrifices it takes to get it. You are willing to work hard, for little or no money, for the chance to make it. You put all of your energy and time into it. Money isn't the goal but a by-product of this mission. It pushes you. Inspires you.

Without passion or purpose, the possibility of making money and having the success you desire is much less likely. You simply won't have the stamina or be willing to sacrifice and suffer, and so it won't happen. Passion is the pull that keeps you in line and the push that makes you try harder. Energy, enthusiasm, excitement, ingenuity, emotion, determination, courage, and resourcefulness all come from passion. When you are on-purpose and find your calling, you have given yourself the greatest gift because you are doing what you want to be doing and should be doing, and when that happens you usually do it exceptionally well, and that attracts others to you, as well as money.

I met a man while on vacation who ran a resort in the South Pacific. He did it all at the resort and loved it. He would greet the guests when they arrived (and even made the leis for each arriving guest), arranged the flowers in the lobby, did a story-telling to kids in the afternoon by the pool, worked the bar at night and came up with wild rum drinks while making sure everyone had a good time, and even sang with the band for a few tunes. This guy was oozing creativity, and he loved his life, and people were drawn to him like moths to light. I came to find out that he started at the resort as a bellman and because of his passion for his work was promoted again and again until he reached general manager. When the owner passed away, his will called for his prized employee to inherit the lavish resort, rather than any of the founder's three children. This guy said what a lot of people who are on-purpose and filled with passion say: "I would do this for free." But when you have passion and purpose you usually do something so well people will pay you.

When you enjoy how you make money you have achieved success, in my opinion. Don't let people tell you that what you want to do won't sell. If you really want to do it, you will find a way. Many of the best books were written with a total disregard for what was selling or not selling. The writer was simply passionate about the subject matter—obsessed, even. Whatever pushes your buttons, go for it, even if those around you try to talk you out of it. Nobody would have guessed that Leon Bean would be a millionaire. He was much more interested in hunting and fishing than the small store he ran with his brother. But when he combined business with pleasure and designed a unique outdoor boot he called the Maine Hunting Shoe and sold them through the mail, he struck gold. The outdoorsman made a fortune with his L.L. Bean catalog company. Who would have thought it? You are limited only by what you think you can and can't do.

• **Others don't live your life.** Work doesn't have to be drudgery. You can make a decent living at what you like to do. One woman was a manager at a public relations firm and the envy of her friends, but she hated it. She was in management and removed from the creative side of the business. All she really did was a bunch of paperwork and deal with personnel problems. Her dream was to run a bed-and-breakfast away from the city. She did it, too. Now she does PR for her own place in a small town in the mountains outside San Diego.

• **Take a look at what is working and do more of it.** This can be a trap if your talents lie in something you are sick of doing. Maybe you restore pianos, but every time you try to do something else, opportunities pull you back to your original skills. Jack Van Mourik, a piano restorer, has wanted to establish a musical retreat for as long as he can remember, but his career got in the way—so he sold his business of forty years and used the proceeds to buy a half acre of land and establish a music retreat that he calls "paradise here on earth."

• **Go with your strengths (whatever they may be)—that's where the money is.** There is a guy who plays in the sand for a living in San Diego. He is a professional sand-castle builder. I was chatting with him one day while on a run (I accidently damaged one of the turrets on his castle), and we struck up a friendship. Passion has a magnetic pull, and I felt I needed to know this guy. He has turned a hobby like building sand castles into a business. He couldn't be happier. Sand castles are his passion. He teaches others how to build them, and he set up a sand-castle-building organization and competitions. He even has a corporate sponsor! To make more money he photographs his work and sells it, and, of course, he gladly accepts donations (which I made since I crushed his castle). He isn't rich, but he makes a good living, and he gets to work outdoors and do what he loves. I say he's a success!

• **It's never too late to make a change—for the better.** To have the courage to chase your dreams and follow your passion and do something different, regardless of the risks, is worth looking into. My wife and I know a woman who was just not happy. She was forty and unfulfilled at work, her home life was a mess, everything was wrong, yet she was making a lot of money with her work. Then she was in a terrible car crash. While she was laid up in the hospital, she had time to look at her life and decided to go in a different direction. Her priorities shifted, and her passion, photography, is now her profession.

• **Follow your heart.** Follow your strengths, your gut, your talent, even if it isn't the safest route. You will be happier and more productive. Remember, success isn't how much you make but how you make it. Elizabeth Pace knew what she wanted to do since she was young, but she chose a different path. From all appearances she was living the good life with all the trimmings (nice home, well-paying job, husband), but she was not happy. To her credit she realized that there might be more to life and prayed for a sign that would show her what to do to have more purpose, passion, and joy in her life. Then one day while on vacation, she walked into a music store and started playing a set of congas. The man in the store said, "You have to buy these. They will change your life." He was right, too. She traded in her house and other luxuries to start Soul Beat, a nonprofit San Diego school where children and adults can learn music and dance. It has not been easy. She lives in one room of the old warehouse that houses the school and subsidizes Soul Beat by running an executive-recruiting business out of another room. Despite the struggle, she says that the school has reawakened her soul.

• **Here's one time when being obsessed is a good thing.** Lorrie Moore, author of *Birds of America,* a collection of short stories, says, "I still think you should become a writer only if you have no choice. Writing has to be an obsession—it's only for those who say, 'I'm not going to do anything else.'" Arthur T. Vanderbilt II is the author of *The Making of a Bestseller* and says, "The moment of holding that first book surpasses the moment of first holding a wet and curious-looking baby." He goes on to explain that later on your book may suffer slow sales and horrible reviews, but the joy of being published for the first time is indescribable. (It isn't until later that you get jaded.) Some of us suffer through and survive the struggles of being an author by remembering why we do it. Getting in touch with that good feeling we get when a book is launched. Your advance money may be minor, the book may not get the proper promotional backing you hoped for, and the reviews may be less wonderful than expected, but if you keep focused on why you write (because you can't imagine doing anything else), you will keep going until everything comes together and you are suddenly an "overnight" success, making the money and getting the acclaim you deserve.

• **Make love, make money.** The stress from hating how you earn your living can be hazardous to your health. Even if what you are doing looks like "the life" to others, if it doesn't make you happy (even if you are pulling in the bucks), doing it for the long term can tear you apart. Mayim Bialik played the title character in the sitcom *Blossom* but quit acting after the show went off the air. She never really wanted to be a part of Hollywood. She made her money and then walked away and is working on her Ph.D. in neuroscience. "You need to know what makes you happy. I love what I do now," Bialik says. Ilan Mitchell-Smith, who co-starred with Kelly LeBrock and Anthony Michael Hall in the movie *Weird Science,* has found his true calling—teaching. "The feeling I had [about acting] was I don't like this very much; it's getting in the way of what I really want to do, which is to be in academia." These actors made more money acting than they do now, but they don't seem to care.

• **Unhappy at work can sometimes translate to unhappiness at home.** Director Amy Heckerling says, "What I hate about making movies is getting up early. You may say you like a script, but then you have to ask yourself, 'Do I really want to get up at 6 A.M. to make it?'" Celebrated soprano singer Deborah Voigt almost gave up her dream of being an opera star because she was overweight. Instead she took a job as a computer operator. She worked full-time for a couple of years but yearned to sing. She would work for eight hours and then take voice lessons at night. She eventually decided to use her gift and went on to become one of the best in the business. You don't have to give up everything. You can keep your corporate job and find another outlet for creativity as a last resort.

• **To make money in a meaningful way is the goal.** When they say, "You can have it all," to me that means you use your natural skills and abilities, have creative freedom, get the respect and admiration of your peers and the public, add value to the world and help others, *and* make money, too. Someone asked me recently if I would be happy in some other line of work. I can honestly say the answer is "N-O." If it were "yes," then I would certainly look into that. It makes me happy, and I am fulfilled. I don't necessarily need a nice car, fancy clothes, or other trappings of success to feel like a success. To me, being able to do what I do, do it well (I hope), and get paid for it is the ultimate reward. I do remember when I first started out as a writer knowing it wouldn't be easy to get where I wanted to go, but because I believed, I found the strength and stamina to succeed. Making it in the arts is not a halfhearted thing. That expression "Give it your all" holds true. Get in touch with the magic and why you want it. So many people during that crazy stock-option gold rush were blinded by bucks. They said, "I hate this job, but they are paying me so much I'll be able to quit after a few years." Hello! The stocks became worthless, and so were those jobs they hated.

• **Do what you love and the money will follow—sometime, somehow.** Author William Least Heat-Moon has been compared to such great writers as Mark Twain and Henry David Thoreau. His books are the result of his traveling the back roads of America and meeting individuals who live in these less-traveled areas of our country. For his book *River-Horse* he traveled the nation's rivers in a small motorboat. It all began when he lost his teaching job, his marriage was on the rocks, and, in need of a break, he loaded up a van and hit the road. While on this journey he made a discovery. "One belief that I'd long held was that human beings need to pay attention to who we were when we were about ten years old, because we're well enough formed by then to have certain elemental passions that never leave us." During his long drives he went back and looked at what he had wanted to be when he was a kid. He wanted to be a writer and photojournalist. So he began his book while on his extended road trip, and when he got back he worked odd jobs while finishing the book and then trying to get a publisher. His first book, *Blue Highways,* was on the *New York Times* Best-Seller List for forty-two weeks. He made (a lot) of money doing what he loved.

• **You don't ever have to retire.** Mexican photographer Manuel Alvarez Bravo feels that a love for his country, rather than any specific school of artistic thought, is at the heart of his work. When asked if he intended to retire (he is nearly one hundred years old) he said, "I cannot say that I work, exactly. It is a part of my life to take photographs, to develop them. It is like eating. It is a spontaneous thing." Speaking of photographers who are passionate about their art, Jeff Devine is probably the most prolific surf photographer of all time. As a teenager he took pictures for fun, until one made the cover of *San Diego Magazine,* which led to a job with *Surfer* magazine. He lived the life (living in Hawaii, spending his days at the beach). Then he tried his hand at commercial photography (where the big bucks were) but found it too stressful and not nearly as creative as his work for *Surfer.* So he focused on his passion, surf photography, and it paid off. He became the magazine's photo editor and has been traveling the world doing what he loves (and getting paid) for over thirty years. Passion pays.

Dreams into Action

"At the parking garage the sign reads, 'Lost Tickets Pay Max.'
What a great deal for Max!"

—Flash Rosenberg

I was a doodler in school. In fact, many of my early report cards mention my "artistic talent" *and* "lack of focus" in other subjects. I dreamed of becoming a cartoonist. There are many of us who had visions of making it as an artist, but when the going got tough we got going—in a different direction. That's why *Dilbert* creator Scott Adams's story is so inspiring. He dreamed of becoming a cartoonist but wasn't sure how to go about it. Like many before him, he turned to *Artist's Market* to find out where to submit his creations. He put together some samples of his work and sent them out but was rejected more times than he could take. So he decided to hang up his Rapidigraph pens and got a job. But an encouraging letter from another cartoonist told him to hang in there and keep submitting his ideas. That's when he created his comic strip *Dilbert*. Adams says that the secret to his success is affirmations. A dozen or so times a day he writes down his goal. He began by writing, "I will become a syndicated cartoonist" fifteen times a day. Today he is wealthy beyond belief. I wonder what I might have become had I stuck with my cartoon characters.

Maybe making money isn't your highest priority, but if you don't earn something from somewhere it becomes difficult to sustain yourself, and the dream dies. So force yourself to think about money and how to get paid. (We cover this later in the book, but sometimes it is just a matter of placing value on what you do and then asking people to pay you. Really.) Think about ways to subsidize your art by working a day job or getting a sponsor, a grant, donations, or financial backing, or finding some other (legal) creative ways to make a buck. More and more people are trading in stress and steady work for spare time and work that means more than just a paycheck. They are trading in the killer job for the killer life. Either way, making some money is needed.

Money made easily is just as valuable as hard-earned income. There is no need to feel guilty. Most people don't realize that "easy money" is usually the result of hard work and sacrifice over a long period of time. It took time to develop the talent to be able to command a high fee. I know when people hear what I get paid to give a speech, they suck in a lot of air and say, "Wow, that's a lot of money for an hour's work." Yes, it is. But it took me years to get to the point where I had something worth saying and was able to deliver it in an entertaining and educational way.

It takes plenty of hard work to make money in the arts. Many times it comes down to the dilemma of whether it's worth it or not. How hungry are you? Are you doing all you can? Really? There are many examples of people who had to put up with so much crap before they started making real money at their art. They were relentless. They were determined. They would not be denied—no matter how long it took. I say: Good for them—they deserve it. We see them as a success but many times fail to recognize or remember what it took for them to make it.

Some see people like Frank Sinatra as a legend—and he was— with over one hundred records, fifty movies, and three Academy

Awards to his credit. That's only half the story. He began as a skinny kid singing for pennies in his family's saloon in Hoboken, New Jersey. He worked hard to make a name for himself and in the '40s was making over a million dollars a year from movie roles, royalties, and concert appearances. But by the age of thirty-seven he was all but written off and struggled to make money. A friend gave him a gig playing in a nightclub on the Jersey shore. When he heard about a movie being made from the novel *From Here to Eternity,* he had to borrow money to fly to Los Angeles and undergo the humiliation of a screen test to get the part. He did, but rather than his regular $150,000-per-picture fee, he was forced to take only $8,000. The role won him an Oscar and revived his career, and he was soon making more than $4 million a year. This is the up-and-down career of a creative person. So if you start to feel sorry for yourself because you aren't making enough money or getting the big break you want so badly, remember that we all go through the same cycles, and those who make it keep our heads held high, put in the extra effort, do the undesirable things that need to be done to keep the dream alive, and it eventually pays off. The Frank Sinatra story also shows us that you can never let up and that it pays to put some money aside when things are going well.

Even if you don't have any money set aside, you can still out-hustle and outwork others who have more money. Things like technology are not a replacement for hard work. Creativity and resourcefulness can overcome a lack of financial resources.

What actions can you take to create more money? Most books do not sell themselves. It is the author who makes it happen. You have got to work your butt off. Having too much money can make you stupid and lazy. When you don't have money for promotion you use innovative ideas that usually work really well. Not many people put in the consistent and persistent effort it takes to make it. They have some fantasy of it all just happening for them somehow. There is no secret to success. You have gotta just put in the time and effort to do it. And when you do finally make it, you have to keep at it. That's why artists have to continue to seek positive publicity and continue to promote themselves. How high you want to go and how much you want to make are in direct proportion to how hard you are willing to work.

You may be saying, "But I have worked hard, and nothing happened." That may be true. The art world doesn't give you total control over your circumstances, but it is more likely that something good will come out of your efforts than if you did nothing. I meet people who have big dreams with lots of dollar signs in them, but when I tell them what other creative people have had to do before making any money at their art, I can see it in their eyes—disappointment or disbelief. Too bad. Talent and effort combine to produce results. You need *both* to make money in this life. Even if you think you are doing all you can, I have to ask: Can you turn it up a notch? Sometimes just when you think you've done all you can, that last gasp of effort is what lands you that lucrative deal you were lusting after.

Making money means doing the things others aren't willing to do. For instance, actors Keenen Ivory Wayans and Eddie Velez would drop by casting offices, agencies, and the lots unannounced and try to charm the people working there. Instead of sitting on their butts, they tried to make something happen (which will eventually mean making money) and had good success. Not only did they meet key industry people this way, they got readings and eventually roles by doing these chat-and-charms. Most people wouldn't be willing to work that hard. But if you force yourself, you force things to happen.

Nobody owes you a living just because you can paint, play, or perform in some way. Just because you are talented doesn't mean someone will discover you and dole out the dollars. But talent and skill do help, along with a little "luck." Hard work leads to luck. Luck is when you win the lottery. Or as Homer Simpson says, "If you really want something in life you have to work for it. Now quiet, they're about to announce the lottery numbers." But working hard at your craft and working harder to get someone to realize how great you are is how you get that "lucky" break.

Bestselling mystery author Sue Grafton begins her day at 6 A.M. with a long walk on the beach before starting writing at 9 A.M. She says, "I treat this as a job, and I wear makeup. I don't work in my pajamas." It's a well-paid job at that, in no small part due to her hard work. When you want something badly enough you need to harness that desire by putting in place a plan and then putting that plan into action. So I ask you again: Are you doing all you can to make it? An

Oxygen.com survey discovered that 57 percent of those under thirty dream about being famous. Daydreaming won't make it happen. So it stands to reason that your dream is the path to success, and hard work and persistence are the vehicles to get you there.

We sometimes see successful creative people as having a cushy life, but they work hard. The difference is that they love what they do and are well compensated for their efforts. Take the band Everclear, for example. That band and its leader are driven. Before they released their first record in 1993, Art Alexakis had paid his dues by playing in punk bands to pay the bills while studying film at UCLA. Then he started his own record label, which unfortunately folded, but not before he learned some valuable business lessons. He then sent in samples of his music to several major record labels. Most ignored his solicitations, but one, Capitol, expressed some interest and encouraged him to keep them posted on projects he was working on. Broke but not broken, he formed a band and recorded a demo on a shoestring budget and tried to get a record deal and gigs. The band played everywhere and anywhere and built up a loyal following and released an EP. Remembering the Capitol executive's invitation to send him what he was working on, Alexakis did, and the band was signed. "Once you get signed to a major label, that's when the work really begins," Alexakis states. Even though they had financial backing from a big label, they still had to do what got them to that point—play and promote. He says in *Roland Users Group* magazine that to succeed you need to be prepared to work the record. "Be prepared to shake a lot of hands, do promo, play stupid promo gigs, and do things for radio stations. . . . If you don't do that, your chances of having a career are slim to none." He should know.

Some may look at what we do and say, "What's so hard about that? You play with clay, or smear some paint on a canvas, or put some words down on paper." Baby, it's harder than it looks! I would say that more than half of what we have to do to stay on top of the game (whatever that is) is tedious and time-consuming, and we likely aren't getting paid to do it. If you are an illustrator, that may mean staying in touch with trends, staying in touch with art directors, and staying in touch with your talent (otherwise known as practicing and learning). It may seem like fun to be able to go to a bookstore and browse through magazines for hours on end and call it research or meet a reporter for lunch, but after a while it gets old. Just like a band on tour—sex, drugs, and rock 'n' roll gives way to finding a place to do your laundry, dragging yourself to yet another radio interview, and spending endless hours on a bus watching bad movies. But when you have a passion for something, you actually don't mind putting up with what goes into making yourself more marketable and thus making more money. And making yourself more marketable can mean practicing your craft ten hours a day or spending time on the road promoting yourself. It pays off.

In the future, machines will likely do all the grunt work, but what will be valued more than anything else will be ideas and creativity and those who *are* creative. "Idea people" will be prized and well paid. We will have risen from the ranks of the underpaid and underappreciated to a vaunted status of both fame and fortune. In an automated world, painters, actors, writers, sculptors, inventors, dreamers, entertainers, architects, and anyone else with a creative streak will finally get what they deserve. Wake up! We're not there yet. Until then we will still have to scratch and claw for every break and buck we get. But it's nice to know that finally those of us right-brainers who have been trapped in a left-brained world will rule.

Oh, the Horror

"If at first you don't succeed, use duct tape."

—Unknown

To reach your dreams may take time. I realize you want it to happen "like yesterday," but I just don't want you to be unrealistic about what it takes to make your money dreams come true. Don't freak out (and abandon your goals) if it doesn't happen for you right away. And please don't say, "It will never happen." You won't be stuck in a lousy life forever, I promise. So sit back and enjoy the journey, because it may be a long one. That doesn't mean don't do anything. Far from it. If you don't work it, then it won't work out. Patience and persistence, that's the formula I'm talking about.

Few creative people start earning money right away. Many struggle for a while before they receive substantial compensation for all their hard work. As an actor, if you earned $15,000 or more a year you would be in the top 10 percent of the Screen Actors Guild.

($5,000 a year puts you in the top 20 percentile.) Hang in there and hang on, do good work, concentrate on your craft, and let your lack of money motivate you rather than hold you back. Many times people who have made it look back fondly on their hard times and the sacrifices they made and appreciate what they have even more because they made it the old-fashioned way—they earned it. Of course, some have gone without for so long that once they get a taste of the good life they go nuts, but that won't be you. You will survive your Top Ramen days and be a better person for it. There really isn't a better way to look at it than that. Just keep plugging away, and things will change for the better. Like a cat, you will always land on your feet. Others have made money at art, and so will you. Sure, some *never* make a ton of money, but they are able to live on less and live the lifestyle they want, which ultimately is what success really is.

April Sinclair used her experience as a community activist to take on the publishing world. She had written the first twenty pages of a novel but had no agent, contract, or connections in the publishing world. But what she did have was a willingness to do what it takes to make it—she hustled. She called a local bookstore in San Francisco and arranged to give a reading (of her unfinished book!). She passed out fliers, called friends, and did what any good activist would do: She started a grassroots movement to get people to hear her work in progress. She got an amazing number of people to turn out (over a hundred), and she mesmerized them with her performance. She was so jazzed that she took her show on the road and the buzz SHE created had agents knocking on HER door. The finished novel, *Coffee Will Make You Black,* reached cult status when it came out, and she received a six-figure advance for her next novel. She quit her job and now writes full-time. Good for her.

Lessons from the Hood
"Five thousand years a wandering people—then we found the cabanas."

—David M. Bader

If you watch VH-1's *Behind the Music* or *Before They Were Rock Stars,* it becomes clear that most who have made it have struggled at one time or another. I think the lesson is that the reason they are being profiled is because they overcame hardship to become either rich or famous (or both). I like to ask myself: What if they had quit? The world would have been deprived of the pleasure of enjoying these great artists' work. For example, Stevie Nicks and Lindsey Buckingham were floundering in Los Angeles after they made a poor-selling solo record for Polydor, but they then were asked to join Fleetwood Mac in 1975. There is almost always a silver lining in each disappointment. Find it.

Bob Dylan's sales numbers were not as strong as you would think early in his career, but that didn't diminish his standing as a great artist. Roy Orbison's early recordings didn't sell, and he was let go by his label. To survive he wrote hit songs for other artists until he got another deal. Raymond Chandler, one of the finest writers of detective fiction, didn't write his first novel until he was over forty and only after he was laid off from his job as an oil executive. Author Sarah Ban Breathnach's book *Simple Abundance* spent more than two years on the *Publishers Weekly* Best-Seller List (in hardback!) and has sold more than three million copies. It was originally rejected (by thirty publishing houses) before being picked up by Warner Books.

Steve Winwood was considering hangin' it up after dismal sales of his first solo album. He was running out of cash and searched for alternative ways to make money. He considered farming but felt that he was more suited to working at a record company or producing other artists. He also came to grips with the fact that he would have to simplify and streamline his life and live on less. Once he realized he could, and would, be okay, he went to work on another record. Without the pressure of having to have a hit, he wrote and recorded *Arc of a Diver,* which was a HUGE success.

Vincent van Gogh sold only one painting during his lifetime (arranged by his brother). It wasn't until 1890 (the year he died) that he started seeing success. Strangely, the prospect of success brought on the madness that led to his demise.

Whoopi Goldberg was a an ex–drug user and single mother living on welfare in San Diego who worked a series of odd jobs like bricklayer, bank teller, and cosmetician at a funeral parlor. She managed (barely) to pay her bills and keep her dream of being an actress and comedienne alive. Before Rickie Lee Jones had a hit with the song "Chuck E's in Love," she was broke. And I mean *broke*. During the day she worked as a waitress but was fired. When her boyfriend left she was unable to pay the rent and slept under the Hollywood sign at night. She didn't give up the dream, though. She played gigs around Los Angeles and wrote, rather ironically, the song "Easy Money" and made it into a demo which landed her a contract with A&M. Mark Slaughter of the band Slaughter felt that his early struggles (he lived in a dingy apartment that had a bed and nothing else) helped make him hungry and gave his music a harder edge that led to the band's success. Grammy winner Beck Hansen was working for four dollars an hour at the YMCA and a video store and lived in a rat-infested shed behind a house when he made *Mellow Gold* for $500 at a friend's house. Mark Knopfler named his band Dire Straits because of the group's horrendous financial situation in their early pub-playing years. Bob Seger worked on a Ford assembly line but quit because he didn't want to give up his dream of making a living at music. For ten years he toiled for an annual salary of around $7,000. He logged thousands of miles in a station wagon traveling from small gig to small gig, but he enjoyed it more than a conventional job. It just goes to show that it doesn't matter where you start—it's where you finish that matters most.

The point I was going to make is that even if you aren't making money and the market for your work hasn't developed (yet), it does not mean you aren't talented. There have been times when I was one of those who saw nothing but bleakness. I would listen to other struggling artists who made blanket statements like, "Nobody makes money as a writer" and "There's no money in the arts." This was on top of my own self-loathing. This double whammy made me feel that life as an artist was a futile pursuit. That there was no way I was gonna make it. My feelings would wander from anger to despair to irritability to indifference to hopelessness. When you are in this kind of state, nothing feels like fun, and it's almost impossible to concentrate because you feel that what you are working on is pointless. "It will never sell. Who cares if I finish this? What does it matter?" Fortunately for me, money was not the biggest concern in my life (even though I didn't have any, I didn't care). I just kept cranking out books and pounding the pavement. I also hung out with creative people who were making it, so it seemed possible. It eventually paid off, and the dark clouds disappeared and were replaced with a more sunny disposition due to the dollars coming in—finally. There is always hope. You can't listen to those who try to convince you that there is *no* way or it will *never* happen. Maybe it won't—for them. But you'll be fine.

 ACTION ITEM

Never Say Never. "I will never make money at my art" is a common complaint. If you remove one word ("never") from the sentence and reread it, it sounds much better and is more accurate. "I will make money from my art."

You Could Use Some Support

"Live within your income, even if you have to borrow money to do so."

—*Josh Billings*

Support can come in many forms, from money to advice to a helping hand, and from many sources: a friend, family member, mentor, or your spouse. There is another angle to consider. Support can come from your label, publisher, employer, gallery, agent, manager, and anyone who has a stake in your success. Get them to give you tools, time, or money. Sometimes sharing your financial frustrations with other creative people can be helpful.

Not everyone who claims to be supportive really is. I have seen so many instances where one person can drag the other person down. This is especially true with couples. One person in the relationship has to pay for everything and is the responsible one. One is a loser and keeps coming up with crazy ideas that will inevitably fail and cause financial duress. One person works while the other goofs off all day. One tries to save while the other spends freely. One keeps jumping from job to job. Many times the artist is kept from his dream because he has to support other people and their dreams and is sabotaged at every turn by people who put him down or by being around people who have basically given up. No matter how much money you have (or don't have), you need friends. It's not easy because they can be jealous and try to sabotage you.

You need a teammate, someone who doesn't resent being the breadwinner, someone who understands that there is a lot of struggle to get going in the arts, someone who believes in you and your dream and will do what it takes to help. Couples need to work as a team and share in the decisions, discuss matters calmly, and establish some common financial goals. The secret to my success is my better half. I married my complete opposite. She's the ying to my yang. Where I am a right-brainer, she's a left-brainer. (This makes us a complete person?) We are a team. This polarity of thought works well. She also has a real job with benefits so that I don't have to. I come up with all these grand ideas, and she deals with the details and planning. She's the voice of reason, while I am more pie-in-the-sky. Over the twelve years we have been together, we have learned a lot from each other.

LOSE THE LOSER

A young entrepreneur was on a roll. His freelance Web-design business was booming, and there was no end in sight. In his personal life he rented and remodeled an expensive apartment and leased a Mercedes. He met and wooed his dream girl with expensive gifts and exotic vacations. When he proposed he presented her with a three-carat engagement ring and flew her family in from all over the country. She was a teacher who made a lot less money than he but over the years had managed to save $40,000. Once they were married they commingled their money. Since he worked at home and she taught class during the day and was working on an advanced degree at night, it was agreed he would manage the money. After having been married only a couple of months (they were still in their honeymoon period), his Web-design business slowed down considerably. When he was short on cash he dipped into "their" savings without consulting his wife. He figured that when he landed another client, he could put the money back and she would never be the wiser. By the time the couple reached their one-year wedding anniversary, he had "borrowed" more than half the money from "their" savings account to pay the bills. He never let on how bad things were with his business. If she hadn't been blinded by his flashy lifestyle, she might have asked more about how he handled money. His whole life had been a series of booms followed by busts, but this time it was both of them who would go bust. It wasn't until she wanted to buy a house that he had to tell her the truth. In her mind, what he had done was cheat on her. Maybe not with another woman, but with her money. When she did look into their finances, she was appalled. She left him after having learned a valuable lesson about love and money.

3

GET OUT OF YOUR OWN WAY

Recognizing potential pitfalls regarding the handling of your finances is the first step to avoiding them. Without any judgment, answer these questions honestly and quickly with a "yes" or "no."

1. Have you ever supported someone else while you, your art, your dreams, your life were put on hold? Are you too afraid to cut lose a loser/deadbeat friend or lover for fear that nobody else will come along?

2. Are you afraid to ask for a raise or to raise your rates, and thus remain underpaid? Do people owe you money, but you are afraid to ask for it back (or forgot)?

3. Are you so disorganized that you don't bill clients promptly or pay your bills (or taxes) on time?

4. Have any of your bad habits hurt your career (showing up late, not at all, or intoxicated)?

5. Do you do things that are dishonest or go against your morals and values to make money? Do you hate your job and do it just for the money?

6. Do you make unrealistic promises that you can't keep?

7. Does your lack of savings put you on the brink of financial disaster?

8. Do you do things in haste (like fail to run a credit check on a client or tenant or not bother to read a contract before signing it) that have caused you to lose money in the past?

9. Do you buy material things to make yourself feel better or to impress others?

10. Do you get angry or jealous or feel inferior when others make more money, have nicer things, or have more success than you?

11. Are you more than $500 in debt or struggling to make minimum payments on your debts? Are you in the dark about how much you owe? Are you near the limit on your credit cards?

12. Do you fail to take care of yourself? Do you not have health insurance?

13. Do you let your possessions fall into disrepair and have to buy new ones?

14. Do you turn down or blow off potentially bigger opportunities to stay within your comfort zone? Do you ignore industry signals and fail to make corrections in your approach to your career?

15. Have you ever been a victim of a scam or get-rich-quick scheme?

16. Do you feel that many of your money problems you brought on yourself?

17. Do you think balancing your checkbook is a waste of time? Have you bounced more than a check or two this year?

If you said "yes" to more than a few of these questions, your money woes may *not* be because of the economy, the art world, or other external factors—it could be that *you* are to blame. If that's the case, that's good news, because it means it's fixable and within your control to do so. Read on.

Are You Your Own Worst Enemy?
"Comparison is what kills most artists."

—Julia Cameron

Ever wonder why the rich get richer? I'll tell you why. Because making and managing money (and making good, sound financial decisions) starts in your noggin. Without wasting their mental capacity on envy, anger, worry, fear, and frustration, they can flourish. (Our brains work better without all that distracting brain clutter.) Instead of worrying about money, they focus on finding solutions and creating great work, knowing that by being more productive the money will come.

Wealthy people (creative and otherwise) usually have a healthy dose of self-esteem and are able to seek and accept money that comes to them without any guilt. They value themselves and their work, time, and talent. They don't waste time on things that don't pay off, because they are cost-conscious and profit-minded. They would prefer to pick a project that has the probability of turning a profit rather than directing their time and resources to something for which the best they could hope is to break even. They know what they want, believe it's possible, overcome their fears, and move forward. And when they make it, they feel they deserve it, so they don't usually sabotage their success. People pick up on their confidence (and can see their success) and want to work with them, hire them, pay them large sums of money.

So remember, if you focus on abundance, that's what your mind believes, and you will find creative ways to get it. The flip side is to listen to naysayers who tell you that nobody makes any money in the arts and that we are *supposed* to struggle. If that's what you believe, guess what—that's what you'll get. Stop saying that money comes to "other" people. No matter what has happened in the past, you have to focus on the work at hand. If your mind is filled with doom and despair, it will be hard to feel that you and what you do have value—and they do. So if you could choose an attitude for today (just try it for a day and see how it feels), would it be negative (nothing has gone right, is going right, will go right) or positive (anything is possible)?

💰 ACTION ITEM

Get a bunch of cash out of the bank, and hold it in your hand. See how it feels to get in touch with YOUR money. It's real, and you deserve to have every penny of it . . . and more! Please put it back when you're done. (Wink.)

No-Limit Thinking

"If you want something badly enough, make an attempt. . . .
A lot of people get scared. They're afraid to fail. Take that
word out of your vocabulary. You don't 'fail,' you've 'tried
your best.'"

—Jane Seymour

Maybe the most devastating effect of low self-worth is that it limits what you think is possible, which in turn limits your growth, which ultimately affects your earning potential. Low self-worth usually equals low net worth. How? Let's say you suffer from confidence issues—are you more or less likely to go for a grant? Your inner critic quickly shuts down the possibility of YOU ever getting the grant with inner dialogue like, "Who do you think you are, a real artist?" We must break self-imposed limitations on what we can do and how much we can earn as creative people. Lord knows, there are others in the arts and business world who will try to beat you down so they can take advantage of you; don't help them do it.

Here's an example of what I am talking about. There were two shoe sales representatives for competing companies who were sent to sell in the Australian outback. One rep called his company to report that the "Aborigines don't wear shoes, so there is no sales potential here." The other rep also reported back that the natives don't wear shoes, but his take was different. "Aborigines don't wear shoes—great sales potential here!" It's all about perception. If you don't feel like you deserve to get the breaks, top billings, and big bucks, you never will. If you don't feel that you are worth anything, it's kinda hard to convince others.

I can't explain exactly how it happens, but your inner beliefs can manifest themselves (in the worst way) in the external world. If you think and feel "I'm no good," I believe others can pick up on that. If you can raise your self-esteem, you can raise your rates and eliminate self-destructive and self-sabotaging behavior. Once you remove the roadblocks you put in your own path, you can make more money, because you'll see opportunities that were clouded in worry, fear, and self-loathing and that life is full of possibilities.

When you suffer from low self-esteem, you will take less than you are worth in wages, allow others to exploit you and your talent, always be underpaid, and struggle. One woman, who is a writer and editor, allows clients to take advantage of her and sometimes does things that she rationalizes as promotion but are foolish and a waste of her time. She will print out hundreds of pages on her laser printer but doesn't charge for this. She will FedEx completed work at her own expense. She will always pick up the tab for lunches, even if the client insists on paying. She feels she is lucky just to have the work, so she goes above and beyond what people expect (which isn't so bad) but passes the point of diminishing returns. When she wanted to work less and started to charge for things she once did for free, people paid without any problem. She had been losing out on that money because of her low self-esteem.

When you lack money and have money problems, it becomes the focus of your thoughts and your life. You may go through periods of anger (How could I be so stupid?) to fear (If I lost my job I would be in big trouble) to hopelessness (I am so deep in debt I will never be able to get out) to obsessing about schemes to get your hands on some money—at any cost. More money is not the answer to your problems. If you don't value yourself and your talents, your mind will look for ways to prove you are not worthy and get you to do things to prove you are worthless. Put another way, you can only accept what you feel you deserve, and if you don't feel you deserve much it will bother you as much as having no money, so you will find ways to discard it. You have to raise your "comfort zone" of what you think you deserve. How else do you explain a singer with everything going for her (talent, looks, charisma) who is mind-blowing at rehearsals, but when it comes to gigs, she chokes by being wasted, showing up late, and screaming at a ball game the night before, leaving herself hoarse. Or the writer who says she wants to make it her full-time job but then screws up her chances by not spell-checking her résumé, wearing inappropriate clothes to job interviews, and failing to finish her first writing assignment. She is more comfortable in her low-wage job and doesn't feel she deserves to be paid better.

The fear of money is called *chrematophobia* (I'm serious), and it's a fact that fear limits how much you make. Afraid to ask for a raise. Afraid to ask for a referral. Afraid to raise rates. Afraid to leave a dead-end (but safe) job for a potentially better one. Fear of not having enough, fear of the unknown, fear of failure is what keeps many creative people from realizing their monetary dreams. Fear can paralyze you and take away any drive you may have had. All of a sudden you can't focus, can't create, and all you can do is make excuses. You are afraid to make that call that can land you a key interview. You are afraid to try out for that band that needs a new singer, so they get someone else, who goes on to become a star. Fear also causes you to stay in a job you HATE and work for less money because you are afraid if you quit, nothing else will come along.

Sometimes playing it too safe is a way of sabotaging success. In the movie *You've Got Mail,* Meg Ryan's character runs a children's bookstore passed down from her mother. Then a large chain store moves in "around the corner" and she has a tough time deciding what to do—whether to close or keep losing money. I won't give it away, but something her character says made sense to me. "I lead a small life. Well, valuable, but small. And sometimes I wonder, do I do it because I like it, or because I haven't been brave?"

There is fear of making a decision about what to do with your money when it comes to investing. Should I or shouldn't I buy that hot stock? You can't decide, and you watch in dismay as it triples in value and then splits four-for-one. Damn! Or you own some stocks and you are afraid to sell them for fear they may go even higher, and to your horror they tumble in value until they are worthless.

There is the fear that you will end up on the streets. What if I can't pay my bills? What if I can't land that account? What if I lose my house? What if I am audited? What if I never work again? What if my book bombs? Most worries are about what may happen in the future. Most things are never are as bad as they seem, and even if the worst comes to fruition, you will find a way to survive it. Right? What are you afraid of? Is it real? Can you control the outcome? What action can you take to ease your fears?

Not all fear is bad. The fear of being a bag lady may be just the motivation you need to work a little harder or save a little more. With the roller-coaster ride that is the creative career, these fears can be real, and if they help you get your act together, I say good. When you are hot it's hard to imagine that things could ever turn around, but, oh yes, they can. Jeff Probst, the host of the reality TV show *Survivor,* said he "partied like it was 1999" when the show first took off. Then he realized that it could all come crashing down, and the fear of that led him to make sure to put some bucks in the bank in case he (or the show) is voted off the air.

Another phenomenon I have noticed is that low self-esteem prevents us from spending time with people who might push us. We may shy away from people who are more accomplished (and more positive), in favor of others who are struggling or those who are worse off than we are. Misery loves company, so they say. But you are allowing others to pull you down rather than putting in time with people who could pull you up. If you need material things to make you feel you are important, worthwhile, successful—to boost your self-esteem—then you are in for some serious problems. You are not your salary or what you own. You think it impresses others (and it does impress people—the wrong people), and you will be in an endless cycle that will leave you broke both financially and emotionally. You need to feel secure in who you are and not what you have. We get into debt because we believe (erroneously, I think) that we have to buy friendship and love.

I had a roommate years ago who spent lavishly on the women he met and, in effect, frightened them off. Then when it came time to pay the rent, he was unable to come up with his share because he'd blown it on gifts for girls. When he went back East to visit his family, he tried to impress them by flying first-class and renting the biggest car he could find (neither of which he could afford). Once, while he was away, he let a girl he had just met borrow his car. He never saw that car again, and his insurance wouldn't pay because he *allowed* her to use it. I think he confused love with money. Love can make you do stupid, irrational things with your money.

Let's say you are able to rein in your brain and you achieve some success. That doesn't mean you let your guard down and let the demons back in. I know a woman who got everything she ever wanted and was more miserable than before. The pressure of her success was overwhelming. That, and the fact that she had struggled so long as a sculptor, made the sudden success she was experiencing freak her out. She had a commission with a university, the city, and two corporations. She was paid very well for the work, but she still had to *do* the work. I had no doubt she could do it, but she did. She did everything in her power to sabotage her success, and it was sad.

You have to feel like you deserve success and money to be able to enjoy and keep it. Otherwise, once you start to make it you feel unworthy and find ways to get back to your comfort zone, which is less wealth and success. The woman in the example above did it by rebelling against those who had paid her by procrastinating and doing shoddy work.

So, how did we end up this way? The reasons why we can become twisted when it comes to our (dysfunctional) relationship with money are many. Let's not go there. Instead of playing the blame game let's focus on a future where we place more value on ourselves and our talents. It's important to realize that everyone suffers from bouts of insecurity, but successful people are able to feel the fear and do it anyway.

💰 ACTION ITEM

Write down all the things you have done to earn money. How hard you worked. All the training you have invested. The dues you have paid. Your track record. What your work means and does for others. The time you put in. You have earned the right to be paid well, to have money, to be rich.

Full Esteem Ahead

"It's like a menu. They can look, but they can't afford it."
　　　　　—Tennis star Anna Kournikova on her body

While actress Renee Zellweger was making the movie *Bridget Jones's Diary,* she began keeping a "gratefulness journal" by her bed. Every night before going to sleep she would add a few of her favorite things, including photos of friends, favorite poems, and positive words. I think that's a good start for all of us in building up our self-worth. If you spend your days thinking about how much money you've pissed away, how hard it is to make a decent living at your craft, all the times you've failed, do you think that is going to help or hurt your chances of correcting the problem in the future? We tend to focus on all the negatives and ignore the positives. Why is that? Why don't we believe, instead, that anything is possible and that the future looks bright?

• **Focus on the positive.** Make a list of all the positive things you have going for you. If you can't think of any, make a list of all the things you think are holding you back, then wad it up and flush it down the toilet (literally) and see how that feels. Then start again and make that list of positive traits. Or make a list of traits you think you need in order to make it, and one by one start working on them. If you say, for instance, "I need to understand money matters better," start learning what some of those ridiculous finance terms mean. Learn one new one a week. Knowledge is power, and it will demystify a lot. You won't feel that you are in the dark when someone on one of those money shows says something you don't understand.

• **Things aren't as bad as they seem.** If all you can think about is how you have mismanaged money and what an idiot you have been, it will drag you into depression and affect all areas of your life. Let's put things into perspective. Money is only one area of your life. You are not a failure. Maybe you have failed at finances (in the past), but that doesn't mean you need to beat yourself up. There are many creative people who are successful but don't have a lot of money. They get rave reviews or the respect of their peers, but their sales are slow. So what? When a book doesn't sell, does that make the author a bad writer? I don't think so. It just means that book missed the mark (or a hundred other reasons outside of an author's control). Also, a lot of very smart people are dumb with money. I don't know if that thought helps you any, but it does give me some comfort.

Okay, try this on for size. It's a cliché, but it rings so true: Today is a new day, and what has happened in the past does not determine your future. Focus on the task at hand. It's a funny thing, but when you don't focus on the money (or money problems) but on enjoying the process of acquiring it, good things usually happen. The past is the past. Events in your rearview mirror are worse than they appear. Keep your eyes on the road. Bad stuff happens to good people (you), but when you are knocked down, you have to get up.

• **Don't believe everything you read.** Much of what you hear and read about the art world and the creative life is rather negative.

Not only does this paint a picture that is inaccurate, it's irresponsible reporting. The people who write that such-and-such a genre is dead and buried are frustrated artists who couldn't make it themselves. No matter what the economy is like when you are reading this or what the state of the arts is, there is always money out there for those who believe it is in abundant supply—and it is. Don't use a slump in the arts or a recession to make you feel there isn't money to be made. By whom? By people who have a clear idea of what they want and are determined to get that goal no matter what obstacles are in their way. No excuses! Start reading success stories and stay away from "the sky is falling" Chicken Little stuff. Also, don't buy into the myth that artists who struggle are somehow morally superior and that to be serious artists we must be starving artists. It simply isn't true.

• **Fear can be your friend.** William Faulkner said, "The basest of all things is to be afraid." So let the fear of being broke and living on the streets motivate you to make more and save more. Fear can be a good thing, if controlled. Once you take action you can quiet those fears. Sometimes it is the thing you (and others) fear most that holds the most opportunity to make money. You have to force yourself past your fears. How? Let go of the outcome and focus on the process, or in other words, remain in the moment and usually the pressure and fear will disappear. Besides, when you remove the fear, everything is more fun, and when you are having fun you tend to do better work. Without worry you can focus on your art and let go of the "what if nobody likes it, what if it doesn't sell, what if they reject the proposal, what if I fail?" Catherine Bell, who plays Lt. Col. Sarah MacKenzie on the TV series *JAG,* is a very talented actress (and a BABE!). Sorry about that. I'm a fan. Anyway, she would not be where she is (on a hit show) if she didn't overcome her fears. "I've always been big on deciding what I want to happen and then making it happen," she says. Anyone can do that.

• **Financial freedom doesn't actually come from money.** You can have freedom from financial worry at any income. Some people worry about money even when they have more than enough. Everyone has anxiety about money. But if you don't deal with your fears and issues about money early, they are still there when you make it. Face your fears. What are you afraid of? Why? Is it real or imagined?

• **Money doesn't equal happiness.** Happiness is NOT a by-product of wealth. Happiness is in your head. If you feel rich, then you *are* rich. There are people who have millions who don't feel it's enough or that *they* are enough. Sad. Making a magical amount of money doesn't make everything in your life all right. You will still have problems, even with a million dollars in the bank. There will never be enough money for some people to feel good about themselves. They never really appreciate what they have or what they have accomplished. It's always about trying to get more and trying to prove that they are worth something because they make a certain amount of money. It's like a rat on a treadmill. They will never get anywhere. They will say that as soon as they make a million, "Everything will be all right and I can enjoy my life." Wrong.

• **Even if you are struggling, keep creating.** The tide will turn. You can't stop at the first setback. Keep busy and keep your mind off money matters for a while and ENJOY the creative process without the pressure of trying to make millions. If you stress on money problems 24/7, do they get any better? Nope. Worrying solves nothing but robs you of your life and the joy that is all around you if you would just put your financial concerns on the back burner. Then you will free yourself up to do better work, and I'll bet things will turn around. A combination of thinking good thoughts along with doing good work leads to good results.

My favorite surf spot has a big rock sticking out and is extremely shallow right where you take off. If you focus on the rock or the shallow ledge, I guarantee you're not gonna make it, and you're gonna get hurt. It happens all the time. The wave is makeable if you do everything right. So you have to first believe you are going to make it and then keep your mind on the matter at hand and off the rocks. Look ahead, and your body follows. Look down, and you will end up on the rocks. Life is like that. Focus on your goal, and usually things work out.

• **Don't compare yourself to others.** The only time comparing yourself to others does any good is when you want to do something that seems impossible but someone else has pulled it off. I am not suggesting you have to be happy for them, but it does prove one thing—whatever you want to do, if someone else has managed to make it happen, you can, too. Never feel intimidated by those who have money. Just because their bank accounts are bigger doesn't make them better people! Besides, when you see others who appear to have it all, you never truly know what their situation is. They may have a nice home, big boat, and fancy car but had to sell their soul to get it or are deeply in debt. You should never want to change places with anyone, not even for a day. You should be your own hero. If you start to compare your accomplishments to others', you never truly appreciate what you have. Make a list of all the things in your life you are happy about.

• **Don't listen to others.** If others are the reason you don't feel worthy, you need to look at that. If others are telling you (no matter how noble their reasoning) that you should give up your dream and stick to your day job, I hope you put your fingers in your ears and say, "Naaaa naaaa naaaaa, I can't hear you." Actor Edward Norton (*Fight Club*) was told by casting director Georgianne Walker that he should give up acting. Even though he was barely surviving on odd jobs (proofreader and temp), he didn't want to take her word for it. In fact, he credits her for inspiring him. He wanted to prove her wrong, and he did. It's okay to have help from others, but be careful of the price you may pay for that assistance. If there are too many strings attached ("Honey, we'll pay for your education if you get a degree in engineering," but you want to make it in music), think very carefully before accepting that help. Don't sell out your dreams and desires for dollars. You also don't want to be too dependent on others. That most certainly won't build your self-esteem.

• **Never let your shortcomings stop you.** Dionne Quan never let the fact that she is blind stop her from being an actress. She now does voice-overs for the *Rugrats* series. People will always have more (and less) than you. You gotta go with what you got. Robin Tovey was born without arms and legs but makes a nice living in public relations. She became a top talent at KVO, a prestigious PR firm in Oregon, by finding ways to work around her lack of arms and legs. (She answers the phone and sends e-mail and faxes using her mouth.) Think about that. Then stop complaining of what's missing and make it happen. If you have a goal so big and the passion so strong, you can overcome just about anything that you imagine is stopping you. People sit around waiting for the right time to begin going after what they want. There really isn't a "right" time. If you wait for it, you will be waiting forever.

• **Some people give up a little too soon.** Jim Morris was a high school teacher and baseball coach in West Texas when some of his kids challenged him to go to an open tryout the Tampa Bay Devil Rays were holding. The kids believed that at age thirty-five Morris still had a shot. It helped that he was once a young phenom until he blew out his arm and gave up any hope of making it to the majors. But years later, he was throwing ninety-eight-mile-per-hour fastballs at batting practice in a little high school in the middle of nowhere. Well, he went to the tryout, was signed, and did make it to the majors. The odds of that happening are a-million-to-one or more.

• **It never ends.** You would think that after having written ten books, I would be supremely confident. Not! Before I begin each book, that old self-doubt tends to creep into my consciousness. To overcome it, I use all of the ideas mentioned in this section. Since you are reading this book, you know for a fact that it works! Even if you don't feel it, act like you are sure of yourself. Jim Carrey wrote an affirmation for himself that read, "I am one of the five top actors. Every director wants to work with me." If that doesn't work, incorporate it into your art. Larry David did. George Costanza, the neurotic, insecure character on *Seinfeld,* was based on the show's co-creator himself.

$ ACTION ITEM

What specifically is bothering you about your current financial situation? Be as specific as possible. Next to each item, write down what you believe you need or needs to happen to make you feel better. Then write a first step you can take for each item.

Difficult Decisions

"Just trust yourself. Then you will know how to live."
—Johann Wolfgang von Goethe

Bestselling author Anna Quindlen had a prestigious and cushy job as a columnist and editor with the *New York Times.* She was clearly on the fast track to a long and successful career as a journalist. While on a long walk in the countryside, she had an epiphany. What she really wanted to do was write a novel and work out of her home. What was holding her back from her dream? The safety and security of her job. She decided to go for her dream, and it has paid off.

Where you are and what you are (and how much money you have or don't have) are a result of the choices you have made. That means what you chose to focus your talent on, the medium you decided to work in, the projects you accepted and didn't accept, and how you spent your most valuable asset—your time. Let's face it, we have all made some poor choices in our past. But we have also made lots of good ones, too. We should learn from our mistakes but not dwell on them. The goal is to have a dream and make choices that support it. Focus on the future and make smart choices each and every day. Little decisions do make a difference, too. You will make hundreds of decisions a day, and over time, they add up. You probably think it's the major decisions that matter most. Oh, they matter, but so do minor ones. Just focusing on the things in front of you and making good choices about how to make and manage your money can mean the difference between wealth and welfare. Anyone can become wealthy. Anyone! So why doesn't everyone do it? They choose not to. What? Think about it. We all know we have to spend less than we earn and save and invest the rest. Simple. So why don't we do it? We *choose* not to. If you were to cut back, live simply, and forgo a few luxuries, you could start to make a dent in your debt, put some money away, invest in the stock market, or finance a project or business that could make you millions.

Money problems are a result of a pattern of poor choices. If you allow others to manage your money and they screw up, you chose to put your money with them. If someone scammed you, again, you chose to give them your money to begin with. If you watched the stock market plummet and did nothing, your inaction was a decision. We can blame others for financial problems, but it usually comes back to the choices we made. Hugh Grant decided (for whatever reason) to get into his BMW and head for Sunset Boulevard and meet Divine Brown. That incident (and decision) did temporarily damage his career, and thus, his income.

I'm not sure about Hugh Grant, but some artists make decisions that damage their careers and dash their dreams to avoid having to deal with the pressure. One writer I know wants to be a published author. Every time she seems poised to pursue this dream, she gets pregnant. She now has four young children, and "the book" is on the back burner again. Oh, did I mention she is a single mom and the children have three different fathers? Decisions determine where you are and where you will be down the road. Decisions do have power!

Maybe worse are those people who are afraid of making the decision to give up good for great. Especially when good is not their idea of "good" but what society thinks they should want. Safe and secure can make for a very comfortable life, if that's what you want. If the idea of a steady paycheck is your idea of success and happiness, then there is nothing wrong. It's a problem when you feel trapped. You hate going to work. You are wasting your talents and making someone else money while you get paid a pittance. If you are afraid to let go of good to get great, then you will never realize your full potential. If you gave up your creative desires in exchange for creature comforts and a dull job you hate, you have made the choice. You can get out of it if you want. If you are miserable, you have nobody to blame but yourself. You dream of a life where you are creating something and doing what you love. (By the way, if you do nothing, that is a choice also.) The strange thing is, when you are a struggling artist you may dream of steady income, home ownership, benefits, and all those perks that come with a real job.

It is best to base your decisions on more than money alone. Sometimes when you don't consider the money, you make the most righteous choice. If you make the right choice for all the right reasons (and maybe money isn't the determining factor), the right choice may just lead you to more money. It happens all the time. Judy McDonald worked for Hewlett-Packard and bought into the American dream—steady income, nice home, and so on. So why risk all that to start her own business with no guarantee it would work? It didn't make financial sense. Her idea was to develop software so that people could use their computers to create crafts projects that they could print out on color printers—HP color printers. Thus, HP would sell more printers (and ink cartridges). Since her employer wasn't interested, she became self-employed, and her business is a success.

It could be that you think you don't have a choice. You *always* have a choice! We all have the freedom to choose what we do to earn a living and how we spend or invest those earnings. Use your creativity to invent new options. Don't automatically accept what others say and do. Maybe they missed something. Maybe you feel you have to sell your house. Look at all your options. You could borrow against the equity, rent it, or trade it.

It may be that you're unsure about what to do next. I'll bet you know what to do but are unwilling to choose it. You really aren't ready to act. Admit it. You know what to do but are afraid (or not ready) to do it. We don't want to rock the boat; we feel overwhelmed, stalled. Take the time to reflect, regroup, and get in touch with your intuition.

If you are always in a go mode, or worse, always in crisis mode, it is harder to make smart decisions. You will make them in haste and without perspective. Your feelings do affect your finances. When you are down, you may tend to see only the dark side of things. A healthy mind-set allows you to see either the upside of things or a way out that you wouldn't see if you were catastrophizing. Since these low moods can come and go, wait to make a move with money until you equalize. Don't take your negative thoughts to heart. Wait for the clouds and storm to pass to get a better barometer on your thoughts.

If you play chess, you know that while you must make a move when it's your turn, you should also be thinking about your next few moves. It's impossible to know exactly what your opponent is going to do, but you read and react to their moves while playing your game. So you have your strategy, but you also stay flexible to answer their threats. You look at the board and what your options are (with your goal and strategy at the forefront in your mind) and ask yourself, "If I did this what would happen?" When you have thought it through, you make your move. The price of a bad decision is that it will lead you down the wrong road, which wastes energy, time, or money, or worse, you get lost and never find your way back. Here's how to consistently make better decisions.

All the Right Moves

"If you put off everything until you're sure of it, you'll get nothing done."

—Norman Vincent Peale

In her book *The Complete Idiot's Guide to Making Money Through Intuition,* author Nancy Rosanoff says she sums up a choice by asking herself this question: "Can I dance to this?" If the choice is right the answer is "yes." If it is wrong, it will feel restrictive and wrong. Although it sounds strange to ask, "Can I dance to this?" I also think it makes a lot of sense. What we are all looking for in a decision is a feeling of rightness, of knowing, without a doubt, that this is a sure thing. How that feels will differ from person to person. For some, it may be a sense of sureness. For others, it is a feeling of excitement. Still others, a kind of calm will come over them as the stress of uncertainty is lifted. The more practical approach is that what you decide to do (either earn, invest, or spend your money) fits into your long-range goals. Look back at your life and how you handled money. Your history of decisions can give you an idea about what would work (for you) in the future (or what won't work).

Don't take decisions lightly. What you decide to do today will ultimately have an impact on what happens to you tomorrow. You create prosperity through the decisions (big and small) that you are about to make. For example, a band may decide right now that the best way to proceed is to sign with a major label. They do, and end up with a single that sells tens of thousands of copies, but the band ends up broke because they didn't sell enough to cover the costs to produce and promote their release and, in fact, they actually owe the label money. In hindsight, they could have gone with a smaller label, sold less, and made more money.

So if you are saying to yourself, "I'm sooooo confused, I don't know what to do," here are some points to ponder.

• **Changes and transitions are not always easy.** One woman decided to give up her job, apartment, and pet to move to Hollywood and make it as a screenwriter. She ended up working as a script supervisor. That wasn't her intent, but it worked well enough to allow her to get her foot in the door, and she had moved closer to her goal. She learned a lot while working on other scripts, and eventually did sell a screenplay. John Paul Jones was very comfortable (and in demand) as a studio musician and producer. He gave it all up to join an upstart band called Led Zeppelin, which led to even more fame and fortune. The same exact thing happened to Andy Summers when he joined the band The Police after a long and successful career as a sideman. Sting also gave up steady income as an English teacher to join the band, and look what happened to him! Also, what sometimes seems like a disaster can turn into a dream come true. When the Eagles broke up, Don Henley was devastated. He never would have had solo success if the band stayed together.

• **Be a trend-spotter.** Pay attention to what's happening all around you. Keep your antennae up and take it all in, and then make your move when the time is right. William Shatner, who *has* lived long and prospered, really hit it big when he accepted stock instead of straight payment to be a spokesman for Priceline.com. The stock shot up, and he dumped it for $3 million before it came crashing down. He went boldly where other spokesmen had not gone before.

• **Be true to you.** Don't ever discount what you want. When you listen to your heart (and your head), you usually are able to make the right choice. Sometimes, what your intuition is telling you to do doesn't seem rational, but that doesn't mean you should discount it. When you go against your gut, you usually pay for it with anxiety, guilt, and turmoil. Know thyself and what works best for you. Listen to others, but do what your heart wants you to do. Only you know exactly what you need and what you can tolerate. The experts might say you should go with an adjustable-rate mortgage, but you know yourself and that you couldn't handle the uncertainty and anxiety (and risk) that the rate could go up, and then you wouldn't be able to afford to make those mortgage payments.

If I had listened to my relatives, I might have become an engineer, and although that may have been a more stable career, with steady income, I would have been miserable. When I would say I wanted to be an artist they would say things like, "A *farkakte* artist? Are you *meshuginah?* What kinda life is that? You'll starve. Why don't you become a doctah or a lawyah like your brothah?" It's more important to love what you do for a living, I would explain, but it fell on deaf ears. When it comes to decisions, father doesn't always know best. Of course, consult with your loved ones.

• **The ends don't justify the means.** One way to cut through the clutter when it comes to making a decision about what to do with your money or your life is to eliminate anything that is less than honest or would damage your reputation in any way. You may be able to make more money by doing something that is in poor taste, goes against your values, is dishonest in some way (to others or to yourself), but the price you pay is usually not worth it. If you will lose sleep over it, it's not worth it. If you could make large sums of money but might get busted—or even if you didn't get caught, you would be embarrassed if anyone knew—the choice is a bad one.

Let's say you need a new headshot but can't afford it, so you decide to steal from your employer. That's a poor choice. You can always find ways to justify it, and you may never get caught, but if you have any morals or integrity, it will haunt you later in life. I think that if you have a code of ethics that you use to judge the merits of a decision, you can't go too far wrong. Or you set up boundaries or limits to what you are willing to do. Remember that short-term gain that causes long-term pain (to yourself and others) isn't worth it.

Actress Lili Taylor appeared with Julia Roberts in the movie *Mystic Pizza* when they were both beginning their careers. The path each took is distinctly different. Roberts chose roles and projects that turned her into a superstar, while Taylor became "the Meryl Streep of independent pictures." Neither path was better or worse than the other. Actress Juliette Binoche makes career choices by the level of challenge, substance, newness, or uniqueness they offer. She turned down *Jurassic Park* but did *The English Patient* and *Chocolat,* both of which resulted in Oscar nominations and her integrity still intact. For creative people, who may have to work on a project for months and years, consider more than the money—but get all you can for your efforts.

• **Look to the left and to the right before crossing the road.** We are right-brainers who use the artistic side of our brain most of the time. But when it comes to decision making, it's best to engage both sides of our brain. The left side is analytical and can look at the facts and come to a conclusion about what we should do. That's fine for a first read on a situation. By reading and doing research on a decision, we can make an "educated" guess and back it up with facts.

We can run the numbers to prove that it would work. It helps to have knowledge and experience before going with a hunch. That way is not just impulsive but careful and smart. Look at the data and do what feels right. But your right-brain (intuitive) can't be ignored, either. How does it feel? This is your internal guidance counselor, and only you know what feels right for you. Pay attention to any signals you are getting, including sensations, feelings, emotions (both good and bad), and a sense of "rightness." It's a feeling. That's why, when you make a list of pros and cons, it uses only one half of the brain. Imagine trying something both ways. Also, imagine what a "yes" would feel like. What do you see? Feel? What impressions do you get? Then try "no" on for size. Write down your thoughts for each. Which option has the most energy or "juice"? As they say, it speaks to you. Go back to a time when you made a right decision. What were you feeling? What did you base your choice on then? Try to get that same feeling again before proceeding.

• **Run "what if?" scenarios.** Where will this decision likely lead me? Listen closely to your answer. What's the worst thing that could happen? Could I handle it? What's the best thing that could happen? Is it worth the risk? Is this what I really want? Is it worth the effort? Think things through. For a moment, get out of your heart and into your head.

• **There is no time like the present.** Act first, fix it later is *sometimes* the best approach. This is aimed more at the left-brainer who will suffer from paralysis of analysis. You know how you say to a salesman, "I'll think about it"? Usually that means "no." So why wait? Too much thinking and it may be too late. Too much information can overwhelm you and cause you to freeze up. It can also scare the hell out of you. Make a decision and go for it and correct as you go. Once you make a choice and start moving in a certain direction, things come into your life to help. There is a lot of risk in this method, but sometimes you have to force yourself out of your comfort zone to have more.

• **Pick the path of least resistance.** What I mean by that is, you hear a loud click. It feels right, it looks right on paper, everyone around you says it's the right thing to do, there is a track record of success in what you want to do, a sales history that has you salivating, it matches your skills and talents as well as your interests. In short, it's the right thing at the right time for the right reasons. Yet we still resist. We are still afraid of the risks. Well, there is risk in staying still, too.

A person I know well (who shall remain nameless) was such a multitalented artist that she was overwhelmed with options. To help her focus, we made a list of all the things she could do, loved to do, and did well and started to prioritize them. We looked at which ones would make money, which ones were her deepest desires, and so on. We began eliminating things that didn't feel right, there was no need for, she didn't have the equipment or experience for things she wasn't suited for, and were things that others thought she should do but weren't her dream. We eliminated what she could do, or should do, and ended up with a list of things that she wanted to do and would likely do well with. The other things she put on the back burner (in a book she keeps for ideas and things to pursue later). She became focused, centered, excited, and committed to her work and as a result has had more success than ever before.

• **Everything happens for a reason.** True. But what is the reason? When everything goes to hell, ask yourself what went wrong. Was it something you did? Is it something you lack? You are looking for things you can fix for next time. You also want to learn from this experience. When you are in crisis mode don't act impulsively. You will make your best decisions when you are not angry, stressed, frustrated, panicked, critical, negative, or depressed. You want to be calm, cool, and collected. Get your head on straight. We need to tap into our inner guide without desperation, despair, and self-doubt, the only way to get a true reading. Relax, recharge, regroup. Use this downtime to reflect, reevaluate, and then go about re-creating your future. Don't worry and think you missed a once-in-a-lifetime opportunity. There is more than one once-in-a-lifetime opportunity. There are infinite opportunities.

💰 ACTION ITEM

Write down a decision you are facing. Imagine you are walking down a path and come to a fork. Walk down each path. What do you notice? What happens?

I Am Forever in Your Debt

"The only time a woman has a true orgasm is when she's shopping. Every other time she's faking it."

—Joan Rivers

Let's start by being positive, then we'll get to the dangers of debt. Not all debt is bad. When you buy a home, for instance, that is okay. You have used other people's money to buy something that will likely increase in value and build your wealth. You pay back the lender (who helped you leverage your purchase) with interest, but you are still left with a profit. Another example is when you borrow money to finance a business venture and you build it into a profitable venture and pay back the loan with profits. There's no way you could have financed this start-up yourself, so you used leverage to get going. When you can buy materials and inventory on credit and sell it before your bill is due, this is good debt. Many creative people use credit cards to get their dream off the ground, whether it's a business, book, or band. This self-financing is a last resort when all conventional attempts to raise capital have failed. I have no problem with this as long as the money is spent on things that make money. If you borrow because you want a new chair and desk for your office, that is foolish. That will not create any income, so it is a poor example of debt.

Bad debt is when you bought something on credit that decreased in value and you have to pay interest on it. A double whammy. When you buy a new car on credit, you have purchased something that will lose its value (quickly), and then on top of that you have to pay interest so that the car costs more then the original purchase price. By the time you are done, the car is worth less and you paid more.

Bad debt is like a virus, and if left untreated it will eventually spread and infect every area of your life (your mental and emotional state, relationships, even your career—not to mention your finances). Every dollar in debt is one less dollar of net worth you could have had. It means that you are working to pay someone else instead of paying yourself. When you purchase with a credit card, you can pay up to 20 percent in interest (which compounds itself), and to make matters worse, if that money hadn't gone "everywhere you want to be" or if you would had left "home without it," you could have invested it in something that would pay you back (like the stock market, which averages a 10 percent return over history). You have paid 20 percent interest and lost out on maybe 10 percent more in the good kind of interest (interest paid to you), for a total cost to you of thirty dollars out of every hundred you make going to your debt; plus you have to pay taxes and need money to pay the bills. So you have to work more for less. Credit card debt is real when you think of it in real terms. There is a tremendous cost to you if you carry a big balance.

Some people have debt that is higher than their annual salary. Yikes! When people try to maintain a lifestyle that is higher than their income, they can pull it off for a while, but it eventually catches up to them. They may be thinking they are one big deal away from being out of debt, but their desperation doesn't help them close that deal. It's a vicious cycle. Making more money can be a solution, if you don't ratchet up your lifestyle and spend to match this newfound wealth as most people do. (And we haven't even talked about inflation!)

A freelance writer I know went from being a starving artist making less than $18,000 a year to becoming the marketing director for a large corporation with a starting salary of $68,000. That's an increase of $50,000 a year. It's hard to believe (and understand) why she is worse off now (besides the fact she has to get up early and punch a clock) than she was when she was working for herself (with no health care). What happened? She bought a fixer-upper house (a lot of money went into renovation and property taxes), but the rest was spent on a nice new car (to get to work), clothes (she had to dress nicer now—no more pajamas in her home office), vacations (her job was very stressful and she needed the breaks, she said), as well as more lunches out with co-workers. She went from being debt-free and living an uncomplicated life to having to get a second job to make ends meet and pay down her debt. Making more money is *not* always the answer.

When the thrill is gone, but you still have to pay for something, that is the worst. Someone once said that there is a problem with buying things on credit: "By the time you're really sick of something, you finally own it." Some of the things you spent money on were fun at the time, but all you are left with is a hangover and the bill. I can't deny that it is more fun to spend money than to save it, but just like most of us who can't eat whatever we want because we'd end up overweight, you can't just go around spending money, because you end up bloated with debt.

It's important to know what you are spending your money on. Don't guess. You never truly know how much it costs just to live until you start keeping track of what goes out each month. Until you do this it is a vague, unrealistic guess at best. I know it sounds mundane and tedious, but it is very important you do this. I think it's equally important to know where your debt comes from. Usually it creeps up on you. I know that when people are out partying, they think they are fine. "Whatta youuuu mean I'm drunk, I'm fiiiiine," they'll say. "Barkeep, another round, please." Then they do that last shot of tequila, and bam, they can't stand. See, it feels good for a while, but all of a sudden you pass the point of maintaining and you're a mess. Then the enablers come to the "rescue." Maybe your folks loan you a few bucks to tide you over. You take an advance against your paycheck, or worse, an advance on your credit card to pay the bills. Before you know it, you don't feel so good again. Then there is the hangover. You borrow money from friends, family, and co-workers and are unable to pay them back, so you either alienate them, avoid them entirely, or piss them off.

People throw their money away for a number of reasons, but most are to satisfy short-term needs and desires, and to hell with the future. "I'll cross that bridge when I come to it," they'll say. Another disturbing thing I notice is that people with low self-esteem use spending to compensate for their lack of self-worth. (Funny, being in debt really does lower your self's worth.) Just because you have a gold card doesn't make you more of a person, and spending money on people to try to win others over, or the things you bought to look like a million, really don't do a whole lot to impress people.

It would be hard to imagine retiring when you blow all of your money on things that won't help you get closer to your goal. If you wonder why some people are able to have the freedom to work when they want, it is usually because they were smart with their money.

For some reason we think everyone else is in debt, too. So it's okay. Millionaires and billionaires usually are NOT in debt (that's how they got where they are). Maybe you are paying the minimum on your credit cards and you feel you have the situation under control, but you may be one bad break away from bankruptcy (so to speak). It could be your computer crashes or a client fails to pay you when they say they will. (The latter happens all the time!) Be careful.

Sometimes being in debt leads to depression and affects other areas of your life, too. You are irritable, have alienated your friends, and snap at loved ones. It's hard to lead a happy life when a lack of money is weighing down your thoughts and taking up your time. You feel overwhelmed and hopeless. You end up feeling like your life is out of control, like your spending. Plus, you are so ashamed, you are afraid to tell anyone, and you feel like you have to keep up appearances, which means day by day you are digging a deeper hole. On *Magnum P.I.,* Magnum was always borrowing things from Rick and T.C., and it was a running joke that he would never pay them back. But after a while, they said, "No more!" That's the danger of tapping into sources like friends and family. If you borrow and don't pay them back, when you REALLY need their help, they will likely turn their backs on you.

Being in debt is a trap. You want to quit your horrible job, but how can you and still pay the bills? You want to go after your dream, but your debt prevents you from doing the kind of work you would love to do, in favor of work that "just pays the bills." You feel locked into your current situation, and you can't get out. It would be better to set aside some money for your dreams instead of having it tied up in debt.

Debt is sometimes a selfish thing. Think about how it affects your family. What would you pass on if YOU passed on? Would you saddle your heirs with your debt? Does your significant other know how bad things are? Do you buy things and hide them? When my wife leaves for work, I will usually say, "That suit looks nice." In my mind I am wondering, "Is it new? I've never seen it before." It's strange how I never see new stuff coming into the house, but her closet is FULL of clothes and lots and lots of shoes. She works at Nordstrom, so I am sure it must be difficult to be that close to all those nice clothes (and shoes) and not want new stuff. How she pulls it off without us being in debt is a major mystery to me.

For some people, *not* being able to shop, travel, and spend is worse than the debt they are incurring. They have ten Armani suits but can't pay the rent. They feel entitled, somehow. "I make a good living—I should have nice things." Unfortunately, they don't make a good enough living to afford them.

If you are in debt but have a great idea and you need money to get it going but are already tapped, that is a shame. I helped a speaker land a contract with a company that would pay her to do seminars all over the country, a really big boost to her career. The only catch was, she would have to pay for travel out of pocket and they would pay her back (usually within a week or two). She was unable to take the job because all of her credit cards were maxed out and she would be unable to check into hotels or rent cars. Not only did she have to pass on a chance to take her career to the next level, she lost tens of thousands of dollars in income. Sad.

Finally, there are the compulsive spenders (a lot like compulsive gamblers) who just can't stop, no matter how bad it gets. For them, there is Debtors Anonymous. Shopping can become an addiction, and those with a real problem will shop whether they need something or not and experience a sense of excitement and a change in mood when they make a purchase. With any addiction, like alcohol, for example, it's hard to resist the temptation, and there is temptation everywhere when it comes to shopping. In fact, Stanford researchers are studying whether a pill could curb your desire to spend.

Quick Quiz

If you are in debt (a lot or a little), do you understand how you got yourself into this situation? Identifying a problem instead of denying it is the first step to finding a solution. Take this test to see if you have a debt problem. If you can say "yes" to more than a couple of these, you do.

1. Have you ever used your credit card (while dining or shopping) and worried that it would be declined due to late payments, nonpayment, or being over your limit?
2. Have you ever used shopping as a mood enhancer? Do you get a rush or physical sensation from shopping?
3. Have you had to ask the credit card company to up your limit so you could continue to use it?

4. Do you carry a balance and pay the minimum on your credit card?
5. Are you getting good at rationalizing your spending? (You buy things for your business that you really don't need only because they are tax-deductible, for example, or you buy something just because it is on sale.)
6. Are you without a savings account right now?
7. Have you ever been afraid to answer the phone because it could be a bill collector?
8. Have you ever had to borrow against your paycheck to pay the bills?
9. Have you ever borrowed money from your family or friends and failed to pay it back?
10. Have you ever gone bankrupt?
11. Have you ever dated someone simply because he had money or in order to get something?
12. Do you play games with creditors (mail them the wrong check to buy time or play the float game)?
13. Have you ever spent an advance or bonus check before you actually received it (buying things with your credit card and planning to pay it off later)? Have you ever felt you didn't have to worry about how much you spend or how deep in debt you are because someone or something would come along and fix everything?
14. Is your checkbook not balanced right now? Have you ever worried that a check you wrote would bounce?
15. Are you worried about how you will pay your bills this month? Is your cost of living higher than your annual salary?

How Did This Happen to ME?

"I'm trying to keep up with the Joneses, but every time I catch up, they just refinance!"

—David Snell

"Bro, I was spending money as quick as I could make it. Clothes, rented jets, a boat, going to the Palm and ordering four-and-a-half-pound lobsters, leaving $500 tips at bars—man, my credit card bills ran from $70,000 to $150,000 a month," admits actor Mark Wahlberg in *Rolling Stone*. He could afford it, but how many people have a Mercedes but can't afford to fill it with gas? Own a home but can't afford to furnish it? Have nice clothes but can't afford to dry-clean them? You aren't alone if you find yourself deeply in debt. Celebrities who spend all of their money on cars, clothes, and other luxuries end up broke. Their mind-set is like a lot of creative people. You spend years trying to save money—for what? You could die.

Another reason creative people get deep in debt is the up and down nature of our careers. A freelance writer I know was $40,000 in debt. How did this happen? The magazine that she did the bulk of her work for folded, but she kept living the same lifestyle she had when she made money. Even though she now had far less coming in (a freelance job here and there). She took out a home equity loan, maxed her credit cards, and tapped her overdraft protection until she landed another full-time gig. But by that time she was in a deep hole.

It's easy to get credit. Credit cards are so easy to get these days that banks even offer them to college students, and they aren't even working! Teens can get cards, for Christ's sake. They practically force them on you then they get mad at you for not paying. You want to say, "When I filled in the application you could plainly see I never paid anything in my life. Why is this such a surprise to you?" The system is set up to get you to buy, buy more, and buy still more. Commercials that spend millions to push your emotional budgets, magazines that hype all the latest, and celebrities are all there to lure you. Once you are in the store you are being set up. That friendly greeter at the Gap is there to put you in the mood to buy. (Shoppers are 50 percent more likely to make a purchase when approached by a salesperson.) The waiter upsells you on top-shelf tequila in your margarita. Baked goods on the counter entice you to get a muffin with your coffee. Subtle, suggestive selling. Then there are the pushy types—those little Girl Scouts and their cookies. It's scary to consider that credit card interest was once tax-deductible. Thank God it isn't now, or all hell would break loose.

It may be that we aren't really cognizant of the real costs of things. When I say the real costs, I am referring to how hard you had to work to get that money in the first place. You gave a little piece of your life in exchange for that money you spent or gave away. If you are still shrugging your shoulders and saying "So," consider that your life is limited and time is more valuable than money. Spending with credit cards makes you feel like you're rich. You are in denial about the realities of your situation. Just because a credit card company gave you the card doesn't mean you can AFFORD to use it. Just because you have checks doesn't mean you can use them. Right? It feels like you have endless money, but it always catches up to you. Next thing you know you're juggling debt by transferring balances to new cards and can't make the minimum monthly payment.

Sometimes bad luck like an accident, a major illness, or divorce can send you into debt. Tina Turner left husband Ike Turner (literally running away from him while on tour, with just thirty-six cents in her pocket). She had no money because her husband handled the finances. She stayed with friends and paid them back by cleaning their houses. Ike then sent the kids to live with her, and she survived on food stamps. Although she started a solo career she was deep in debt, mainly to the IRS, and to promoters because of breaking appearance contracts after leaving Ike. That was extreme but see if any of these debt-incurring scenarios seem familiar to you.

___ Maybe you bought into the notion that you need to have credit to get credit. Many young people believe that they need to go into debt so that others will loan them money. They think they have to prove themselves worthy to creditors. You're worthy, trust me.

___ Do you have the little devil on one shoulder whispering in your ear, "Come on, you know you want those shoes. Go for it. You deserve it. It's only $1 a day if you pay it off in a year. What's a dollar a day?" Then before you know it you have a closet full of clothes and a mountain of debt.

___ Maybe you are a bit impulsive and want instant gratification. Like a man dying in the desert who must have water. Need now . . . Must have . . . Pay later . . . please . . .

___ It's like Lucille Ball's classic scene where she is working on a cake assembly line and at first is able to handle it. Then the cakes start coming too fast, and she is overwhelmed. She can't keep up and eventually gives up. Are you on a treadmill just trying to keep up by paying the minimum balance, but your debt keeps growing due to the interest?

___ You never think about how interest can kill you or how you will pay it back. You're living in the moment. You get enticed by those low monthly payment offers. Make sure you understand the total cost after tax, interest, and maintenance. Don't be fooled.

___ Maybe you used your credit cards to get a project off the ground that never had liftoff, and now you are left with the debt. Bob Seger left Capitol Records to sign with Reprise but was dropped. He was broke and had run up $4,000 in bounced-check charges. He had to borrow $1,000 to remix his master tape to get another deal.

___ You think you make more than you actually earn, and so you spend more than you really have. You may have no idea what's happening with your finances. Or worse, you have a distorted view of money and don't understand how it works.

___ Maybe the stock market "adjustment" put you in a hole.

___ Friggin' taxes!

___ You use purchases as a reward. Do you spend when you are "up," but after you come down from a shopping high, you are down so low? And what do you do to feel better? Go out and shop!

___ Do you feel like the world owes you a vacation? New car? Nice dinner? You're broke, but you somehow rationalize that you should still be able to buy what you want. You justify purchases by saying it's something you need, but it's really just something you want.

___ Do you feel you are different and that it won't happen to you? Rapper Will Smith had earned a million dollars by the time he was twenty, but spent it all and had to get a second job to pay the bills. That second job, acting, paid the bills all right.

___ Social spending is like a leaky faucet. Your debt starts out as a drip but ends up in flooding.

___ Peer pressure. You don't want to be left out when all your co-workers are going to lunch. You are expected to take your date to a nice dinner. Or people see you as a success and you don't discourage that, so when the bill comes they give it to you.

___ The twelve days of Christmas. Holidays put a lot of people in debt, and some are still paying off gifts from last year's holiday spending spree. Friends and family don't want you to go into debt for them, so give them memories, not money.

___ You just love to shop. It keeps you from thinking about life.

__ Student loans are an investment in yourself, and the interest is tax-deductible, but it's not free money. Someone I know spent most of her student loan on pot. She's so afraid to graduate and start paying the money back that she has been in college for TEN years.

__ You have no savings for emergencies, and a crisis sent you over the edge.

__ One spouse decided to be a stay-at-home mom and you made less but spent more.

__ Going for frequent-flier miles tripped you up.

__ You expect miracles, don't see down times coming, or that bonus doesn't materialize.

__ Maybe it's a midlife crisis. The hair plugs, Harley, and happening clothes add up quick.

__ You lost a job and used credit cards to get through the rough spell. Or you got a promotion and raise, and instead of paying down your debt you crank up the credit card.

💰 BY THE NUMBERS

You are not alone. Consumer debt is at an all-time high. One-third of all adult Americans are having trouble paying their monthly bills. If given an extra $500, women admitted they would spend $278 of it on clothes. Men said they would spend $202 on clothing. (Facts from American Express Retail Index, CNN/*USA Today*, Standard Register, and *Newsweek* polls.)

Ready, Set, Charge?

"In God we trust, all others pay cash."

—*sign*

Let's do a little plastic surgery. Dr. Silber says the first step is to admit you have a problem. Come to grips with the fact that you are going to have to make some changes. If you keep doing what you've been doing, you'll keep getting what you've got. (I'm guessing that if you have already made and saved millions, you wouldn't be reading this book—and I wouldn't be writing it.) So let's try something new. First, forgive yourself. You aren't a loser if you are in debt.

Yes, you want to jump out a window, but that will only pass your debt on to your next of kin. Take a deep breath. It's going to be okay. You can do this. You aren't a failure. You may not be worth much on paper, but you aren't worthless. Who you are shouldn't be based on your bank balance. Debt is a temporary problem and one that is fixable. It doesn't make you a bad person. I'm not saying you can ignore it, but like any condition, there is a cure. You're going to get out, and it's all going to be fine. Don't let debt ruin the rest of your life. You can still be happy and enjoy your life. The sunsets are still free. So relax.

Maybe you are in denial about your debt. "Oh, that $50,000 I owe. Ah, it's nothing. I could pay it off if I wanted to, but I like paying 20 percent interest and dodging creditors." Sure you do. Once you get past the denial stage, then you can grieve, get angry, and go through all the other stages until you get to the point of acceptance. Accept responsibility for what you've done with your debt, make a promise (and take action), and do something about it. You don't have to bottom out before you can realize that the path you are heading down isn't leading to where you want to be. I know, you have a long list of reasons why you'll start as soon as . . . or some real fears: "My girlfriend will bail on me if I don't take her out to dinner and a movie and buy her nice things." Or you believe you will pay it off as soon as . . . "But I need new shoes for my job interview—when I'm hired I'll pay them off then." Or you think it's an investment or tax write-off. "I must have a new laptop so I can start on my book. I mean, it's tax-deductible. Right? I'll pay it off with my advance money or royalties." And so it goes.

The problem is, we are all-or-nothing types, and we want a quick fix. We want to wipe the slate clean all at once. If you can do that with one high-paying project, awesome. But try to avoid acquiring new debt to pay off the old debt. (However, a home equity loan does make sense. You can consolidate all your debts into one payment, the interest is going to be better than the 19 or 20 percent a credit card charges, and it's tax-deductible.) Getting out of debt can happen in one fell swoop (and I'm not talking about bankruptcy) with a big payday, but usually you just have to chip away at it. It will seem hopeless. Impossible. "There's no way!" You're wrong.

People have gotten out of more debt than you. If they can do it, you can do it. "But, but . . . " I hear you, but believe it or not, your situation isn't so special. The solution isn't unique, either. You need to spend less and/or make more and use the difference to pay down your debt.

It's not easy, but much like a fitness program, once you begin and see some progress, you'll want to stick with it. You have to make some changes to your lifestyle that will be difficult at first. I know that when some of my friends were contemplating getting married, they would ask me (I've been with my wife for twelve years), "But don't you miss the wild times and the variety?" Then they'd give me the old cereal analogy. So I'd ask them, "Were those single days really so wonderful? Doesn't it feel great to be in a stable, loving, peaceful place with someone you care about and who cares about you?" They'd just stare at me with a blank expression. But my point is this (as it relates to getting out of debt): You can be free to have all the fun you want, it's just different (and more meaningful). Get off the fast track and focus on things that feel good but don't necessarily cost money. You don't want to cheat yourself. The wild and crazy days aren't over, but you need to put *some* of them behind you. Maybe it doesn't give you the same thrill as a one-night stand, but believe me, the good life isn't a life of goods. Being debt-free is such a weight off your shoulders that it's worth the sacrifice. Without the debt hanging over your head, it's like you have a new lease on life. It's freedom, baby.

💰 ACTION ITEM

I want you to imagine you don't owe anybody anything. Make a mock-up of your credit report showing a zero balance. Then free-write about what that means to you and how it feels.

Start small and take it one day at a time. Maybe the first thing you do is say, "I'm going to go one day without any new debt." It's a start. It's like you are in a boat that's filling fast with water. If you don't start bailing, you will sink. Even if you just get rid of the water that's coming in, you are staying afloat. You are either moving further away or closer to a goal. That would be a small step in the right direction. Fight the urge to say, "Screw it, what's the use" or "What's one more charge, anyway?" Don't buy something unless you can pay it off in full. Find ways to get what you want and need without going into debt.

The average consumer debt is $13,000, from credit cards, car loans, student loans, and mortgages. Yikes! Cut off access to any new debt. Close accounts. Use only one card for things that you WILL pay off when the bill comes. Get a low-interest card. Lower your limit. Cut up your other cards. I mean, what's worse than having a waiter do it in front of you and your date for failure to pay? You want to tell them, "Hey, just take the damn card, you don't have to humiliate me." When solicitations come in the mail, shred them. Put your cards in a safe-deposit box for a while. If you need them they are there, but you will have to think before you spend because you have to trek to the bank to get them. Freeze them in a block of ice and break or melt only in case of an emergency. Ask your family to hold them (this is if you trust them). If you want to use them you have to plead your case to a "jury of your peers," and they will agree or not agree to let you use them. When you go shopping, leave your credit card at home. Spend cash or don't spend at all. Thankfully, ATMs don't give out thousands. Lauren Velez's advice is, "When I don't know if I want to spend the money, I go away. If I can't stop thinking about something, then I come back and buy it."

Set some money aside for emergencies, or else you'll just use the credit card again. Sell off some stuff, and use the proceeds to pay off creditors. Moonlight for money. Put in overtime. Put all "extra" money toward paying down debt.

The phone rings (during dinner, of course), and you expect it to be a friend or family member, but instead it's a collection agency asking when they can expect payment. You tell them they can always *expect* payment—whether they are gonna get it is another story. One guy has a great reply when they ask if he has a payment plan: "Sure, I put all the creditors' names in a hat," he says, "and I pick one. The lucky one that gets picked gets paid." Remember the movie *Fletch,* where Chevy Chase's character would enter his apartment by using the fire escape around back to avoid his wife's lawyer? That's no way to live.

Birds fly high to get a better perspective. We also need to see the bigger picture. We need to know specifically what we're dealing with. List every single debt you have right now so you can gain some perspective. (Car loan, credit cards, store cards, home equity loan, back taxes, overdraft, unpaid invoices, back rent, and so on. Everything.) Maybe you should also request a credit report to see exactly what you owe. Hey, it may not be as bad as you thought. Whatever you come up with, it's just a number. List who you owe the money to, how to contact them, and how much you owe. This is VERY important—don't skip this step. Write all of your debts on index cards (one creditor per card), along with the amount and interest rate, and then shuffle them highest to lowest and keep track of balances as you make payments.

Make a wall chart with a "goalometer." Keep a reduction record for your debt-repayment plan. Note when and how much you have paid and how much you have to go to get to zero owed.

The goal is to be debt-free (except for your mortgage and maybe a student loan, which both have tax benefits) as quickly as possible. You can't wish it away. Don't be tempted to try to recover it all with one risky get-rich-quick scheme. You need a plan. You need to know what you owe, to whom, and how much you can afford to pay. Don't wait another day to do this. Set up a realistic time frame to pay off all of these debts. That is the goal: ZERO debt. If you are deeply in debt then you should make that priority number one, and starting an emergency fund and investing your secondary goals. When you get a tax return or large lump of cash, allocate a third of it or more to paying off your debt. Can you sell anything to pay down debt? Use savings. Earning 3 percent but paying 19 percent doesn't make sense. You can save 16 percent. Get a home equity loan if you have to. Pay more than minimums on high–interest rate cards or you will never get ahead. Ask card companies for a lower interest rate. Threaten to move your money if they don't. Pay off the highest interest rates first. Or, if it would give you a boost, pay off the smallest balances right away, and you can get a small sense of satisfaction. Consolidate to one lower-interest card. Be careful. It's a weight off of your shoulders but it can give you a false sense of security. It's so easy to get deeper into debt at this point. Your monthly payments are lower, so you think you have extra money that you don't—or should use for anything BUT paying down your balance. Call credit card companies and anyone else you owe and ask for a break from your bills. Get some breathing room. You'll be surprised at how often they will work with you. Most creditors want to work with you and it is in their best interests that you don't go belly-up or that they don't have to pay a collection agency. Just don't promise something you can't deliver. Now you are a debtor *and* a liar. No matter what, don't mess around with the IRS. Most important of all is *no new debt*! While in the debt-reduction phase make a promise to yourself that you will *not* add any new debt to your load.

Makeover

I guess you could say I had a hand in this makeover, but really it is a self-help situation. A reader wrote to me about how she had turned her life around after reading my book *Career Management for the Creative Person*. She agreed to let me use her story after I told her it could help others in the same situation (deep in debt). She agreed, as long as I changed her name. So here it is. "Susan," an artist, was overwhelmed (and consumed) by her overconsumption and the debt that resulted. If it were just her, maybe she wouldn't have wanted to change her ways, but she was a single mother with a young daughter. To keep up with her bills she had to work three jobs—none of which involved any creativity. (She worked as a receptionist five days a week, as a waitress three nights a week, and on Saturdays in a chiropractor's office.) This left very little time to spend with her daughter. She worked hard (and long) but couldn't get ahead. She had no idea where her money went and how she had gotten so deep in debt (over $15,000). So on New Year's Day (a rare day off), she took a step back to examine where she was and how she got there. (Here's where I come in. She bought my book and was working through the section on goals and realized that she was so far from a creative career that she needed to make some changes.) She started by looking back at old credit card statements to see where all of her debt came from. She was shocked to see that most of her money was spent on discretionary items she could do without. (She admitted that she felt guilty about her divorce and spent a lot of money on her daughter—but not enough time with her daughter.) Then she totaled up how much she had made in the previous year. If she wasn't depressed before, she was now. She realized she worked too hard for too little. She made it her New Year's resolution to get her financial life in order and get back on track. She started by setting a goal for how much (or I should say, how little) she would spend each month. This worked well. She also kept track of where her money went and looked for—and found—creative ways to cut back. She realized she had a knack for finding ways to save and found she was charged (so to speak) by the challenge. She was able to save over $500 a month. She also found a better paying "day job" (she was grossly underpaid in the past, but now that she was resolved to rectify her situation, she was determined to make more money—and she did). She quit her weekend job and started waitressing one night a week—the best night, Saturday night. Now that her nights were free she didn't have to pay a baby-sitter to watch her daughter while she worked; her mother watched her on Saturday night or she was with her father. She began pursuing her art again and was able to spend more time with her daughter. In under two years she was debt-free due to her discipline, diligence, and debt-reduction plan. Here is what she did.

1. The most important step she took was finding out how much money was coming into and going out of her life. That led to a new awareness and step two.

2. She began tracking every penny and looked for ways to either eliminate or cut back on her expenses. Susan wasn't a compulsive spender, but over time her lack of awareness for how much she was spending had brought her to where she was now. So she went cold turkey. This approach isn't for everyone, but it worked well for Susan. She realized that if she bit the bullet now, later she could, within reason, have some luxuries when she could afford them.

3. People on budgets (or diets) usually don't stick with it once

the initial desire to get out of debt (or lose weight) wears off. Susan was determined, and once she saw progress it motivated her to keep going and not fall back into her bad spending habits. She also had a goal to be debt-free and wrote and drew what that would mean to her. It was a work of art, and that's how she looked at her situation. She was turning her life into a work of art. A masterpiece. That also kept her focused and motivated and helped her make choices and kept her drive alive.

4. She also created a colorful wall chart to track her debt and its reduction. She got a thrill out of seeing and reaching these goals. Money was now real to her. She made more, saved more, and steadily paid down her debt. Her decisions were now less impulsive and emotional and more rational. She gave up the apartment she rented and accepted her mother's offer to have her and her daughter move in rent-free. At first the idea made her feel like a failure, but she realized it was the best thing for everyone. Her mother, daughter, and even she benefited from this arrangement.

5. She attacked her problem on both fronts—one, by cutting costs and controlling the outflow of money, and two, by increasing what was coming in. Before she was trading her life for very little. Meaning, she worked hard and was worse and worse off. Her time was worth more than what she was getting paid, and she simply wasn't willing to trade it for so little any longer. She was good at what she did at her day job and demanded more money. When her employer, who was accustomed to paying her a pittance, refused, she gathered up the courage to quit and got a better job (closer to home, too) that paid nearly *double* what she was making. She takes on freelance work on the side for both a boost to her bank account and the boost it gives her self-esteem.

Some of the e-mails "Susan" sent me were so long they could have filled a whole chapter. I left out a lot of the details of her debt-reduction story so that it would fit in the book. But I do want to mention that this is a creative, right-brain person just like you and me. She was once disorganized, disinterested, and ultimately distressed about debt (and money in general). But she used her whole brain to tackle this problem. To hear her talk about the time she is able to spend with her daughter as well as her mother, and the pride she feels (and exudes) for turning her life around and getting her debt down to zero and her income up to levels she never thought possible, put tears in my eyes. I hope it inspires you, too.

The Lighter Side of Debt

Sting says, "I've given up tantric sex. I'm trying to get Trudie [his wife] into tantric shopping now. That's where you shop for five hours and don't buy anything." (Tantric sex is an Eastern technique for lengthy lovemaking.)

Bankrupt

"They say you can't take it with you. I can't even afford to go."

—*Milton Berle*

I was hoping this chapter would end up being Chapter 7 (bankruptcy that gets you out of your debts) or Chapter 11 (restructures your debt), but alas, it's not. That doesn't mean we can't discuss this option. I mean, if you feel that the situation is terminal, and you can't find any other way to get out of debt, bankruptcy is one way to be debt-free (however, Congress is making it harder to do so) and at least get creditors off your back. It's not a cure-all, and it's a tough pill to swallow (it hurts like hell). It doesn't deal with or fix the root cause that got you into this mess in the first place. It gives you a fresh start, but it screws up your credit for ten years, and it makes you feel like a failure. (At least you won't lose your home or retirement—usually.)

There were a record 1.3 million bankruptcy filings in 1999 despite some of the best economic times ever; some famous creative people have sought this remedy, including Meat Loaf, Toni Braxton, Isaac Hayes, Tom Petty, and Sly Stone. Mick Fleetwood of Fleetwood Mac (a hugely successful band) found himself $2 million in debt after some bad investments in Australian real estate in the 1980s. Wayne Newton also filed for bankruptcy when he ended up $22 million in debt despite earning $250,000 a week. He turned to his good friend Donald Trump for advice, who told him to get rid of the lawyers, call his creditors, and come to a settlement agreement. He then began paying more attention to his financial affairs. That's good, because half the people who file for bankruptcy do it again.

Back in Black (How to Stay Clean)

"Just remember, I am spending your money foolishly."
                                                    —Jimmy Buffett

Some people could pay off all their debts, and they would be back in the same situation within a matter of months. You must make it so it won't happen again. Take away the means, motive, and opportunity. It's easy to get into debt, but *much* harder to get out.

• **You need a credit card . . . one.** I would not try to sell you on the idea of not having one card. You can rent a car, check into a hotel, and even buy online without one, but it is a LOT easier and provides the purchaser (you) with some protection. One card, low limit. It's hard to give them up, but if they are there, it's too easy to rationalize why you can use them. Close the accounts and cancel the cards. Don't use any other credit cards from stores, gas companies, or even store credit. Use a credit card but only if you have the money in the bank to pay off the balance. Shop around for the best deal. Get a teaser rate and get the company to waive the annual fee. American Express is ideal because you really have to pay it off every month. The interest rate is then irrelevant. Or go for the perks. Get one that "pays you back" or gives you frequent-flier miles.

• **Keep a spending journal and balance sheet so you can see where you are.** Break expenses down by week or month and then by category. Get a snapshot of where you spend your money. Go back through charge slips or statements to see. Do a daily, weekly, and monthly summary. It's the best thing I ever did! It takes the mystery out of spent money. You won't wonder where the money went. You will know for sure. Notice all the places you get into debt, and reduce access.

• **Think before you spend.** Mark Twain in *Following the Equator* talks about ways to keep from spending frivolously. He says that by counting to forty before buying you will save half of the money you would have blown. By counting to sixty you will save 75 percent and if you can count to sixty-five before buying you will save it all! Better yet, wait thirty days. Keep in mind that it is much easier to buy than to sell.

• **Know the difference between needs and wants.** Do I *need* this or do I *want* this? If I really need it I try to wait until I can afford it. All our friends were buying bigger homes. We decided we didn't *need* (or even want) a bigger house. List all the things you are lacking. Make a list of all the things you want to do and have. Next to each, estimate the cost. Then determine the level you want it. Prioritize. You can't have it all, so choose the things you can afford or really want.

• **Stay busy.** The main thing is to keep your mind off spending and focus on how it feels to be debt-free and the peace of mind you feel. Then remember what it was like to be in debt. The pressures that went with it. The strain it put on your life and relationships. Replace destructive behavior with constructive behavior that doesn't require you to spend money, and stay away from people who pull you from the goal of being debt-free.

• **It's not play money.** Come to grips with the fact that *you can't spend what you don't have.* The reality is, you can't afford to do or have everything you want (at least not now), but a lack of money can lead you to come up with creative solutions, like bartering. Cut back on other areas to free up funds for things you want to do. Do something on a smaller scale. This sounds trite, but you need to take it one day at a time. Celebrate a day without debt. Try to go one year without spending money on holiday gifts. Maybe you make the gifts you give this year. There's nothing wrong with others knowing you are trying to cut back. They don't have to know the degree to which you are in debt, but be honest, many of them will be relieved at not having to exchange gifts, and I bet they'll envy you for your discipline and desire to be debt-free. Try to find ways to have fun without having to go into hock. This means making some lifestyle changes—for the better.

• **More money isn't always the answer.** In 1864, John Washington Steele inherited more than a million dollars (that would be like a billion today) and spent it all within one year! Deprivation isn't the answer, either. Once you get out of debt you don't have to deprive yourself of things you want and need. You can still travel, for example, but save up for it. Make it more real by paying in cash when you can, and as a last resort, use a credit card. (But pay off the balance every month!)

WHAT IS YOUR TIME WORTH?

In the book Your Money or Your Life, *authors Joe Dominguez and Vicki Robin make an interesting point. Distilled down (you should really read their book, it's great), it shows how (if you figure out your real hourly wage after all the hidden costs and not-so-hidden costs have come out) you make a lot less than you think. If you take that figure (let's say it's ten dollars an hour after all things are considered) and divide that by the cost of an item you want to buy, you come up with a figure that reflects the real cost of an item. Let's say you bought beers for yourself and your buddies, and the bar tab was $100. That means that you spent ten hours of your life for this pleasure. (If you add in the lost day to the hangover, it's even higher.) Those are hours you can never have back. The cost is you traded your life's energy for that privilege. Try dividing your rent by your hourly figure. Yikes! You realize you use up your life to put a roof over your head, a car to drive, and clothes to wear. It hardly seems worth it, does it? This puts spending in proper perspective.*

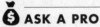 **ASK A PRO**

CINDY LEE BERRYHILL, RECORDING ARTIST AND AUTHOR

What are some pitfalls musicians face when it comes to dealing with their finances?

Like many musicians, I'm a fool for the music. I've invested most of my paychecks and time in support of my music. Not to say I've had much money to invest, but proportionally it's been most of what I've made minus rent, gas, and food. Most musicians I know are this way. Whereas someone else might buy boats and recreational equipment, a musician may spend their money on musical equipment and mailings. It's very easy to justify because it's going back into your work and true love—music. Instead I've relied a lot on help from other musicians and band members, asking them to donate their time to recording sessions, or I'll borrow musical equipment for certain sessions. I've also learned to keep my needs extremely modest. Most musicians I know don't have much money to manage, and we end up doing more TIME management—juggling jobs, family, friends, rehearsals, and creative time.

Other Pitfalls Beyond Debt

"We love our habits more than our income, often more than our life."

—Bertrand Russell

Some of the most talented and creative people are also the most self-sabotaging. They struggle with money not because of external forces but, rather, because of their own lack of judgment. Sometimes these problems mask deeper problems. How many times do we see the artist who makes it big, only to blow it? (Of course, there are the less publicized people who use the money they make from their art to make more money and set themselves up for the future.) So what makes some creative people sabotage their success? I have a few theories.

One is that *some* creative people have such low self-esteem that when they do make it big and get their hands on a lot of cash, they don't feel they deserve it, so they do everything in their power to squander it. There are other artists who think that if they make too much money, they will get soft and their art will suffer. I know some writers who relish the struggling stage of their career and thrive on the excitement that comes from pursuing a goal—but lose interest once it is reached. So they find ways to get back into a crisis mode. They prefer chaos and drama to stability and success. Others prefer to be also-rans and wilt under the pressure and expectations that come with fulfilling their promise. So they self-destruct and have to start over or wallow in their self-pity. Something that strangely feels comfortable to them. Some artists just never took the time to learn what to do with money and keep making the same mistakes over and over again. (Merle Haggard has been divorced four times, went bankrupt, and spent two years in prison.) Some creative people couldn't care less about money, so that's how they deal with it: carelessly. Finally, many people just aren't ready to handle their newfound wealth, so they go crazy and blow it all not knowing any better or figuring they will just make more. Let's look at some of these and other potential pitfalls in more detail. These are here to serve as a warning.

• **A day late and a dollar short.** Natalie Cole was, by her own admission, doing so much drugs she even considered dealing. This was during the height of her career. But when she blew off gigs and didn't show up for recording sessions, her record label dropped her. (This was all on VH-1's *Behind the Music.*) It can happen to anyone, no matter how talented. Procrastination and general flakiness can be costly. Sly Stone was a genius! His band's greatest-hits album alone sold three million copies, and he had a number-one hit with "Everyday People." So how did he end up living in his van after being evicted for not paying his mortgage? He was legendary for missing tour dates and being unreliable. In fact, he didn't show up for a show to benefit muscular dystrophy. It all caught up with him and effectively ended a brilliant career.

Some creative people who rely on their right brains have no sense of time (that is a proven fact), so they take on more than they can chew (or do) and end up overcommitted, unable to do the work or do good work—both of which can ruin their reputation and potential for future work. For many of us earning a living at creating, it is the rule that if you don't do the work, you don't get the dough—or worse, they sue you. Nothing can be a bigger bummer than being dropped or denied the work because of your "reputation." Profits come from producing. Do what you gotta do to get the work done, *then* go goof off. On a similar note, procrastinating has a price. There can be penalties for late payments, or you end up paying a premium for waiting until the last minute.

• **She got the ring, I got the finger.** Divorce can be a disaster on many fronts, but monetarily, it can become a bigger burden than you ever could have imagined. Don't just split up—terminate all joint financial obligations. You may be liable for things you didn't deal with. "I didn't believe in divorce until after I got married," announced Diane Ford. That's why Catherine Zeta-Jones signed a prenuptial agreement when she married Michael Douglas. "Prenups are brilliant because it's all sorted out," she says. It's like you aren't supposed to see the bride the day of the wedding because it may be bad luck. We think that discussing money matters may also be a bad omen. But if things don't work out you will wish you worked this out in advance. If you own a business, have stock options, or real estate, you have to split that. You also split the debt, even if it's debt you didn't know about. So if you are unlucky in love don't be left for broke. It's better to be up-front with money matters before getting married. Talk about how you feel about money, find out what your partner wants and how he handles finances. Does he like to shop till he drops, gamble, or is frugal to a fault? Flaky on bills? Been bankrupt? What are his dreams? Do they match yours? For example, he tells you that he wants to go back to school and that you will have to work two jobs to support him while he focuses on his studies. It would be nice to know that.

Money is the leading cause of divorce, with sex being the second biggest factor. Divorce is a legal issue, but it is also emotional. Many divorces start out civil, but when lawyers get involved it becomes a civil war. Couples end up spending more on lawyers and end up with less. When the dust settles the reality sinks in. Now you have to live on less income or pay alimony and child support.

Now, divorcing from your significant other is hard enough, but breaking up with a business partner can be even worse. Be very careful who you go into business with. I don't know what's going to happen to Artie Bucco, the restaurant owner on *The Sopranos,* but going into business with Tony Soprano can't be a good thing. When you run with the wolves you tend to step in wolf shit.

• **Kick the habit.** I can recall when being a journalist meant you worked long hours, drank a lot of coffee, smoked a pack or more of cigarettes a day, and had a few pops after meeting your deadline. Those days are gone—or are they? Many writers have bad habits that aren't healthy and can be quite costly. Some of my favorite writers are from the old school, and I thought that in order to emulate them I should try to be like them. So I tried drinking and writing. It doesn't work for me, thank God. I know the fate that befell some of my favorite writers (they ended up isolated, depressed, tortured, and broke). That's not me, or you, I hope.

• **Party all the time.** Going out and partying once or twice a week is cool, but when it becomes an obsession, it gets to be kinda costly. I have seen it time and time again. The creative person finally hits it big and collects a big advance or a fat royalty check and instead of putting it away goes nuts. He rationalizes it by saying three words—"I earned it!" I knew a guy who got a BIG amount of money for one of his inventions. He blew through it ALL in less than a year by partying it away. We all tried to tell him to "cool it," but he would not listen. Frank Zappa said it best: "I would like to suggest that you not use speed, and here's why: It is going to mess up your heart, mess up your liver, your kidneys, rot out your mind. In general this drug will make you just like your mother and father." Charlie Sheen, the baddest of the bad boys, conceded that he spent millions on partying and all the things that go with it. Maybe you are just a "casual" user, but the cost can be more than a "dime bag" here or there. It can kill motivation. You end up sitting at home all day eating sweets and watching *Matlock* reruns. Ask Jenna Elfman—she'll tell you. "I was still dreaming big, but I was *not* on the road to it at all. I was smoking too much pot, doing nothing with my life."

• **Letting success go to your head.** When things are going good, you assume that there is no end in sight. It's onward and upward, baby. But then all of a sudden a pink slip here, a canceled contract there, and you are in trouble because you never saw it coming and didn't plan for your own economic slowdown. Another phenomenon I noticed is that when you start to see some success you don't feel the need to market yourself anymore, and then when your current workload dries up, you have nothing on the books. To start again takes time. You have to write a proposal, pitch an idea, and wait and wait and wait for something to happen or to get paid. Plan for the worst, but expect the best.

I know a lot of us have to take our act (whatever that may be) on the road. When you are away you are living in a fantasy world, and things at home (like bills, bank deposits, and taxes) don't seem real. Maybe you decide to take a year off. After all that inactivity you realize you are out of the loop and find it hard to get back in the game. Once you reach a goal, automatically set a new (and bigger) one and try to keep the momentum going. Joni Mitchell said it well: "You wonder about people who made a fortune, and you always think they drank it up or they stuck it up their nose. That's not usually what brings on the decline. It's usually the battle to keep your creative child alive while keeping your business shark alive, too. You have to develop cunning, shrewdness, and other things which are not suited to the arts."

• **Easy come, easy go.** Why is it that the easier money comes to us the easier it is to throw it away? Maybe it's because it feels like found money. You know, when you find a Ben Franklin in your pants pocket and call your friends and say, "Dinner is on me." What if we used found money to start saving or pay down our debt and let someone else buy dinner?

• **You are not a bank.** All of a sudden you have more money than you need, so you decide to spread it around. My rule is, I don't lend money. Period. In my opinion, it never has a happy ending when you lend money to someone. MC Hammer blew more than $3 million, much of it spent on his "posse" or so-called "friends." When he went bankrupt, most of those who helped him spend his money were gone. "A fool and his money are soon parted. I want to know how they got together in the first place," says Cyril Fletcher. Don't tell your friends how much you make, or they'll expect you to pay. When others know you have money to burn, they always bring matches.

• **Too good to be true.** It's our nature to be open-minded—just don't have an open-wallet policy. Speaking of which, I was doing a book signing in Seattle and since I hate to have funny bulges in my pants when I speak (don't go there), I usually take my keys, change, and wallet and hide them. Someone must have seen me do this, because they rifled through my wallet, wrote down my credit card number, and ran up almost $10,000 in charges checking out porn on the Internet. As they say, "People will rob you blind if YOU let them."

Some of scams are pretty sophisticated, and they push that magic button—greed. Be wary. Use a credit card with a low limit exclusively for online shopping. Clean out your wallet or purse, and purge cards you don't use any longer. Don't leave bills with checks in them out for mail pickup. Shred important papers.

Some writers would do just about anything to see their words bound into a book. That makes them an easy target. Not all vanity presses (or vanity galleries) are bad, but there are all kinds of things that could cost you time and money. Please, be very careful. Use your intuition *and* common sense. Do your homework. You need a website, so you hire a guy who promises the moon, takes an up-front deposit, and then doesn't deliver, disappears, or gets distracted, and you have half a site. A little background checking (check out his site and ask for references) could have saved you time and money.

When a broker you don't know calls you on the phone and asks to handle your investments, there can only be one answer, and that is NO! If he won't take no for an answer, you can get creative. Tell him, "My brother works for the Securities and Exchange Commission" or

"I work with Big Tony. He handles my investments. Send him your information."

There are all kinds of warning signs, like "You better act fast." Or he will FedEx you information (so it's not mail fraud) and ask you to respond right away. Maybe in the background you hear the sound of hundreds of other "brokers" "helping" clients (better known as "marks"). Never buy anything over the phone. Don't fall for the free vacation if you send $1,000. If someone outside a convenience store says he just won the lottery and asks you to front him the cash and you can have the ticket, what do you say? Right, "Go screw yourself." Trust no one. There are so many scams, everything from the "make millions working at home" to the "investment clubs." The Internet is inventing new scams or bringing old ones to new people but push the same buttons as before (greed, laziness, hope) and it still works on some people. Basically, the pitchsters get rich, and the receivers get poor.

• **Viva Las Vegas.** There is the everyday gambling like the lottery (a tax on people who are bad at math), and then there is more hard-core gambling. Remember the movie *Indecent Proposal,* where Robert Redford wins a night with Demi Moore for a million dollars, or *Honeymoon in Vegas,* when Nicolas Cage gambles away his fiancée, Sarah Jessica Parker? One of my buddies was in Las Vegas with some friends and took full advantage of the free drinks they provide while sitting at the blackjack tables. Before he got wasted, he was up a few thousand dollars (and this is a guy who can hardly afford to be gambling). One of his quick-thinking friends snatched $3,000 in chips when he wasn't looking. On the ride home my friend was distraught at losing everything he brought. Then his pal presented him with the $3,000 he had held for him. Was my friend grateful? Yes, but he wanted to go back now that he had more money! Rodney Dangerfield once joked, "I joined Gamblers Anonymous— they gave me three-to-one that I wouldn't make it." It's no joking matter. Stay away from the track, casino, and places where the pressure to bet is great, like concerts and shows held at Indian casinos. Thankfully this isn't "one" of my vices. Maybe I could be tempted into a all-night dreidel game, but . . . I once met a potential client who offered me the chance to do some design for him if I would arm-wrestle him for it. Are you friggin' kidding me? This guy was a compulsive gambler who would wager on how long it would take a waiter to bring some water over.

• **Crime doesn't pay.** I read somewhere that the average take in a bank robbery is less than $1,000 and that 70 percent of the perpetrators end up getting caught. Now, I am sure that robbing a bank never crossed your mind, but when we are desperate we can come up with some pretty crazy ideas about how to get money. I mean, wouldn't it be great to be able to pay off all your debt and buy anything you want? That's the fantasy. There are so many ways to make easy money in a dishonest way. The downside is so depressing that it stops most of us (that and a lot of Catholic guilt). It can be a constant battle between good and evil for the creative person who just wants a chance to show off his talents and would almost be willing to push people in front of cars to have it happen for him—finally. How else can you explain someone stealing, lying, or cheating to get ahead? Even if they pull it off, they have to live with what they did, and believe it or not, that's a heavy burden to bear. Do you think an actress who slept her way to the top never has that haunt her? Or the guy who steals stuff from the music store where he works to use for his band's demo, only to get caught and then prosecuted by the law and persecuted by fellow musicians? Or you could deny it. "I didn't steal this. It was differently acquired." One woman worked at a department store and was stealing customers' credit card numbers and buying stuff for herself. She got caught when she used her employee number to get her discount. Dumb, very dumb.

• **We all have problems—deal.** Grammy Award–winning singer Shelby Lynne writes songs about love and loss with such conviction that you would think she had gone through them herself—and she has. Her song "Life Is Bad" sums it up. Her life has included almost every tragedy you can imagine, including seeing her father shoot and kill her mother and then turning the gun on himself. Lynne is no saint, but I have enormous respect for her talent and her tenacity. After the death of her parents she moved to Nashville, and after five CDs with three different labels, she moved into a small $250-a-month house and just kept writing songs, which led to interest from Sheryl Crow's producer and a new record deal.

• **Drop the deadbeats.** Daryl Hannah describes the type of guys she has been attracted to, "Oh, you're a drug addict? And down on your luck and fucked up and depressed and suicidal? I love you!" Many times I see a "couple" where one of them drags the other into debt (or worse). I know a writer who has a stable job and lives a simple life. Her husband, on the other hand, can't hold a job and has one harebrained scheme after another. She has such low self-esteem that she gladly lets him walk all over her, and she supports them without regard to her own financial welfare. Then the love of her life left her, and guess what? Not only did she have to deal with despair, she had debts to pay, too. To those of us looking in from the outside, it's easy to say, "Dump the loser," but I realize it's much more complicated than that. Or is it?

• **Ideas are NOT a dime a dozen.** Intellectual property is an asset and one that you don't want to lose. I designed a logo for my father's business. I *gave* it to him to *use*. For some reason he let his "partner" at the time use it. Then when the two parted ways (this guy was a L-O-S-E-R and a crook), my father didn't want to be associated with him anymore. So I said, "Dad, why don't you use the logo I did for you?" He told me that the other guy was using it. "But Dad, I did that for you. I let you use it. It's not even really yours, it's mine, and either you use it or I want it back." Fortunately, the other guy went out of business and my father was able to resurrect the logo. But I have to tell you, that is just a tiny example of what can happen to your work if you don't protect it.

Intellectual property is more than just a logo—it's also patents, copyrights, and trademarks, and in today's world, it's your company's branding. Just like physical assets, your customer lists, supplier relationships, name, logo, tagline, ideas, products, processes, and such have value—to you. Now with the Internet there are all kinds of ways these can be stolen and used without your permission. Do what you can to protect them, and be diligent about going after people who pilfer them. However, don't let the fear of your work being stolen stop you from putting things out there. Pursue and protect.

• **Careless does NOT equal carefree.** If you haven't got a care in the world, then you aren't paying enough attention to what's happening around you. If you let others manage your money you still have to pay attention. Blind trust could allow someone to rob you blind. I understand that we are too busy to be bothered by pesky details about our money. "Hey, I'm too busy making money to manage it." My buddy simply could not believe he was being ripped off by his partner and his partner's wife. They owned a business together but were also best friends. It was his girlfriend who came to work for him who noticed the missing money—almost $100,000! The result was a complete meltdown. The business failed, his friendship was over, and he felt like a fool.

Another way carelessness can cause financial problems is by not protecting what you own with insurance and/or alarms and locks. You might also get lazy and leave your purse out in the open at work and have money (or worse, your identity) stolen. Maybe you leave your wallet or laptop in the car overnight, and someone breaks in and steals them. You realize your PIN number is on your ATM card. Maybe you didn't back up your computer files. This can be very costly in time and money. Listen to this. Sharon Stone's former housekeeper stole $300,000 worth of the actress's clothes and jewelry. When Stone started to notice items missing, the housekeeper simply said, "Oh, you gave that to your sister" or "It's at the cleaners." Then she was caught. The bottom line—Watch out.

YOUR STORY

Look at your life and recall all the highs and lows that led you to where you are today. Put these events on a lifeline. If you want, you can put the positive things on one side and the negative events on the other. Next to each event look at the lessons learned and ask yourself what happened, why it happened, and what was the end result. Write this next to each event. Then see if you can spot any patterns. What conclusions can you come to about how you handle success and failure and how you make decisions about what to do?

4

GIVE YOURSELF A RAISE

*"John and I literally used to sit down and say,
'Now, let's write a swimming pool.'"*
—Paul McCartney

My agent tried to impress upon me early on that most authors teach, speak, or have a day job to supplement their meager advances and earnings from writing. Did that deter me from making writing my career choice? No. I can't think of anything I'd rather do for the money. Besides, I don't do it for the money. That said, I gotta live. And why not live well? It is the limiting belief that I couldn't or shouldn't make more from writing that kept me from making more money. I decided to aim higher. The average author makes about $4,000 a year from their writing, according to the Authors Guild. I know I can do better. In fact, there are plenty of writers who are talented and motivated, who are able to write about what they love and make money without compromise, many making over $100,000 a year. I'm staying focused on them. If someone else is making good money in your field, then it's possible. But, but . . . NO! If you work hard, continue to improve and start to believe in yourself and your talents, combined with placing a higher value on your time, uniqueness, contribution, and so on, you can and should make money. People with far less talent are making more than you (I meet them all the time), so drop the limiting belief that you aren't good enough to be paid well and to make a fortune.

You must make money, enough money to keep the dream alive (and your spouse and parents off your back). Far too many talented and creative people had to quit and give up because they weren't able to make enough money to keep pursuing their dreams. Having to pay the bills and constantly not having enough money to do so killed their motivation. For this (creative life) to work we need some money coming in. Where does it come from for the creative person? That's the beauty of it. There are all kinds of ways to boost your bottom line and bring in bucks other than straight salary. There are royalties, licensing agreements, speaking fees, product sales, consulting, teaching, advances, endorsement deals, and so on. There are also some straightforward ways to make your money make more money, including savings, investments, real estate, stocks—things that generate income. (Things like cars, trips, and clothes do not produce a profit and are thus not income-generating. I know, Duh.) We want to focus our energies and money on things that will make us more money without having to work for it. Right?

The goal is to make more doing what we enjoy. That said, why not try to get the most you can for yourself? To do that, you must value your time (and energy) enough to demand that you get paid what it is worth (usually more than what they are offering) and seek out higher-paying opportunities, because you put a price on the time you are trading for your wages. You want more so that you can work less! (Many creative people make enough to take large blocks of time off after a project. Wouldn't that be nice?) You want to be able to not only survive but to thrive. To make enough so that you can actually start to save, pay off your debt, travel, work on pet projects, relax, and most of all, have peace of mind. Many times these take creative approaches; other times it is just putting in the time and doing whatever you have to do to make a buck.

To me, freedom has always been and will always be my number-one goal. I also realize that to achieve this you need two things, one of which is money. (The other is a mind-set of making choices that lead to freedom.) I could write a whole book about freedom (maybe I will), because it is that important. I believe that's what every artist wants (that, and a lot of love for their work and for them). The freedom to choose how you spend your time, what you work on, how you go about that work, and where and when (and how) it is displayed and distributed is HUGE. Money is more than a little important in making it happen.

My attitude toward money has come full circle. When I was a kid, I worked hard and saved what I earned. I would faithfully take my little bankbook to my friendly neighborhood bank to make monthly deposits and would watch with glee as my savings account grew and grew. I started my first business at age eleven and a second at age sixteen. Then, for some strange reason, I got careless with my money, and it dropped from number one to number nothing in my list of priorities. I could care less what I was paid (or whether I was paid at all) for my work and felt no thrill from what little money I earned. When I did make large amounts of cash, I tended to spend it as fast as I made it. But I have gone back to the beginning, where I am putting money as one of my highest priorities, because I now know that money is the fuel that gets my dreams off the ground. Once I got money back up to where it should be, I have been able to do more of what I want to do, which is basically nothing. What I mean is, I can take the entire summer off and travel and wait for projects that I am passionate about without worry.

Start thinking about things that generate money. Do good work, of course, but become money-oriented. There were times when I would work for next to nothing because I wanted the chance to show people what I could do. Maybe it was to get love or make others happy. Who knows? Like a slut, I gave it away too easily and wondered why I got no respect. When I finally realized I was giving up a lot more than I should, time I could have used for things that pay, having to work harder and longer just to be where I wanted to be, I wondered why I was exhausted as well as angry and bitter. What was once fun had begun to be a burden. I was overwhelmed with work that wasn't paying nearly enough (and sometimes nothing at all). I finally said enough was enough. My wife was getting pissed, too. I couldn't go to the movies or dinner because I had to finish something I promised I would do for someone, usually for free. I then realized I have limited amounts of time. I couldn't get to paying projects with all the freebies piling up. So I did something that went against my normal giving nature. I sent back a bunch of work, explaining that I just couldn't do it. It was like the weight of the world was lifted off my shoulders. I am now very careful about giving away my time or talents for free. How about you?

At first, it's hard to put a price on a creative project, because each piece is unique, each job is unique. But once you know what your time is worth, it becomes easier. You may still underbid, because as a rule, right-brainers chronically underestimate time. I started to keep a time log and a cost log for each project. Then I charged for time plus costs. Simple. I'm also realistic. Not everything we do we get paid for (promotion), but that's an investment in *us*. There should still be a payoff. Is it high enough? Is it worth your time? Remember, you have a limited amount of time, and what you give away can't be used for things that pay. Or you find you have no time to promote yourself. Why not? It's possible you gave away your time to help someone else. Your time and your income are linked.

I used to think that some people just couldn't afford to pay, and that's why I would help them out. Then one guy bragged that he had also hired another "professional" to work on the design project he had asked me to consult on—only he paid the other guy. My work was better, of course, but I was a sucker.

It motivates you to have a specific income or earnings target to shoot for. It gets you off your ass and pushes you to work harder and ask for more when you are going for a goal. My agent was the one who set what I thought was an unreasonable number to aim for. But because we both wanted to reach it, we worked extra hard and hit it— and then some. We looked at all kinds of ways to make that goal, including collecting past-due invoices, charging more for expenses, negotiating better deals, and selling books at the back of the room to attendees. I concentrated more on my income and ways to build it up and looked for things I could add on that would generate cash. This included things like encouraging existing customers to buy more, bundling items together to move slow sellers by packaging them with hot items, and raising rates. I also started focusing on profits and not just sales.

Creative people usually are uncomfortable admitting they want to make money and even more reserved about asking for it. They don't see their worth, so they either don't try to make enough or are ashamed if they make too much. Ever notice how nobody talks about what they make? Guys would rather talk about their need for Viagra than divulge what they make in a year. (Well, maybe that's a stretch.) That isn't to say we don't like to look at what others are taking home each year and make judgments on that amount. There is nothing to be ashamed of if your paychecks are big or small. (It's how you use it that counts.) But isn't bigger better?

ⓢ ACTION ITEM

When you cash your paycheck, do you feel you are paid enough for all the time, energy, and effort you put forth? If you aren't making enough money (and who is) ask yourself, why? Before you begin blaming others—the art world, a lack of time, yada, yada, yada—do some soul-searching. Have you truly given it your best shot? Do you have trouble charging what you are worth? Are you hustling and looking for new business as hard as you can? Do you do enough to market yourself? Are you getting repeat customers? Are your skills dated? Is your art stale? Do you do shoddy work? Have a reputation as being difficult to work with?

Money Is Power

"With money in your pocket, you are wise, you are handsome, and you sing well, too."

—*Yiddish proverb*

Noah Wyle, one of the original cast members of *E.R.*, has made millions from the show. "You don't walk around with an air of desperation all the time. Suddenly you're walking into rooms with a completely different frame of mind," he says. "It carries over to friendships and family relationships. Your family starts seeing you as a success, as opposed to the kid they had to worry about because he didn't quite make it through college." Maybe my parents were right. If I had become a doctor, dentist, or lawyer, I would have had one of the highest average annual wages. (Rounding out the top five are podiatrists and pilots.) Some parents see income as the only barometer of success. How you make your money is more important than how much. That said, it seems that society seems to respect those who make more over how one makes it.

That's just the way it is. It's the same with the business of art. The more money you make (or generate), the more respect and opportunities there are. Hey, I'm just the messenger. At a panel discussion on the book business, one of the panel members, an executive for a large chain of bookstores, revealed that one of the other panelists' books sold only 1,100 copies the previous year. That's how they see us, in terms of dollars and cents. The more you sell (and make) the more clout is given you and the more you can get away with. Take director James Cameron. His big-budget action-thrillers made millions (*The Terminator, True Lies*), and this gives him a lot of leeway. Many in Hollywood are willing to put up with his "eccentricities" because he makes money.

People are still impressed by the big corner office with a view. In fact, one firm decided to do away with fancy offices and made them all the same size with the same decor. At another firm a woman was hired, and after a few days her office windows were covered with duct tape. Why? Because she was told that only managers get windows. Man!

In the arts, a good portfolio is *almost* as important as a strong sales record. I'm thinking I may start carrying my sales history around along with samples of my work. Hey, if that's what it takes! I know that when I try to book our band, club owners are almost more interested in "how well we travel" (can we pack the place) than in hearing a tape. Agents use strong sales to negotiate larger advances. Also, once you have a hit, people start to return your calls. If you don't have a strong sales record but have the *potential* for strong sales, you are okay.

There is a myth that the artist has no negotiating power. That's not entirely true. If an editor wants to buy your book, you have some leverage. Don't dare let them know how desperate you really are. When they offer you a ridiculously low amount of money and a contract with unfavorable terms, you can negotiate both the size of the advance and some of the terms of the agreement. They expect you to. When you can afford to walk away, you can usually get a better deal.

FAST FACT
Believe it or not, one out of five women makes more money than her husband. Women are also playing a bigger role in financial decisions that affect the family.

ACTION ITEM
Add up every source of income you can think of. (Look at old invoices, checkbook registers, deposit slips, pay stubs, and so on for clues.) Look

for areas where you can make more money. Which of these can you build on?

_____

Why We Don't Make More Money

"I don't want to make money, I just want to be wonderful."
—Marilyn Monroe

There are some artists who almost expect to be poor or have gotten used to it. You read about the struggles of "starving artists" and come to expect the same. Like it's a rite of passage to go through poverty before the big bucks come. (It's a victim mentality, when you come right down to it.) You feel that the wages you want are out of your reach and control—the "suits" will decide what your art and talent are worth. You can't fathom monetary success. Or maybe you are a money martyr, wearing your poverty as a badge of honor, as if the fact that you can't sell anything or do anything commercial is a sign of success. When you see less qualified, experienced, and talented people making big bucks, it pisses you off. Admit it, you envy them—maybe not the money but the respect they get because they make money. You can keep your integrity intact and still have commercial success.

You can be loved by the critics and still have strong sales. The goal is to not be recognized as just a struggling artist. Maybe money isn't the most important thing, but it should be more important than you likely think it is. Having been around a lot of successful creative people, I can tell you that even the most hard-core, pure, respected artists think about making money.

• Let me ask you a question. Do you feel that you are getting paid what you are worth right now? If you said "no," that's good. It's a start to realizing that there is more money on the table. And you deserve a piece of it. In the art world it pays to remember that others are making money from your work. Be grateful and generous to them for their efforts on your behalf, but don't let them take advantage of you. Aren't you tired of being abused and used—of being chronically underpaid? Could it be you don't see the correlation between the fee or price you charge and profits? Yes, it's art, but it's a business, too.

Get serious—about your career and your business. Is it a hobby? Are you a charity? Or is this a creative career?

• Maybe fear keeps your fees too low. You are afraid to charge more for fear that all your current clients will leave. You think you'll have less volume. Good. You can't make it on a small margin and large volume. You'll have to work harder. You want *less work* at *higher fees.* You can be busy but not make much money. Are you missing out on a lot of lucrative work because you are so busy with the lower-paying gigs? Look at who makes what in your industry. Are you surprised to find that those making more than you are far less talented and may even have less experience? They just had the chutz-pah to ask for more and felt they deserved it.

• You are good enough! Many creative people undervalue them-selves and their work. I know many artists who are willing to work for nothing. Maybe they think that it will lead to something bigger, and it can. But usually they are needlessly giving away their time and talent. This approach has even backfired. When a client was ready to hire someone, they didn't respect the artist enough to pay her after she was willing to work for free and hired someone else. Doing freebies gives others the impression you are less than profes-sional, and desperate. You don't have to compromise your art. If the money makes you uncomfortable, use it for greater good. Just put a little aside.

• Sometimes NOT knowing what is fair leads to more money. You don't realize that authors get only $15,000 advances and you ask for more, you may just get it. You think that you don't have the expe-rience or education to make more—even though you can do the job just as well—go for it anyway, and you might get it.

• Maybe you hate discussing fees. You would prefer to take out the trash, clean the toilet, or dig a ditch. Do you have a problem ask-ing for and accepting money—even when you know that the work is worthwhile? You may never lose this feeling, so distance yourself from this part of the business. Have your agent, manager, partner, or someone you trust deal with it for you. Or have several strong open-ing lines you can use depending on the situation. You could be direct, "My fee is . . ." or "It won't exceed . . ." or ask them, "Do you have a budget in mind?" or "Let's discuss my fee structure." If you don't do well with math you may just guess at what you should be paid and underbid. Factor in your time and expenses before blurting out a figure for your fee. You don't have to compete on price. Focus on value.

HOW MUCH IS YOUR TALENT WORTH?
ANSWER: WHAT PEOPLE ARE WILLING TO PAY.

Value Added

• I remember when I was starting out as a graphic artist, people would ask me to design a logo or T-shirt for them, and I'd do it for free to build my portfolio. After a while I had enough stuff for two portfolios. When you don't charge enough (or anything at all), people don't respect you. Bette Midler's character in the film *Ruthless People* has a great line after her abductors are holding her hostage and making lower and lower ransom demands to her husband. "I'm being marked down?" she asks. "I've been kidnapped by Kmart!"

• Here's another observation I have. When we get paid in one lump sum, it seems like so much money. But when you do the math (hours it took or takes to complete a project divided by the advance), you realize you are making minimum wage. When you sit down and actually calculate your hourly fee, you are sick to your stomach. That isn't even factoring in your overhead, the time it took you to get where you are. You've spent half your friggin' life in class and apprenticing to get where you are. That's why, just because it takes you only five minutes to do something, it doesn't mean you don't charge full fee. It took you a long time to get good enough to do something fast and good. That's valuable, and they should pay. If you are like most creative people, when your name is on something you've created, you can't help but do your best work, even if it is for less. Others know this and take advantage.

• A money mind-set means you are always on the lookout for money-making opportunities. One guy I know was giving away his time and expertise for free. He would be working on a project doing computer graphics, and in addition to the work he was hired for he would come up with all kinds of neat ideas for the company that contracted him, but instead of charging extra for his time, he did it for free. We had a little chat, and he now contracts himself out or consults for cash—a lot of cash. He was leaving tens of thousands of dollars on the table.

💰 ACTION ITEM
Repeat after me. "I am special. My work is worthwhile. I deserve to be paid well for what I do."

Make Yourself More Marketable
"Sales figures are to authors what batting averages are to baseball players."

—Betsy Lerner

Andy Warhol once said, "Success is what sells." He was right. In a perfect world we would all be rewarded (handsomely) for doing quality art, not just commercial art. But doing good art doesn't always guarantee monetary gain. Many hacks make a fortune while talented artists struggle. It could be the kind of art that is limiting you. If you want to be a poet, you are probably not going to get as much as a songwriter. (Jewel is the lone exception here. Both her poetry and songs sell a ton.) So you could turn your poem into lyrics or resign yourself to the fact that poetry is not a well-paid endeavor. The art world is not plotting against you. It may seem that way, but the reality is that they want to see you succeed because that would mean they have succeeded, too. They make money, you make money. The problem is, they are under a lot of pressure to produce. That's why it seems to get harder and harder for less-established artists to break in. Those who make decisions about what (and who) gets a chance are becoming more about going with the sure thing. "It's not what they [studios] do. They look for home runs. For a studio, it takes just as much time to hit singles as a home run. So why try to hit singles when your whole philosophy is built on home runs?" asks Tom Sherak, a film executive. That's not to say that discovering the next new thing isn't still the Holy Grail for the "suits"—it is still a thrill. But being able to prove your worth (in sales or potential sales) is part of what it's about these days.

It is imperative that you understand and embrace the concept of profitability. It's actually not a novel premise that those artists who can produce (in dollars) get deals. Early on, the Rolling Stones convinced the owner of the Crawdaddy Club in West London that they could bring in more people and hence sell more drinks than other bands. Sure enough, the first time they played the West London club there was a line out the door. Art is a business. Period. You can wish it were different, or you can deal with it. Only one of these two options is going to produce positive results. So if you can somehow show how your art or idea will make money, you have nothing to worry about. If not, then maybe you can scale it down and do it yourself if you so desire. But don't expect others to want to drop money on something that won't make them a dime. Harsh? Yes! Reality? Yes! Sadly, your previous sales record can become more important to a publisher than the quality of the creation. Sure, they would love to have both—a good book with strong sales potential— but if they were to have to choose one or the other, it would be a bestselling book.

It's also a fact that the more they think they can sell, the more support you get. Sales are your "juice." So you'll want to do anything and everything you can to promote and push your previous projects. All this big business versus quality art is giving me a headache. Let's get to some good news.

Thankfully, good work will usually find an audience and sell well. Whew. Sure, some utterly crappy movies make millions, but the fact remains, clever marketing can take an inferior idea or product only so far. But when you combine even a mediocre marketing campaign with amazing art, the results are almost always awesome. This is when big business and art can coexist. Hey, I hear you. You're saying, "How can commercial work be considered serious, important?" It can, and it is. Just because a lot of bad stuff makes big bucks shouldn't take away from the fact that sometimes groundbreaking and breathtaking creations have mass appeal and make money. You want more? Okay, bring it on. Someone may say, "Well, he's just doing it for the money." So? What's wrong with making something that makes money and gets you paid well for your work? Other professionals make big bucks when they are the best. Do we really have to remain starving artists in order to create great work?

Don't answer that. Let me just tell you a little about my own experience with this.

I worked on one of my earlier books for eighteen months. That is a long, long time. I have never worked that hard on a book before or since. When the book first came out the reviews and reactions were all magical. Everyone loved it—except it didn't sell all that well. Since I self-published this book (and gave up more than a year of my life to write it), I began to understand the importance of marketability. I vowed to never let that happen again. I won't work on projects like that one, which was a labor of love, unless there is at least the chance for a payoff. I can't afford to. You can't afford to. Things have certainly improved for me since that painful lesson. I worked hard to make myself and my books have a more mainstream appeal, and it has paid off. It wasn't easy. Publishers don't really promote authors like they used to, but I knew how important it was to get my sales numbers up so that each time it came time to sign a new deal, I could demand more. Why? Because I have proven myself a marketable and profitable property. It's all about the profits, baby. I am telling you all this because I learned the hard way. I wouldn't say I wasted two years of my life on that slow seller, because it did prove to be an important piece and earned me a lot of respect as a writer, but I wouldn't do it again. No way.

The way I see it, my publisher and I are partners, and we both benefit from a book that shows a profit. If I were in their shoes, I would honestly have to say I would look for the talented writer who could also make money. So you can try to fight the fact that books, paintings, films, and music have become a commodity with a bottom line, or you can try to boost yours up. "I'm sick of musicians saying, 'I don't care what you want to hear, I'm gonna play whatever I want 'cause I'm an *artist.*' You're an artist? Paint my house, bitch!" This is Gene Simmons of Kiss's take on this whole subject. Whoa! Where you choose to spend your creativity and time can determine your level of success and income. Focus on those things you do well, enjoy doing, and have a passion for and that have at least a chance to pay off. As I said earlier, great works usually sell well. Thank God! I think consumers can tell the difference between art from the heart and art made for money. So how can we charge more for what we do? Make sure there is a market, and then make yourself more marketable.

• **Choose a path with a chance for a payoff.** Why struggle if you don't have to? If you choose a niche market that motivates you, where you can honestly say you wouldn't want to do anything else, that's success. Hopefully it can happen like that, and people will pay for what you want to produce. That isn't always the case. I know an author who wrote a book about hiking in the Southwest. She sees herself on *Oprah,* making millions. I don't want to be the one to burst her bubble, but it will be an uphill climb, so to speak. It's a small-market book. Nothing wrong with that, but if she put the same effort into something that had wider appeal, she would make more. Some jobs just don't pay.

• **Be better.** Make it your mission to be the best at what you do. Continue to practice and improve. People pay for performance. If you are known as the best at something, even if it's playing polka tunes on the accordion (like Grammy-nominated Lynn Marie, who all of a sudden got offered a record deal and a chance to play at the Grand Ole Opry after being nominated), you will make more. Whatever you have to do to improve, do it. Not only will this boost your confidence (and confidence sells) and your ability to sell yourself, it will make marketing much easier (word of mouth will do the trick when you are at the top of your game). Practice, improve your game, give better customer service, promote your success. You can charge more when you are known as the best. Look at Alex Rodriguez, the best shortstop in baseball. He signed for $250 million. In fact, the difference between a baseball player who hits .250 (average) and one who hits .333 (rare) is only one more hit every twelve tries. That's one more hit every three games. The difference in salary between the two players is millions.

• **Is your attitude worth catching?** Marketability may not have anything to do with your talent level but more to do with people's tolerance of your "artistic" attitude. There are some "difficult" people who others won't work with for any amount of money. Life is too short. Improve your reputation as being reliable, likable, and bankable, and work will come your way. For example, a photographer who is known in the industry as being on top of technology, very efficient, organized, reliable, and works well with models gets more work than he can handle. Conversely, a more talented photographer who has been known to be less than professional is having trouble getting good work. A little attitude is okay. Michelangelo had quite a temper and would quarrel with even his most powerful patron—the pope! Raphael was the exact opposite personality type—reasonable, reassuring to those he worked with, and generally a nice guy. But of the two gifted artists, who do you think is better known?

• **Be reliable.** Bassist Nathan East is best known for his work with Eric Clapton and Phil Collins and as one-fourth of the band Fourplay. He's known as "everybody's bassist" because he is very talented as well as likable and reliable and works constantly. How can you make yourself more marketable? When a director is working with a tight budget, she has to be practical. If she can get an actor who can hit home runs without any hand-holding, it makes more sense to use him because he won't take a hundred takes (expensive) to get it, and he won't be constantly asking, "What's my motivation?" Don't discount things that come easily to you as not being valuable to others. Don't assume that because "it was nothing" you shouldn't charge for it. The key is to package these assets (talents and skills) and get them to people who will pay. This is where what you do well (and like to do) crosses paths with what others want and need.

• **Produce and you will prosper.** You may work extremely hard on a project and it will still bomb. Believe me, I understand. But you have to keep plugging away and build a body of work and a track record. You have to get your work out there. Make sure you get proper credit and that people know what you are doing and the success you are having. The people who get promoted usually have a higher profile than those who don't. (Call them "ass-kissers" if you like, but they get the big bucks.) The goal is to get in on the cool projects (or make mundane ones more interesting and important) and make sure others know that you had a hand in their success. As Tom Peters says, these are projects that "make a difference, projects that leave a legacy—and, yes, projects that make you a star." This is true if you work for a corporation or company (like Apple designers who worked on the iMac) or if you are a freelancer. You want projects you will be able to brag about.

• **Success by association.** If you've worked on a hit, you can get some of that to rub off on you. Name drop. It builds you up. Get testimonials. Fashion designer Zandra Rhodes is known as "the queen of shock chic"; her clothing has been worn by the band Queen and THE Queen and she uses that fact to her advantage. Sony signed a select set of screenwriters to a deal that pays them 2 percent of the worldwide take on their films. This was not open to everyone—initially it was offered to only the top tier of writers who had been nominated for a major award *or* made over $750,000.

• **Big fish, small pond.** Be the best in a small niche. Sam Walton went against the grain by opening his Wal-Mart stores in small towns where Sears, Target, and Kmart weren't located. Brilliant. Look for expanding markets because there is a higher rate of return in growth areas. Or look for areas that are small but overlooked by others. Artist Holly Christian designs greeting cards that feature people of varied ethnicities. Brenda Green opened a store for left-handers in her hometown. What trends have you noticed that you can identify with, that interest you, and that involve some of your skills and abilities?

• **Strike while the iron is hot.** When you are new, there is a honeymoon period. You are all potential. Milk it for all it's worth. The power of threes, it's called. You need three big things back-to-back to really build up your fee rate. Nobody was hotter than Regis Philbin in 2000. He saved a network, for crying out loud. He also cashed in with a book, a line of clothing, and ads, in addition to his hit shows. When you're hot, keep the fire burning. You don't have to reinvent yourself every four months, but build on what you've already done. Sometimes a first deal sucks and needs to be renegotiated. It's best to do this while you are hot.

• **Start small.** Writer-director Amy Heckerling was looking for a "name" actor for her movie *Loser* but looked to Jason Biggs. Jason who? The "pie guy" (Jim) from *American Pie*. Heckerling joked that "Next year, I wouldn't be able to afford him." Before he hit the "Biggs" (sorry, I couldn't resist), he was working as a "sandwich artist" at Subway. Now that he is a hot property he will be able to cash in and get a bigger piece of the "pie."

• **I'd like to thank the Academy.** Children's-book writers are often relegated to the bottom of the rung of the literary world. To break out of that literary ghetto, one has to be recognized by big sales numbers or do something dramatically different. There is another way to get respect (and maybe more money), and that is to win an award. Few authors have won as many awards for literary excellence as Virginia Hamilton, and she was able to have the kind of success other children's-book authors dream about. Your stock goes way up when you can add "award-winning" to your title. This is true for almost every creative endeavor.

• **Higher learning, higher earning?** According to the Census Bureau, an individual without a high school diploma earned an average salary of only $16,124, while someone with an advanced degree earned an average of over $60,000. ($40,478 with a bachelor's degree.) In the creative arts a degree is *not* always needed to get top dollar. In fact, I hear that what employers will pay for in the future are people who are able to use the right side of their brains. Hooray!

• **Go where the money is.** According to a study by the Segal Co., pay for CEOs at smaller companies varies by geography. In the Northeast a CEO can expect to earn $324,000 while that same CEO would make *only* $304,000 in the South. Cozy Powell was the drummer for Rainbow and Whitesnake, as well as a session drummer known for his precision and timing. He made a nice fat fee for his studio work until he was replaced by a drum machine. He became a solo artist and did more live gigs to make money. Is there a demand for what you are thinking of doing? Will people pay? As Steve "Woz" Wozniak, the co-founder of Apple Computer, once pointed out, "If it's not making money then it's not being done the right way."

• **Go where the money WILL be.** No matter what you are working on, you have to start thinking about the next big thing down the line. When I owned a chain of retail stores (specializing in action sports gear), the secret to our success was that we (my brothers and I) were into the same stuff as our customers and we were tuned in to what was happening in our industry. We saw Rollerblades as being a big thing. Bingo. We were big into wakeboarding, too, well before it became the booming business it is today. We also experimented with making longboard skateboards, a popular trend today. When the Quiksilver rep showed me a line of board shorts and bathing suits for women called Roxy, we said, "Yes!" The point is, we made a lot of money by being the first on a trend and riding the wave for all it was worth. This is as true today as it was when Thomas Edison made the first recording of Johannes Brahms for his new phonograph in 1889, to Neil Young embracing DVD technology. The fact is, the super-wealthy are people with vision. They have the creative ability to see something that others didn't.

 ACTION ITEM

Make a stack of cards of your talents and skills, abilities, experience, gifts, and strengths. Pull out the cards that will make you more marketable. Make a top-ten stack. Do the same for any projects you are working on, or thinking of working on. Which are the most marketable?

Raise Your Rates

"If you don't go for as much money as you can possibly get, then I reckon you're just simply stupid."

—*Mick Jagger*

Your prices say a lot about you. It's how people perceive the quality of you and your work. It's the image. Low prices make you seem second-rate. You can always come down from higher fees, but it's hard to go up. You can give discounts if people are willing to pay cash or your full fee up-front. Money indicates your value in many art forms. The more you make the more respected you are, and strangely, the more work comes your way. Weird, but true. More money means you can choose meaningful work and walk away from projects that don't push your buttons, or you can pass on poor-paying clients. (Don't price yourself out of the market, either. Sometimes the client has a budget for a project and can't exceed a certain amount no matter what.) Stay competitive. What is fair market value for comparable work? Where do you fall? Is profit possible at current rates? Do your rates cover your costs?

Don't forget about inflation. (Inflation means that your money won't buy as much today as it did when you didn't have any.) Review fees and costs annually, and adjust for inflation. Inflation affects you in a big way. It eats into profits if you don't keep up. Have canvases gone up? Film processing? Studio costs? Compensate. You deserve to make a profit! Profit is what's left over after all your costs are covered, and that includes materials, overhead, advertising, commissions, postage and shipping, and time invested (including conceptualizing time as well as attending meetings).

WHAT THEY EARN*

Actor	$42,100	Keri Russell	$920,000
Newspaper editor	$22,500	Barbara Walters	$10,000,000
Graphic artist	$50,000	Website designer	$65,000
Waiter	$16,000	Performance artist	$35,000
Composer	$140,000	Britney Spears	$15,000,000
Author	$40,000	Dean Koontz	$34,000,000
Software developer	$37,500	Steve Jobs	$90,000,000
Radio talk-show host	$30,000	Dr. Laura Schlessinger	$13,000,000
Children's-book author	$40,000	John Grisham	$36,000,000
Orchestral musician	$30,020	Shania Twain	$48,000,000
Public-relations writer	$49,100	TV writer	$410,000
Magazine editor	$41,500	Rosie O'Donnell	$25,000,000
Music teacher	$47,000	Record-label promoter	$95,000
Potter	$12,000	Art gallery manager	$29,000
Jewelry maker	$28,000	Tommy Hilfiger	$22,000,000

Startling Statistics

According to the Bureau of Labor Statistics, the median weekly income for an artist in 2000 was $727. For all Americans, $576, and for physicians it was $1,340.

💰 HIDDEN COSTS

Don't underestimate what it costs you to be in business. What about day-care costs, supplies, phone, utilities, office supplies, commute, postage, shipping, rent, car, lease on equipment, costuming, depreciation on equipment, services, outside labor, travel, repairs, sales taxes, self-employment tax, insurance, sick days, commissions, marketing? Come up with a total from last year, and divide by twelve months. Then divide by 2,080 hours. That's what you need to charge an hour just to break even! Will what they are paying cover these costs?

*Parade Magazine, "What People Earn," February 25, 2001

The Price Is Right?

"Never mistake your salary for your income."

—Lillian Gish

Most right-brainers don't want to deal with the details like figuring out expenses and profit margins, so they wing it and may be losing a lot of money without doing the math. You are not a nonprofit. You need to know what you are making. You have to do your homework. You need to know what your overhead really is. Know what the market value is for your type of work, and poke around to find out what they are willing to pay. You have to arrive at an hourly rate and what your bottom line is. The minimum rate you are *willing* to work for. Don't go below it. How much do you want to make a year? ($100,000?) How much do you want to work? (Eight months?) Take the total desired salary and divide by the total hours you want to work. Look at that number. Not enough? (Fifty-two weeks, five days a week, eight hours a day comes to 2,080.) $100,000 divided by 2,080 equals $48 an hour gross. Do the math. If you want to work only eight months out of the year and make $100,000, you'll need to make $78 per hour. So either you can work more or raise rates or cut costs. It's not some fluff thing. There are realities you have to deal with. Arrive at break-even and desired figures.

Granted, it's hard to put a price on art, and each project is unique (as is your situation), so it is like comparing apples to oranges. What is the competition getting? Do your homework. Request others' fee sheets, go online, ask newsgroups, ask associations, read catalogs, go to a gallery, talk to other artists. Base your fee on that number. You want to know, what is the most you could get? Ever wonder what Carrie Bradshaw (the sex columnist played by Sarah Jessica Parker in *Sex and the City*) would make in the real world? I do. I asked around—about $45,000 a year. (I was surprised that writers could get $1 a word, $500 a page for Web content.) Charge based on past performance, what the market says, based on hourly rate, your overhead expenses, self-confidence (what you are willing to ask for). Also, ask yourself, if you didn't take this job, what else could you have done with this time?

You must first believe they can afford to pay. Who would pay $750 to teach people how to perform impromptu sketches? Leo

Burnett (an advertising agency) is paying people at the Second City comedy company to do just that for dozens of employees. People will pay. Sometimes it doesn't matter how much time it takes you to do something—they are willing to pay a certain amount, and that is that. It's up to you if you want to do it. Is there a way you could get it done faster? I have found that when you give a project price, it can seem high to them. Tell them how many hours, the costs, and so on and that this is actually cheap. Point out that if you were an employee how much it would cost them in benefits. For you, it's more profitable by the hour, but a project price is most popular. Here's an example where an hourly rate *is* better than a salary. In Hollywood, if you are a "day player" on a movie set, you may make $1,000 a day and work for four days for $4,000. If they make you a "weekly player," you'll still get $4,000 but have to work six days for the same money. Either way you must have an hourly rate to work with and from. By the way, if they say "Such a deal" and jump at your rates, then you are too low. If they freak out at your prices then they are too high—for *them*.

How to Make More

"Does giving birth make you a real woman? No, earning less than a man makes me a real woman."

—Suzy Berger

Have you ever been out to eat and had a ballpark figure of what you wanted to spend but left wondering how the bill ended up being triple that—before the tip? A good server who knows how to work a table (and you) can take a $50 dinner and make it into a $150 dinner before you can say, "I'll just have water to drink." How does she do it? Most of it is just the power of suggestion and a willingness to ask for the sale, plus a warm, friendly persona. "Would you like a cocktail before the meal? We make a mean margarita. If we use Agavero, it will be even better." "Ahhh, I see you are looking at the appetizers. May I suggest . . ." You were just going to have a salad, but those little shrimp things sound yummy. You then order wine. You agree to add chicken to your house salad. She recommends the special (but fails to mention price). Instead of coffee, you upgrade to an espresso drink and split a dessert. Before you know it your bill has ballooned. There is a lesson here. Ask (or suggest) add-ons, and they may just go for it. Always look for ways to increase your earnings from existing clients. You work just as hard but now it's for more money. Here are some other suggestions to up the ante.

Make a price list. Carry it with you. Post it where you'll see it. Make one with your real fees and another with the fees you really want to get—your goal. Make a list of what you would like to charge, your ideal rates. (Maybe you could get your hands on an industry leader's rate card and use it to inspire you to get yours up to that level.) Having a rate card or price list is professional and essential. Set rates in advance, in writing. It's easier to get money out of the way and have them pay up-front rather than trying to collect or discuss it later. You will likely need an hourly rate to show how you arrive at your project prices. Spell out terms and discount prices clearly. Charge more for quick turnaround times and change orders. The more rights they want, the more you charge. Watch what you say and what you sign. They may try to get you to hastily agree to a fee and hold you to it. Agreeing to a price is only half the battle. To get paid, make sure you have a letter of agreement and have filled out all the necessary forms (theirs and yours), and if possible, get a purchase order and approval from the person who is authorized to give it. Include a kill-fee clause. This is usually 15 to 50 percent and protects you in case the client pulls the plug and cancels the project. It doesn't matter what price you agree to if you can't get paid. Check with others to see if this client is a slow payer. If you find out they are, get paid first or stay away, no matter how tempting the project is.

If you plan to raise rates, let everyone know well in advance, and get them to place orders or book you before the price goes up. You will usually get a ton of work this way. Raise rates while you're hot, like after you've won an award or had a big seller. Increase your marketability through increased experience, improved skills, exposure. You don't have to raise all your rates. You can still have a "loss leader," a low price to entice someone to do business with you, but you make the money up on other (high-priced) products and services. If you want to get rid of problem people, raise the rates that would directly affect those people. When people complain about price, demonstrate how what you do can boost their bottom line. If you really hate discussing money, then maybe an agent or manager can negotiate the deal for you. Agents can get you more than you can usually get for yourself.

INFLATION IS A BITCH.

You would think that with a booming economy for much of the 1990s, most Americans would be making more. Some are making more, but when you adjust for inflation, the annual pay raise for the decade was just $111—about 0.03 percent a year (nothing!). The average family was worse off in 1997 than it was in 1977 and took home less. Want more sad news? According to a recent study, a minimum-wage job isn't enough to cover the rent on an apartment in most parts of the country. The average hourly wage to afford rent in a standard two-bedroom home is at least $12.47. Or as Joe Weinstein pointed out, "My dog is worried about the economy because Alpo is up to ninety-nine cents a can. That's almost seven dollars in dog money." Where does your money go? Here's an angle you may not have considered—inflation. You have to raise your rates to compensate.

Who Put the "Free" in Freelance?

"I never write—indeed, am physically incapable of writing—anything that I don't think I will be paid for."

—Truman Capote

Even though Samuel Johnson said, "No man but a blockhead ever wrote, except for money," should you ever work for free? Sometimes in the creative arts you don't have a choice. You have to do work on spec and hope that you can find a buyer and get paid. It depends what the potential payoff would be. How serious are they about buying the finished product? Are they a potential client that could be worth big bucks down the road? Or is it an existing client who just needs a "favor" for free? Again, is it worth it to you? What is your time worth? Are there other paying jobs to support you while you do this? Would you possibly miss out on a paying job because you committed to this? How much will it cost you in materials? Will it look good in your portfolio? Will it lead to more work? Is it challenging? Will you learn something new? Could you sell this somewhere else when you're done? Is it an opportunity to prove yourself? Get your foot in the door? When someone says to me, "I just want to pick your brain," what is that? I picture someone opening the lid on my head, rummaging around until they find what they want, then leaving without paying. Don't get me wrong, I want to help others, but there are times when I feel violated. You have to choose who to help and who to charge for that help.

On the other hand, there are reasons to waive your fee. If a client is willing to fly you in to speak, teach, or perform in a tropical locale, all expenses paid (but no fee), it sure gives you something to think about. Jimmy Buffett was flat broke, so when he got an offer to go to Paris (all expenses paid for him and his wife) to score a documentary film on tarpon fishing, he jumped at the chance. Maybe you can sell your creations at the back of the room, or you'll get some media exposure. That's good. Other reasons may include the chance to build your portfolio, make contacts, get referrals, or it's a form of free marketing. Maybe there is a chance the product you create for a client is something you can turn around and sell later, like an article (don't sign away the rights), or you can use the work as a sample. Maybe you want the byline in a prestigious publication. Maybe the gallery or bookstore is willing to do a massive mailing if you do a free signing or showing.

Just don't become a charity case. Clients will always cry that they don't have any money to pay you. Okay, so hand them a tissue and get something in trade. If they don't want to pay, offer a budget version of what you do. Negotiate down if you really want the work. Actors take less than scale to work on films that can be a showcase for their talents and result in higher fees later. A lot of writers were writing articles in exchange for stock options in start-up e-zines. This obviously didn't pay off. Clients have the money—they just don't want to give it *to you.* Try for partial payment up-front. Ask for payment installments. Assume some of the risk and take a percentage of the sales or profits. If they do well, you do well.

How to Get a Raise Out of Them

"I hated to go in and ask my boss for a raise the other day, but my kids found out that other kids eat three times a day."

—*Milton Berle*

"I'm tired of begging people for money. Can you find me a job?" "How long have you been out of work?" "Who said anything about not having a job? I work for PBS," laments James Wilkes. The goal is to find enjoyable work that is stimulating and fulfilling. Doing something just for the money is NOT the goal. That's not to say you shouldn't be paid well for what you do just because you enjoy it. You trade your time (and a piece of your life) for the employer's or client's gain. You should be paid well for that, regardless if you would do it for free. First you must feel like you really deserve more. Consider that William Farley, the CEO of Fruit of the Loom, was paid over $60 million from 1994–98 despite the fact that the company lost $247 million and had to file for bankruptcy. "It is unfortunate we can't buy many business executives for what they are worth and sell them for what they think they are worth," said Malcolm Forbes. You are a lot like an athlete. Part of a team but you want to be the superstar. Put up good numbers and you can negotiate a good deal or request a trade. Get a piece of the action if possible (stock options). Did you generate "wins" for the company? It doesn't have to be in dollars, either. Players who are "good in the clubhouse" or "field their position but can't hit worth a darn" are still valuable in baseball terms. Same for you. You had a brilliant idea that made the workplace a better place to be, made a difference, stand out, maybe somehow you have proven your worth. You may have to become a free agent to get what you're worth. Don't be modest when going for more money. You don't get paid what you deserve—you get paid whatever you can get them to pay you. Okay, let's look at other ways to get a salary like a superstar.

• **It's you or them.** Companies don't care about you, so get what you can. Don't get emotionally attached or you're dead in the water. They'll use you and abuse you if you let them.

• **Prove your value.** One of the nice things about creative careers is that many times it doesn't matter if you have a degree or what experience level you have. If you can do the work, that's all that matters. The more they need you, the more they'll pay.

• **Be ready to rattle off your accomplishments.** Have your portfolio and résumé ready. Update it regularly. Pick the right time to make your pitch (after you have just hit a home run for the company). Know what your contribution to the company has been (in real dollars if possible) and be able to say, "The accessories I designed resulted in (fill in the blank) of additional revenue, and there has been a growth of (fill in the blank) in my area." Keep a journal of your successes.

• **ASK!** Most people are too timid to ask for a raise. Only 20 percent of men and 24 percent of women are willing to ask for a raise. Fifty-nine percent of the men that asked for a raise got one. Forty-five percent of the women who asked for a raise were successful.

• **Do your homework.** Are you getting paid what you are worth? Could you make more elsewhere? Is it worth the hassle of moving? Ask around. Go online. Know what you want to make. One footnote: Some creative careers have set fees that are nonnegotiable. You get scale, and that is that. Union scale is set at roughly $1,752 a week for an actor working in film and $580 a week for an hour-long television series. Acting in a Broadway show should pay at least $950 a week.

• **Stock options made many millionaires.** The business does well and you do well—or vice versa. You reap the profits you helped to create. Is this great or what? The catch is, you take a risk that you are working on "The Next BIG Thing." You gave up a cushy job with steady pay and perks for long hours and the excitement that only a start-up can provide. Are you willing to work hard and make sacrifices for the potential payoff? Why should you work sixteen hours a day for someone else? Stock options offer the potential to get a big payoff. (Warning: They don't always pay off—stock options can end up worthless.)

• **People want perks and pay.** Pay attention to the value of bennies like learning opportunity, health benefits, and retirement programs. Many record executives have enormous expense accounts, but their salaries are lower. Nice perk, but it's not pay. You may be giving up things that are worth money. Review your benefits at least once a year.

• **"Hop" for a higher salary.** Many times creative people have to change companies to get promoted and paid what they are really worth. (Beware that when you hop you may be affecting your retirement total. Each time you hop you have to wait until you are eligible to participate in the company's profit-sharing and retirement plans.)

💰 ACTION ITEM

Write down every job you have ever had and what you were paid for each. Make some mental notes about how you feel while doing this.

Negotiation Made Easy (or at Least Easier)

"The strong inherit the earth—the meek inherit shit."

—Gene Simmons

In the book *The Forest for the Trees* by Betsy Lerner, she tells a great story about the late golf legend Harvey Penick and the negotiations for his bestselling book. For years he kept all of his golf secrets in a little red notebook. Simon and Schuster wanted to publish the book and made an offer. Harvey's agent called Harvey's wife and told her that the publisher was interested in publishing the book for $90,000. She said she needed to talk to Harvey first. The golfer's wife called back and said the two had talked it over and wanted to go ahead with the book, but first they would have to get a second mortgage on their home. "Why?" the agent asked. "So we can come up with the $90,000 to publish the book." Of course the editor quickly explained that the publisher would pay THEM $90,000. *Harvey Penick's Little Red Book* went on to become the most successful sports book of all time. If only negotiating a good deal were this easy (and lucrative).

The problem is that many times the artist has very little leverage and would be willing to do the work for almost nothing if it meant recognition and exposure for himself or his creations. He is so thrilled to get a deal, any deal, he almost blurts out, "I'll take it," before the contract is taken off the table. Don't think gallery owners, publishers, employers, clients, record executives, and other power people don't know this and use it to their advantage and your disadvantage.

In order to get what you deserve you need to be a little more savvy about negotiating. Malcolm McLaren said it best: "What most people don't realize is that the whole thing is about getting as much money as possible in as short a time as possible with as much style as possible." Amen. The art world doesn't always treat an artist fairly. It's a buyer's market, and you get the feeling that if you don't take what they offer, someone else will. The other side has more experience and skill at the bargaining table, and that's why you need to improve this skill or hire someone (for a percentage, of course) to represent you. A bad deal can cost you down the road. While no amount of money will seem like enough to cover all the struggles and sacrifices you have made, there must be some number that will at least ease some of the pain.

When two installers came to lay tile in my friend's new home, they began by moving all of the appliances that were in the way. When my buddy asked them to put the appliances back, they said there was an additional charge. So he reluctantly paid them an extra $50. After the two workmen went to leave for the day, they realized my friend's car was parked behind them, blocking them. Being a lawyer, he charged them $50 to move *his* car out of the way.

ACTION ITEM
Repeat after me: "There is plenty of money to go around, and I deserve some of it."

The Negotiator
"Sure I lie, but it's more like tinting. It's all just negotiating theatrics."

—Irving Azoff, manager of the Eagles

The mind-set must be, get all you can! You are NOT a charity. "Greed, for lack of a better word, is good," said Gordon Gekko in *Wall Street*. I don't know that I agree, but it is important to realize that this is what drives most people in business. They (the client) don't deserve your pity. Don't be apologetic about your fees. You are a professional and should be paid like a professional. Many times they will cry poor in order to get you to lower your fee. They say they are taking all the risks. Then they hop into their Mercedes and drive away happy while you try to start up your twenty-year-old piece-of-crap car. You are good and deserve to be paid well. Don't give the store away because of any insecurities you may have. You don't want the reputation of being a bargain-basement type. You want to be top-shelf and thus top-dollar. Do whatever it takes to build your confidence level so that you feel you deserve to be paid better. If your fees are too low or you are too quick to cut them, they will start to wonder about your ability, and it may reduce your chances of getting higher fees in the future. Find creative solutions to impasses. Make a concession, but get something else in return.

• **Think first.** Some of the personality traits that make us great artists can work against us when it comes to negotiating. Traits like being big-picture people not even remotely interested in the details, our short attention span, being overly emotional, our tendency to speak without thinking, our impulsiveness, and our low sense of worth.

• **"Free" agent?** I have found that having others negotiate on my behalf is the best way to get a dynamite deal. Sure, they take a cut, but they almost always pay for themselves by getting you more than you could have gotten for yourself. They are experts at this kind of warfare, while you are an artist. They are informed about what others are getting, and they can remain neutral and unemotional. They are driven to increase the amount you will get so they will make more. (Not all agents are great, but the good ones are worth their weight in gold.)

• **You want win/win agreements.** You do well, they do well. Then there is less pressure, less guilt, and no hard feelings. Don't tick them off during the negotiation, because you still have to work together after the deal is done.

• **Have a goal and know your bottom line going in!** Remember, things always take longer than you think.

• **Leave room to negotiate down.** There will be times when you really want the gig and they want a deal. Jack up the price so you can cut it down. You need room to move. Go in assuming you'll have to negotiate, so a little wiggle room is a must. Make them feel they got a bargain. I have found that a flat fee doesn't work (I think some car dealers named after planets are getting this, too). People love to haggle.

• **Charge more for jobs that you really don't want or you know will be a big hassle.** If they want a rush job and you have to drop everything else, you should charge more.

• **Bundle things together to get a better deal.** Throw something in to get the price up.

• **Wait them out.** Sell them on the benefits before discussing price. Let them go first. They may make you an offer that was higher than you expected. Don't guess or assume what they want and are willing to pay. Do your homework or at least ask some leading questions, like "So, what is your budget for this project? What did you pay the person last year? What were you thinking of spending on this?" When they pin you down and say, "What's this gonna cost me?" you don't want to be evasive, but you also don't want to undersell yourself with some figure off the top of your head that will come back to haunt you. Either do a quick calculation and give them a range or say, "I'll get back to you later today." Knowing what they are likely to want and expect to pay is very helpful. Remember, listen about 75 percent of the time. Pause to get them to keep talking, and eventually they'll say something you can use.

• **When they make *you* wait you lose your edge.** Self-doubts start to creep in. They play on this insecurity. Relax. Work on something else. If you settle just to get rid of that awful anxious, upset-stomach, paniclike feeling, you may be selling yourself short. "I just want to get this deal done and move on" is not the way to be. Haste makes waste.

• **When they say the price is too high, you don't necessarily have to lower it.** If they can't afford you, you should refer them to someone else who is willing to work for less (and take the referral fee) and leave yourself open to getting a better offer elsewhere. Why tie yourself up for less than you deserve and then have to pass when something more lucrative comes along? You are good. Explain that they are going to get their money's worth. If they won't pay your price, give them what they can afford. If they want a twenty-minute promotional video but can't afford it, scale it back to a ten-minute video. If they can't afford a string orchestra, use a synthesizer instead.

• **Term limits.** Maybe you can improve the terms of your deal (more money up-front or a better royalty rate) in exchange for taking less money in total. You may also be able to get more promotional support, have your expenses paid, get stock options, or have your name appear more prominently. There are issues concerning your rights you may want to work out. For me, I realized that I was buying a lot of books, so I negotiated a better buy-back clause where I could purchase my books for resale at a discounted rate, which means more money in my pocket. Maybe you take less but get a longer-term deal. That security is worth something. Just be careful about being locked in to a bad deal.

• **Creative financing.** When one client said they couldn't afford my fee, I asked them if they could get a large company to sponsor the talk. They did, and I got paid my full fee. Lucille Ball and Desi Arnaz were shrewd negotiators. They wanted to do their show in front of a live audience in Los Angeles. The network bigwigs insisted it be done in New York. To settle their differences, Arnaz proposed that their own company, Desilu, would foot the bill to film it in a Los Angeles studio with an audience as long as they retained complete ownership of the shows. As you can imagine, the syndication market for the show is huge and lucrative.

• **Know your bottom line.** Appreciate what your time is worth! Know how long something will take and what your hourly wage is. Go in with a goal. Don't forget your agent's cut. If you cut costs too low not only will you lose money, you'll lose that time that could have been devoted to a higher-paying and more profitable project, so you lose twice.

• **Know the market.** What do others in a similar situation get?

• **Put yourself in their shoes.** What would they want to hear, have, or need? They are afraid you will say "NO." Trust me on that. It turns out that women entrepreneurs (who own about 40 percent of the businesses in the United States) only got 2.3 percent of the venture-capital money doled out. Most of the billions went to men and were from men. Man! (Oops, bad choice of words.) Going in to negotiate a deal, you've got to read and react to men.

• **Confidence sells.** Without it they will eat you alive. If you don't feel it, fake it. Put up a front. To get some self-esteem, practice negotiating. Do a dry run, and have someone grill you. Make a list of all your accomplishments and carry it in your wallet. Take it out or touch it when you need a boost. Do whatever you have to do to look and feel your best. Have a solid track record (along with samples, examples, and testimonials) to show them why you deserve more money (or at least a fair deal). If you look like a slob and your marketing materials or portfolio are shabby, or the sound quality of your demo is bad, it's hard to command higher fees. You gotta look like a million dollars to get a million dollars.

• **The most powerful negotiating tool (besides having a good agent or manager negotiating on your behalf) is to have walka-way power.** The ability to get up and leave. When you are buying a car and threaten to leave, what does the salesperson usually say? "Wait, wait, perhaps we can work something out." Don't get too attached too soon. It's the same thing in many creative fields. If you threaten to walk away unless they come up with more money, they may just be thinking, "What if this person walks and goes on to become a big star? She sure seems awfully confident. Maybe it's better to pay her what she wants now rather than later. We do need new acts, and here is a good one right in front of me. What's an extra $50,000 anyway." You have to put the fear into THEM. If you can't or won't walk away from a potentially poor deal, you lose. You don't actually have to walk—you just have to be WILLING to walk. The kind of attitude we want is not obnoxious and overconfident but, rather, self-assured. By saying, "Thanks, but so-and-so offered me more," or "My last gig paid such-and-such, and I've got to pass unless we can get the numbers up."

Certainly there have been instances where artists have walked away and were replaced to their former band's benefit. (Peter Gabriel left Genesis, and they became a bigger band. The same with David Lee Roth and Van Halen.) At the height of *Three's Company,* Suzanne Somers's contract was up for renegotiation. Somers asked for a raise. She ended up being booted off the show and blackballed for a decade and seen as greedy.

Ever notice that when you are dating someone, there are all kinds of other people who want to date you, too. But the minute you break up they are gone. Why is that? It has something to do with the way you carry yourself and the fact that others are interested in you, so you must be quite the catch. Don't seem desperate. When you don't need the work, all of a sudden there it is. You aren't desperate any-more. Or you have some money saved up so you don't feel you have to just jump in the sack—oops, I meant jump into a deal right away. You aren't under any pressure, and you perform better. Where was I going with this? Oh yes, you don't make stupid decisions and rush into bad deals that may damage your reputation or cost you money.

• **Leverage** comes when you have compromising photographs of them doing things they shouldn't be doing, or being able to name-drop that so-and-so is also interested is leverage. Leverage is also when they need you more than you need them (at least lead them to believe that). Take the six stars of the hit show *Friends*. They threatened to walk away from the show if they didn't get a substantial raise. (This was before *Survivor* kicked its ass in the ratings.) Although they asked for $1 million per episode each, they settled for $750,000 per person per episode. (That was a sizable raise from their previous salaries of $125,000 per episode.) The key was, they really would have walked. That, and the fact that they stuck together.

• **When you have a track record of success or a hot property, you can call the shots.** When George Lucas was negotiating a deal for licensing his latest installment in the *Star Wars* series, he took equity in Hasbro in lieu of licensing fees. His 7.5 percent stake ended up being worth almost $200 million.

• **Good cop, bad cop.** Have a CPA (or agent or manager) with you to say "no" so you don't have to. Having someone (like an intellectual-property lawyer as well as your agent) to look over an offer is a good idea. Know exactly what you are agreeing to. You can defer to him when you have to turn a deal down. He may also be able to make some suggestions that will help you earn more.

• **Don't get all emotional.** It's not personal (to them, anyway). It's true that most decisions (on both sides of the bargaining table) are emotional and we rationalize them out later, but if you let emotion (fear, greed, anger, or any other feelings) get in the way of rational thinking, you lose your edge. You can feel them, I guess, but try not to let others see them. Put on your best poker face. Certainly don't freak out and essentially kill a deal. Understand that it's part of the game for them to try to lowball you. The two emotions that are good are intuition and hunches. Trust them!

• **Go to the top.** Try to deal with the decision-maker. If it's just some lackey, demand a quick decision. It is almost always better to be face-to-face when working out a deal, so you can engage all of your senses in reading the other person.

- **Remove risk.** If you are at an impasse in a negotiation and they are reluctant to move ahead, do what you can to eliminate or minimize the risks to them. It could be the boulder in the way. One guy duct-taped himself to a chair until he got his price. There is a better way.

- **Money talks.** When you are the buyer, having cash or a cashier's check ready to go (even for a lower amount than you discussed) can push them over the edge. By seeing a briefcase full of cash or allowing them to hold the check in their hand, they will almost always cave and take it. When buying something and they won't budge, you could buy the item with your credit card and get frequent-flier miles or cash back. When you are the seller, taking a little less in exchange for cash in hand is worth it. Trying to collect down the road is a nightmare.

- **Ask for the moon.** One of his four-year-old twins asked actor Ray Romano for "everything and a kite." Pretty clever. You always ask for more than you want so you have some room to negotiate.

- **Don't underestimate what a solid reputation and good credit is worth.** A lot! You can get all kinds of great terms with it. People will want to work with you.

Seven Creative Solutions to Your Money Problems

"'Mommy, we're not going to be poor again, are we?' 'Not as long as you have that rare blood type.'"

—*Brett Butler*

1. My business is (fill in the blank). What other areas could I expand into that are related to what I already do and use the talents and tools I already have? How else could I use my talents? What am I positioned to do? What assets and resources do I already have at my disposal? Make a list of your talents, and see if anything clicks as something that you could sell to earn some extra money. (What do people tell you that you do well? Would they pay? If you're doing it anyway, you may as well be paid.) It's best to make extra money (and spend what little free time you have) doing something you enjoy and have a natural affinity for. What else could you sell to the same people?

Author Joyce Maynard had a "novel" idea for her third book,

Where Love Goes. She compiled a CD of love songs to serve as a soundtrack for the book. Sometimes money-making opportunities are right under your nose. What add-ons could you sell? Like related gadgets and goodies.

Emil Brach sank his entire life savings into a small candy store and factory in Chicago. He quickly realized that he couldn't survive on the neighborhood business alone. It was his sons who came up with ways to expand their dad's business. They started selling the candy via mail order as well as wholesaling it to department stores. The youngest brother gave demonstrations at city emporiums and moved mountains of the Brach caramels.

One image consultant I know expanded from consulting to providing a wide variety of services: public speaking; running a personal shopping service; manufacturing and selling her own line of makeup, clothing, and posters; preparing how-to videos, a television show, CD-ROMs, booklets, and a paid-subscription newsletter; conducting in-home parties and workshops on cruises; consulting with attorneys; writing books, newspaper and magazine articles, and a column; teaching others how to become image consultants with individual coaching as well as her self-study course; and following her interests in interior design and feng shui.

2. In the middle of a sheet of paper, write down what you want to make per month. Then draw six lines out from it, and at the end jot down the first word that pops into your mind. Then draw more branches from those topics and repeat until you run out of ideas (or room on the paper). This forces you to make associations and triggers income-generating ideas. Sift through and pick out the most practical. Use some of your other talents.

Actor Jon Favreau (*Swingers*) spent his weekends sketching caricatures of tourists in Greenwich Village for two dollars each. One drummer turned the front of his home into a retail drum store. He began selling stuff he wanted to get rid of, but it turned into a booming business. He also sells online. An artist started a walking tour of galleries. Another collected driftwood and made it into art without any additional expense and sold it online and at flea markets. Sylvia Munoz left her corporate job to spend more time with her children. She turned her hobby of making gift baskets into a home-based business.

3. List everything you could sell for cash. "Wilson," the volleyball Tom Hanks talked to in *Cast Away*, sold for $18,400 in an Internet auction. Believe it or not, Ripley's was interested in buying Pamela Lee Anderson's removed breast implants to be used in its museum. Mike Turk could not get rid of the thousand teak trophy bases he had bought in bulk, so he used a little creativity and turned them into novelty desk ornaments. He bolted a disarmed Army-surplus hand grenade on each one and added a plaque that read, "Complaint Department: Take a Number." The number hangs from the detonation pin. They sold.

One couple in Pittsburgh sold ads on the back of their wedding program to help pay for the event. These advertisers included a photographer, florist, and four other businesses that helped sponsor their special day. An artist I know has been making money on eBay by selling off stuff in her garage for an insane markup and then started finding things at flea markets and garage sales and turns around and sells them for a profit. (She bought a vase for $5 and sold it for $500.) This generates about $10,000 in extra income.

4. Collecting unemployment is demeaning and demanding. Demeaning because you have to wait in line with others who are down on their luck and demanding because you have to fill out a bunch of paperwork and actually *look* for employment. But it's YOUR money based on past earnings that you paid in. This is money that can be used to support the arts—your arts.

5. There are other options. A truly starving artist traded her skills for food. She did beautiful murals on restaurant walls (beach scenes) in exchange for meals. Patrons liked to watch her work, and she'd get commissions.

The other night my wife attended a candle party and came home with some cool stuff and a great story. The woman who hosted the party is making enough money from doing what she loves (socializing with other women) and was able to go from being deeply in debt and working two jobs she hated to being able to get out of debt and quit both jobs. She now has time to sing in a band.

One guy put a coffeemaker on his back and sells coffee to people stuck in traffic in Boston. He loves meeting people. A dog-walker makes $30,000 walking several dogs at a time. A massage therapist working in the Seattle airport does fifteen-minute rubdowns between flights. Another artist became a house-sitter who will wait for deliveries and repair people while you work. Charges $50 but loves the solitude the empty homes provide.

6. Have you ever bought a T-shirt at a concert? Not gonna admit it, are you? Back-of-the-room sales generate a lot of extra income for everyone from singers to public speakers. The people in the audience get caught up in the moment and want a memento to take with them, so why not oblige them? It doesn't have to be as sleazy as it sounds. If people like what they hear you performing, you don't even really have to pitch it, just have them available for sale as a convenience—one that can mean big profits. Selling tapes and CDs you produce and package yourself can be sold at full price but cost you very little. (When you sell a CD to a distributor or retail outlet, you have to give a deep discount.) Things like programs, posters, and other paraphernalia are a nice bonus to put in your pocket. Many artists sell their paintings at sidewalk art shows, bypassing dealers and galleries and pocketing the profits themselves. You aren't going to get rich going this route, but it does give the artist control over his or her market.

George Parker decided to sell pens to his students as a way of making more money than his meager salary as a teacher provided. He bought a batch of pens but spent more time fixing them than preparing his daily lessons. He said to himself, "I could build a better pen," and he did. He formed the Parker Pen Company and became wealthy beyond his dreams. That's a lesson for his students to learn.

7. Make a list of all the money that is owed to you (go through past invoices) and collect it! List all the projects and ideas that you haven't finished, and choose one to complete.

When I lived in Hawaii and worked on the beach, I used to put on a mask and snorkel at the end of the day and go hunting for lost money (and stuff). I almost always came back with something valuable. You do what you gotta do. Would any of these income ideas work for you?

__ Do some modeling   __ Be an extra in a movie

__ Charge for referrals   __ Do carpentry

__ Landscape or mow lawns   __ Become a palm reader

__ Be a party planner   __ Sell some herbs on the side
                                          (and I do mean *herbs*)

_ Turn your home into a B&B

_ Teach arts and crafts to kids

_ Collect unemployment

_ Use gear to make more money

_ Be a consultant

_ Speak for a fee

_ Teach a cooking class

_ Start a home-based business

_ Sell ad space on your website

_ Ask for a raise

_ Play gigs for pay

_ Tutor

_ Ask for cash next holiday

_ Produce a video or audio

_ Start a newsletter or directory

_ Do some desktop publishing

_ Be a creativity consultant

_ Collect material fees up-front

_ Return stuff and get money back

_ Sell home movies to news

_ Deliver flowers

_ Be a poll worker

_ Get a sponsor

_ Have a rummage sale

_ Teach software you've mastered

_ Manage an apartment for
free rent

_ Be an information broker for a
referral fee

_ Rent your gear when you're not
using it

_ Write reviews

_ Be a pet-sitter or baby-sitter

_ Develop a how-to booklet
or course

_ Make jewelry

_ Rent a room

_ Appear on a game show

_ Work overtime

_ Endorse something for free stuff

_ Empty your piggy bank

_ Do freelance work

_ Hold a fund-raiser for yourself

_ Write a book or booklet

_ Host your own radio talk show

_ Desktop video editing and
production

_ Make stress-reduction tapes

_ Barter your services

_ Cut hair on the side

_ Participate in market-research
groups

_ Give blood

_ Work a convention

_ Hold a contest

_ Package a program about what
you do

_ Get a day job

 ACTION ITEM

How can I make more money doing what I enjoy? Start by doing a
mind-map. Relax your mind and eliminate negative thoughts. Then put

your name in the middle of the page, and start branching out things you enjoy doing. What hobby could lead to extra income? _____

 $ FAST FACT

Two out of three people asked would not sell their spouse for a million dollars—or even lend them out for the night. (But one-third would!)

Support for the Arts

"The phrase 'working mother' is redundant."

—Jane Sellman

Bestselling science-fiction writer Raymond Feist was a social worker until budget cuts put him out of work. He moved in with his mother and began writing. Flat broke, he applied for a job as a management trainee for a hamburger chain. Fortunately, a few friends offered to lend him some money so he could concentrate on completing his first book. We need people like this in our lives. Supportive friends, family members, fellow artists, and others who believe in us and the dream and are willing to help with the details of surviving until we hit it big.

Having someone in your life who understands that you need both emotional and financial support is one of the ingredients that help us rise to the occasion. That could mean watching the kids while you work (as Steven Spielberg did while his actress-wife, Kate Capshaw, made the movie *The Love Letter* in Gloucester, Massachusetts) or stuffing your newsletter into envelopes. Mary Engelbreit was a struggling artist who flew to New York to find work illustrating children's books, something she had always wanted to do. Every publisher she saw turned her down. One even suggested she try doing greeting cards. Even though she and her husband had no money, he never told her to go get a job. Instead, he became her biggest booster. After doing some freelance work, she decided to start her own greeting-card company, selling millions of cards each year and making her (and her husband) rich. For many of us, having a spouse who pulls down a steady paycheck and has health insurance is a godsend.

Sunshine Smith was raising two kids on her own in Key West,

Florida, and was about to lose her home to foreclosure when her good friend Jimmy Buffett made her a business partner, and the two opened the first Margaritaville store in 1985. The first day the store was open it sold out of almost everything, and the business has boomed ever since, with several locations making millions. Having someone to show you the ropes is worth its weight in gold. Seth MacFarlane was studying animation at the Rhode Island School of Design. A professor sent MacFarlane's student film to Hanna-Barbera, where he was hired right out of college. That led to a three-year, multimillion-dollar deal with 20th Century Fox. Who is your "Yoda"?

Do you ever get the feeling that noncreative people don't have a clue what we go through to create? They think we spend our days goofing off (and even if we are it's all part of the creative process) and don't understand why we don't just get a real job with a steady salary and benefits. Noooooooooo way! Just because I am still wearing the same clothes I had on when my wife left for work and I'm sitting in the same spot (in front of the TV) doesn't mean my *mind* isn't working. When they do see us working hard, they don't understand that not everything we do will pay off right away—if ever. They wonder silently (or sometimes out loud) why we don't have the riches that some other, more famous artists have. It doesn't help when we are in one of our manic states, feeling depressed and defeated after some sort of rejection, or we continue bitching about the current state of the arts.

Support from Above

"There used to be a time when a person could make a decent living writing crime stories. Back then, a hard-working individual could earn two cents a word for a short story. Three cents, if he was exceptionally good."

—Evan Hunter ("Ed McBain")

In a classic *Peanuts* cartoon, Snoopy is reading a letter from his publisher that says, "We printed one copy of your book. It did not sell. Your book is out of print." You don't have to go it alone. The Indigo Girls wanted to go the "indie" route, and did with some success, but it was becoming a burden. So they signed with a major label. "We'd taken this very serious independent stance, and we wanted to do it all on our own. It was working—we were making a living. But we had so much to do, we were just falling apart," admits Amy Ray. The less you have to spend on promotion and distribution, the more money stays in your pocket. Getting your publisher, label, the gallery, or employer to cover costs is the same as making more money.

My feeling is, you are the struggling artist and can hardly afford to pay for the things that would barely make a dent in their bottom line. Don't let them plead poverty, either. Go for all you can. Bleed them dry if you have to.

Don't think the grass is greener elsewhere. Maybe you take a little less to stay with them, but a supportive partnership is rare and that sense of security you feel from them is rarer still. Don't undervalue a long-term and mutually beneficial relationship. Jive Records was so behind Britney Spears that they made her a star through persistent promotion BEFORE any of her songs were even released.

As the cost of travel rises and publicity budgets shrink, it's harder to get a publisher or label to underwrite your promotional tour. Harder, but not impossible. When you sign with someone, make sure that you get paid *and* that there will be sufficient support for your creation. You want a financial commitment. This means promotion, distribution, and anything else that will help sell what you've done. You want promises, in writing—make that in blood.

Day Jobs

"To all the people who said my show wouldn't last, I have one thing to say: 'Good call!'"

—Jon Stewart

It's not always possible to prosper (or even survive) on our creative pursuits alone. John Steinbeck once said, "The profession of book writing makes horse racing seem like a solid, stable business." Maybe your parents told you a career in the arts wasn't practical. That may be true, but if you are like me, there isn't a choice. It is art or nothing. Still, you have to be able to make some money. It can happen, but it may take some time to get there, and in the meantime we have bills to pay. Getting to the point where all your pay comes from your art is your goal. But before you get there you may have to make money from sources other than your art. There is nothing wrong with this, and many creative people before you have had to go down this same road. The fact is, there are many art forms that never will pay enough to be able to support you. You'll need to supplement your income in order to stay true to yourself and your art rather than sell out and compromise your vision. Since the arts can be feast or famine, there is nothing wrong with doing something on the side during the "famine" part. Make it part of your plan. So how do you survive until you thrive? A day job that pays well, you can tolerate, and doesn't burn you out. It's good if you can use your existing talent to earn that extra income.

• **Having a day job means steady paychecks.** Most home-based businesspeople have full-time jobs at first. Gail Berman, co-producer of the 1982 Broadway production of *Joseph and the Amazing Technicolor Dreamcoat,* accepted a position with Fox Broadcasting because, "You're risking everything—financially, creatively—and you're out there, without a net. I spent a great deal of time not making any money. It's exhilarating when it works; very scary when it doesn't. This is easy compared to that. I come to work every day and I get a paycheck."

• **Support the arts—your art.** Bestselling horror writer Dean Koontz has sold more than 200 million books but received only $1,000 for his first novel. It wasn't enough to live on, so he taught high school English while continuing to write and sell his books. His wife then told him that he could quit his day job and concentrate on writing (for a maximum of five years), and she would support him.

• **It can lead to bigger things.** Peter Caporilli makes and markets cedar garden furniture, thanks to a break he got on his day job working for the Burpee Seed Co. John Burpee knew that Caporilli did woodworking as his hobby and asked him to make him a bench. The bench became so celebrated among the Burpee staff that Caporilli was soon making benches for co-workers and their friends. Eventually, this became his full-time business, and Tidewater Workshop was born. Rob Brown made his film debut as the gifted writer befriended by Sean Connery in *Finding Forrester*. The irony is that he went to the audition as an extra hoping only to make a quick $300 to pay his cell-phone bill.

• **A change of environment can be stimulating.** Bassist Tina Weymouth and drummer Chris Frantz were one-half of Talking Heads. On the side, they were all of the Tom Tom Club. The couple hit it big with 1992's *Dark Sneak Love Action*.

• **It motivates you to work harder on your REAL career.** "I used to work at Burger King to save up enough money to get into the studio. I'd say to my boss, 'One day, you'll see—I'm going to be a big star.' And he'd say, 'Listen, give me nine Whoppers, six fries, and hold the dream,'" says recording artist Wyclef Jean.

• **You can learn the ropes.** Before Faith Hill became the superstar she is today, she learned a lot while selling T-shirts at Fanfare (a country music festival), working as a receptionist for singer Gary Morris, and managing Reba McEntire's mail-order business. She also filled in as a backup singer on demos around town before her big break. British singer Dido was a literary agent and law student, which has come in handy for the pop star, who says, "I read all my contracts with a fine-toothed comb." Bestselling mystery writer Sue Grafton took an extension course in writing that was taught by a book editor for the *Los Angeles Times*. He encouraged her to write a novel. While working on her book she held a series of day jobs, including working as a secretary for Danny Thomas Productions in Hollywood. In her off hours she continued to write. Her first book finally came out in 1967, with another in 1969. Her second book was optioned by MGM, and Grafton was asked to write the script. This led to a contract adapting novels by others for television movies. Her frustration with the work led her to go back to book writing, and the rest is history.

• **Free from worry.** Singer and songwriter Cindy Lee Berryhill has been described as an "obscure cult hero" and an "independent cult artist" who has never enjoyed mainstream success. But after ten years of building a grassroots following and with innovative ideas, she is taking that knowledge and applying it in her job at Neil Young's label, Vapor Records, and its sister company, Lookout Management, in exchange for a steady paycheck. She is now able to focus on her craft knowing she has the basics covered. "I needed to put an emphasis on basic survival skills. I want to be an artist, but not a starving artist."

• **Make connections.** Hector "Chef" Boiardi was a real person. After immigrating from Italy at age seventeen and working at the

Plaza and other hotel restaurants, Hector opened his own restaurant in Cleveland. His spaghetti sauce was so popular with customers that Hector and his brothers formed a company to market spaghetti dinners in a can. They called it Chef Boy-ar-dee. Back in New York, Hector's brother, maitre d' at the Plaza's Persian Room, served a sample to John Hartford, president of grocery-store chain A&P, while he was dining at the Plaza. Hartford must have liked the meal, because Chef Boy-ar-dee dinners were soon found on A&P shelves.

• **Flexible hours.** Bryan Ferry of Roxy Music fame was working full-time at various manual-labor jobs to survive but felt he was going nowhere. He decided to take a part-time job as an art teacher. This left him enough free days to write songs and take demo tapes to record companies.

• **Earn enough money to do what you really want to do.** Considered one of America's finest actors, Sean Penn admits that he would rather be behind the camera than in front of it. To finance his films he takes acting jobs. Kevin Bacon and his big brother Michael are both known for something other than performing in a band together (the Bacon Brothers) and recording an album. Kevin Bacon is best known for being on screen as an actor, while brother Michael works behind the scenes as an Emmy-winning composer for television.

• **Get closer to the dream.** Camryn Manheim has won an Emmy Award for her role on *The Practice* but has also appeared in several movies and written a book, *Wake Up, I'm Fat*. Early in her career she worked various day jobs related to the theater, including as an usher at plays, reading lines with auditioning actors for $6 an hour, and teaching classes at New York University, all the while continuing to act despite the fact that all she ever got were "fat parts." So she wrote a one-woman show aptly titled *Wake Up, I'm Fat*.

• **Benefits.** When editorial cartoonist Steve Kelley was working his "other" job as a stand-up comic, someone yelled, "Don't quit your day job," and Kelley agrees. "I'm far too practical to quit the newspaper. Comedy is great, but there's no dental plan."

There are plenty of other examples of highly successful artists who made ends meet with a day job. It's both fun to read about the odd jobs they had "before they were stars" and inspiring to know that how you make money now doesn't have to be a dead-end deal. So let's look at some examples of what the rich and famous used to do for minimum wages.

Before They Were Stars Quiz: (True or False)

"I was a lousy waitress because I had to serve meat to people, which pissed me off."

—*Vegetarian singer Chrissie Hynde*

Stevie Nicks was a Bob's Big Boy hostess.
Henry Rollins managed an ice-cream shop.
George Michael worked as a movie-theater usher.
Courtney Love of Hole was a stripper.
Cyndi Lauper was a racehorse walker.
John Goodman and Garth Brooks were both bouncers.
George Clooney sold insurance door to door.
Joe Cocker was a plumber.
Peter Gabriel was a travel agent.
Lorenzo Lamas was a french-fry cook at McDonald's.
Sandra Bernhard was a manicurist.
Kevin Costner was a stagehand.
David Duchovny was a teaching assistant at Yale.
Dennis Franz worked as a postman.
Pat Benatar was a bank teller.
Vince Neil was an electrician.
Belinda Carlisle was a gas-station attendant before
she was a Go-Go.

Amazingly, these are all true.

Because They Were Stars

Herb Alpert was a trumpeter and producer who co-founded A&M Records with his friend Jerry Moss. The success of having his own label allowed him total creative freedom, and he had a string of number-one albums in the mid to late 1960s. His biggest hit, however, was when he sold the label to Polygram in 1989 for a half-billion dollars. Steve Katz of Blood, Sweat and Tears fame became the East Coast director of A&R at Mercury Records when the band broke up and then went on to become the vice president of the label.

After They Were Stars

Counting Crows lead singer Adam Duritz took a job as a bartender during the height of the band's huge success in order to stay grounded. Dee Snider of Twisted Sister fame can still be heard on the radio, but this time it's as a disc jockey, as he hosts the nationally syndicated '80s metal show "The House of Hair." Guitarist Lenny Kaye, who also co-wrote the autobiography of Waylon Jennings in 1996, became a rock historian and taught a popular class on the subject at Rutgers University.

Spend Less, Work Less

It should also be noted that instead of finding extra work, the other option is to spend less and simplify so you need less money and thus less work. Are you working two or three jobs to support your art or an extravagant lifestyle? Could you cut back so that you work on your art three days a week and work your job four? Don't live for work, work to live. Do you know any bitter creative people who have sold their souls for a few bucks and a little "security"? Don't let your day job dominate your life. Never sell your dream for a few dollars. It is easy to complicate your life and become dependent on your day job. You hate the work but need the money. Meanwhile your dream of a full-time career in the arts is off in some distant place called "Someday I'll." It is better to be bankrupt financially than emotionally.

You may have to make a few sacrifices if you want financial freedom or creative freedom. You can have one without the other. Put your art first and other stuff last. You may have fewer material things, but I bet you'll be happier, and you won't have to suffer through a nine-to-five job that you hate. You want to make money without burning yourself out, leaving enough time to pursue your own projects. If you are always working or tired from working, you may find it difficult to create space for your art. Leave enough time and energy to practice, create, and MARKET. Marketing yourself can be a full-time endeavor. Don't let this slip. You want something stable to keep you going but isn't so taxing that by the time you get around to your art, you are too tired (mentally and physically) to create.

Many creative people like jobs that leave their days free so they can go to auditions and market themselves during business hours. At the Turtle Bay Hilton on Oahu, they pull from a large pool of what they call "casual employees." These are workers who are on-call and can fill in if someone is sick or, more likely, the surf is up. You probably want low pressure, good hours, and maybe most important, something you enjoy. You don't want anything that leaves you exhausted, ashamed, or frustrated. Make the most of your situation. One actor practices her craft while she works by "acting" like a waiter. She plays the part, tries on accents, and memorizes lines. Consider that a mundane job allows you to look inward and to think, good for creativity, insights, and breakthroughs, and you can use your experiences in your art.

Your day job doesn't have to be a dead end. Find something related to your field so you can network, practice, study, learn, grow. It can lead to opportunities to boost your creative career. One freelance writer taught computer courses and did some consulting on the side for extra cash. When asked to fix an editor's computer problem, he left several article ideas on her hard drive along with a Post-it Note. She read them, and he got a full-time position at the magazine. Another woman, who works for a developer, was able to get some of her pottery pieces into the model homes. They kept getting stolen, or people would ask where they could buy them. Eventually, pottery became a big business for the artist, but she kept her day job for the benefits. A writer could also become a consultant, teacher, copywriter, freelance writer, columnist, Web-content contributor, reviewer, ghost writer, grant writer, technical writer, script editor, newsletter editor, speaker, or write press releases, proposals, annual reports, direct-mail letters, ads, business plans, trade-magazine articles, catalog copy.

Many artists have what is called a "B-skill." This is something they can do to make a few bucks during a downtime. It's a practical skill that pays the bills. One fine artist does CD covers, posters, and book covers and has a contract with a large publisher that keeps her very busy. This gets the word out about her art. Most creative jobs and projects are given to people who can do the work and have proven themselves through experience and have built a portfolio. Where am I going with this? If you take a day job that pays the bills and helps you gain valuable experience and build your contacts along the way, that would be huge. Film school can cost over $100,000. But if you were to work on films and get on-the-job training, that would be even more valuable. Or maybe by working on or for someone in the area of the arts you want to get into, you can learn while you earn and have access to their equipment. One designer worked in retail to better understand that side of the fashion business. A drummer I know worked in a music store, met many people in the industry, and got gigs. He learned about gear and got free samples and access to cool stuff. He also picked up students. He was on commission, so he worked when he wanted to and was free to record or audition when he needed to.

I know a girl who wants a career in the arts and is interested in photography. At least that is what she says. Her actions indicate otherwise. She wastes what little money she has on partying, trips, a new car, and clothes instead of concentrating on her career. To support herself she has to work as a waitress. It pays fairly well, but she is in danger of making food service her full-time career. It's so easy to get sucked into that whole cycle of easy money. The problem is, she works late and then stays up later to party with co-workers. Every time I see her she says, "I'm going to do this or that," but never does. Someday she is going to wake up and realize that she has wasted a good portion of her life, and although it is never too late to make a go of it, she would have been better off going for it sooner, rather than later.

What Do You Want in a Day Job?

Circle those that apply, and think of some more: Flexible hours. Pays well. It somehow relates to your dream. Low stress. It's fulfilling. Fun. Good benefits like medical and dental or free materials. Flexible schedule. Close to home. Learn something new or gain life experiences you can use in your art. Make contacts in your industry.

What Do You Have to Offer?

Circle those that apply: ability, creativity, entertaining, experience, intelligence, knowledge, know-how, language, looks, problem-solver, skill, style, talent, travels, uniqueness. Keep going and list some more. Have you ever considered selling some of these assets?

ASK A PRO

ERIC MAISEL, PH.D., AUTHOR OF A LIFE IN THE ARTS AND AFFIRMATIONS FOR ARTISTS

What are some of the biggest mistakes writers make when it comes to dealing with finances?

Writers are faced with regular expenses and irregular income. That is one vexing problem. Another is engaging in natural wishful thinking, hoping that your book will do better than it is likely to do and spending money (on credit) that you will never see from your publisher. A third is believing that a middle-class life is possible from writing. That is quite rare: Some writers make a fortune, but even those writers who manage to publish regularly still may only make $5,000 to $20,000 annually. So other sources of income—day jobs, teaching, mate's support, parents' support, and so on—remain a necessity for most writers. The main problems writers have are not having enough money, dealing with the unhappiness of necessary day jobs or being dependent on a mate, and dealing with lump sums (from advances, royalties, sales of articles, and so on) that must be managed wisely.

Multiple Streams of Income

"Mostly, we're on the road working, because that's how we earn our living, by playing."

—Jerry Garcia

In addition to being a party animal, Andy Warhol was a painter, film-maker, writer, and even a band manager (for the Velvet Underground). Before he started doing paintings of Coke and Campbell's Soup cans, he was a very successful commercial artist, earning over $100,000 a year (in the '50s!). In the '70s he made a sick amount of money doing commissioned portraits. When he died he left behind an estate worth about $100 million. Creative, right-brained people have the natural ability to be able to juggle several different things at once. Why not use this, as well as our natural curiosity and notoriously short attention spans to produce some profits? Leonardo da Vinci "dabbled" in science, math, philosophy, and music in addition to art. Pablo Picasso tried his hand at writing plays. Ben Franklin was a bestselling author, media mogul, printer, editor, publisher, inventor, statesman—and a very rich man. Samuel F. B. Morse (the guy who invented Morse Code) was, in addition to being an inventor, a painter, a sculptor, and an art professor at the National Academy of Design, which he co-founded. Why do we want income coming from several sources? I'll tell you.

• Having several projects going at once increases the odds that something will work and you'll hit it big. Leonard Cohen's novels (*The Favorite Game* and *Beautiful Losers*) each have sold more than a million copies, yet he has also scored gold as a songwriter with "Suzanne" and other songs.

• You do what you gotta do to make a buck. So you are a comic and you haven't gotten your big break. Couldn't you do a little corporate training? As a musician you could teach, write reviews, or work on the fringe of the industry. A fine artist could also design websites or do portraits. An entrepreneur could consult on the side. Cheech Marin held a number of odd jobs, including janitor, tattoo artist, and mariachi musician, before becoming one-half of the successful comedy duo Cheech and Chong. Primarily an actor (co-starring with Don Johnson in *Nash Bridges* and *Tin Cup*), he also writes, directs, and does voice-over work.

• You go where the work is. When there was a recession the film industry was still cranking, so one artist I know went to work in Hollywood doing set designs. He drew the line at doing any work in front of the camera, but I bet with his looks, he could have. Others in Hollywood are diversified and can and do any number of jobs.

• You can underwrite your art with other lucrative gigs. Faith Ringgold is an artist, writer, and activist who for four decades has produced works that deal with the lives and experiences of contemporary black Americans. She keeps branching out and in the 1990s began writing and illustrating children's books. She is also an educator who has taught at almost every level from public school to university. Avant-garde composer Morton Subotnick was in New York doing two concerts for which he was to be paid $500, but he had to pay for his own travel expenses. Unfortunately, the audience booed, one angry attendee even threatened to kill him. When he got back to his hotel room after that first show, he got a message informing him he was hired to compose a 22-second commercial that would pay nearly $10,000.

• Putting all your eggs in one basket (either with one client or in one area of the arts) can be dangerous. Yes, it's good to focus, but don't be myopic about other money-making opportunities. Jonathan Frakes is known for his role as William Riker on *Star Trek: The Next Generation,* one of the most successful syndicated shows in television history (residuals, baby!). Frakes decided he would also like to direct and learn other aspects of the business behind the camera. He started spending time in the editor's booth and sitting in on casting sessions before he directed an episode of the show himself and went on to direct other television shows as well as the film *Star Trek: First Contact,* making him an A-list director.

• There is also a lot of waiting when it comes to making things happen. Then you have to wait to be paid. You have to have something coming in while you're waiting. It's your best defense against bankruptcy, boredom, and going bananas. Tom Corcoran has made leather handbags, been a professional photographer, and authored a book in order to survive. As his friend Jimmy Buffett says, "He's invented a good number of phony-baloney jobs that have kept him afloat till this day."

• You are extremely limited by what you can make from wages and fees, but revenue from royalties and residuals can continue forever. Spike Lee first began selling stuff related to his successful film *She's Gotta Have It* via mail-order, selling $50,000 a month worth of T-shirts, hats, books, and posters. This led to Lee opening a retail store called Spike's Joint as well as starting an ad agency. Lee also diversified himself and began directing commercials and feature films and somehow found the time to write six books (and attend Nick's games).

• Gets you through the lean years or a slump in your career.

Buffett saw his record sales sagging and decided that as a hedge against having to get a real job, he could sell merchandise inspired by his 1977 hit song "Margaritaville." Who knew it would turn into a multimillion-dollar business venture that includes retail stores and restaurants in addition to his bestselling books, sold-out tours, albums, and now his own line of tequila and margarita mix. There are also cycles and seasons in many of the arts, and having something to hedge against the slow times is smart.

• So you won't get complacent. Rosie O'Donnell has seen success as a stand-up comic, actress, and talk-show host, and she is now in the magazine business. There are lots of stand-up comics who struggle and possibly begrudge Rosie her success, but she is savvy, and there is nothing wrong with that. Of course, she is following in the footsteps of Oprah Winfrey, who earns a reported $150 million-plus a year from her hit TV show (the highest-rated TV talk show in history) and acting, bestselling books, magazine, Internet ventures, and various other products handled by her company, Harpo Productions. Besides, it's how we work best. We need new challenges and ways to channel our creative energies to stay fresh and sharp. Look at how many musicians have turned actors. You've got Jon Bon Jovi, Flea, Sting, Alanis Morissette, Jewel, Henry Rollins, Phil Collins, Roger Daltrey, and the list goes on.

• When one door closes another opens. Suzy Spafford's line of greeting cards called Suzy's Zoo had some success, but she found herself competing with the big boys (Hallmark and American Greetings, who control nearly 90 percent of the market) so she is taking her cute characters, like Ducken, and creating a line of products aimed at the infant market and licensing her art to other companies. After a few years of flat sales, she has seen a steady increase in revenue from these revenue streams (and profits are up, too).

Maybe the strangest example of an artist finding other ways to make money is Jethro Tull's frontman, Ian Anderson. The British rocker has become one of the biggest salmon farmers in the world, which has made him a millionaire. It's refreshing to see someone take his music money and turn it into something positive and profitable. Anderson wanted to do something with his money that was socially redeeming and would create jobs in his community.

• Strike while the iron is hot and take advantage of momentum. Christopher Lowell has introduced a new collection of linens and paints and a new book that complement his popular Emmy Award–winning decorating show.

• What talents or resources do you have that could be used to bring in additional income? Look at what you do and ask yourself, Is there any other way I could apply the same things I already do to another market? Many successful singers write and sell songs to other artists with amazing success. The list is too long to name them all, but considering the writing royalties you would receive from a hit song (whether you sang it or not), it could be a way to make extra money.

• In previous books I have said that it is important to be focused (and able to clearly and concisely articulate that to others), or you risk being all over the place. My advice is, focus first, then you can branch out. Be the best at something before you move on to other areas. Russell Simmons co-founded Def Jam records and oversaw Run-DMC's success before becoming a media mogul. He produces films (*The Nutty Professor*) and TV shows (*Def Comedy Jam*) and also has his own line of clothes (Phat Farm).

Make Money While You Sleep

"I've been living off the royalties from "Sister Morphine" for ten years, which is really bizarre—don't tell me drugs don't pay."

—Marianne Faithfull

I don't know where you stand on the Napster issue, but most creative people realize that above all else, they have to protect their rights and royalties. I do know that people like Diane Warren, who has written more than sixty top-ten hits, makes millions every time one of her songs hits it big. It is hard to turn on a radio and not hear one of her songs. Even though she doesn't perform them herself, she has penned hits for some of music's biggest stars. She owns her own publishing house, Realsongs. Songwriters and publishers make most of their money from royalties. The writer's creation is a property, and to use it someone has to license it. This means that whenever you hear a song you can hear a ringing sound in your ears: it's the sound of a cash register.

We're not just talking about the music industry, either. John Bolton patented a collar design for dress shirts and sold the rights to his invention to another shirt company. The royalties from the collar brought him millions, which he used to develop other neat things like a nonslip shoulder strap for women's lingerie. Ralph Lauren both manufactured and licensed out his Polo designs. How about Dolby Sound? The guy who invented that gets money every time the noise filter is installed in a stereo. Some books become like an annuity, providing the author with income years after its release. Gary Larson, the creator of *The Far Side,* doesn't work anymore, but his stuff still sells. That's the dream.

When advertisers were pushing to replace all residuals for actors in commercials with a flat fee, it was met with an amazing amount of resistance. Kevin Bacon, among others, claimed that he survived for years on commercial work and the residuals that resulted from it. "Residuals meant the difference between working as a waiter and as an actor." (According to the Screen Actors Guild, nearly half of the income that actors receive comes directly from commercials and residuals.)

Ever wonder what happens to television stars after their hit series and sitcoms get canceled? Most live comfortable lives from the residuals. I'm a big fan of the show *Magnum P.I.* We all know that Tom Selleck went on to other work following the demise of that show. But what happened to the other actors on the show? I'm sure they are kicking back at the King Kamehameha Club, living large off their fat royalty checks. It can be the same way for musicians who may see their music used in a movie soundtrack, a home video, a theater production, a TV show, or a commercial ad; covered or performed by another artist; translated into another language; or printed in a book or magazine. All of these earn the writer/composer more money. I was reading an article about theater director Trevor Nunn where it mentioned his salary as the artistic director of Britain's prestigious Royal National Theatre. It said he would earn between $130,000 and $135,000. I thought, "Not bad." Then I read the next sentence that mentioned this was in addition to the estimated $20 million annual income he makes from royalties, mainly due to his lyrics from the song "Memory" from *Cats*. Holy meow! That sums up the importance of residual income pretty well, doesn't it?

Do everything you can to protect your rights. Many music people never got paid what they were owed, and trust me, they were pissed. Songwriter Percy Ivy was so infuriated about not getting paid that he shot record-label president Johnny Dolphin in 1958. Songwriters should be paid when their song is sold (broadcast fee), played onstage (performance fee), and played on the air (broadcast fee). These fees can really add up. Make sure you are very careful about what you do with the rights to your work and spend the small amount of money it takes to file and copyright everything.

Negotiating your "cut" can be very confusing. A good lawyer and/or agent is very important here. The ways you can get ripped off when it comes to royalties are unlimited. There are so many ways a gallery, publisher, label, or licensor can reduce the rate that your royalties are based on. Do you get 10 percent of the cover price or the *wholesale* price? When do you get paid? If you want to move on, can you get your rights back? If your product is in the "trash bin" or "shelved," can you resell or resuscitate it? You can now resurrect it with new technology or more marketing. You want the chance, at least. So please be very careful before you sign away any of your rights to royalties. You never know if something will take off, and if it does, you want a piece of the pie. When Pete Best was asked to leave the Beatles, he had no idea it would end up costing him *millions*! (Ringo Starr replaced him.) At least he was able to see some royalties when some of the songs he played on were released on the Beatles' *Anthology 1* album. I heard he made plenty.

I know that twice a year I get a check for royalties for past books, and it's a blessing, believe me. Royalties are such an important part of an artist's income. Yet it can be one of the most confusing and confounding things when you look at your contract or royalty statement and try to figure it out. I look at that royalty statement and wonder if they make it so light and hard to read on purpose. Many agents and editors don't even understand it. But because they are integral to your income, it pays to pay attention to this part of your salary. "Honey, I Shrunk the Profits" would be a good title for a film about the movie business. Movies that appear to make millions are actually losing money. How can that be? Some of it may be creative accounting; the other reason may just be the high cost to produce and promote a film. Get someone to explain your royalty statement to you. There are royalty specialists and some associations, like the Authors Guild, who will review royalty statements and put it into plain English for you.

You want staying power. Keep creating, and when you hit it big it will pull your older work up, too. The longer you are out there, the more you create, the more money you can make. In today's disposable society and with society's short attention span, it's becoming harder and harder to have a lengthy career. Nick Reynolds of the Kingston Trio is someone I interviewed in the past for my radio show, and something he said really stuck with me. When I asked him about the Trio's biggest hit song, "Tom Dooley" (over a million copies sold and it was number one for eighteen weeks in 1958), he said, "That was the only hit song we ever had, and we've been going strong for thirty years off that single record." By 1965 they had sold eighteen million records, and each band member made $1 million a year. It may not happen right away, but hang in there and keep creating. Some of the best early blues records by Muddy Waters and John Lee Hooker didn't sell or chart at first. It wasn't until years later (when other artists began recording their songs) that the royalties started rolling in. Barry Mann and Cynthia Weil are a powerhouse writing team who have penned hit songs for Lionel Richie, the Pointer Sisters, and many more. Even if they never wrote another hit, the money keeps coming in. Keep promoting and plugging. According to the chief financial officer of Barnes & Noble, the top twenty-five bestselling titles in both fiction and nonfiction amount to less than 10 percent of the chain's total book sales. The bulk of the business comes from titles that are "backlisted" (books that have been around a while) and smaller, steady sellers. Do what you can to keep your product in the stores, on the shelves, or online.

Create things that you can replicate and recycle. "They can take fat from your rear and use it to bang out the dents in your face. Now, that's what I call recycling," jokes comedienne Anita Wise. She has a point. If you have something you created once that can be sold again, the work is done, but the sales keep on and the income keeps coming in (even if you are incarcerated). Jim Gordon was a successful drummer in the '70s who played with a veritable who's who of rock, including George Harrison, John Lennon, Eric Clapton, and Steely Dan. Unfortunately, he went nuts and killed his mother with a hammer, but he still receives royalties for songs he co-wrote, including "Layla." (He's serving a 25-year sentence.) Ex–Grateful Dead keyboardist Vince Welnick said, "Paul Newman came to see us play a couple of times at Giants Stadium in New Jersey, and it was funny, because Paul said that when he walked through the audience, all people could say to him was, 'Hey, man, nice salad dressing!'" They'd never seen any of his movies, but they bought his sauces. Moby made $16 million from licensing his music for commercials.

This also means more exposure. Sting's 2000 release was slow-selling until he did a commercial for the car company Jaguar. This instantly sent his album to the top of the charts. It's always nice to have something that sells and sells so that you don't have to. In 1976 the song "Popsicle Toes" was to be Michael Franks's only big hit. He's had an enduring career and solid sales, but that remains his most commercial song. In 1999 Diana Krall recorded it on her album *When I Look in Your Eyes,* which means more money than he can count on his toes.

ASK A PRO
JOHN COSBY, FINE ARTIST

One area many artists struggle with is pricing their work and believing that they can and should be paid well for what they create. How do you deal with this area?
First of all, the price of art is determined by the last piece that you sold. As you sell more pieces, the demand for your work grows, and as you reach the point that you can't keep up, you can raise your rates. The price of art is also supported by the confidence of your collectors. The more confidence there is in the intrinsic value of your work, the more prices become no object. I learned early on that there are collectors for every level of artist. In my experience I have found that people want to pay a lot for a painting. They don't want it for

free. They want to feel like they have invested in art. For example, in the very beginning of my art career, I had a collector who asked me to bring a large painting to his house for a trial. I hung it up over the couch, and he said, "I love it, how much?" I said it was $2,500, and he said, "Hell, the couch cost me $20,000. I don't want a painting that costs less!" He didn't buy the painting.

_____

5

COVER YOUR ASS-ETS

"Being intelligent is not a prerequisite for being a rock star."
—Sting

The funny thing about the above quote is that Sting himself was defrauded by his accountant in 1995 for $9 million. How can you *not* notice that amount of money missing? Easy. We are a trusting bunch who will ask others to handle our finances (because we don't like to). Most of us never learned about finances in art school. So we have had to teach ourselves or rely on others to manage our money. Good financial advice can be invaluable.

Even if you do it yourself, it's nice to go in for a once-a-year financial checkup just like you would with a doctor. If you think you can't afford a "money doctor," there are usually places you can turn to for free (or almost free) advice on money matters and taxes. Many organizations for artists offer free consultations about financial and legal matters. No matter who helps, the number-one thing you want in a financial adviser is T-R-U-S-T. You want to be able to trust that they have your best interests at heart and that they aren't going to rip you off. You want to be able to trust that they know what they are talking about. If you see them shaking a Magic Eight Ball before picking a stock or hear them calling up the Psychic Friends hotline to determine which mutual fund to go with, you aren't going to trust them.

You are good at what you do, and it would be wonderful to have someone to just "deal with it" when it comes to money so that you can focus on what *you* do best. Or maybe you want to do a lot of the work yourself but want someone to use as a sounding board. Ideally you are setting up a team to help YOU make decisions.

A word of caution: Don't overdo it with advisers. They can end up costing you and eat into any profits you may make. If you have just come into a large sum of money (if only we could be so lucky), that's a good time to ask for help. But before that happens consider doing some of it yourself. It's never been easier to manage your money. There is so much information available (too much?) on the Internet, and you can do things today (like buy and sell stocks) that would have required a broker before. Advisers don't always have to be paid for. Maybe a family member, friend, or colleague could give you advice, but you should always remain a part of the decision-making process. If you do pay for planning, take an active role and learn all you can. Ask questions and demand they answer in plain English. I don't think you want to be taken care of—you just want some help. Right? Be interested, informed, and above all involved in money matters. Just don't let it distract you from your role, which is to create and make money from your art. Balance between letting them worry about all that money stuff (indifference) and being obsessed with every little detail.

Advisers can include an agent, manager, coach, therapist, publicist, guru, accountant, bookkeeper, or even a CEO. An article in *Allure* magazine profiled actress Salma Hayek's twenty-person team. The team was made up of stylists, publicists, business managers, and assistants, plus a masseuse and an aromatherapist, who said, "I prepare a mist for Salma to carry around to protect her aura." Only in Los Angeles! Bestselling author Stephen Covey (*The Habits of Highly Effective People*) built an empire with the help of others. He knew his strengths lie in writing, teaching, and training and in interviews has said that he needed help with managing costs, inventory, accounts receivable, and cash flow. So he hired people with the skills to handle that end of his business. Sometimes you hire experts in areas you don't do well or don't want to deal with.

A women who is a professional dancer and owns a dance studio and teaches decided that she was spending too much time on managing her money. She didn't have the time to stay up on tax laws, rules, and such that kept changing. She got a bookkeeper and an accountant. She can now see more clients and make more money. They have a monthly pow-wow, but she leaves the details to them.

Maybe all of a sudden you got a big bump in income and feel

like it's too much to manage all by yourself. I read somewhere that Jason Alexander's wife, Daena, handled their finances until he got a substantial raise (over $100,000 per *Seinfeld* episode). Daena had done everything right, but there is a lot to managing a portfolio of that magnitude. Someone with more experience can help you make your money grow or help you make decisions on what to do.

In many fields there is a real need for representation. Know your strengths and weaknesses. Ask yourself: What do I need help with? Who can help? Then ask around for a referral. Then when you meet with potential professionals ask yourself: How did I FEEL about them? Many will agree to outline a plan for you so you can see if you are on the same page and that they understand your situation and the business you are in. Then begin to surround yourself with people who can do your taxes, negotiate on your behalf, and deal with details you just aren't suited for. When you choose the right people to help you, they end up paying for themselves ten times over.

My team includes two agents, a business manager, a bookkeeper, a lawyer, a mentor, and a financial planner. I look at it like casting a play. Of course I am the star, but I need a supporting cast. So to fill those roles I held auditions. For the most part my cast of characters has remained the same. The agents get the work, handle the paper-work, negotiate the fees, and collect the money. No fuss, no muss. I can focus on what I do best. (We still aren't sure what that is, but that's beside the point.) I do what I do best and delegate the rest to these competent, trustworthy, and smart people. They are all also creative people themselves who have worked their way up and yet still understand the life of an artist and the arts in general. Almost all of them get a percentage of what I get so they don't nickel-and-dime me to death.

I do want to point out that I don't just blindly turn everything over to others. I have tried to become as knowledgeable about finances as I can. Creative people usually wouldn't perform surgery on themselves or even fly their own plane—those two tasks are both dangerous and complicated. So when it comes to big money deci-sions, go to a money doctor (but be awake for the procedure) and get help piloting your financial decisions (but sit in the co-pilot seat and observe). You want to be as informed and educated as possible so you don't get burned by unscrupulous or incompetent financial advisers.

Don't forget that a broker is essentially a salesperson, and salespeople don't always have your best interests at heart. Educate and empower yourself so that you can make the big decisions, but have help carrying them out.

Be Your Own Guru

"I don't think creative people are very good at following directions—nor should they have to be."

—Amalia Mesa-Bains,
former San Francisco arts commissioner

Do not walk behind me, for I may not lead. Do not walk ahead of me, for I may not follow. Do not walk beside me, either. Just leave me the hell alone! That's how a lot of creative people feel. For good reason. They have had horrible experiences with their agents, accountants, and advisers and wonder why the hell they pay someone so much money to do next to nothing. Much of the mumbo-jumbo language in money-management circles is there to mystify money and make it seem like it is more complicated than it really is. Why would the industry do that? So you are forced to work with investment advisers and brokers, that's why. Do these experts really know what the hell they are talking about? Do they know which way the stock market is fixing to go? Do they know which stocks to buy to guarantee a good return? No! They are probably guessing, just like you. They are making more educated guesses, but with some insights and your intuition you can do a pretty good job yourself at managing your money, if you wanted to. Just because they have a degree doesn't mean squat. If they pull up in a beater car reeking of pot insisting that you pay them in cash—now, chances are they don't know what's what any more than you do.

Let me say this: Nobody cares about you and your money like you do. Only you know your tolerance to risk, fears, and worries, as well as your dreams and goals. You can try to convey them to an adviser, but it may fall on deaf ears. Brokers make money when you spend money. It is in their best interests to get you to buy and sell stock rather than buy and hold. There is the flip side of the coin, too: advisers who are too conservative. To cover themselves they paint a pretty bleak picture that scares you into inaction. Another possible problem is that you start trusting others more than you trust yourself. You have a gift as a right-brainer: being able to make tremendous leaps of insight and possessing an increased sense of intuition. Many creative people rely on themselves to manage their money.

Debbie Fields (you know, Mrs. Field's Cookies) was once a foul-line ballgirl for the Oakland A's (I just thought that was neat, so I included it) before starting her cookie company. Along the way she learned about bookkeeping, accounting, and taxes. But as the business grew it got to be a burden, so she hired a chief financial officer to take care of the day-to-day details, which freed her up to concentrate on creating new ideas as well as on promotion and people problems. Maybe the best bet is a combination of having someone to offer financial advice that you take under advisement but acting as you see fit. I mean, you are the captain of your ship. You can have people telling you what to watch out for, but ultimately you decide when to turn and when to stay the course. (Hopefully you will listen when someone warns you there is an "iceberg dead ahead!")

Others are able to thrive on their own. MCA founder Jules Stein was in a band when he received two offers to play dances the same night. His group played one gig, and the resourceful Stein found another band to play the other gig for a 25 percent commission. He went on to build his empire by advising acts for a fee and dominated the music business before taking on Hollywood. He became an expert in business, finance, and legal issues and fought for the rights of artists.

However, the business side of creativity can be complicated. Have you ever heard of creative accounting? At least if you know how you are getting screwed, you can do something about it. Many arts organizations offer free or low-cost accounting, legal, or business assistance. (They may not do the work for you, but they'll help you put together a system or advise you about your rights. You have to be willing to ask for help.) Dineh Mohajer and her sister Pooneh started Hard Candy (a company that sells cool-colored nail polish) for $200. They relied on themselves and a friend at first for financial matters, but when they couldn't keep up they hired help. The qualities that make a good entrepreneur—passion, risk, creativity—are not always what you want in a business manager. You want a conservative, boring, back-to-basics kinda gal. A good accountant or tax person can pay for themselves by saving you money. How do you know if a tax person is good? She has a loophole named after her (or you get good referrals for her). Or better yet, ask her if she is honest. If she says, "yes," then you know she is a liar. Just kidding. It's nice to have access to someone's opinion you value and be able to tap into her experience and expertise. There is also the fact that we are busy creating and don't have the time or inclination to learn about money matters. It's okay to admit we may need some help. Neil Peart of Rush is one of the drummers I truly admire. He's a drummer's drummer. I was surprised to find out he still takes lessons. Some people are too proud to admit they need help. Others ask for and accept assistance.

Quick Quiz

Should you ask for help? Answer these questions and then decide.

1. I hate negotiating deals and dealing with money.
2. I hate reading contracts and the fine print contained in them.
3. I have no interest in managing my own money.
4. I am easily intimidated.
5. I don't trust myself when it comes to money.

One or more "yes" answers, and I think you should at least consider it.

• **Starting out.** Many money-management firms require a minimum investment and just aren't interested in you until your wealth rises to that level. Some managers and agents won't take your calls until you have risen to a certain level. In fact, many creative people had to get deals lined up and then take it to an agent to close before the agent would work with them. Especially in the early stages of a career. Nobody cares about you in the beginning. Jimmy Buffett was his own agent, accountant, manager, and roadie for his first tour (headlining at Steak & Ale restaurants all across the Midwest for $500 a week). He would book the shows and deal with all the business details for being on the road. Once he achieved a certain level of success, he hired help but remains very hands-on.

• **More money in your pocket.** You can spend a fortune on advisers. A professional publicist may want a retainer and $5,000 a month, guaranteed for six months (with no guarantees from them). That's a lot of money for something you could do yourself.

• **You really can do it yourself.** One writer I know created his own (fictitious) manager complete with a separate phone line and business cards so he could do his own deals. Be a student of money. There's TONS of information (including sample contracts, information on royalty rights, and so on) at the library and online. There are clinics and classes. Look at other creative people who have a lot of money and find out how they did it. Get involved and pay attention to what the professionals are doing and learn from them. Country star Trisha Yearwood says, "I want to see everything. Every contract that goes through, anything to do with my career and my money."

• **There is safety in numbers.** You could join an investment club. There you can learn about investing and get help with decisions about what to do with your money. It's usually in a casual setting and thus less intimidating. Plus, you pool your resources (and research) and have greater pull as a group. You could also start your own group. It could be just a support group and investment club with other creatives. You would then bring in speakers, discuss financial decisions and concerns, and commiserate.

The Billy Joel Story

Billy Joel began his career when he joined a band called the Hassles (ironic name) and recorded two albums with the group. The band broke up, and Joel's girlfriend also broke up with him. He regrouped (literally) and formed a new band called Attila. In 1972 he went solo and cut an album but made two major mistakes. One was the quality of the recording, the other was that he sold off most of the rights to his royalties. He was able to renegotiate his deal, but Artie Ripp's Family Productions would still get a quarter of every dollar Joel made from subsequent albums. Joel signed with Columbia Records and released *Piano Man* in 1973. It was a hit and sold over one million copies, but Joel reportedly made only $7,763. He was so upset that he asked his new wife (a graduate of UCLA's school of management) to sort out his financial affairs. She did, but the couple divorced in 1982. From 1974 through 1989, Joel had a number of hits and should have made a lot of money. When he had his manager (also his former brother-in-law) audited, he uncovered (allegedly) millions missing and more invested in some very risky ventures. Joel filed suit for damages (to the tune of $90 million).

Suze Says

"Whatchu talkin' 'bout, Willis?"
—Gary Coleman ("Willis" from Diff'erent Strokes)

Financial adviser and author Suze Orman has had money problems in the past and discusses them in her bestselling books. You get the feeling when reading her work that she not only cares but also understands. Her advice seems nonjudgmental and compassionate. I hope I come across the same way. Like many creative people, my career has had several highs and one very uncomfortable low. When I sold my retail stores to become a writer, I had to pay my dues and face some lean years during that transition. It got so bad I was forced to sell my car, my home, my clothes, and even my dog before I was able to claw my way back. If you have never been through something like that, there is no way you will be able to understand and emphathize with people who have struggled or are struggling just to get by. There is nothing wrong with asking for guidance, but find someone who will help make you feel better about your future rather than dwell on your past mistakes. If you are afraid to ask for help because you have dug yourself so deep you don't want anyone to know, understand that a *good* financial planner is like a shrink in a way. They can help and will use discretion. Talking to them should make you feel better even if your finances are a mess. You need someone who won't berate and belittle you but help you fix what you broke (or made you broke).

I'm Going Broke with My Broker

"A lot of musicians that get real famous have this feeling that everyone that's dealing with them wants something from them."
—Flea of the Red Hot Chili Peppers

You can save on rates and commissions if you shop around and negotiate. Be careful, however, because you generally get what you pay for. If you give your money to a guy who cold-calls you, then you are probably not getting a top-of-the-line adviser. Who knows, this adviser could be calling you with his last quarter from a pay phone. It happens! Remember the *Saturday Night Live* skit with Chris Farley where he is a motivational speaker who lives in a van by the river. Go with a pro. Most problems with financial advisers come from a lack of trust and unrealistic expectations. Explain in detail what you expect, and let them explain to you what you can expect. Then formulate a plan together. Have them explain everything that is being done and send you regular reports. Get an agreement in writing. Don't let your adviser tell you that you can't make money. If others are, why not you, too? Remember, they work for you. If you are frustrated or disappointed, you want a way out.

There are all kinds of artists, including rip-off artists. In Hollywood not everyone is trustworthy (no kidding), and they use "creative accounting" to get out of paying you, or worse. Dana Giacchetto was living large—on other people's money. He was palling around with Leonardo DiCaprio, and his clients read like a who's who of the entertainment business. He got these celebrities to trust him and then ("allegedly") ripped them off. Harry Nilsson got a $5 million deal from RCA (despite modest sales of previous records), but after his manager stole all of his money in 1992, he ended up destitute, and many feel this led to his death of a heart attack two years later. Please be very careful.

Reduce risks of being ripped off by being more involved. Set up some kind of checks-and-balances system. Ask for an accounting from time to time. One artist and entrepreneur left all business matters to the partner to deal with. It wasn't until a few years later that she realized he had placed their profits into some very risky investments and failed to pay taxes. Even though she didn't know what he was up to, she was still held liable for the $60,000 owed in back taxes. Another artist had an agent who would tell him his art sold for less than it really did and pocketed the difference. Give them a test first before giving them all of your money.

Trust your instincts. Use common sense or horse sense—as W. C. Fields once said, "Horse sense is the thing a horse has which keeps it from betting on people." If it feels wrong it usually is. Other would-be authors call me from time to time and ask about hiring a "book doctor" who promises to help them write a proposal and get an agent and a deal—for a fee. I get asked this so many times that I copied an article from the Authors Guild newsletter that outlines all the pitfalls of working with these people, who have in the past taken advantage of writers.

Do your research, get referrals, and never buy from a broker over the phone. It's usually not a good sign if they have to cold-call you or even advertise. Watch out for the promise of huge returns that seem unrealistic. They'll use the "you don't want to miss out" (fear) or the "opportunity of a lifetime" (greed). Many people are unhappy with their broker. They want results, and sometimes it's not the broker's fault. YOU made some bad choices. To them it's a game. They are playing with your money. They are under a lot of pressure, and many take unnecessary risks, steer you to something they get extra commission on, or outright defraud you. But *you* let it happen.

They shouldn't ask for their fees up-front. This is usually not a good sign. If you succeed, they succeeded. Golfer Tiger Woods's caddie (like all caddies) gets a percentage of the golfer's winnings. Tiger's caddy reportedly earns about $800,000 a year. Don't let them nickel-and-dime you to death. One musician had a manager who deducted all kinds of fees from his royalties and she ended up owing the manager money. This included ads for the manager, travel expenses, and some other questionable costs.

You probably don't want to hire friends—it's hard to fire them. Brian Wilson's father managed the Beach Boys until the band fired him. The fallout from that disagreement cost Brian Wilson millions of dollars. His father sold all the songs Brian had written between 1961 and 1967 for $700,000. Those songs became some of the most exploited pieces of music in history and were used in commercials and covered by other artists, generating millions of dollars for everyone BUT Brian Wilson.

Lawyers, Guns, and Money

"Lawyers are like beavers—they get in the mainstream and dam it up."

—John Naisbitt

In a recent study respondents were asked how often they read the fine print in financial agreements. Forty-seven percent said always (liars), 25 percent said often, and 17 percent said never. That's interesting.

It's a fact that we (right-brainers) are not known for being detail-oriented. When I try to read that foreign language known as legalese, my mind tends to wander. When it comes to matters regarding our rights, we maybe perk up a little, but in most cases we want to know what the bottom line is. "How much do I get?" we will ask. But the nitty-gritty stuff we leave to others (or don't deal with it at all and hope it all works out okay—and sometimes it does). That's not to say every creative person is uninterested in details. Some have even become lawyers, like Barry "The Fish" Melton (Country Joe and the Fish), Jackie Fuchs (the Runaways), Elliot Cahn (Sha Na Na), and Manny Caiati (ex-bassist for Joan Jett). The bassist in my band is an attorney; so is the guitarist, now that I think about it, as well as my brother and some of my best friends. Yikes! I'm surrounded by lawyers. Actually, that's a good thing. Most contracts you come across as a creative person will favor the dealer, label, publisher, studio, and so on, because they are prepared by *their* lawyers to benefit *them.* Since they don't have your best interests at heart, it's nice to have someone on your side to fight for you. As an artist you have rights, damn it. You don't have to feel beholden to those who you make deals with. Make all the jokes about lawyers you want—when you have a lawyer looking at contracts for you and, heaven forbid, defending you against any litigation, you'll sleep better at night. As they say on all the cop shows, "If you can't afford one . . . " I would reply that you can't afford NOT to have one.

If you are really in a financial bind lawyers volunteer for the arts and some associations provide access to legal advice. Contact a local arts council for a referral for a lawyer who understands the arts. In many cases an hour with an attorney beforehand will pay off by helping you dodge different dilemmas before they become legal matters. (An hourly fee to review a document should run between $200 and $300.) You can negotiate the fee down, too. Lawyers, in many cases, work for themselves, and their fees are negotiable. Maybe they work on a sliding scale; you should ask. Some lawyers have even been known to ask to see a tax return to determine if you really are destitute. (And they wonder why we despise them.) Figure out what would be the best way to pay (by the hour, a flat fee, or a contingency fee). If you can settle a dispute rather than litigate it, you will probably save some money. You don't need Johnnie Cochran to handle a smaller dispute, just a competent attorney. You can have an attorney draw up a form that you can use yourself rather than have them review and write a custom one for each transaction. Do the research or legwork yourself and have the attorney handle the rest. When you do go to see them, be organized and try to cover as many items in one meeting. Get to the point, because with a lawyer, time is money.

Don't let a lawyer scare you into inaction. They may paint a bleak picture. That's their job. But don't allow these worst-case scenarios stop you from getting your work out. I have seen creative people scared out of their mind by "diligent" attorneys who point out every single potential problem. They also try to talk some people into overprotecting their ideas. Don't overdo it! Inventors can spend thousands in patents, trademarks, and lawyer fees to protect their ideas. Just because they have a patent doesn't mean someone won't rip them off anyway, and it certainly doesn't mean the invention is worth anything. Just get the damn thing out there, and be the leader. Be better than the rest. Reinvent yourself as you go. Don't let the fact that someone may want to emulate you or copy your idea force you to waste valuable time and money defending yourself. Ideas are a dime a dozen. Lawyers, like the police, are there to serve and protect you, but I think they do a disservice if they advise you to spend every last dime protecting your creation and you have little left to produce or market it.

To protect us from ourselves. Little Richard renounced materialism and signed over all of his royalties for $10,000. When he tried to get them back he was unable to. Aretha Franklin, the Queen of Soul, was sued for breach of contract when she didn't appear at rehearsals for her Broadway stage debut, and the producer won a judgment and damages exceeding $200,000. Jerry Lee Lewis was shooting holes in his office door one day when his bass player wandered by and was shot. Of course he sued Lewis. It's not likely you'll shoot anyone, but it's nice to know what your rights are. Sometimes we are so anxious to sign a contract where the other party tempts us by dangling thousands of dollars in front of us, we inadvertantly sign over the rights to them. You need to know who owns your art. Who gets the master, the original, the right to reproduce the art? A lawyer can really help you here.

To protect us from others. The band Judas Priest was sued by the parents of a teenager who attempted suicide while listening to the album *Stained Class*. (Hey, I listened to that album all the time, and I'm fine.) Anyway, the band was exonerated with the help of their lawyers. Sometimes litigation is the only way to resolve a dispute, and unless it's in small-claims court, you need a pit bull for a lawyer. Someone to whom you can say, "That lawyer is a real a-hole, but he's *my* a-hole!" Sometimes you can resolve disputes better without a lawyer. For example, let's say you had an oral agreement to do some creative work for a client, and all of a sudden you are doing a lot more work than you originally agreed to and not getting paid for it. You can probably work this out yourself.

To protect our creations. Getting a patent is an expensive and tedious project that really requires the help of an attorney. A trademark also is easier with the help of a lawyer. (Although I do my own trademark searches at the library for free.) Copyrighting your work is something you can and should do yourself. If you do need assistance you'll want an attorney who knows about intellectual property and maybe even specializes in your area of the arts.

Someone to Watch over Me

"A fat lawsuit is never as smart as a lean compromise."

—*Unknown*

I watch a LOT of *Law & Order* reruns. Sometimes I think I know a little about the law (just enough to be dangerous), but when it comes right down to it, contracts are complicated. Stevie Wonder's 1976 contract with Motown was reportedly worth $13 million and was 120 pages long! Most of us have no interest in reading through a contract, and if we did, we wouldn't understand it. Also, when dealing with a major label, publishing house, or corporation you have to realize they can afford to hire top-notch attorneys, so don't try to be a Perry Mason. Let the professionals watch your back. You don't have the experience or the knowledge, and it's highly likely you'll get all worked up and emotional. That's why it's harder for you to negotiate on your own behalf.

There is no question that Shawn Fanning is amazingly talented.

He may have invented the single most popular computer program of the past decade. Napster enabled millions to share CD collections over the Net. One problem, though—it infringes on artists' rights and royalties. Losing a lawsuit can ruin your life; so can fighting and winning. It is VERY costly to defend yourself, and it takes a great deal of time. The Righteous Brothers used Phil Spector's "wall of sound" on the song "You've Lost that Loving Feeling" but then tried to get out of a contract they had with Spector to cut costs. Spector sued and won. John Fogerty was sued for plagiarizing his OWN song. The song "The Old Man Down the Road" sounded a little like "Run Through the Jungle." Even though he wrote both songs, the latter was written while with Creedence Clearwater Revival, and to get out of his record contract he had sold some of the rights to his Creedence output. The person who now owned those rights sued, but lost.

Creative people (right-brainers) prefer metaphors, analogies, and anecdotes to boring basics. That's why I like to ask my attorney "what if?" questions. Then he lays out a scenario or tells me a story about so-and-so who lost his shirt, and the fuzzy picture starts to get a lot clearer. What if I agree to this clause or that clause? What could happen? Try this with your attorney.

Contract Killers

"Beware of dealers who won't use contracts."

—Caroll Michels

The meek shall inherit the earth . . . but the strong will always retain the mineral rights. It should be so simple. You produce art and somebody else sells or distributes it. So why is it so complicated? For one thing, when disputes have arisen over all matter of things relating to the relationship between artist and publisher/dealer/distributor/label/ employer/gallery owner and others, lawyers are including more and more C.Y.A. (cover your ass) clauses and contingencies in contracts. Then there is the language, "whereas" and "therefore" instead of just saying what they mean—in English. Finally, there is a lot at stake (for both sides), so review more than the correct spelling of your name before signing. Lawyers who concoct these contracts on behalf of their clients (not you) don't do all this work to protect you, the artist.

Maybe they aren't trying to figure out how to screw you, but they are working to ensure that the other side is covered under every possible scenario. (If you think they *don't* want to take advantage of you, I have some dot-com stock to sell you.) It's a power struggle, and the one with the most leverage has all the power. You probably have more than you think. In fact, many creative people are so afraid that if they make too many demands the deal may fall through, they sign the contract as is, thinking they have no choice. That and the fact that the darn contract is so long and confusing you wouldn't know where to begin to make suggestions.

They have you by the balls. Jazz great Charles Lloyd commented on this by saying, "Some guy from a big record company told me: 'I love your art.' I asked, 'What does that mean?' And someone else told me: 'He doesn't love art; he loves to *sell* art.' Then he gave me a forty-page album contract that was literally about slavery, and this music is about freedom. It would have been a disgrace to me, and all my elders whose shoulders I stood upon, to accept it." Richard Bach, the author of *Jonathan Livingston Seagull,* signed what he thought was a movie contract but ended up signing away his merchandising rights. That was then and this is now—and there are more ways you can make a mistake when it comes to signing away your rights. For example, a group of freelance writers found out that a major newspaper was going to sell its archive of articles and not pay the writers a red cent. Why should they when they didn't have to? If the freelancers wanted to work with this MAJOR publication again, they had to agree to sign away the rights to their work.

Even when you think you got the best of the other person, you can still end up getting punked. Apple Computers was pressuring Bill Gates to sign a statement agreeing not to use Mac technology in Windows 1.0 (which worked a hell of a lot like the Mac interface). Gates agreed he would not use the Mac technology in Windows 1.0. But the agreement said nothing about using it in future versions of Windows. Stupid, stupid, stupid! Speaking of Apple Computers. When Steve Wozniak worked at Hewlett-Packard he essentially had a lot of the workings of the future Mac computer all mapped out. By contract he had to offer the computer to HP—they passed.

Then there is out-and-out fraud and deceit. Actor John Cusack, describing the people you deal with in Hollywood, said, "There are some good people. . . . But a good chunk of them will lie for no reason at all—it'll be ten o'clock and they'll tell you it's nine. You're both looking at the clock, and you can't even fathom why they're lying." They say "Trust me," "Sign here," and "It's a standard contract," and the next thing you know you are in deep shit. Don't be a fool. You won't lose the deal if a lawyer looks at the contract. If you don't agree it's okay to suggest changes. Have an attorney review the contract and make suggestions; you can pick which points to discuss or challenge. Don't feel like you are powerless. They want you—on their terms, of course—but you can make *some* requests. Look, if you are at the contract stage, they are interested. You made the grade. But beware of the euphoria of finally having someone show interest in you and your work. Don't get giddy and sign whatever they stick in front of you. Think about things like, "Am I signing away rights I may need and want later? If there is a "no compete" clause, how does that affect my ability to make a living down the road? What if I am unhappy with this deal but there is an option clause that gives them first crack at my next project?" You are ready to move on (and maybe even up), but you have become an indentured servant to them at a rate below what you could get on the open market. What about those royalties? Are they based on the retail price, net price, or some other funky factors? Can you deliver what they want when they want it? Don't promise what you can't deliver, because there can be dire consequences.

You don't deserve to get ripped off. You should feel fine asking for what you want. If you don't, they will think you are an idiot and unprofessional. They expect it. So many things can go wrong that you need to know what signing this contract means, because it could cost you a fortune down the road. Better to take the time to get it right now. You can never review a contract too carefully! What you don't understand, ask for clarification. You won't look dumb—in fact, it's the smart thing to do.

Some things a creative person should consider before signing. How long is this agreement going to last? How can I get out of it if problems arise? How and when will I be paid? Who will own the art when I am done? How much promotion will be provided? What about insurance? How and when will my work be returned to me? How can I get my rights back if I need or want to? If you don't understand a contract, don't sign it! Don't leave things vague. Make sure you agree to the terms. Let the attorney simplify it for you. Always keep a copy of your contract.

Maybe you have heard that the arts is more informal than traditional business and works better by simply getting someone's word and sealing the deal with a handshake. I have deals in place like that, so I can't say it doesn't work. It does—to a point. If nothing goes wrong, you're fine, but how often does that happen? I am beginning to believe that a contract can generate trust (rather than just taking someone's word). I believe it is more binding than an oral agreement because it is harder to wiggle out of. The contract doesn't mean you don't trust someone—it says, "I'm professional," and it helps you to expect the unexpected and plan for it without having to wonder, "What if I want to leave?" or "Do I have to pay commission in this?" It gives structure where chaos and uncertainty are not a good thing. Put everything in writing, and try to cover all contingencies. By spelling it out everyone is in agreement. There is no excuse. Even if you make arrangements over the phone, write up what you talked about and agreed upon and send them a copy to sign. You can draw up your own contract or purchase one from an office-supply store. If the client refuses to sign your letter of agreement, purchase order, or contract, that is a huge red flag. Sometimes they try to stall. Have a version you can fax or e-mail so there is no delay. Leave a paper trail. Have them confirm things in writing. Keep a log of the dates and times you talked to them and what was said.

Sometimes we focus too much on the money and ignore the terms. Getting the price set is only half the battle. Then you have to clarify (and agree on) what is expected of each party, who will pay for what, how you will be paid, and other considerations. What happens if the client cancels the job midway through the contract? Do they have to pay for the work you've done to date? What about any expenses you've incurred? That's why it's important to have these issues raised and resolved by at least a letter of agreement or, better yet, a contract. Then you can state what kind of "kill fee" is in order if the job is halfway done.

Here's an example: When you display your art at a gallery, or any other place, for that matter, agree who is responsible if a piece is lost, stolen, or damaged and who will collect the sales tax. Or in some contracts the band must pay for recording costs and other expenses out of their royalties. That's just one of the possible disagreements that can arise. There are also pricing issues, accounting practices, payment, and legal and other business issues. It may be there is no malice on either party's part but rather a lack of understanding. Or the artist signed the agreement because he couldn't get a better deal— take it or leave it, and he couldn't afford to leave it. Then all of a sudden stuff starts to sell, and he is still stuck with a crummy deal. That's why sometimes short-term deals are in the best interests of the artist.

A work-for-hire agreement can mean you don't own the rights to your work. You are paid a onetime fee for the work, and the rights revert to the person who is paying you. Matt Groening was invited to a meeting to offer him a chance to bring his successful cartoon strip *Life in Hell* to *The Tracey Ullman Show*. But just before the meeting he found out that Fox wanted to own whatever he was going to do for the show. He really didn't want to sign away the rights to his *Life in Hell* cartoon characters, so fifteen minutes before the meeting he invented a new cast of characters that we now know as the Simpsons. Work-for-hire agreements should usually be avoided. It costs you control over the work, and if the thing hits big, you have already been paid your fee. That's that. Even if it sells a million copies, you won't be compensated. It's far better to license the rights to your work so you can be compensated based on sales. Employment contracts are similar in that they may own the rights to whatever you have created while working for them. There are pluses to signing an employment contract—it clearly defines the rules and what is expected and how you will be compensated, all in writing.

Protect Yourself

"I've learned to pick my battles. I ask myself, 'Will this matter a year from now? A month? A week? A day?'"

—*Valorie Jackson*

When you create something of value of course you want to take steps to protect it. The law is on your side here. Copyright protection is available for creative people in most mediums. Yet artists are getting robbed every year by businesses that use their work in order to make money without compensating the creator. That's bad enough; what's worse is when they take your art and use it (without your consent) for something that could damage your reputation. So why don't we take the time to register our works or patent our ideas? It can be a hassle, time-consuming, complicated, and we don't know how. Learn. A copyright is potentially worth money. If your art is protected you can license it for big bucks. Or you can collect in a lawsuit. It can be costly to go through the patent process or to do trademark search through a high-priced lawyer, but there are ways to either do it yourself or get it done for less.

Singer/songwriter Tom Waits is well known for his gravelly voice and sued (and won a multimillion-dollar judgment) against a potato-chip company that used a soundalike in their ads. His win prompted Waits to say, "Now by law, I have what I always felt I had, a distinctive voice." Dustin Hoffman has carefully tried to protect his marketability over the years and felt he was damaged when a magazine used his likeness (dressed as Dorothy from the movie *Tootsie*). He won a $1.5 million judgment plus punitive damages. Madonna won control of the Internet domain name Madonna.com. (It had been used by a New Jersey businessman as the address for a porn site.) Celebrities know that their domain name has value.

💰 FAST FACT

Three out of ten wives and husbands don't know how much their spouse makes.

Book-Keeping

"What the world really needs is more love and less paperwork."

—Pearl Bailey

Would you agree with me that most of us are allergic to paperwork? We just weren't programmed to deal with it. Besides, I became a writer to write books, not *do the books*. Yuk. It's nice if you can afford to hire someone to deal with it for you. (Beware: You must stay on top of the person doing it or you may be robbed blind.) We may need another remedy. The symptoms of this condition are usually pretty severe. For starters, doing taxes is a headache. Someone once told me that when playing "rock, scissors, paper" with the IRS, "paper" always wins. That's why you need to keep good records. Another reason is if you don't stay on top of things like billing, there isn't enough money coming in to nourish us because we didn't get around to it and collect what's owed to us. Most freelancers fail for three reasons: not enough money, no plan, and bad bookkeeping. Having some system to keep track of what you have coming in and going out is critical to your financial (and mental) health. But being the big-picture thinkers we are, this kind of detail work is drudgery, and we will avoid having to deal with it all costs (and when I say "at all costs" I mean that literally).

I think it's safe to assume that many club owners and managers who offer your band a percentage of "the door" or a cut of "the bar" are not going to be honest. Many times the band gets to drink all they want, and be honest, how much do you care about the money after you come off the high of giving a great show and have a good beer buzz going? Right! Not much. You're more concerned about finding some food. (Yes, I've been there many, many times.) You just assume the person paying you is forthright and trust that whatever amount he gives (minus whatever expenses he takes out) sounds about right, so you take it on faith he isn't screwing you. Then there are creative people who record everything, double- and triple-check statements and the like to make sure they aren't getting punked.

It's true that some people make mountains out of molehills by doing paperwork that doesn't need to be done or is redundant. But I know for a fact that being a freelancer requires a lot of paper-pushing. It's endless. I also know it's an important part of the profession. Ask yourself, Why do all the people on the business side of the arts have all the money? They are better businesspeople, and they run their careers like a business, with the bottom line always in their field of vision. We can learn a lot from them (just don't turn into one of them), and the first place to start is by being a better bookkeeper. I hear you, you don't want to do it. You may even be under the illusion that you thrive on total chaos. That you need your creative freedom and this business stuff will just bog you down. If you want to take chances in your personal life or even in your career, I say go ahead, but when it comes to managing money I know you probably equate safety with boring, and structure as stifling, but by being better with the business side of your career you will have more freedom. Too much clutter and chaos can get in the way of creativity. If you are worried whether you paid some bill (and if you could even find it if you needed it), then your mind is already wandering in the wrong direction. (You'll know when they turn your electricity off.)

We want to be somewhere between out of control and controlling. Even if your system for doing the books is to write down everything you buy and sell on the wall, if it works, it works. Whatever system helps you get a handle on your books is a good thing. Without a good bookkeeping system you will have a tougher time with taxes, forget to bill (or double- and triple-bill), never really know how you are doing, suffer cash-flow problems, and worse. Even if you have someone helping, get involved, even in a casual way. Know what's going on with your money. Have them set up a system for you that you will use consistently. The key is that you use it yourself. If someone else deals with your dough it won't feel real to you. Money doesn't seem real to you until you are actually subtracting the amount of a check from your balance. Gaining control of your finances starts with good bookkeeping.

ASK A PRO

PATTY BROWN, SINGER FOR CROWDED HEAD AND PRESIDENT OF BLACKBALL MUSIC

What are some of the biggest mistakes musicians make?
Not saving receipts and keeping track of expenditures are probably the two biggest mistakes musicians make. Money spent on equipment and supplies as well as mileage to and from gigs should all be accounted for. Most bands starting out don't have two things—time and money. There are software programs available to help you keep track of your money. Keeping accurate records is very important, even if it means just dropping receipts into an envelope labeled with the month and the year. I also believe that all band members should be cognizant of the finances. Run the band like a small business. Even if you are losing money, keep good records—there are tax advantages.

How to Cook Your Books (So to Speak)

"I never ask about sales. It's better not to know. I feel like I write a book, I give it to my editor, then I go back and write another one."

—Alice Hoffman

I think we agree that most of us have no patience for the mundane and maddening task of bookkeeping because it is both boring and a burden. The only way I have found to deal with it is to make it as simple and fun as possible. All most artists really need is a simple spreadsheet. It's also common to use the simple cash-basis method (record income when cash is received and expenses when cash is paid). Come up with some way (it's okay to be creative with how you force yourself to do it but not with what you write) to add what you earn or have coming in and subtract what's going out (pay out). You can buy software to make it easier (I don't think it does; I use an old ledger book and a pencil myself). You can be creative and make a mind-map to track your money. Maybe you just staple receipts into pages of a notebook or stick receipts into a shoebox and add them up once a month. Fine. (Try using an accordion organizer, and just drop receipts into the month or category they fall into. It works!) When I am on the road I grab an envelope and stick the receipts in there at the end of the day and write the totals on the outside. Maybe you use an index card for each area of your business and write down expenses or income right on the appropriate card. You could even make a wall poster and write the numbers in crayon. Whatever works! I find it easier to write transactions in as they happen rather than letting them pile up. It takes discipline, but it's really simple. It only takes a second, and I do it while I am on the phone. I still have to force myself, but these pesky tasks have become habits. My wife, on the other hand, thrives on this kind of stuff. She triple-checks the credit card statement. My job is to just answer "yes" or "no" as to whether I actually made that charge. Once you set the system up it and make some of the difficult decisions, it gets easier. Maybe you get some new supplies to make it seem more fun to start. Get someone else to help you set this up. Take a class. Read a book. Model your system after someone successful. If all this seems overwhelming, start small and get a handle on something easy, like your checkbook.

Quicken is NOT quicker. Someone I know who works for Intuit doesn't even use it. Quicken does have the ability to print out all kinds of reports and can make filing taxes easier. Plus it *does* the math for you! You can link Quicken to your bank, and it will balance your checking account automatically. It can help you automate payments. It can create budgets and help you plan. But it also can be a BIG burden. Using it also won't magically make your money problems disappear. Darshan Thakkar wrote me about how she prefers her Palm Pilot to Quicken. "I have found it very difficult to use Quicken," she says. "Managing finances with a Palm Pilot is as easy as writing data in an address book. Everything is in one place and at your fingertips. It is definitely the machine for a right-brainer."

Most married couples fight about money—it's a fact. It's best to pick a person to be the banker, but you need to be a part of the process. James Brolin is married to the diva of all divas, Barbra Streisand, so who do you think manages the money in that marriage? If you guessed "Babs," you are right. Brolin says, "She handles both of our money. She has a knack for trading and investing, so she's in charge of our investments." Have one person in the home be the banker (like in Monopoly). This should be the responsible one. One woman wrote in to Dear Abby saying that when she handled the family finances everything was fine. Then her husband offered to take the burden from her. A few months later she was getting calls at work about bounced checks and unpaid bills. He said he was on top of it. Then her car was repossessed. He wasn't gambling or giving the money away—he was just lazy and a major procrastinator. His irresponsibility cost the couple a great deal. Not only was their credit ruined, they had to pay all kinds of late fees.

Make it easier by automating as many payments and transactions as possible (automatic investing, direct deposit, bill-paying online). Keep everything in one place. One woman who handled the couple's finances said to her husband, "We have to get all of our finances in order and put them in one place. What if something should happen to me? You wouldn't know where our assets are." He looked at her and replied, "If something happened to you, I wouldn't need any money."

You know how you clean up the house and call it your annual spring cleaning. Do the same thing with your finances. Once a year check your credit and order a credit report. Go through everything and decide what to do with credit cards you don't use, accounts that are inactive, and investments that aren't performing; inventory your art (and see what is "on loan" and where), see if any money is owed to you, and so on.

Remember when it took at least two business days for a check to clear so you could, if you wanted, overextend yourself on paper knowing that you had a day or two to cover the check. Those days are disappearing due to debit cards and technology making for faster transactions. Of course, you can still tell people you owe, "The check is in the mail" (now it's e-mail). Start with a new register each month in your checkbook so you can reconcile with the bank and get a fresh start. What did you start with? How much came in? How much did you spend? On what? How are you doing? As a creative person there can be many ways money flows in and out, and tracking them all will be a burden without a way to accurately deal with your accounts receivable (everything from royalties to retail sales) and accounts payable (including production, promotion, and other payments).

The thing that has helped me the most is that I stopped fighting my natural tendency and now organize things in an unorthodox and creative way. I created colorful wall charts for sales and expenses that include stickers and symbols instead of plain old boring and mind-numbing numbers. I color in as I go, and when I reach certain benchmarks I set up little rewards. I know this goes against conventional thinking, but if it works how can that be a bad thing? Michelle Downey, an artist and designer, concurs. She wrote me to say, "Managing money is boring. I try to find ways to make it more fun." (Like using her favorite color marker for balancing her checkbook.) She's also responsible. "The first thing I do when I get a bill is open it and immediately write the date the bill is due and the amount I plan to pay in the far left corner below my return address. I keep a small red basket on my desk and file the bills according to the date they are due, and then I check up on them daily."

Bill Me

"The most beautiful words in the English language are 'check enclosed.'"

—Dorothy Parker

Have you ever noticed that people don't pay unless you bill them? The faster you invoice the faster you get paid. That all depends on them, but at least you did your part. Let's get something straight— you are NOT a bank! Don't feel like you have to extend credit to others or take risks on people who never pay promptly. If they never pay you (and this happens all the time) it's the same as if they broke into your studio and stole a painting. They are stealing from you. Not getting paid in a timely fashion can kill a business that is overextended.

Make them prove themselves worthy by starting small or with COD and then issuing terms or at least get some money up-front. Make sure they have agreed to your terms by having them sign a contract or letter of agreement. The more paper the better. Make sure you have jumped through all of their hoops, too. Are they waiting for your Social Security number or tax ID? Did you fail to get a purchase order? Approval? Lisa Kanarek in her book *101 Home Office Success Secrets* says to make a copy of a client's first check so that you will have all their bank-account information in case of future problems with payments.

Is their website outdated? Have they suddenly stopped advertising? Were they on the news announcing layoffs? Have they stopped shipping orders? Are their shelves barren and inventories low? It's important you stay in touch and pay attention. Ask around—others will usually tell you who the deadbeats are. Don't do business with people who are problem payers. It's not worth it. Don't be a fool. It's well worth the time it takes to check them out if it's a large amount (and only you know what a large amount is and if you could survive if they failed to pay). Is the company a chronically slow payer (don't get me started about trying to collect from government agencies)? Are you willing to wait?

The best thing is to get as much money up-front as you can. No contract or credit report is as good as having their money in your hand before you do anything. That sense of security is worth something (to both you and them), so give them a reason to want to pony up. Maybe it's a discount, deal, or other incentive to pay you now. Services have the highest value when you render them. The longer you have to wait to collect, the less likely you ever will. Pay me by this date, and you owe this amount. But if you pay by this earlier date, you owe me only this amount. People usually respond to this. I came up with a plan to collect more money up-front. I would gladly cut my fee if someone paid me the bulk of the money on the front end. That still left money to be collected, and I have always felt funny asking for money owed. So I have someone who handles it for me. I do like having someone else handle billing to keep myself out of it. But I did make a form that lists who owes what and when. That way I can nudge my agent when money is past due.

Submit a bill with the job *and* mail one. That way it's less likely they can lie and say, "We never got it." Set a deadline in writing, and put it on the bill and highlight it. *This* is when it's due. Not ten days after that date, but on that date or before. Have them agree and sign. Include an SASE to make it easier. Accept credit cards, pigs, goats— whatever it takes to make them pay. Bill them electronically for the fastest way to get the invoice to them. On your invoices and letters of agreements make your terms VERY clear, including penalties for nonpayment. Again, put all relevant information on the invoice so they can't say they need your tax ID number or Social Security number to cut a check. Put your address on there as well. Offer a discount for early payment. People will take you up on this, but they are usually the prompt payers anyway.

Set up a tickler system to remind you to check back. Drop the invoice in the month or day slot it's due. Or write the date in your day planner. If they don't pay or agree to pay, put it in past due or the date they *promised* to pay. Number your invoices so you can track them more easily. Be the squeaky wheel and stay on it. See why keeping good records are critical? Make it a weekly thing. Don't let people run up a big tab, or you'll have to get a goomba to collect. Keep track. Sloppy billing (and overbilling or double-billing) can cause a client to question your credibility and shake their confidence in you.

What if it's too late? You can freak out and demand that they pay you (usually this won't work) or try to work with them. Why aren't they paying? Are they in financial trouble? Set up a payment plan. Were they unhappy with the work? Try to resolve any problems and collect full payment or cut the amount they owe and consider it promotion. Sometimes people are just difficult to deal with. I am not saying you let up or forget about it until you run out of options. (Small-claims court is always an option, and even the threat can be enough to collect. You can also turn it over to a collection agency.) Step it up and send a certified letter. You can set up your contracts or agreements so that they will owe interest in overdue bills (You can charge a 2.5 percent service charge for bills thirty days late.) Or take back product if they aren't paying and resell it. Hold back on finishing work until they get current. Worst case is you never get paid, and then it becomes a tax deduction and you can write it off as ad debt.

When it comes to "friends" who owe you money, it is important to keep a log and track it. My friend (who owes me money and never pays for anything) and I were at a Padres game, and we ordered nachos, and I had them pile on jalapeno peppers. He looked at the spicy treat and said, "I'm gonna pay for that tomorrow." I corrected him and said, "No, you're gonna pay for it now!"

Banking on It

"I don't have a bank account because I don't know my mother's maiden name."

—Paula Poundstone

Some ancient Chinese coins have a hole in them so they could be strung together, making them easier to carry. Elvis Presley wrote a check to Roy Brown on a paper bag. When Brown went to cash the scrap of paper at a Memphis bank, what do you think happened? If you said, "They cashed it," you are right. Ahhhh, the good old days. Or were they really so great? Sure, our bills are higher than ever, but bill-paying and banking have never been more convenient (and expensive). According to a Harris Poll, the reasons people pay bills late include: They didn't have the money to pay them (51 percent), forgot (46 percent), procrastinated (32 percent), and couldn't find the bill (23 percent). The key to reducing stress is doing all your bill-paying at once, in one place, using a simple, convenient way to file your receipts that is logical and effective for you.

Electronic bill-paying can save a ton of time. Electronic bill-paying means no stuffing, stamping, last-minute dash to catch the outgoing mail, paperwork, writing checks. No waiting in line, less paperwork, automatic, no having to remember to do it. There's still a paper trail. No stamps to buy, no envelopes to lick (there is actually one calorie in the glue on envelopes), and it is easier to automate. It may help you pay bills on time (avoiding late charges), stay organized, and can make bill-paying less of a burden. However, it doesn't always work the way it was advertised due to technical glitches and it can be a hassle and time-waster to set it up in the first place. Software for finances takes time to learn and may be more trouble than it is worth to load checks and envelopes into the printer each time, but it does do fancy expense reports, so you can see where your money goes. It can also make it easier to do taxes.

It's a Wonderful Life?

"I bank at a women's bank. It's closed three or four days a month due to cramps."

—Judy Carter

Remember in the movie *It's a Wonderful Life* when George Bailey was an advocate for the customer? He went to war with the evil Mr. Potter to keep him from taking over. Well, there aren't any George Baileys left in the banking world, and the mergers with the evil Mr. Potter have instituted long lines, fewer services, and insane fees. But wait, you say, the movie has to have a happy ending. Doesn't Clarence get his wings? Uh, no. He missed his deadline by one day, so the bank closed his account and took the wings as a penalty for trying to talk to a teller one too many times. What about all the money the town raised to save George from bankruptcy? Gone. "B . . . b . . . but that's not right." Tell me about it.

Fees, fees, and more fees. It really makes me mad that we now have to pay the bank instead of them paying us. We pay more for less. I switched banks when they started charging me just to come in and talk to a teller. The goal, of course, is to get everything you can from a bank for the least amount of money. If you pay a ten-dollar fee per month just to have a checking account, that's $120 a year. There are hoops you may have to jump through to avoid these fees (direct deposit and keeping a larger balance). But they can save. Watch out for hidden costs like a limit of how many times you can use the ATM or deposits you can make or a limit on how many checks you can write. Eighty-three percent of U.S. banks collect surcharges from non-customers. Look at some of your past statements, and add up the fees. Crazy, isn't it?

Union dues. My wife belongs to a credit union, and one day I went in with her, and it was such a contrast to my bank. At my bank they yell, "Next!" and then do the transaction without even a "How are you?" or "Thank you." At my wife's credit union they called her by name and cheerfully processed her transaction. So you get better service with less fees. Sounds good to me. So why don't more people stash their money there? You have to qualify, and many freelancers don't unless they belong to a union or trade organization. But if you can get in you are in the "alternate" world where George Bailey lives. Hear that bell? Clarence got his wings, and you got a great interest rate on a car loan and an interest-bearing checking account with no hidden fees. Hooray!

Banking made easy? Drive-in banks were invented so that automobiles could visit their *real* owners. Now everyone is banking online or by phone. This easy access from home makes it easier to review, update, check, transfer funds, or pay bills from the road with laptop and modem. (I have to be honest, though—I miss my passbook account.) We've come a long way. But my parents are a blast from the past. They have never used an ATM! So they have to wait in long lines, withdraw more money than they need, set their schedules around the bank's hours—basically, it's a hassle and extra work. Why won't they use an ATM? They claim that it's too complicated to learn. (I guess online banking is out of the question!) Banking online isn't for everyone. Sure, they promised it would be better, faster, cheaper. We'll see. There are still a lot of "real" brick-and-mortar banks, they haven't all been turned into Starbucks. That's because to bank online you need compatible software, to some it doesn't seem safe, and others just want some freakin' human interaction. If you hate long lines and still want to bank the old-fashioned way, visit the bank during off-hours, or use branches that are inside the supermarket so you can do two things at once.

A.T.M. = Access To Money. One of my pals (I better not mention his name) is always short on cash. To his credit he doesn't like to use his credit card, but I can't tell you how many times we have had to wander around looking for an ATM machine so he could pay for the privilege of getting his own money out. Once, we were having a grand time at a "club" until my buddy couldn't settle up his bill with the "dancer." Next thing I know there is some big bouncer pulling me up by my shirt. "You know this guy?" he asks as he points to my friend. "Yeah. What did he do now?" I innocently asked. "He says he ain't got no money. He owes the lady $120." "What! How much? I don't have that kind of cash on me!" "There's an ATM across the street— your friend can go get more money there, but I'll need to hold something of value before I let him leave." "I'll stay here and wait," I offered. "No, I said something of value, you piece of s—." Nice. From now on I make sure my friend is packing, and by that I mean a wad of ones. It's been proven that people who go to the ATM more often not only pay more for their money but also spend more. The best advice I ever heard was to take out what you need for the week and make it last.

Checking it out. Please balance your checking account, including debit card purchases. If you bounce a check, what once cost a couple of bucks will now cost twenty (and that's twenty you don't have if you are bouncing checks in the first place). Whether you enter a transaction or you don't, the balance is the same. I prefer to balance my checkbook as I go. Or drop ATM slips and receipts in a bowl and enter at the same time you pay bills. The fact that you don't know what the receipt is for doesn't do a damn thing for you. Denial is never a good thing. Deal with it. You don't want to dip into your overdraft protection (there is usually a fee), or worse, bounce a check (more fees and major embarrassment). Try carbonless checks that provide a written reminder of where and to whom you wrote checks to as well as the amounts. Did you know that a brokerage account is nearly as easy to open as a checking account at a bank? It's a lot like a traditional checking account—you can deposit money (you do need a few bucks first) into the account and then use it to make purchases. The best part is that it is invested and earns interest, which makes it better than a bank's checking account.

Debit cards are not credit cards. For one thing, they don't offer purchase protection. When you check into a hotel or rent a car, the company will put a hold on your account that can take days to clear and may cause checks to bounce, and you have to remember to enter purchases into your ledger.

On loan. I once worked for my father selling art supplies to art-supply stores. After I had proved myself in the warehouse (and got my driver's license), he gave me some of his accounts to service (I was only in my teens, but I was an ambitious little booger). When I first started making sales calls to people who had done business with my father for years, they would always welcome me with open arms. Many times it would go like this: "Look, everyone, it's Harvey's boy. Isn't he cute." After a while it started to get to me. But let me tell you something—when I went to my father's bank (where he did a lot of business) for a loan, I was sooooo glad to hear them say, "Look, it's Harvey's son. What can we do for you? Your father's a *very* good customer." (If you could have seen the grin on my face.) It's better than going to one of those "quick cash" places; they will take about $50 in fees when cashing a check for $300. You may as well go to a loan shark.

It's a Chart-Topper

Being visually oriented, I had a hard time picturing the amount of debt my wife and I had incurred several years ago. (A giant mountain comes to mind.) We decided that our goal was to be completely debt-free. So to help me see the big picture, we made a wall chart to show how much we owed and to whom. As we paid each one down we would color in a box until it was full, which meant the card was paid off. I could now see exactly how we were doing at a glance, and I could see progress (So this is why I can't have this or that). I am proud to say we are completely debt-free. It feels great!!!

An Ounce of Prevention

This could be you: "I came running out of my house naked with my pig, Max . . . and my buddy Ben, who was in the guest house, came running out naked with a gun, because he thought someone was breaking in. So we're naked like this,

> *and my biggest fear was that we would end up getting killed*
> *and they would find two naked guys, a pig, and a gun."*
> —George Clooney, describing what happened
> during an earthquake in San Francisco

Reknowned jazz vibraphonist Lionel Hampton lost a lifetime's worth of memorabilia when there was a fire in his Manhattan apartment. Lost was his vintage record collection, sheet music, photographs, letters from past presidents. New York Mayor Rudolph Giuliani presented the jazz great with copies of several photographs and city proclamations that were lost in the blaze. Most of us aren't that lucky—or well connected. There is insurance for this kind of thing, plus other pitfalls.

"It will never happen to me" is the catchphrase among people who haven't been a victim of a robbery, fire, flood, or mudslide (and if you believe what you see on TV, a meteor or alien abduction). There are only two kinds of people when it comes to a disaster: those who have had it happen to them, and those who will. Be prepared. Get insurance to protect what you have worked so hard to acquire and to limit the amount of money you will personally need to raise in case disaster strikes (and by "disaster," that could mean a natural disaster like a flood or fire or a man-made one like a lawsuit). What are your biggest fears? If you have enough insurance to cover them, you can have some peace of mind.

Something nobody thinks about is that as a creative person we make money by creating things (and hopefully collecting on those efforts for years to come). But what if you were unable to work for a while? What would happen? How would you pay the rent? One carpenter moved to Miami to build custom cabinets in boats. He was renowned for his attention to detail and his creative touches. He was seriously injured in a motorcycle accident and was unable to work for weeks, plus he didn't have insurance on the motorcycle or health insurance. He lost everything (including his tools, which were auctioned off). Could a weekend sports injury or a lawsuit wipe you out? What if a patron came to your studio and slipped on some wet paint and broke her neck? What if you were to lose something you were entrusted to hold? You can protect yourself from these (and other horrific) tragedies with insurance. Talk to your insurance broker (and your attorney) to see how you can protect your assets. Get the most coverage for the least amount of money.

• Put valuables and irreplaceables in a safety deposit box or fire-proof safe. Also, store your art out of harm's way. (I put my books on Zip disks and store them in a safety deposit box.) Inventory, photograph, and document your artwork. Save contracts, receipts, and invoices in a safe place in case you have to prove that your art was valuable. I know that sucks, but it's the way it is. Make an inventory or video of your home.

• If you lost your wallet what would happen? Record all cards and emergency numbers or photocopy everything and store it in a safe place. Play the "what if" game. If I had three minutes to grab everything of importance before my home burnt to the ground, what would I want to take (other than people and pets)?

• Many bands cut costs by traveling around in a beat-up van. One band traveled around in a panel van with their name painted on the side. This basically said to thieves, "Gear inside—steal me." And they did. To cut costs the band dropped their insurance. As an artist, what would happen if a piece were to be lost in transit or stolen while on display? Make sure you are covered in case of emergencies. You may have to add a rider on your insurance in case your gear is stolen. Don't assume you are covered—ask! I ask questions like, "If all my gear was stolen from my garage, would I be covered? How much would I be able to collect? Is that replacement cost? How much would I have to pay? Is my art covered? What if it is in transit? Is it protected from theft and damage while on display? (We are risk-takers, so here's a way you can gamble a bit: The highest deductibles usually mean the lowest premiums.) You can usually save money by consolidating all of your insurance (car, homeowners, life) with one company.

• Put some money away for emergencies. If having to rebuild your engine is going to wipe you out, you are living too close to the edge.

Types of Insurance

__ Health insurance. "Fame hasn't changed my life or who I am, but I have health insurance now," boasts Heather Donahue from *The*

Blair Witch Project. No small feat for the creative person. Nearly 85 percent of adults are insured through their spouses' employers, according to a survey by the Aragon Consulting Group. And according to another study, less than 75 percent of artists (of all types) have any form of health coverage. The reason given was that they couldn't afford it. Which stands to reason: Artists are seen as a risk because of a negative bias about our behavior, so they are charged a higher premium. (By the way, part of the premium is tax-deductible.) If you are self-employed (or single) you can sometimes get good rates through a trade association or union. Consider this: Americans spend an average of $906 on medical bills annually, and that number is expected to rise to $1,172 by 2005. Many theatrical performers complain of respiratory problems and other ailments from theatrical fog.

"I'm living out my dreams. And I have health insurance, which makes me successful, according to my mother," says jazz violinist Regina Carter.

__ Disability insurance protects you in case you are unable to work. This covers accidents and illness and not just those that occur on the job. Can't create or perform—you still get paid. You get to kick back and watch TV while you recover, and you are covered. My friend hopped off the side of my boat and sliced his foot open. As he was hauled off to the hospital, he said, "I'll meet you back at the marina bar in a couple of hours." Three days (and a lot of morphine) later he was released from the hospital.

__ Life insurance. Do you want someone to cash in when you cash out? What would happen if you died? A lot of people get ripped off when it comes to life insurance. As an investment it usually isn't your best bet. If you are single, you probably don't need it. Don't buy so much that your loved ones are considering having you whacked.

__ Automobile insurance. Hang up the phone and drive and get the most car insurance you can afford. (At least get liability.) You'll want at least $10,000 per person, $100,000 for property, and $300,000 per accident. You'll also need collision coverage if it's a nice car. (The cheaper your car, the less insurance costs and the less you need.) Don't skimp if you can afford it. You may save a few bucks now but pay later. Do I even need to mention that every ticket or DUI is VERY costly? Insurance rates for artists are very high anyway (we are considered self-employed and high-risk, go figure).

___ Homeowner's or renter's insurance protects you and your assets from theft, natural disasters, and even lawsuits. Look for the limits on your policy. If you are a photographer and have a bunch of expensive equipment, you'll need more than a poet who has a pen and pad. Sculptor Martin Puryear had most of his work destroyed in a fire in his studio. He made a freestanding work out of the ash, but . . .

___ Umbrella insurance provides some safety from being sued. If you have a lot to lose, this is something to think about. Even if you don't have a lot now, they can go after your future earnings. Umbrella insurance goes beyond homeowner's insurance to protect you against libel, copyright infringement, slips and falls, and other potential problems. It kicks in when you exceed the limits of other insurance coverage. There is also something called liability insurance that covers you against lawsuits. Virtually all publishers carry it, and as an author you can be covered by it, too. The only hitch is that you may be on the hook for half of the deductible paid by the publisher. Keep in mind that every dollar you spend on insurance coverage can save thousands in legal fees and lawsuits. Add up what you could lose if you were sued, then add in legal expenses, and then ask yourself: Should I maybe look into some umbrella insurance?

Taxed to Death

"We don't seem to be able to check crime, so why not legalize it and then tax it out of business?"

—Will Rogers

Will Rogers overpaid his income tax one year but was unable to collect the money owed him. After his requests were ignored, Rogers evened the score on the following year's return by listing under deductions: "Bad debt, U.S. Government—$40,000." Would it surprise you to learn that 28 percent of Americans don't file a tax return in any given year? You don't want to be looking over your shoulder and worrying that they will come after you. Only 1 percent of returns are audited each year, so the odds that yours will be flagged are pretty low.

Taxes are an example where there is a penalty if you don't do it. They're boring but must be done, or delegated. Many of us are paid in cash or in lump sums without any taxes taken out. It's up to us to put some aside to pay Uncle Sam. If you are a slave (Oops, I mean employed by someone else), your goal is the same—keep as much money as you can. If you don't trust yourself then by all means have the max deducted from your paycheck (or better yet, contribute to something that will reduce your taxable income). If you feel like you could invest that money wisely, have them take out less and put it somewhere where it can earn a little interest.

We derive income from so many diverse sources that it can get complicated. Keep good records, please. Then there are our unusual expenses. I write off magic tricks used in my workshops. An actor attends plays, and that can be a deduction. A writer deducts his travels for research. A craftsperson purchasing tools at Home Depot should save the receipt. A hairstylist who subscribes to several magazines for the latest trends and to have around for people waiting may want to claim that as an expense. So will a musician needing strings and a new strap. One big benefit if you are a freelancer (most artists are) is that most expenses are tax-deductible, even if it's not your full-time gig. The distinction the IRS likes to make is whether what you do on the side is a hobby or a legitimate business. (You have to show a profit every few years, or it's a hobby.)

The best bet, in my opinion, is to get someone else to do your taxes. Tax law and tax returns can be complicated for the freelancer. An accountant can actually save you money by uncovering hidden deductions, not to mention freeing you from the details and allowing you to do what you do best—create and earn income (taxable or otherwise). The language the IRS uses—oy. I have read passages several times, and I still don't get it. A tax specialist can also alert you to things you can do to lower your taxes in future years. There are special tax breaks for artists (for example, artists can deduct expenses from art activities that exceed income). That is the goal—reduce the amount you must pay and put more money in your pocket (or back into your business). The amount of the typical workday that goes to pay taxes is almost three hours, and the percentage of all income owed per household went from 27.9 percent in 1955 to 38.2 percent in 1997. Uncle Sam is not the lovable uncle. Of course, it's up to you to be responsible for keeping receipts and records regardless of who does the final figuring.

No matter how screwed up your tax situation is right now, there is a way out, and the sooner you deal with it the better. It's that or move to some island that doesn't have an extradition agreement with the United States (or get a presidential pardon).

TAXING PROBLEMS

Comedian Redd Foxx lost everything he owned because he never paid attention to (or paid) his taxes. Same with singer Dottie West. James Brown had all kinds of money problems, including the $4.5 million the Treasury Department claimed he owed in back taxes. The IRS filed liens of $2.2 million on his land. He had to sell almost everything to get them (and his ex-wives and lawyers) off his back. Artist Peter Max concealed $700,000 in income from art sales and got a two-month term in prison (plus 800 hours of community service). Willie Nelson owed $16 million in back taxes before settling for $9 million.

"ONE FOR YOU, NINETEEN FOR ME"

I saw a truly E-Z tax form that said: "1. How much did you make? _____ 2. Send it to us."

You Are No Uncle of Mine, Sam

"The rich aren't like us—they pay less taxes."

—Peter De Vries

A seventeen-year-old baby-sitter was surprised when she got a 1099 form and was considered an independent contractor by the parents (who owned a business and put her on the payroll, so to speak). The baby-sitter owed $100 in self-employment tax. I guess it wasn't a hobby. You do matter. Try not paying your taxes (no matter how insignificant you think they are) and all of a sudden you become popular (with the wrong people). This includes estimated, quarterly, as well as annual taxes. On the news every year they have the long line at the post office for people who have to get their forms in by midnight. Mark your calendar for estimated taxes. Schedule time to work on it (and not in early April). This gives you time to prepare, find all the papers you need, and find the money to pay the darn taxes. You can get an extension if you are really in a pinch. But it's better to break it down and do a little at a time. I know, we right-brainers would rather wait till the last minute and charge through in one fell swoop. At least I tried, right? (Pay on time and there's no penalty.) If you are going to get a refund, you want it as soon as possible. Why wait? It doesn't get any easier if you wait to do taxes, and if you rush you may miss something or make a mistake. If you are fearful of what you may owe, set some money aside for taxes. You can even pay with a credit card. There is a fee to do so, but think of all the frequent-flier miles. (Can you dispute what the IRS charges?)

Being self-employed, it was bound to happen sometime. I was audited by the IRS. At first I was terrified. Then I relaxed because I knew I had done nothing wrong, and I could prove it. When the day arrived to meet with the IRS agent, I confidently strode into his offices with a portable file box under each arm. Everything was alphabetized and categorized. He would ask me about something, and I would instantly produce the receipt. My audit was over very quickly and went smoothly because of the sheer amount of my paper. I think it frightened him—he probably thought I was going to spill all those papers on the floor. He also tried to be my buddy. "I see here you went to Maui to do a book signing. Maui has great snorkeling, eh?" I wasn't going to give him anything!

What's a red flag? Any money left in your bank account (ha, ha, ha). Wait, this is the nicer, kinder IRS. Doesn't matter. Red flags include a home-office deduction, and big "other" expenses (so break them down). Messy returns or ones they can't read. Cash businesses like a hairdresser. When you exceed the rule of thumb. Small businesses with higher than normal expenses. If you didn't report "all" your income. (Oh, they know.) In the case of an IRS audit, documentation is the key. Keep track and report the sources of your income. Even the small sources of income (each source that pays more than $600 a year). I have some bad news: When you barter with another business you are supposed to report what you received as income (fair market value). Per diems also count as income.

For the creative person deductions can be, well, creative. Supplies used in your art can be virtually anything (depending on your medium). Artist Eleanor Antin would order stuff from the Sears catalog to help her invent people for her art. When she needed a peace sign for her art, she would go to the local head shop and then deduct it off her taxes. "It was the funniest thing when I had to take it off my taxes as art supplies." Load up at the end of the year if you need deductions. Whatever you claim, make sure you have proof.

IT'S NOT A LICENSE TO BUY
Just because something is deductible doesn't mean it's free. If you went out and bought a digital camera for your work and spent $1,000, it doesn't mean you'll save $1,000 on your taxes. It's not dollar for dollar—it's more like 20 to 40 percent (depending on what you earn). So don't use saving on taxes as a license to buy what you don't need. The goal is to reduce your taxable income through deductions and expenses (or by deferring it through a retirement plan or investments).

What expenses are deductible? Wages to band members and roadies, models used in a shoot, art supplies, your studio or home office, business travel, your business phone, courses and classes, union dues or association fees, and so on. Matt Groening, the creator of *The Simpsons,* says, "I watched way too much TV. The reason I went into television is to justify all the hours in front of the TV. I can say it was research."

Save old returns forever, as well as receipts. They don't take up much room, and what could it hurt to have them just in case you need them? The more organized you are the better you will be able to find and take deductions and defend yourself in case of an audit. Having documentation is like having a shield to deflect their swords.

💰 ASK A PRO
DAVE KAPLAN, PRESIDENT OF SURFDOG RECORDS

What is one of the ways musicians seem to get into financial hot water?
The most common pitfall that I have seen is the underprovision of taxes. Musicians do not typically have taxes withheld on any of their earnings, so they must allocate a portion of all their royalties, performance income, and other earnings for taxes. Most of the artists these days have business managers whose job it is to look after all

financial affairs, including taking care of taxes. There are many horror stories in the earlier days of rock and roll where bands made enough money to be financially secure for life only to find themselves broke after a few years. That is less common now due to the fact that most successful artists have personnel specifically hired for financial matters.

💰 FAST FACT
A *USA Today* survey found that most people begin preparing their taxes early for the April 15 deadline. (Only 13 percent wait until April, and just 1 percent begin after the deadline.)

Paying Your Penance
Every year Pam, a dancer and dance-studio owner, cleans up the papers and paperwork that have been accumulating for the past eleven and a half months. It's a ritual, and one that works for her. "By December, my office is cluttered with piles of paper, unfinished projects, things to file, an overflowing in-box, and a bulging file of things to do. Not to mention, my bookkeeping is in complete disarray," she muses. So during the holidays she will spend an entire day alone organizing her office and books. No calls, no interruptions, and no excuses. She calls it her "day of atonement." She'll sift through the papers, past invoices and bills, and file some, toss others, and get everything in order. She's well aware that one month later things will go back to the way they were before, but she likes this system for the following reasons. "I like to do it this way because it's my way to look back on and review the previous year. Seeing what got done and what didn't is very enlightening. It's sort of like therapy in a way. I celebrate the successes and examine the failures and then move on."

6

IT'S WHAT YOU KEEP THAT COUNTS

*"Every Friday, I withdrew eighty dollars in cash to last me
the week. If I had extra left over the following Friday,
I'd put it in an envelope marked 'Florida Trip.' I managed
to save $700."*
—Sunny Anderson

In 1790, Ben Franklin (a very creative person, I might add) bequeathed to two cities (Boston and Philadelphia) 2,000 pounds in sterling silver, with a slight catch. The money was to be used to loan to young apprentices (he was once one) to help them out. The two cities had to wait 100 years to withdraw part of the money for themselves and another 100 years to get the rest. In 1990, the two cities ended up splitting $6.5 million (which went into their general funds). The lesson here is that saving some of what you make is a good idea. This is not an easy sell to the right-brainer who likes to live in the moment and probably spends everything he makes instead of saving for the future. When you are a "starving artist" living day to day (barely), saving some money for the future is probably the furthest thing from your mind. That may be, but even if you just put the pennies from your pocket into a piggy bank you are better off than spending every last dime. So let's just look at what it would be like to have some money saved and how to start putting something aside for a rainy day (or more likely, a drought).

Nobody can go back and start a new beginning, but anyone can start today and have a new ending. So even if you have never saved money in the past, it's never too late to start. You must have heard this before, but I'll say it again, "Save some of every dollar you make." Now say it with me. "I will save something from every dollar I make." It's easiest when you get a big payday. Simply take some off the top, and then do what you will with the rest. But to do it the other way, after you pay all your bills, buy some clothes, a new car, take a trip, and so on, it is less likely you'll have any left. Take it out and put it away first, then live on the rest. Come on, stop laughing. I'm serious.

In the past when I made large amounts of cash, I tended to spend it as fast as I made it. It was almost as if I didn't want it sitting around. But over the past few years I have been saving some. I now know that money is the fuel that gets my dreams off the ground. Once I got some money socked away I have been able to do more of what I want to, which is basically nothing. What I mean is, I can take the entire summer off and travel and wait for projects that I am passionate about without worry. I am an active saver and investor, with enough money to survive for years without work. Enough about me, let's talk about you.

Let's just pretend for a minute that you are concerned about your financial future and how you'll support yourself down the road. (And hopefully it's not by collecting aluminum cans at the beach.) Start by adding a zero to what you currently earn to get a good idea of how much money you'll need by the time you stop working so that you'll have enough cash flow to keep your current lifestyle. If you make $60,000, then you would need $600,000, earning a 10 percent annual return, to have enough income to live like you do now (and that isn't taking into account inflation and taxes). Something to think about, isn't it?

Lifestyles of the Rich and Frugal

"I would rather be rich than famous. That is, more rich and slightly less famous."

—John Lennon

Aaron Spelling is so rich that his handyman is actually Tim Allen, bada bing. Creative people *can* make money from their ideas. I used to think that you had to inherit money to be really rich. Now I know that you can become wealthy with your talents and skills. Then you have to make that money make more money. Although inheriting money is still an option. One man said to his wife, "Admit it, the only reason you married me is because my grandfather left me $10 million." "Don't be silly," she said. "I don't care *who* left it to you." But even if you did inherit great wealth, if you didn't save some you'd probably end up right back where you started. For some clues, let's look at what the wealthy do.

The rich (who save and invest) actually do get richer. Money begets more money. They make prudent choices. Because they have money they can take advantage of opportunities. They can get loans. During downturns in the economy they can buy up bargains and afford to hold on to them. Then there is the mind-set that once you've made money you know you can do it again. There is also a sense of security that makes them less anxious and desperate. They have an air of confidence, and confidence sells. They feel they are predetermined to be wealthy. Artists don't.

Those who aren't wealthy have squandered their money and made poor choices, spending money on trivial things. Wealthy people are usually frugal. I know a waitress who told me blue-collar customers are the best tippers, while the wealthy are not. They come in for happy hour and eat like they were just voted off of *Survivor*. They are "smart with money" or "cheap," depending on how you look at it.

Who wants to be a millionaire? Okay, you can put your hand down now. Let's play *Who Wants to Be a Millionaire*. For a million dollars answer this question. The *best* and most certain way to become wealthy is to: A.) Ask for and get a raise at your work. B.) Write a book about finances. C.) Start a business. D.) Save and invest wisely. I'm guessing you are going to want to use a lifeline here. Let's use your "50/50" and eliminate two. Answer "A" will not make you wealthy. You'll make more, but likely also spend more. "B," unfortunately for me, is a long shot. Okay, so it's either "C," "start a business," or "D," "save and invest wisely." Tough one, isn't it? Both are good, but one is better. Go ahead, ask the audience. They are telling you to pick "start a business." It's sexier than saving and investing. But the correct answer is "D," save and invest wisely. Many made millions in the last dot-com boom. But the collapse of Nasdaq killed many companies. I'm talking about a conservative, sensible (I can't believe I just said that) approach. I know this sounds sooooo dull, but it works. Be creative in other areas of your life, not with your life savings.

Creative people are not the best savers, sadly. But setting up a savings plan and sticking with it is the key component to most millionaires' wealth. Set a goal of becoming a millionaire, and with time and some smart moves, you can make it happen. Increase your income and/or cut back on spending (and get out of debt). Find a safe investment, and put your money to work. See, now you don't need to buy another book on money management. That's all you need to know. I bet I'm not telling you anything you haven't already heard—but don't want to hear. Right-brainers are risk-takers, and that is a key to *giant* wealth. It can also wipe out a savings account faster than you can say, "I went belly-up." But it's hard (impossible) to change who we are. We thrive on change, excitement, chaos, and immediate gratification. Not good when it comes to saving money. When you hear how Warren Buffett made his *billions* by buying low (undervalued) stocks, holding them, and waiting for the market to recognize their hidden value, it sounds so . . . mundane. But that's where wealth comes from. Saving, investing, and long-term thinking. Bummer.

This is an especially hard pill to swallow because the latest wealth that was created quickly by technology stocks allowed people to become very rich, very fast. But the market has a way of humbling people. Some made a fortune but got greedy and lost it all. Others took their money out and put it into things that were safer and invested wisely. Still others lived so large that when the stock market took a tumble they were caught with their (very expensive) pants down. They spent their (paper) riches on new clothes, eating at the best restaurants, travel, or renting a nice home. They were really just one bad market away from being in trouble.

Let me say this to you: Luxuries are not as important as your dreams. The Joneses are idiots, so stop trying to keep up with them. Isn't it more important to pursue your passion and not possessions? What is your idea of wealth? To lie on the beach all day, every day? To have happiness, contentment, focus, direction, passion, freedom, fame, purpose, or critical acclaim? This doesn't require money. Even so, how much money would make you *feel* wealthy? Why do you want wealth? What would you do if you didn't have to work? If you do what this chapter tells you, it's possible. Being an artist isn't easy. You may never have the security and riches of someone with a regular job, but if you play your cards right, you can be better off.

By not paying 18 to 20 percent interest on your credit card debt, you would be earning 18 to 20 percent more, tax-free.

Your Net Worth

"A rich man is nothing but a poor man with money."
—W. C. Fields

Let me begin by saying you are wonderful the way you are. Your value is your talent, skill, and ability. Your gift of being able to create things is *invaluable.* I know, if only someone else would recognize that and drop large bushels of cash at your door just for being you. Actually, that's not as far-fetched as it sounds. When David Bowie went public (not about *that*) and offered to sell stock in himself by creating "Bowie bonds," which Prudential bought, he became human capital. But the definition of your net worth is more mathematical and material than putting a price on your talent. Your net worth is what you own minus what you owe. You take your assets (your assets include cash, of course, plus any investments you own, your personal property, art, clothes, and the equity you have in real estate) minus liabilities (debt), and that gives you your net worth. (Yes, it can be a negative number.) When you do the math and you get a negative number, then you have a negative net worth. Yikes! Figuring out your net worth may also surprise you when you learn you have more than you thought. No matter what the number, you'll always want more. Why do we never seem to appreciate what we have? Either way, this is a snapshot of your life at this time. The health of your finances can change. That means the diagnosis of your condition is reversible and not terminal. This is just a test or biopsy to determine what's wrong. There is a cure that can make you (financially) healthy again that we'll discuss in a minute.

In the book *Stop Worrying About Money!* author Mitch Gallon came up with the best way to figure out your net worth that I have ever come across. He says to pretend you are going to Tahiti for a job with the condition that you have to start next month and you can take only cash and the shirt on your back. How much money do you think you could get your hands on after selling off everything (after paying off your debts)? The answer is your net worth. What you have minus what you owe. Once you are done you may say, "Wow! Look at all those zeros." Yes, but two of them come after a decimal point. Ouch!

💰 ACTION ITEM

Your net worth should be one to three years of your annual income. More than three years is awesome! The average median household's net worth in the United States is $79,600. (Examples are in parentheses.)

What is your age?	_____(36)
What is your income? (Before tax.)	_____($24,000)
Multiply your age by your income.	_____($864,000)
Divide the above number by ten.	_____($86,400)
Now double that number.	_____($172,800)

This is what your net worth should be now to get ready for retirement. How do you stack up? _____

Marry Rich?

"Money is always there but the pockets change."
— Gertrude Stein

Did that subhead get your attention? "Marry rich"? Puh-leeze. That's so wrong, I agree. So does Cher, who said, "My mom once told me, 'Honey, you marry a rich man.' I said, 'Mom, I *am* a rich man.'" There you go. You want to create your *own* wealth. How? The answer is simple, but putting the principles into practice is not. Rules number 1–100 on how to become wealthy are the same—spend less than you make. Repeat after me. "I will spend less money than I take in." Simple, right? Uh, no. But doable. This book includes all kinds of creative ways to make money and even more ways to spend less. All you have to do is pick a couple and put them into practice.

Making more money but spending more does not increase your

wealth. My buddy got a big bump in salary but still had to do side jobs to stay afloat. He was deep in debt. He makes over $250,000 a year but never saves and actually spends more than he makes (if you can believe that) on stupid stuff. He does own a beautiful, BIG home in a nice neighborhood, but he put down the minimum and then almost immediately took out a second mortgage on the home. His nice new car is leased, for which he pays $600 a month plus insurance, gas, and repairs. Basically, he spends everything he makes—and then some—with nothing saved. When he lost his job he was in deep excrement. What you spend has nothing to do with your wealth (except to lower it). When you spend and spend you can never save anything. If you look at my friend's net worth, it's a negative number. People spend money they haven't even made yet to buy things they don't need to impress people they don't like (and who don't care).

Another guy lives in a modest home, drives a used car, is a compulsive saver, doesn't make much a year, but what he does make he reinvests in his business. By reinvesting in his business he doesn't pay tax on that money (which is growing and thus increasing his net worth). The more you take home the more Uncle Sam takes. If you make $100,000 a year, does that make you wealthy? Nope. You need to build something or buy something that will increase in value or pay dividends. You can't get rich working by the hour. You must invest money and make it work for you. Or invest in yourself. Increase your assets (real estate, stocks, art) by investing in something that appreciates. You just put your money to work and watch it multiply while you lie on the beach sipping a piña colada.

Look at those creative people who have wealth—not just super salaries, but real net worth—and do what they did. Success leaves clues. It's no mystery, and you don't have to be Sherlock Holmes to figure out what it takes to make millions, and better yet, be worth millions. The question is, are you willing to pay the price? If you model yourself after the masters of money, you will at least know which path to take. The choice is yours. Do you buy a new car or start your own business? Take a trip or buy stocks? Your choices affect your wealth.

It's also a mind-set. What does "rich" mean to you? How much money would make you feel wealthy? There isn't a whole lot of difference between $1 million and $10 million except the sacrifice it would take to make the other $9 million. Is it worth it to you? Wealth is more about security than it is a dollar amount. After losing money in the market, many people feel insecure even if they still have a million. As John Updike once said, "Sex is like money—only too much is enough."

Quick Quiz

What is stopping us from increasing our worth? Take this quiz and see if any of these apply to you.

1. I spend more than I make, and I often spend money without thinking.
2. I owe a lot in credit card debt.
3. I could die tomorrow, so why save? I like to live for today, the hell with the future.
4. I don't know how to invest, so I don't.
5. I work for someone else.
6. I rent instead of own a home.
7. When I do get a big payday I tend to blow it on things that decrease in value.

 FAST FACT

Do you have what it takes? According to *Forbes*, of those who made the current *Forbes* 400 (average net worth $3 billion), 263 were entirely self-made. One hundred and eight never graduated from college. Forty-six were women (as of 2001).

"Budget" Is a Dirty Word

"I've been sort of crabby lately. It's that time of the month again—the rent's due."

—Margaret Smith

In 1971 it was reported that Rolling Stones guitarist Keith Richards was spending roughly $1,000 for food, $1,000 for booze, $2,500 for illegal substances, and $2,500 for rent each week. Yet all of this was well within his means. They say don't spend more than you make, so I wanted to find out if I was living below my means. According to the Bureau of Labor Statistics, the average annual household spending was $35,535 in 1998. Here's where the money went: $11,713 on housing, $6,616 for transportation, $4,810 for food, $1,746 for fun, and a few thousand for this and that. Budgeting doesn't have to mean deprivation. Still, "budget" is a bad word to the creative person. As we've established, we'd rather live for today, the hell with tomorrow, with very little concern for accumulating great wealth or saving some money for later. But budgeting means you move some money around so that you are still able to do what you want, but eliminate some of the things that cost money and give you little in return (either in pleasure or helping you reach your goals). It's not so bad. Let's start by looking at where your money goes.

A REAL LIFE STORY

"I was having a real problem managing money. My biggest weakness was spending like crazy on my credit card. I just couldn't help myself. One day when my defenses were down, I told my mother about my financial woes. The scolding she gave me reminded me of when I was a kid. So I had a creative idea. I pasted a picture of my mom on the front of my credit card. Nothing, and I mean nothing, has worked as well as this in helping to curb my credit card use. One look at my mom and I am feeling so guilty about charging something that I will pay cash or just go without. It has made a big difference to me and my debt and spending habits," wrote a reader to my website.

Where Does It All Go?

"I was street-smart—but unfortunately the street was Rodeo Drive."

—Carrie Fisher

Write down what you *think* you spend in a month. We'll get back to that figure later. Now you need to know what you *really* spend each month. It's not as tedious as it sounds. I did it, and so can you. I went out and bought (not a good start, is it?) a little notebook like reporters or cops use and began keeping track of *every* dollar I spent. The first month I did it without judgment. I simply wrote down what I bought and how much it cost. If I didn't have my notebook with me, I just put the receipts in my pocket and entered them when I got home. It became a habit (a good one), and almost instantly I became very aware of where my money went. I started to get in touch with my money and where it disappeared to. Before, I would pull some money out of the ATM on a Friday, and by Monday it was gone. Where it went I couldn't tell ya. Now I could—and it was eye-opening!

I totaled what I spent each day and came up with a monthly figure. After doing this for two months, I started to set some goals of what I would (and wouldn't) spend in a month. You can take this exercise as far as you can tolerate. You can total up how much you spend each month in each area, such as "food," "clothes," or "gas." The advanced course is to record what you spend and why. "I was feeling flush so I bought gifts for my friends" or "I was feeling down and I thought I needed a pick-me-up, so I bought some new strappy sandals." Even if you do this just for an awareness of what you spend, it's worth doing. Once you start tracking how much you spend, you quickly realize how much you waste every month (then multiply that number by twelve, and it gets really frightening). It's funny: You think you know how much you spend in one area, and then you realize you were way off.

I also went back and found all the yearly expenses that I pay once or twice a year, like gym dues, property taxes, and insurance, plus any unexpected one-time expenses, and I prorated them. I added that up and divided by twelve. I did this by going back two years, looking at my check register and old credit card statements for clues. The mystery was now solved. I knew where my money went, and I was appalled to discover where I was overspending and where I was neglecting. I highly recommend you go through old credit card statements and your check register. You will quickly realize how much it costs just to live. It's a wake-up call, that's for sure. Reality and clarity don't just rhyme, they go hand in hand. That's what you get when you explore where your money goes. It should make you more determined to either make more money or spend less (or both). At least try to rearrange your spending so that your money goes to things that mean more to you. Run "what if" scenarios to see what would happen if you made some changes in your spending. At the very least, it will help you get a little more organized.

Are you happy with where you are now, financially speaking? If you said "no," then you need to pay attention to this. Fix what's "broke," and that means you need to diagnose the condition. It's the perfect first step to getting your finances in order. So why doesn't everyone do this? As they say, "Ignorance is bliss." Or is it? It's like a lot of things. You think by ignoring it it will fix itself or "I'll make a big score soon, and that will take care of everything." Even if you are about to score, you'll just be that much better off, and if you don't hit it big, you'll still be okay. If you are lucky enough to have created something that makes you a ton of money, this will not set you up for life unless you make some life-altering changes.

Many of the nouveau riche went nuts when their companies or stocks skyrocketed. Instead of buying a plane, they would buy a fleet of planes. Instead of a one-carat engagement ring, they were buying rings worth millions! Instead of a thoughtful gift, they would buy Rolexes by the dozen. I can't tell you how many times I heard people with stock options or start-up companies tell me they were going to retire in a year or two. I think you can guess what happened. They spent and spent and spent while times were good, and when the stock market tumbled, they were left with nothing (or next to nothing). Retire? I think not. Your friends, co-workers, or colleagues may get a new car, and your old clunker, which was fine last week, will suddenly feel like a pile of poop. Just because they got a new car shouldn't make you feel inferior. You don't know what their financial situation is. Besides, new cars are not good investments. So smile and drive on (rust, rattle, and roll, baby).

Success and financial security are not about creating wealth and wasting it. They're about using your money to create more money or to further your career. To start saving and paying off your debt. To have some set aside to survive for a few months in case it all turns to hell, or more likely, you wait to collect on a contract or have to wait for a check to clear. Actor Christopher Walken (*The Deer Hunter, Pulp Fiction*) and his wife (a casting director for shows like *The Sopranos*) live a normal life in Connecticut. He drives a Volvo (I thought it would be something sinister, like a hearse), and they are smart with their money. Says he, "I've been married over thirty years [and] I don't owe anybody money." They don't try to keep up with other celebrities and their wild spending—and neither should you. Try this for a while: Take money out for the week or month and live off that. That's a budget, by the way.

After you have tracked your spending for a month, look at the number you wrote at the beginning of this section for what you *thought* your monthly spending was. Totally unrealistic, I'll bet. The bottom line of this exercise is to get you to realize just how much it costs you to live (and how much you really spend). This awareness is key. Then take steps to try and cut down on your spending or rearrange it so that you are getting more (of what you want and need) for your money.

Incoming

"The more you get, the more you get."

—Tom Petty

In an early episode of *Friends,* Rachel (who had never had a real job before) was excited to receive her first paycheck from Gunther at the coffeehouse. When she opened it she was appalled. "That's it?" she exclaimed, "Who's FICA? And why does he get all my money?" Just like with our expenses, we *think* we know what we make, but it's a safe bet that your estimate is off. (Especially for the creative person who makes money from a multitude of sources.) Write down all the money you have coming in (under the table and otherwise). This includes rebates, refunds, residuals, and real income. When you know what you have coming in, you know what you have to work with. Then you can decide where you want to spend it for the best results—or most bang for your bucks. Go back and figure out how much you made (from everything) during the last quarter, and then project that over the rest of the year. What do you expect to make this year? Surprised? Do you need to make more? Are you both excited that it was more then you thought and alarmed because your checking account shows a zero balance? Either way, it's a very good exercise to determine how much money is coming into your life. One thing I found helpful was to get a year-at-a-glance calendar and at the top of the year write my yearly income goal. Then I figure out what I need to make each month and write it at the top of that month. Then I put in gigs and what they pay plus advance money and royalties and subtract that number from the goal to see how much more I need to earn. Any extra or a deficit rolls over to the next.

💰 ACTION ITEM

Run your personal life like a business. Think profits and bottom line. What's the minimum you need to live on to cover your basic expenses? How much more money do you need for the "this and that" stuff? Add those two numbers together to figure out how much money you need/want to spend each month. Keep in mind that expenses include fixed things you can't get rid of easily (like loans, alimony, taxes, child support, rent, car payments, and insurance. Variable costs include phone, utilities, gas, clothes, vacations, supplies, food, postage, ads, travel, and so on). Then multiply by twelve. Calculate your work. (Forty hours a week × fifty weeks is 2,000 hours a year, divide that by your yearly expenses.) Two thousand divided by yearly expenses equals the hourly rate you need to earn just to break even. Is it a negative number? Are you just breaking even? Start to look for things you can live without. What do you feel you can cut back on? You can probably trim expenses without even noticing it. The word "budget" doesn't conjure up images of wealth, but believe me, it is the key. If you can associate living on less as a positive thing, you'll be better off for it and may even embrace it. Remember, your options are to make more money or spend less—or both. Try this affirmation on for size: "I handle money well. I am debt-free. I save money."

💰 FAST FACT

We are living longer. If you are a man you can expect to live to 75, and a woman's life expectancy is 81 years. Having something saved for your "golden years" is important.

Jesus Saves

"It doesn't matter if you're rich or poor, as long as you've got money."

—Joe E. Lewis

Okay, so Jesus saves people. But we can save ourselves, so to speak. When I say "save," I mean putting something aside for our future. We all know that we should, but most don't do it. In 1999 the personal savings rate in the United States dropped below zero for the first time since the Depression. Man, oh man. The question isn't, can I save? It's am I willing to pay the price? Are you willing to do without something now so you can have it (and more) later? You can either pay now or pay later. When you pay now (meaning pay yourself by putting something aside), you are ahead of most creative people. It gives you an edge. Do you want to be able to achieve a dream? Have a feeling of peace and prosperity? Have a huge burden lifted off your shoulders? Or does living paycheck to paycheck or project to project mean living dangerously? Is being one crisis away from disaster stimulating? I find it stressful—how about you? When you are strapped for cash it can mean being strapped down to a project or job you hate. You feel like your life isn't your own. The bank, boss, and other buggers own you. You have very little control over your life. There are a lot fewer options for someone who has to make money or die a painful (debt-ridden) death. Maybe what could motivate some of us to save is to look at all the good things that can happen if we set some money aside. It's worth a shot, anyway.

• **Save Face.** Having some money saved equals freedom. Freedom to choose what you want and don't want to do. Freedom from worry (at least about money) and the freedom of doing things you want to do. "Money frees you from doing things you dislike. Since I dislike doing nearly everything, money is handy," cracked Groucho Marx. You don't want to be in a position that you have to do something that could be detrimental to your creative health. Not that I would ever be asked to pose nude (the thought should scare you), but some do desperate things in desperate times. You need "screw you" money. Then you can tell people to go to hell and still pay the bills. You may not even have to temp or work a real job, either. Instead, you can do work you are passionate about without worrying about money. If you have some money socked away you may not have to raise money or, put another way, you won't have to grovel.

• **Save Your Sanity.** There is a lot less pressure when you have money to fall back on. You'll feel more secure, and you can concentrate on your art. You definitely don't want to be desperate. Money in the bank is a boost to your brain. It's one less thing you have to worry about, and so it's less of a distraction. You can rest easier. Have a sense of security. If you lost your job would you become a bag lady and be homeless and mumbling to yourself? Although that's an unlikely scenario, worrying about it can be very real and taxing. With some savings, you can take a break between projects and even take some time off! Maybe even take a vacation. Increase your savings, and you increase your self-esteem and self-WORTH. You'll be worth more, and more importantly, you'll *feel* like you are worth more.

• **Save Your Career.** It takes a long time to build a creative career. You will likely have to do a lot of things that don't pay right away—if ever. *Down Beat* magazine named bassist Dave Holland "Bassist of the Year" in 2000. He was a sideman for some of the biggest names in jazz before breaking out on his own. Critics loved his solo work, but it didn't translate into sales or bookings. It took him a long time to build up grassroots support for his quintet. Projects can take forever to get going. The time lines are very long for many creative endeavors. You have to budget for these long waiting periods. You need cash flow. It's also smart to have an emergency fund, just in case.

• **Save Some for Later.** Save so you can retire one day. According to my Social Security statement (everyone should have gotten one in the mail by now), I would have to live on less than $1,000 a month when I retire. What a wake-up call! It's distressing to see how little you've made and how much you won't have waiting for you. Most people don't understand this. To avoid paying taxes, maybe you took your taxable income down to as close to zero as possible and less was set aside. You are supposed to save for yourself. If you work for someone else, you should take advantage of your employer's retirement plan. By the way, the retirement age for those born after 1960 is now sixty-seven (not sixty-five years old) to collect benefits.

What About Your kids? It can cost tens of thousands to send a kid to college. Only 56 percent of families with kids twelve or younger have begun to save for college. "We are just going to do the best we can and hold our breath and hope that we've set enough money aside for their therapy," jokes Michelle Pfeiffer.

• **Save for a Rainy Day.** Mae West once said, "Save a boyfriend for a rainy day, and another in case it doesn't rain." How can I spin that into something useful? Ah, I know. A woman I know owned an ad agency and was living LARGE. Times were good. She landed a major client (a national chain of restaurants) and spent everything she made on a high-rent office and other trappings. She spent all of her time working on this account, instead of marketing to get other clients, she put all of her eggs in this basket. Suddenly the client decided to "go in a different direction" and fired her firm (even though they won several awards for their ad campaigns). She had based her expenditures on that money coming in and went out of business three months later. There are cycles in the lives of creatives. When it rains it pours, followed by a long drought. It's inevitable. You must live on LESS than you make, or else you won't make it over the long haul and through the tough times. You *know* what I mean. Publishers don't care about your rent, so you have to. Also, as a creative person you can be dropped at any time. You are only as good as your last project, as they say. If you experience slower sales than you expected, you may be cut loose—or have no royalties coming in. My buddy got a nice advance check. He started spending like crazy. He was so busy partying that he never finished his book. When he didn't turn in the book on time, they asked for the money back. Of course, he'd spent it, so they sued him. It was *ugly*.

• **Save Yourself.** The expression that "you need money to make money" is true. If you are unable to find someone to produce or publish your work, you can always produce or publish it yourself—if you have some money. Once you have something in play, you will probably need to promote it. This can be done cheaply, but you will still need some cash. Another saying, "Buy low and sell high," is true when it comes to buying and selling stocks. If the market is sagging you want to have a stash of cash to buy stock in the next Microsoft.

It's also nice to not have to depend on others. In an emergency your parents will probably bail you out. But what if they start going to the "tough love" theory of parenting and cut you off? Besides, what money doesn't come with strings attached?

💰 ACTION ITEM

If you keep going the way you are, where will you be in ten years? What is the worst possible outcome? Now write a happy ending. Think for a minute about how you want to live when you are older. How much money will you need? Where do you see it coming from?

Ten Reasons Why We Won't Save

"Save a little money each month, and at the end of the year you'll be surprised at how little you have."

—*Ernest Haskins*

1. "When I make more, then I'll save" is our excuse. Some people make $250,000 and can't save. Yet some teachers, who make far less, *are* able to save. For example, a former teacher of mine who taught art and *loved* what he did (and didn't do it for the money) was able to save. Teaching was his calling. He also didn't want to be destitute when he was older. He wanted to paint. He wanted to travel. So he had $100 a week deducted from his paycheck automatically and put into a mutual fund. He now lives the life he envisioned when he sacrificed that $100 week after week. Don't procrastinate. Do it now, even if it's just a few bucks here and there. If you are waiting for the right time, it will never happen. Forty percent of all women worry that they will be living in poverty when they retire. So do something about it now, even if you can barely pay your bills and say, "There is *no* way! It can't be done!" You are probably thinking you need to put aside a lot of money or why bother. Just set aside a little when you can. Once you start, it gets easier and you actually start to enjoy it.

2. We feel like the good times will last forever. Getting that first big paycheck is a rush. You feel *rich* and figure this is just the start. So you say things like, "I friggin' worked my tail off for this money, and now I am going to enjoy it." Or maybe after a little success you decide to quit your day job and now have less money coming in but are spending like crazy. Sometimes when you are flush with success it gives you a false sense of security. When times are good many people get complacent. Some of the younger people today (I can't believe I just wrote that—I *am* getting old) have never seen tough times. It's a good bet they will.

3. You have nothing to save for. When you have a plan for the future, it seems a little less stressful when you have some money set aside. Let's face it, the future will be here sooner than you think, and it's more than likely you are going to need some money to enjoy it. You don't want to look back and say to yourself, "Damn! What was I thinking? If only I had stashed some of my earnings when I had the chance." Live for today and *plan* for tomorrow. Ask yourself, if I continue on my current path, where will I be (financially) in a few years?

4. You don't want to give up the good life. Saving money means (to many people) that they'll have to give up something today to be able to put something away for tomorrow. Well, that's true. You may have to live on a *little* less. But you can still have a life! This is a hard sell to the right-brainer who wants what she wants when she wants it. Saving? Boooooooring. It goes deeper than not wanting to be responsible and an adult. I suspect it has something to do with our DNA. "I totally appreciate being able to buy, say, this thousand-dollar cashmere blanket. I do. Because if I couldn't, I would hate the fact that I would have to go back to real, regular blankets," says Stevie Nicks. Hmmmmm. Damn the consequences, we want to spend!

5. Not to worry. Someone or something will save me. I have seen creative people spend all of their money and then some while waiting for a deal to go through. Then, when all of a sudden the deal doesn't materialize, they are *deep* in debt. Some actually believe they are going to win the lottery. Others figure their parents are saving for them and will bail them out if they get into trouble. On *Friends* (I realize there are a lot of television references in this book, but I think you can learn a lot from watching TV, anyway), Monica, who was terminally single for so long, told her parents that she was finally going to get married (to Chandler). Her parents had to break the news to her that they had spent "Monica's Wedding Fund" on a beach house. Fortunately, Chandler was a "little saver" and squirreled away enough for the "scenario A" wedding. But waiting to be rescued or for a windfall is a little too iffy for me.

6. Some simply don't believe in saving. "Saving is for sissies," they will say. They think that saving money is something left-brainers do, not them. In a strange way, I think some creative people like being perpetually starving artists or are afraid that too much money will make them soft. There is also the "Oh, what's the use" syndrome. The thinking is, it's hopeless. They are in such dire financial straits that they feel there is no point in putting anything away. Whatever the mental block (and we didn't even get into the influence our parents have had on us and how we are either emulating them or rebelling against them), some people just don't see the value in saving for the future. What're you gonna do?

7. Some of us start to save, but life's little tragedies keep getting in the way. We get a tax return, but the car breaks down. The journey of a million miles begins with a flat tire and a busted fan belt. Maybe we finally earn some royalties, but Nordstrom is having a sale. (I'm kidding about that last one.) In truth, if we have even a minor setback, we bail on saving altogether. Admit it, I'm right, aren't I? We figure, "Aw, screw it. I give up. I'm just gonna spend it all." Wrong approach.

8. The future will take care of itself. We may feel we can work forever, so why save for retirement? We love what we do, so why stop doing it? It may be that you'll want to work forever, but will there always be a market for what you do? Just something to think about. Tiffany Darwish's career fizzled after two albums in the '80s. Her mansion, cars, and shopping sprees ("If I liked it, I bought it," she says) made her monthly bills in the five figures. She has since downsized dramatically.

9. Don't know how to save. Maybe we never learned the value of a dollar or how to save and invest and don't realize how wonderful it is to have some money saved up. Maybe we don't realize we have control over money and that it doesn't have to slip through our fingers. It's never too late to change.

10. Easy come, easy go. We don't appreciate money because it comes in a lump sum and it seems like it will last forever. But as your savings slowly but surely dwindles, you start to realize how wrong you were. When you get a big paycheck, earn a bonus, collect an advance, make a big sale, finally see some royalty money, get an inheritance, Uncle Sam kicks you back some money, or you win a lawsuit, this is the *best* time to save some.

How to Save Yourself

"Saving is a fine thing, especially when your parents have done it for you."

—Winston Churchill

A Merrill Lynch study says that 70 percent of youngsters between the ages of twelve and seventeen save and 22 percent have mutual funds or own stocks. So what the hell happens when we turn eighteen? For one thing, we can now drive ourselves to the mall. Two, our parents no longer control the purse strings, so we are free to do what we want with our money. And three, we learned what "Visa" and "Master-card" mean. You have to have the strength and discipline to give up a little now for financial freedom later. This is not a concept that people seem to get until it is nearly time to retire. There will be a tomorrow, and God willing, you will be in it. Do you want to be homeless, combing the beach for aluminum cans, or kickin' it in your beach-front home?

Maybe projecting yourself that far into the future isn't doing it for you. Try this on for size. Add up your monthly expenses and multiply by four. This is the minimum amount you need to save so you won't have to be out on the street if you didn't work for four months. If we don't put some money aside before our right-brained selves spend it, we will never save. That's why the advice of "pay yourself first" actually works. You think you can't possibly live on less than you do, but you'd be surprised. No matter what your situation is now, you can save some money. You may have to force yourself, but if you make it a habit it becomes second nature to put away a piece of everything you make. Go ahead and open a savings account or stick it under your mattress, but whatever you do, start building your net worth. Here's some suggestions.

• **Take small steps.** A little at a time adds up. Years ago actor Robert Hays (*Airplane!*) lived in his van and made $45 a week working at the Old Globe Theatre in San Diego and other odd jobs. "I was collecting $47 a week unemployment, and then I lost the unemployment because I got a job making $45 a week. Then I got an apartment with a friend of mine. I think the rent was $110 a month, $55 each. From when I was little my father taught me how to save money. Before you pay your bills, you pay yourself first. So take 10 percent and put it in the bank. Ten percent of my $45 a week was $45, so I rounded it up to $50 and would always stop by the savings and loan and stick $50 in there. I'd use the rest to pay my bills. At the end of the season, I remember some of the Equity actors at the Globe getting paid five times as much as I was every week, and they were tapped out. They'd spent all their money, and I had $300 saved up."

• **Make it automatic.** Your employer can do it. A bank can do it, too. You can even have your agent pull out 10 percent from your checks (That's in addition to the 15 to 20 percent they take for themselves—bastards). Have them put it into a mutual fund and monitor it yourself. (If you make automatic payments to a mutual fund, they will usually wave the minimum initial requirement.) Some artists are on an allowance (so are many husbands) and can spend only so much a month. Make saving a habit. Treat it like a bill to pay, and just write that check like you would your rent. Wouldn't it be nice if we could use a credit card and a percentage would automatically go to savings?

• **Maybe you need something to save for.** When you know what you want (the pot of gold at the end of the rainbow, so to speak) you can see how this suffering will pay off. What do you want? How much will it cost? How much/little do you have saved? What do you need to save to get it? It's easier to say no to wasteful spending when you have a goal. Put up a picture of it. Buy a mini version of it. Put the number on your wall, and in your wallet. I made a piggy bank with a picture of a new longboard I want to buy on it. (The piggy bank looks like an old Woody surfmobile.) At the end of the day I throw my change in it. Then I started stuffing ones in it. I would deduct the amount from the total needed as I added to it, which left the amount to go. Or make a savings chart and watch it grow. (It is very inspiring.) Make a reward for reaching a savings goal. Celebrate your success. When you save up for something you are a better consumer. You buy smarter, take care of it better, enjoy it more, and make it last longer.

• **Increase earnings or reduce spending.** If your dream is to quit your job and work on your novel for a year, let's get real, shall we. How much would you need to have saved to hold you over without any money coming in? How can you cut back? (Two biggies are car and rent as well as your debt.) Are you doing all you can do to cut back? When you begin to live on less, you'll feel a slight sense of loss. Go ahead and grieve. Better yet, find productive ways to replace your excessive lifestyle with healthier and fun alternatives. So you skip your annual trip to the tropics this year. Do something closer to home. But don't give in to the feeling of "what's the point" and give in to your urge to go back to spending everything you make. Reward yourself occasionally with a luxury, but for the most part put needs before wants. Don't ignore the other side of the equation. Look for income opportunities. Just think, if you make $4,500 a month but can earn $500 more and put that away, by the end of the year you will have $6,000 plus interest. Live off the other $4,500 a month.

• **Quit a bad habit and use the savings to start a savings.** Give up a bad habit and put the savings in a savings account. Guitarist Walter "Wolfman" Washington had a weekly gig at the Maple Leaf Bar in New Orleans when he wasn't on the road performing and promoting his albums. Early in his career he toured with singer Lee Dorsey making $500 a week (a lot back then) and made it a point to take $100 for spending money and send the rest home for his mother to hold. After two years he asked his mom how much he had. She told him he had saved up $43,000. So he decided to stay home and go solo.

• **Try to save 10 to 40 percent of any big checks you get.** Save half of any raises or royalties. Put it right in the bank. Maybe this year you could use your tax refund to open a savings account or pay off any credit cards. If you are paying, say, 19 percent interest but could only earn at best 10 percent by investing or saving your money, you would be better off paying down your debt. At the very least start an emergency fund that can be used for, well, emergencies. In case "it" hits the fan, you'll be all right as long as you've set aside some for a rainy day when your house floods, for instance, or you need new tires. Only then can you tap into this fund. Need a new suit for a job interview, debatable, but go ahead and tap in. You're not going to go broke as long as you have this money. If you have to dip into savings, set a minimum amount you will not let it dip below. No exceptions. Put it into something that will earn more than a savings account but you can get your hands on it without paying a penalty. Keep it simple. Investments that grow without a lot of muss or fuss are best.

Investigating Investing

"The safest way to double your money is to fold it over once and put it in your pocket."

—*Frank Hubbard*

The above quote isn't entirely true. January is one of the most dangerous months to speculate on stocks. The others are February, March, April, May . . . Ha, ha, ha. There aren't many things in life that you can count on like the growth in the stock market. Investing probably isn't the area in which you want to flex your creative muscles. Stocks and mutual funds (and maybe real estate) are better than investing in coins, collectibles, or cars. Many successful artists have some strange ideas about what to do with their money, and it makes for interesting reading but not something you want to emulate. For example, musician John Entwistle collects teapots, Morrissey is into 1950s wrestling magazines, and Eric Clapton collects guns. I want to suggest some safe and secure (maybe even boring) ideas for your money that will work for you while you do what you do best—create. You can go your own way, but at least I feel I gave it a good shot to get you into something that is less like gambling and more of a sure thing and will grow at a steady rate.

We want to create a money-making machine that pays you without you having to work. Oh, now you're interested. Good. Now that I have your attention, how would you feel about having money coming in that you didn't even have to work for? You would be free to do whatever you wanted with your time without having to worry about money. Sounds like a dream, doesn't it? If you wake up and smell the coffee, it can be your reality. It IS possible, and it ISN'T that hard. Again, I have to ask, If you keep going the way you are going, where will you be in five, ten, fifteen years? Instead, create things that pay you back and earn income. It makes sense. The goal is to replace your salary with cash flow from income-producing assets like your art, rental property, a business, retirement funds, investments, and stocks. At the least, you want to have something put aside so that if, heaven forbid, there is a slowdown, you lose your job, or go through a slump, you don't go deep (or deeper) into debt, or worse. If you don't do anything about your financial future, it will remain a dream—or worse, a nightmare. Start small and make some minor adjustments now.

 ACTION ITEM

What Have You Always Dreamed of Doing, Being, Having? When you have a dream you can see how the things you do TODAY will affect you tomorrow.

Putting Your Money to Work (So You Don't Have To)

"I'd like to live like a poor man with lots of money."
—Pablo Picasso

If you gave up a latte a day you would have over $1,000 a year to invest. You'd be awfully grumpy, but you would be on your way to financial freedom. You can open a money-market account with as little as $100. Could you do something with your art that would generate an extra $100 a month that you could use for your future financial freedom? Could you live on $100 less a month? Try putting some money in a piggy bank or under your pillow before you pay your bills, to use for investing. Take some off the top and put it toward the dream. "But I'm so deep in debt I think I can barely pay the minimums on my credit card bills." You don't *have* to wait until you are debt-free (or you may never invest!) before beginning to invest. Pay down that debt AND also invest. Invest in a place to live. This is your biggest single expense, it can also be an investment. It serves two purposes. It can appreciate, and there are tax benefits on the interest you pay—plus it gives you a roof over your head. Invest in yourself, too. Use your money to buy supplies, equipment, education, and whatever you need to do your art. Don't go overboard, but put 10 percent into the best investment of all—you.

Keep it simple. You don't want your investments to take up too much of your time, and you certainly don't want them to be a burden. Simple, somewhat safe, and something you understand is the goal. It should give you peace of mind and not use a piece of your mind. Investing can be an overwhelming proposition, you can end up paralyzed. Things like high-quality, no-load mutual funds come to mind. You can pick a mutual fund by yourself and start to build your portfolio (the other kind of portfolio). Choose to invest in things that interest you and involve something you enjoy learning about or already have knowledge of or experience with.

Think long term. Most day traders lose money trying to outsmart the market and make a big score. They would make more if they bought smart stocks and just held them. They would have less ulcers, too. Think about tax implications. Getting a good tax break will help you in the short term (we like that), and the investment itself will be beneficial in the long term. Money invested over the long haul does almost as well as short-term big scores. Slow growth is the best way to be rich.

Risky Business

"Growth, income, and stability are like the three primary colors. They can combine to create any desired variation."
—Jason Kelly

No investment is entirely risk-free, but some are certainly safer than others. Risk is what you are willing to give up in order to get a goal. The key is the words "give up." When criminals are asked why they did something like steal a car, they may say, "I never thought I would get caught." When the weathercaster says there is a 25 percent chance of rain, we focus on the word "rain." Same thing with investing. Look at the worst-case scenario, and let it sink in. If the worst were to happen, would that be cool with you? Run this worst-case scenario through your mind. The younger you are the more likely you'll be able to bounce back. They say it's like betting on horses. "The higher the risk, the higher the reward." You know, longer odds pay off more when your horse comes in. Not always! Sometimes things are very risky and will never pay off. Safe isn't sexy and we are daredevils.

Don't be Evel Knievel with your money. You can play it safe and earn 5 to 10 percent a year without a lot of risk. What's so bad about that? If you had $500,000 and put it into something safe, you could earn $25,000–$50,000 a year. Careful investments like this would allow you to quit or scale back your work (if you wanted to) and do what you really want. It's freedom. Focus on that for a minute. Being able to spend your time the way you want.

The advice to the creative person is this: Take some money and put it in a safe place and then take some risks with the rest. Not all risk is bad. It depends on your tolerance level. There is also the risk that if you leave your money in one place you may miss an opportunity to invest it elsewhere for a higher rate of return. Safe isn't always all good, either. Inflation is roughly 3 percent per year, so you need to be making at least that or you are losing money.

All that said, many of the portfolios of the super-rich have a portion of their assets in risky forms. If you were on *Millionaire* and could walk with $250,000 or take a guess on an answer for a possible $500,000 payday, which would you choose? Remember, if you get it wrong you would walk away with only $64,000. Keep in mind—you don't have to get the highest return possible. It's not always worth the risk. Greed has gotten a lot of smart people into trouble.

Truth or Dare?

Do you like taking risks? Answer the following true or false questions and see.

- Do you like to push the envelope and take chances in whatever you do?
- Drive too fast or don't wear your seat belt?
- Are *not* afraid to get up to sing, play, speak, or talk to complete strangers?
- Ever took off alone for a vacation? Hitchhiked?
- Shaved your head or went with a crazy hairdo?
- Went skydiving or bungee jumping? Gone nude at a beach or pool?
- Went on a blind date? Don't wear a condom or require a partner to wear one?

- Sneaked into somewhere for free?
- Fudged on your taxes?
- Quit a job with nothing lined up?

I'd say that four or more "yes" answers and you are a risk-taker.

I SAW IT COMING

We are visual people—that's why I made a wall chart for my investments that allowed me to track them. Along the left side of my chart were these terms (in descending order): "I'm Rich," "It's Cool," "What I Paid/Break Even," "This Sucks," and "Bail!" Then I made a long line across the middle, coming out from "What I Paid/Break Even." Along the bottom of the chart were the months starting with when I began investing. Each month I would plot each stock's progress. This worked well because at a glance I could see how the investments were doing. I could follow them month by month and watch them rise and fall. I was able to sell most of these stocks at the "I'm Rich" point and the rest at "This Sucks" before they got to "Bail" and eventually became worthless.

Invest? Who, Me?

"If you aren't willing to own a stock for ten years, don't even think about owning it for ten minutes."

—Warren Buffett

The first time I sat in the front seat of a Cessna for my initial flight lesson, I looked around the cockpit and thought to myself, "There is no way!" There were gauges, switches, and levers everywhere—and this was a simple aircraft. But after a lesson or two (and with a lot of studying) it wasn't so bad. I knew what every switch, lever, and gauge did. Investing is the same way. You can learn how to invest. It's not that hard once you know what you are doing and if you choose investments you understand and not something someone told you would be hot. In the past, stocks have outperformed all other investments. When you are reading this the stock market may be down, but overall it goes up. Don't try to outsmart it—hold on and watch your investment go up. Simple and easy.

Let's say you just got an advance of $50,000 and used it to go on a vacation, throw a party, and get some new clothes, a new car, and a watch. Let's fast-forward two years into the future. None of these will increase in value. What you bought are worn, worn out, or gone. If you just took two-thirds of that advance and invested it, here's what would have happened. You could still have had the party (I say celebrate your success) and the watch (Rolexes actually hold their value). But buying things that don't pay you back like a car, vacation, clothes, treats, and other luxuries just isn't being smart with money. Your money isn't working for you when you buy things that decrease in value. Sorry, but putting some of that advance aside to invest is being *smart* with money. How much you put away depends on YOUR dream. Paul Simon bought a red Impala convertible with the few thousand dollars he split with Art Garfunkel as a result of their song "Hey Schoolgirl." The car burned to the ground, and so did all of his share of the record. Fortunately, he was only sixteen and had a few (hundred) more hits left in him.

With investing, time is on your side. Years ago my grandfather offered my brothers and me a few dollars at the holidays or we could wait while he took a dime and doubled it for eight days. I took the fifteen bucks and ran. But if I had waited for eight days, that dime doubled (cumulatively) would have been worth fifty bucks. Is your money growing now? Has what you are doing or have done produced wealth? If it isn't earning interest, it isn't working for you the way it could. If all your money is going to Visa or Mastercard, then it is working against you.

Are You Ready to Invest?

1. Is using a Magic Eight Ball your method of choosing stocks?
2. Do you look at investing as gambling?
3. Do you expect a 50 percent return on your investment?

The correct answer to all three questions is "NO!"

Take Stock

"Why, I oughta . . ."

—*John Wayne*

I am going to make a good guess here that day trading is not for you. God, I hope I am right. It is a full-time, high-stress, and dangerous proposition at best. I bet you like the excitement that comes with high-risk investments. Fine, just like in Vegas, decide how much you can afford to lose and take some chances, and then stick the rest in a safe place where it can grow. Avoid investments where you could lose it all. Anything that grows or pays you back at least a reasonable rate of return with the least possible risk is okay. Don't gamble with your future. It feels like "funny money," but it is not free money. It can easily stop rolling in, and "this thing of ours" can end. Take some of your earnings and be selective with it. Don't fritter it away. Keep some safe and secure. Many, many people have made money in the stock market. You can also lose money in the market, but you have a better chance to make money if you don't gamble and take unnecessary chances. It's not for everyone, however, and as I am sure you know, some have lost their shirts. As I like to say, the stock market doesn't kill, people do.

• **Don't overcomplicate things.** (The industry doesn't help in this regard with all that mumbo-jumbo language.) Buy and hold. Trying to figure out when to buy and sell a stock (or a bunch of different stocks) is not the best use of your time. That isn't to say it's not possible to "play" the market. Remember Gabe Kaplan, Mr. Kotter on *Welcome Back, Kotter*? It was a big hit in the 1970s. So where is he now? He did some stand-up, hosted a radio talk show, and even played professional poker for a time. Now he plays the stock market, which he contends has made him very wealthy. How does one of the most successful investors of all time, Warren Buffett, do it? He invested in Disney, Gillette, Coca-Cola, and American Express and held on to them—for years.

• **I've got a tip for you.** Just because someone else is excited about a stock doesn't mean it's right for you. You figure they did all the homework and they can save you time. So over the backyard barbecue they tell you about Webistics, it's a sure thing. First of all, nothing is a sure thing. Secondly, does it fit into your OWN investment strategy? If what you are doing is working, why blow it on a long shot? Just because this person is going to jump off a bridge, does that mean that . . . ? If your inner guide is yelling, "Don't do it, dummy," listen.

• **Become a student of the game.** At a Padres baseball game fans can stay in the game and know the score on a thirty-foot scoreboard. When I say "game" and "score" I mean the stock market. On the scoreboard, along with the score of the game they also flash how the top stocks did that day. The San Diego Padres lost a lot of games, and investors lost a lot of money. For a long time everyone was into the stock market. Everyone. It was everywhere you turned. The problem was not everyone knew what the hell they were doing in it.

Knowledge and understanding is key to making money in stocks. Four out of five people don't know what the Dow Jones Industrial Average is. (It refers to the combined price of the stock of thirty major corporations on any given day.) You don't need to know a lot. Common sense and some math skills help. So does buying stock in things you understand and are interested in. Go for what you know. David Gardner, the co-founder of the Motley Fool service for investors, tells the story of a motorcycle gang leader he met outside a bar. The biker had $5,000 to invest in the stock market. He didn't know what to buy, so he went with the recommendation of a few friends and put it all into a restaurant chain. The investment went down to $250. Had he bought stock in Harley-Davidson, a company he knew a lot about, he would have made money.

• **Trust yourself first.** David Geffen, according to *Forbes,* is worth $3.3 billion. He pulled most of his money out of the stock market and wasn't affected by the big correction that killed other investors. I bet you know as much as many "experts" do, but having someone distill everything down and then make a presentation to you and narrow your choices (that are best suited for you) makes sense. Do you want to waste your valuable time becoming an accountant, economist, or tax expert? I didn't think so. Get good help. Stocks can be complicated, and the language is written in some foreign dialect. If I want to go to sleep I will pick up a prospectus. Just holding one in my hands makes me vewy, vewy sweepy. You will pay for this advice, but it may be worth it. They can tell you when you should buy or sell, but the ultimate decision is still yours.

• **Choose wisely, grasshopper.** What stocks should you buy? Ask yourself, what kind of company would I like to own? When you buy an individual stock you are investing in a company. Invest in things you are interested in and know something about. Rocker Joan Jett made money on the market. She bought stock in things she herself consumed, including Snapple and Starbucks. "I drank it, wondered if it was public, bought it at a very low price. It became the hot drink, and I looked like a genius. Same thing with Starbucks." If you know a little about a particular industry, it gives you a little edge. You may know what people will need and want. Maybe you are a customer yourself. If you are interested in fashion, for instance, you can learn from reading the trades and other magazines you might already read, and by being an insider you can easily spot trends. Individual stocks are fun, and everyone is doing it, but it is also risky. If you don't understand an investment, don't do it. Use a whole-brain approach. Combine insight and intuition (right brain) with research and reading (left brain), and you get a balanced approach. Using your left brain you might look at a company and ask yourself, "Is this a quality company? What is the right price? Will it grow? Are there any red flags I should look for?" Then consult your right brain. "Does this feel right? What is my gut telling me?"

• **Just because you can doesn't mean you should.** The Internet is SUPERB for research and analysis. Access to tons of information is just a click away. You can get real-time quotes and accurate information twenty-four hours a day. (Warning, not all information can be trusted.) You can, if you choose, become a very knowledgeable investor. You can buy and sell stocks without having to pay commissions to a broker. The downside is that it's easier than ever to make impulsive, stupid investments that can cost you thousands. Easy access and the fact that trades cost only a few bucks can lead to meddling instead of having a long-range plan and sticking to it (better). More trades, the more you pay, and this cuts into your profit.

• **Diversity is more than a buzzword.** Being the divergent thinkers we are, you'll be happy to hear that you probably should have diversified investments. Spread the risk around. Just don't end up all over the place. You don't want your eggs all in one basket, but you want to be able to find them when you want to make an omelette. You don't want an Easter egg hunt, either. Too diversified and you'll end up with papers coming at you from all angles. It can be overwhelming and confusing. If it's too hard to stay on top of all those different investments, get a mutual fund instead and diversify within that fund.

• **Buy low, sell high.** Hot stocks as an investment strategy can work well, but it's better to buy undervalued stocks and hold them until they increase in value. When the market takes a downturn, that is the *best* time to buy. You get the marked-down version. Be a bargain shopper. Others see poverty and you see profits and prosperity. Buy and hold. Reinvest the dividends you receive in more shares. Those dividends, over time, can be a bigger boost than the rising stock price. If you are really concerned that a stock may be heading for trouble, set a scenario under which circumstances you would want to sell. It's not just the price of the stock but the industry as a whole and that company's role or position in the industry. Just in case I haven't said this yet, most people are poor at predicting the stock market. The average investor can eliminate most of the risks by buying into stable companies and being in it for the long haul.

• **The kind of stock you would bring home to meet Mom.** Sexy investments are great if you seek publicity, a high profile, and prestige. But you can do well with investments in less desirable, shall we say, areas. On *Frasier,* Niles was in the middle of a bitter divorce with Maris, his high-society wife. It turns out her family made their fortune in urinal deodorizers. Oh, the horror. There are a lot of stable investments that aren't sexy, but solid. How about a simple, stable business? Boring, but profitable. No giant gains, but safe. They make good products and provide things people will want and need. They are an industry leader (no matter what that industry is) and you can easily check them out.

Horror Story

Trying to *play* the market is dangerous, and what it really amounts to is gambling, and we know what the odds of winning at craps are. It's about not trying to make a killing but getting rich slowly and safely. The long-term trend of the stock market is upward.

I know a guy who won a large settlement after being injured at work. He decided to try to turn his thousands into millions. For a while he looked like a genius. He invested online and played the market. To him it was like playing a video game, only the stakes were much higher. It turns out he wasn't that smart, after all. He got rich, but then lost it ALL! He could have been set for life if he would have pulled the plug sooner. Instead he lost everything he had, plus some of his parents' money, on tech stocks. It was like the Gold Rush days, and he had gold-rush fever. But like the boom and then the bust of the Gold Rush, what goes up must come down. His parents didn't like the wild swings and got out. (Keep family and friends away from risky ventures. There is way too much downside.) His girlfriend left him because he spent all day watching tickertape, and his mood swung with the market. To try to redeem himself he cashed in his 401(k) and borrowed against his credit cards and invested that money in the market, which fell again, and he lost that, too. I wish this story had a happier ending, but it doesn't. If he had kept his money in something safer, he would have *earned* money.

Unlike past investors we can do it ourselves and have instant access to information. People follow the stock market on CNBC and react to every fluctuation. You can watch your net worth grow or decline in real time. I say, why suffer needlessly? This pain and pleasure takes its toll. Some will put their life on hold and live like monks while trying to outsmart the market. They usually end up with nothing. Less than nothing.

Stock Options Are an Option

It would seem that everyone was getting rich from stock options. In Silicon Valley nearly one out of three households receives options (it's more like one in twenty nationwide). This is the latest way to get rich—or not—by going to work for a start-up company that offers you stock options. They do well, you do well. That makes you loyal and willing to work eighteen-hour days for next to nothing or the promise of a pot of gold (that may never come) at the end of the rainbow (which you never see because you work so much). Stock options are shares of a publicly owned company that are offered to their employees as compensation. People already making six figures are making millions. Watching what happens to people is frightening. It makes smart people do stupid things. The wild ride causes severe anxiety. The worst part is that you are at the mercy of the market. Stock options don't guarantee anything. Like a nor'easter, one storm and you can lose everything. With the ups and *downs* of some companies (like Enron), you can lose your paper fortune in an instant. Even in a best-case scenario, if you take money out by exercising your options, there are serious tax implications. Most people don't understand the risks or how they work.

Mutual Funds Are Mutually Beneficial

A mutual fund is a collection of stocks chosen by a fund manager who makes the decisions about buying and selling. If you were to try to keep track of such a diversified portfolio, you'd never get anything else done. If you don't feel like dealing with the details of individual stocks, you can spend your time creating (and making money) and leave the rest up to the professionals. They are managed by a full-time (usually competent) professional money manager for next to nothing. Of course, do your homework and choose the right fund and the right manager. The same as for individual stocks, choose something in an area you are interested in and wouldn't mind studying up on, and like a broker, check the track record and philosophy of the manager. You want no-load (no commissions) mutual funds. If you don't want to take the time to study stocks and don't have enough money to spread around and diversify, then this may be the way to go. You can get detailed account statements and have the freedom to sell.

Some of the smartest investors say the best way to beat the market is to own every stock in America and hold it. "How the hell do I do that?" you ask. With stocks you invest in one company. With a mutual fund you are buying pieces of a lot of different companies. You can invest in a mutual fund that mirrors a stock-market index that includes all stocks in America, and hold on to it. Sounds simple. For the most part it is. It also sounds boring. It is, but boring is good when it comes to investing. If you want a thrill take a little money and invest in individual stocks, but the bulk should be safer and more secure. Stock mutual funds offer maybe the best chance for the highest possible return on your investment. You should buy bonds for income, stocks for the growth, but mutual funds for some stability. It's less risky, and there is less worry with a mutual fund than with individual stocks since they contain assorted stocks. In fact, it's a great way to make a statement about your values and beliefs. If the environment is an issue for you, you can easily find funds that target stocks that are environmentally friendly—and friendly to your bank account.

Other Investments

• Invest in yourself. Tracey Ullman is diversified. She has starred in her own TV series, appeared in films, and even had a hit single ("They Don't Know" in 1984), and now she is an entrepreneur. Her Web shop is called Purple Skirt (and Purple Pants for men) where she spotlights celebrity fashion trends and sells chic brands of clothes and accessories. "This is a business venture for me," says the star.

• Invest in others. Seth Thomas was a carpenter who was asked to construct some clocks for a Connecticut clock maker. He found his calling. Six years later he took his $1,500 savings (in 1813!) and launched his own clock company. It was wildly successful. He took the money he made from his clock company and invested in other ventures that ended up making him one of the wealthiest men in his state. On the other hand, some big stars became major investors in Planet Hollywood restaurants, which expanded like crazy before filing for bankruptcy.

• Invest in Beanie Babies? Collectibles can be very unpredictable. Collect for fun, not for funds. There are a number of reasons why this is not the safest way to go. Is it a hobby? A habit? Are you really going to be able to part with your Kiss action figures when you need to raise money to fix a leaky roof? Bob Grove collects airsickness bags and has them framed and displayed in his home. Do you think there is a large market for that? There are all kinds of crazy get-poor-quick scams or highly risky investments, like coins, commodities, futures, penny stocks, time-shares, and other "investments." Watch out.

• There are other types of investments, like Treasury bills and bonds as well as CDs, but you aren't going to get as high a rate of return as with the stock market and mutual funds.

The 4-1-1 on Your 401(k)

Singer Brandy says, "I don't want to have to work when I'm 23." Hmmm. How will she accomplish this? "I want to open a hair salon.

I want to own some buildings and rent them out. I want to be a model—you know, Gap jeans and stuff like that. I want to do the whole TV and movie production thing and have my own label." Hey, it's good to have a plan for your retirement, no matter, like, what that plan may be, "you know." According to a study, more than 56 percent of women said they were the primary investors in their families. This just reinforces what I already know: Women control most of the money in the United States in one way or another. That's not a bad thing. Many are smart with money. Their preferred investment is a 401(k) plan as well as mutual funds and stocks (and shoes?). Let's talk about investing for your future and why a 401(k) plan can be a big part of that and what makes them so important.

In 1978 the government wanted to give working Americans a tax incentive to save for retirement, and so the 401(k) plan was born. This can be an even more valuable asset than your salary. You save on taxes and save for retirement almost painlessly if you have part of your paycheck deducted and placed in this investment vehicle. Yes, it makes your paycheck smaller, and you can't touch it until you are sunning yourself in Florida at age 59½, but boy, can you save on taxes. It will reduce your taxable income, and the investment appreciates (except at Enron). Then when you retire and tool around the country in an RV, you'll have plenty of money. This is a tax-exempt retirement account that the government can't touch, and some companies will even match the money you put in. This is a great thing!

I think people are picking up on that fact. The average 401(k) balance was $40,740 in 1998, up from $31,700 in 1994. The same study by the Spectrum Group found that 54 percent of those polled had under $25,000 in their 401(k). That's okay. *Don't put all of your money into your company's 401(k)* just in case things don't go well. If the company goes belly-up you could lose your money. These investments can make you rich fast or in a worst-case scenario can be mismanaged by the employer. Since they are NOT federally insured, you could lose a lot. How healthy is your company anyway? There's a lot of risk in having all of your retirement money in one place. Would you buy that much of one stock? Probably not, so contribute accordingly and spread the wealth (and risk) around. There are penalties when you withdraw from these accounts. Touch it and you pay taxes. You also may not be able to get your hands on the money until you are vested. Also, don't borrow against your 401(k) if you can help it. If you get laid off you'll have to pay it all back plus be required to pay taxes on the amount you took out.

Intuition: Your Sixth Sense

"Money is like a sixth sense without which you cannot make a complete use of the other five."

—W. Somerset Maugham

Bruce Willis starred in the movie *The Sixth Sense* and trusted his intuition when he took a pay cut to play the part and instead took a percentage of ticket sales. The picture made more than $650 million, and Willis made millions, too. Your intuition is like having your own Yoda. The force is IN you. Trust your inner directors. Advisers are helpful, but ultimately decisions about what to do (and not do) with your money are yours and yours alone. Once you tap into this source of knowledge, it's easier to make decisions. It's like having an inner compass. When my wife and I sailed a 44-foot Benetau sailboat around the British Virgin Islands with another couple, I always felt I knew where I was going even without using a compass. He was an engineer and a TOTAL left-brainer. He sailed by the book. When it was my turn to take the helm, I think it bothered him that I sailed totally by intuition and feel. (I wasn't the one who ran us aground, either.) Is it luck or intuition that puts you in the right place at the right time? Good question. I think it's trusting your intuition that makes you seem lucky.

You know more than you think you know. For a promotional video the director asked me to put my notes away and speak off-the-cuff and from the heart. It was magic. Where did that come from? It was there all along, I just had to trust myself more. Designer Donna Karan looks into her closet at the beginning of every season and intuitively sees what is missing from her wardrobe, and then designs it. Daryl Hall says that throughout his career hit songs came to him just as he needed them. It works! You may not be able to articulate and calculate it because it is a feeling. You may have been told you are irrational, a flake, or emotional, when in reality you were actually being insightful. So even if you can't back up a feeling with hard facts, it doesn't mean it isn't right on. You have to believe in yourself and your intuition. As Ralph Waldo Emerson said, "When in doubt, trust yourself." People will try to tell you what to do, but *you* need to decide to trust yourself. If you have to ask others about a decision, then you aren't sure and may need to rethink the decision. When you have had some success you know how it feels and can duplicate it. Pay attention to how it felt when you used your intuition and it worked out. It's that source of KNOWING that can guide you. When it is so easy to decide what to do, I suspect your intuition is at work.

On the Money

Why do people lose money? Many times it is because they ignored their intuition. They trust others more than themselves, or they let their ego or left brain get in the way of their insightful side. Lee Iacocca once said, "The only mistake I ever made was not listening to my gut." Haven't you ever ignored your instincts and intuition and paid the price or had a hunch about something but did nothing and missed a golden opportunity? On the other hand, you may have listened to your inner guide, and like magic, struck gold.

With stocks you are supposed to buy low and sell high. That works only when you KNOW when that is. How do you know? Do some research, talk to the experts, read everything you can, examine the trends—*and* trust your gut. That's how you know when to cut your losses or leave an investment alone and let it ride. As Kenny Rogers said, "You gotta know when to hold 'em, know when to fold 'em." Sometimes no action is the best course of action. But how do you know? Knowing when to expand and when to pull back comes from combining both halves of your brain.

Your intuition can be beneficial when dealing with your finances. Here's an example. In early 2000 several financial analysts (I should say so-called analysts) projected a huge increase in technology stocks, singling out a few of their favorites. By December of 2000 those shares had dropped by an average of 90 percent. My friend had an uneasy feeling about tech stocks and ignored it. He let his investments ride and lost a LOT of money. If he had trusted his gut when it told him to get out, he would be wealthy. Instead, he looked at the numbers and trusted the experts. People have made bold moves that made no sense on paper but paid off even though others said it was crazy or would never work. The payoff came when they were right and everyone else was wrong.

Those who use their intuition as an early warning system, guide, and barometer are right more than they are wrong. They are able to make good decisions *without* adequate information. They can anticipate and solve problems. Have giant leaps of insight. Read people. And if you combine intuition with analytical information, you will make good, sound decisions and avoid a lot of grief. I should know. I was about to sign a contract but backed out at the last minute because I had a bad feeling about it. I was right! I would have lost a lot more than the temporary loss of face I suffered when I pulled out. On the flip side, when I met my wife for the first time, I just knew that she was *the one*. I even told the person I was with, "That's the girl I am going to marry."

 ACTION ITEM

Next time you are about to make a money-related decision, ask yourself, "How do I *feel* about this?" Get quiet and relax. Picture a stock. See if it goes up or down in your mind. Put stocks (or any decisions) on one side of a stack of cards, turn them over, and shuffle. Close your eyes and pick one (without looking at what you wrote on the other side). What images come to mind? What do you feel? Put your thoughts on the back of the card. Do this for each one. Then look at your stocks and your notes about them.

Let Your Conscience Be Your Guide

We all have the ability to use this valuable tool. Somehow school and just living in a left-brained world have squelched it. It's never too late to get in touch with the little guy warning you. It may be a click when everything comes together, a kind of epiphany. Or things don't line up and are out of alignment, and it feels wrong. Unforseen forces are at work that will bring you what you need when it's right and make it much more difficult if it's wrong. We just don't pay attention. You have a hunch, dream, gut feeling, some symbol appears over and over, coincidences, a bad feeling, an epiphany, a feeling of discomfort or desire, a sign, delays, stress, unhappiness, no energy, a creepy feeling, events feel like they are in slow motion. Recognize the signs and act or react to them. You may get a feeling of "rightness." It's a pit-of-the-stomach excitement that makes you feel like you have to make a bowel movement. (Nice picture, eh?) It is visceral. You feel the urge to act. "Come on, let's go," your little inner guide tells you. It's like a surge of energy. It's a good vibe. When Eric McCormack from *Will & Grace* got his hands on a script for the hit show, he just knew it was the one—and it was. Sometimes it is something just out of your consciousness that is bothering you. The signs that something is wrong produce a strong case of procrastination or flakiness. It's a knot in your stomach. Or the minute you say "yes" your whole being says "no." You know it is a mistake. You don't want to disappoint; you gave your word. I still say stop and go in another direction. Whatever you do, at least check in with your "little voice" before going forward. We all have one. It's just that some of us choose not to listen. Take the following quiz to see how intuitive you are.

Quick Quiz

___ I am good at reading people.

___ I have a strong sense of direction.

___ I will often get a feeling of knowing.

___ I hear voices in my head.

    (I could make a comment here, but I won't.)

___ I didn't feel right about a situation, and darn it, I was right.

___ I get flashes of insight.

___ I have had a recurring dream that came true.

___ I have had a strong yearning for something.

___ I have had a feeling of "rightness" before and I was right.

___ I have a metaphor or symbol (or sign) that keeps popping up.

___ My life is full of coincidences. I am lucky.

___ I will get severe discomfort (or a gut reaction) about people, places, or things.

___ I had a hunch, played it, and it was right.

___ I can recall a time when I could not get something going, let it go, and it was the right thing to do.

If you were able to check three or more things, you are an intuitive person.

To get in touch with your intuitive side, try these tips and techniques.

• **Slow down.** If you get too busy going from one thing to the next, you'll never hear your inner voice above the rush and roar of the traffic in your life. To have the signals break through the clutter and congestion in our lives, we need to get quiet. Some people meditate, do yoga, walk on the beach, go for a drive, run, hike, read, or just stop and think. If you do something else, even work on something else, sometimes it will allow your right brain to talk to you and send a message while the left brain is busy. Once you start to get signals, capture your thoughts and feelings either on paper, in a planner, or in your Palm Pilot. For more insights start a journal, do some free writing, mind-map, draw, doodle, or talk into a recorder, and watch universal forces flood you with signs. Or simply think about a situation and then write down or draw whatever comes to mind.

• **Use it or lose it.** Try to engage your intuition every day. I do it for what I want to wear (which always worries my wife) and where I am going to go. I let my internal guide point the car to which part of town I want to work. Sometimes by driving about aimlessly looking for a coffeehouse to stop at and do my writing in, I have made some super discoveries. I'm *not* talking about testing your intuition by not balancing your checkbook and then trying to guess how much money you have left.

• **Stay open-minded.** Knowing too much about something can get in the way of your intuition. Too much left brain and your intuition shuts down. I'm not saying you should make money-related decisions based on your hunches alone. Numbers are important, but so is your intuition. Run the numbers, gather information, and then you can make an informed *and* intuitive decision. Some say your intuition is an inner knowing. Information and input are what fuel it. Just the act of gathering information about an investment can stir up feelings. Keep doing research and all those left-brain things like a pros-and-cons list, but for the ultimate decision you must get approval from your inner guide.

- **Go back to past success.** How did it feel? What images come to mind? Colors? Energy? Words? Then do the same for a failure. What were you thinking? Compare how you are feeling about a current choice with feelings you had before. Then compare how you feel about a current situation to your past feelings. Or gauge your reaction to something you are thinking about doing now on an excitement meter. How excited are you? Is this a one or a ten? How does it feel? Do you feel energized? Then go to your left brain. Does this seem to fit with your goals? Does it make sense? Can you see it? Can you imagine completing it or enjoying it?

- **Sometimes the best thing you can do is to do nothing.** Put the decision on the back burner and do something else. It's not foolproof, but it's effective. If you feel funny about something, ask for more time to decide. Let it sit. Does it still feel wrong? Why? Is it the whole thing that seems wrong? Do you need more information? Time? When you are sure you have to act on it, if you think *too* much you'll never act. You'll overanalyze. Plus, fear is a function of the left brain.

- **It's a sign.** Get an object that reminds you to consult with your inner guide.

A REAL Estate

"Whoever used the term 'dirt cheap' probably hasn't bought any real estate recently."

—P. Flynn

Recent research reveals that your home is crucial to your net worth. It can be more important than stocks or any other investment you can make. Despite the stock-market run in the 1990s, home ownership (for people earning less than $100,000 a year) proved a solid investment, and equity in those homes was where wealth came from. Between 1995 and 1998, homeowners saw home values jump by 20 percent. As they say, "Home is where the equity is." You can borrow against your home and deduct the interest from your taxes. Or you can refinance, basically replacing your old mortgage with a new one, and pull cash out at this time if you want. It will cost you to do this and could take a while to break even, but the money is there if you need it. But in reality, you buy a home because you want to live there.

Sting found the inspiration to write the album *Brand New Day* at his family home in Italy. While wandering the grounds of the 500-year-old villa, he found peace of mind. Let me just say, this is a twenty-room estate complete with two lakes, a forest, and a vineyard. Who wouldn't be inspired?

People do make money from buying and selling homes, but it can be risky and time-consuming. In a hot market you can buy and "flip" a home for a quick profit. In a depressed market you may not be able to give a place away and cover your costs. Fixer-uppers can be a good way to make money, but boy, are they a lot of work. And being a slumlord isn't for everyone. You have people calling at all hours, skipping out on rent, and in general being a pain in the neck. One creative guy turned his troubles with buying and renting places into a board game called "The Slumlord Game" so others could experience being a landlord. You can buy a building or duplex and rent out some of it to cover the rest. There are also income-producing properties. Bruce Willis and Demi Moore bought a town, basically. They own a diner, club, and movie theater as well as a home in Hailey, Idaho.

Some of my friends bought big homes because they didn't know what else to do with their money. It's not a bad idea, but there *are* other options. There are all kinds of costs when purchasing a home, including points on the loan, property taxes, upgrades, moving costs, landscaping, painting, decorating, maintenance, and improvements. Some of these you may never recoup—like a pool. With a home you don't get paid cash in the future unless it appreciates. It may just not be affordable for you at this time, either. In places like San Francisco and Hawaii, the median home price is over $300,000. (Property taxes are based on the price of the home. Whoa!) If you are able to put down only 5 percent, that is a HUGE amount of money you have to come up with every month. If you already own a home but have the urge to move up, be careful. You don't always have to buy up. Bigger isn't always better.

"Never leave a place where you're having a good time to go somewhere else where you only think you'll have a better time," says Rich Leblond. Right-brainers thrive on change. We switch jobs and may move often. In that case, home ownership may not be the best bet. Being emotional, impulsive people, this is not something we should do in haste. This is a BIG deal with big consequences. It's a huge commitment that may be hard to undo. A home will likely be the biggest and most expensive thing you will ever buy. It can be exciting and frustrating (at the same time). At the very least, it can be confusing. Be very careful before you talk to someone in a gold jacket. It's not something you do on a whim. Spontaneity is a good thing, but not here. Emotion can work against us when we are in the market to buy a home. Think with your head *and* your heart. It's hard, I know, because you are about to become "involved" with your home. But if your head is telling you no, pay attention. Buying a home is an investment, so you have to make decisions like what to add and/or upgrade based on whether it will it pay off.

You will have to do some math to figure out your total payments. Find out what you can qualify for. Factor in a worst-case scenario (no work for months) and see if you still want to commit to a $4,000 monthly mortgage, or you can downsize. Sure, you can buy a home with next to nothing down, but go for low monthly payments instead. Only one in four people can afford to buy a $200,000 home with 10 percent down and a 7 percent fixed thirty-year mortgage. If your family offers to give you the money for the down payment, take it! (Couples can now register at a bank for contributions to fund their home instead of wedding presents.)

Mortgage payments should be 28 percent of take-home pay. A $100,000 mortgage for thirty years at 10 percent (which is high) is an $878 payment each month. If you had to, you could always rent out a room to help cover some of the costs. If you are going to actually stay in your home for the full thirty years, you will save tens of thousands of dollars by paying it off faster. (You don't need to pay someone to help you do this. Making extra payments is easy.) You can pay off your house faster if you prefer with a few extra payments a year. But with low interest rates a home is a good example of leverage. Invest the difference. The home still appreciates, and you profit.

It goes without saying that you want the lowest possible interest rate. If you get an adjustable, pay attention to the cap, ask how high it could go, and then figure out what your payment would be. That's when reality starts to sink in. Switch to a fixed interest rate if it goes way down. If I were to have a mortgage, I would go for a fixed mortgage rate because it is easy to understand and I would know what I need each month.

Cash in your home isn't earning any interest (you're not paying any, either). But you may want to own your home outright when you retire. I paid my home off. I made sure to get a mortgage that didn't penalize me for paying it off. If you need a tax break (and who doesn't?) interest on your mortgage is tax-deductible. (So is the interest from a home equity loan.) But for me, owning a home outright gives me peace of mind and a hedge against a slowdown in my career.

For Rent

When it comes to renting a place, I am sure everyone has his own horror story. That doesn't mean that renting can't be a pleasurable experience. You just have to pick the right place, in the right location, for the right price, with the right terms, from the right people. Don't get emotional, make a hasty decision, and sign a long-term lease. Ask "what if" questions. What would happen if (fill in the blank)? You never really know what a place is like until you move in, but you want to try to cover as many bases as you can. I mean, who could have foreseen that the couple living above my wife and me would be such, how can I say this, an "active" couple? Thankfully, the guy could only go for a few minutes and then the whole thing was over. But it *was* very noisy. Still, I really liked that place, distractions and all. We rented for a while after we sold one of our homes (at the peak of housing prices) and then waited for the market to drop before we bought again. Is renting for you? Take this quiz and see.

__ Don't have the down payment needed to buy a home.

__ Don't think you will be living in one place very long. (It can be costly to jump ship.)

__ Don't want to pay property taxes, homeowner fees, maintenance, upgrades, insurance, water, association dues, trash-collection fees—and many of the other "hidden" costs of owning a home.

__ Couldn't make the monthly payments on a mortgage.

__ Could make more money by investing elsewhere. (You need only a few hundred dollars to get into the stock market, while real estate can be a big investment.)

__ It's cheaper to rent. (It's almost always cheaper in big cities to rent.)

___ Would rather use your money to build your business.

___ Are on the road a lot and all you really need is a crash pad.

___ Don't want to deal with repairs, maintenance, and general upkeep.

___ Not ready for that kind of a commitment.

___ Are currently living cheaply and saving up to buy a home down the road.

___ Have bad credit or no credit and couldn't qualify for a home loan.

___ Interest rates are too high.

___ Want your money more liquid.

___ Don't want to have to worry about the real estate market fluctuating.

___ Don't want to clean out your savings.

___Don't really need a tax break. (It's not as much of a break as you think, anyway.)

Invest in You

"Success is one thing you can't pay cash for. You've got to buy it on the installment plan and make payments every day."
—Zig Ziglar

When it comes to investing, maybe the best investment is in yourself. As Dolly Parton once said, "It takes a lot of money to look this cheap." That's funny, and true. If you are an entertainer, then maybe the hair, makeup, clothes, shoes, boob job, and collagen injections are an investment in your career. Plus, you need headshots, résumés, demo tapes, business cards, fliers, one-sheets, coaching, lessons, a cell phone, a pager, Internet access, and a website, among other things, just to compete. As creative people, we must put our money where our careers are. You laugh, but an actor I know who was trying to make it in Hollywood didn't have a car or a phone, and his agent was getting frustrated. He spent all the money he had in his savings (about $1,200) on a phone and voice mail (and was compulsive about checking it). He also went out and got a cheap car and a couple of outfits. He was now ready to roll on a moment's notice.

To coincide with his New York debut and a gig at the

Copacabana, Sam Cooke spent $10,000 of his own money to buy a 20 × 100–foot billboard in Times Square that read, "Who's the biggest cook in town? Sam's the biggest Cooke in town." The group Bam Bam rented a flatbed truck and performed in front of a record company's office. Beck invested $60 in the acoustic guitar on which he wrote and recorded his first album. Stephen Perkins, the drummer for Jane's Addiction and Porno for Pyros, used his bar mitzvah money to buy his first drum set. (Barry Manilow got a piano for his bar mitzvah.) Brian Setzer made money from the Stray Cats and spent most of it. He struggled for six years. He wanted to make big-band music. The problem with playing big-band music is just that you need a BIG BAND. His was over eighteen people. Plus, there was no market at the time. But he believed so much in what he was doing he decided to use the last of his money. "Jump, Jive and Wail" sold 2 million copies and was a chart-topper. He also won a Grammy Award and started a whole swing revival. Frankie Valli bought back the master tape for the 1974 song "My Eyes Adored You" and released it on the small Private Stock Label. It hit number one on the charts. There were all kinds of disasters during the filming of *Apocalypse Now.* The cast and crew endured typhoons, cast changes, the star's heart attack, logistical location nightmares, and bad press. Francis Ford Coppola was hot off his *Godfather* successes and decided to bet it all on this film. (Much of the $30 million expense was in credit that he guaranteed himself.) It turned out to be a land-mark film. John Travolta plowed most of his money from *Welcome Back, Kotter* into PR. Melanie Griffith tried to boost her, uh, career when she went in for a little "work." "I had my tits done after my sec-ond child. But I didn't make them bigger. I just had them put back to where they were," she says.

Don't skimp when it comes to your career. Materials, marketing, and other miscellaneous costs of getting started and keeping it alive are worthy and legitimate expenses. What you create can become a valuable commodity and pay dividends like a stock or bond, so I say go for it! I mean, if not you, then who is gonna back you? You gotta spend money to make money. Just be careful and calculated. Watch your "burn rate" and don't blow it on things that are frivolous.

There are things you can do for free, too. Work on your posture, handshake, and approach (all free). Get your personal life in order first. Don't be a flake because your car broke down, your phone was disconnected, or the power was shut off so your alarm didn't work.

So forget the lottery—invest in yourself. The odds are a lot better. You are your best asset. Invest in marketing yourself and making yourself more marketable. Frank Zappa was an aspiring musician who was selling encyclopedias to make a buck, but when he was paid $1,500 to score the film *Run Home Slow* he invested his earnings to set up a recording studio. Then he and the Mothers of Invention released *Freak Out,* and he never had to sell encyclopedias again. That was then, this is now. Creed's 1997 debut album, *My Own Prison,* was made for $6,000. The band would save up and record, save some more and record, until the thing was done. The CD sold four million copies and yielded four number-one Rock Radio singles, and their follow-up record was even bigger.

Maybe you want to start your own business. Great! You can never really feel secure until you are your own boss. William Burroughs was a bank teller in the 1880s when he realized that human error was costing the bank money, so he invented a machine that could automatically tabulate numbers quickly and accurately. We now know this was a great idea, but then people weren't so sure. It took him seven years and thousands of his own dollars to build prototypes before he made money, but then it took off and he became so wealthy he could have bought the bank he once worked at.

Berry Gordy was a boxer who used his winnings to open a jazz record store. Although this was his dream job, the store went out of business, but this didn't diminish his love of music. He took a day job at Ford Motor Co. and spent his spare time writing songs for local acts. Although the job at Ford paid well, it wasn't what he wanted. He saved his salary and went to New York to make some contacts in the music business. He had some success but still kept the job at Ford even though he had hit records as a writer (including "Lonely Teardrops"), because he barely broke even. That's when he decided to do it himself and borrowed $7,000 from his sister and used $700 of his own money to set up a makeshift recording studio in a run-down house he dubbed "Hitsville USA." That was how Motown Records was born, and it eventually made Gordy a very rich and powerful man.

Once you say "I'm a pro," people treat you differently—better. Are you a pro? Give your career a priority. Get serious. That means marketing materials, attitude, equipment, and whatever else you need to be professional. Confidence comes from having a website and nice business card. Get a place that accepts packages and has an expensive name. Confidence also comes from being good at what you do and knowing what you are talking about. Spending on training, a tutor, or classes is always okay. Maybe you would be more confident with a working prototype. In the toy business you need a prototype, and you may have to come up with a hundred ideas (and prototypes) before something sells.

Tools and technology. Before you buy, ask yourself, Will this help me make more money? Is it worth the investment in money (and time it will take to pay for it)? Is there somewhere else you can gain access to what you need? Accomplished guitarist Kat Dyson says, "Some women buy clothes, I buy gear. I try to stay current." If you are a hairstylist you need top-of-the-line shears. A graphic artist needs a computer and software (among other things). A painter needs brushes, canvases, and a beret. Okay, maybe not a beret, but brushes would be a wise investment.

Where do you get the money? Put off a purchase and use the money for your career instead or you'll never reach your goal. Spend it on expensive meals, movies, men, and manicures when you need new paint, canvases, equipment, video, and so on, and you'll never get there. When I started making some money I resisted increasing my lifestyle and used the money for marketing. You want to turn a profit at the end of the year and put that back into your career and dream. Shoot for 10 percent of your income to go to building your future. If there is no extra money, then use another asset—time. Invest five to ten hours a week.

It's in the Planning Stages

"There aren't enough people who care about the future. They are busy worrying about today and what they can do now."
—Berry Gordy

Planning is like looking in a crystal ball. It's your future, so shape it the way you want it. You need to manage money to reach goals. Have a blueprint that gives you something to shoot for, not some vague, abstract idea. It's tangible, gives you vision, it's motivating, energizes you to work harder, save, and sacrifice because you can see the reason why. Deadlines are motivating, too. Where do you want to go and how do you get there? The planning process stimulates ideas. A plan frees you up for more creative pursuits. Get it out of your head and on paper. Your mind and intuition work better when you have some ideas about what you want to do. The universe will provide for you. A benefit of this is less stress. "I was in bed by midnight on New Year's Eve. I already know what I'm doing for my whole year, all the way up to next New Year. So I feel very calm," says Jenna Elfman. Calm? Her?

With planning you will make better decisions, identify potential pitfalls and problems, and turn chaos into order. Without planning you are easily overwhelmed, lose interest, and quit. Break down anything, and it becomes easier to digest. It is also a reality check. It helps you stay focused so you don't end up spending on whatever comes along. Otherwise you're going around in circles, or worse, sinking into debt and getting further from your financial goals. You don't have to be locked in. You can still live in the moment and be spontaneous or plan for it. Start wherever you are. You don't have to have extra cash to plan. It's simply what you want and steps to get it.

Planning the RIGHT-Brain Way

"A good criterion for measuring your success in life is the number of people you have made happy."

—Robert Lumsden

Having a financial plan is a lot like flying. In the movies the star climbs aboard the plane and takes off. No preflight checklist (checking the fuel!) or filing a flight plan with the control tower. Dream on. You need to know your plane and yourself intimately. You need to know how to fly. You *should* check and triple-check the plane before you leave the ground. You select a destination and submit a flight plan and get necessary clearance. You also check the weather. You want to know what you are in for and if you can fly the course you chose. Only then do you start the engine and taxi onto the runway. Now you can throttle up and take off. Once in the air you have a bird's-eye view where everything looks small and insignificant. While in flight you keep an eye on your airspeed, altitude, compass, and fuel. Then, and only then, do you sit back and enjoy the ride, adjusting as you go.

Financial plans are the same way. You need to look at what you want and do a checklist to make sure you are both motivated and willing to do what it takes to get it. You may talk to a few people for advice and check the "weather" to see how stormy the ride may be and if it's worth it at all. Then you select your destination and take off and set a heading for it. From this vantage point you keep an eye on your progress and adjust as needed, but from where you sit the little stuff doesn't bother you because it's small stuff that will pass. You keep adjusting your course, but the destination is the same—financial freedom. And while you are en route you enjoy the journey with the knowledge that you know where you are going and how to get there, and with a little luck (like a tailwind) you'll get there soon.

A right-brain financial plan needs to be visual, flexible, simple, and if at all possible, fun. No problem. Here's some suggestions on how to make the linear, left-brain act of planning more creative. You could start by making a time line beginning with where you are and ending with when and where you want to be. Along the time line you can write, draw, or paste pictures of what you want to happen and when (roughly) they should occur.

You could simply write out a plan (like a business plan, but this is for your personal finances) that spells out what you want and what you have to do to get it. Include any resources you'll need and how you expect to get them. I recommend writing a short summary that you read over and over.

You may want to write a short story about your future (as you want it to be) with characters, plots, and, of course, a happy ending. You can start with "Where I want to be in five years." Then craft a story of how you will get there. This project is more of a "how to" than a "mystery." Along those same lines you can write an article or interview yourself as if you already have what you want and explain how you got it. Piece it together by working backward. Fast-forward to the future, and then trace your steps to figure out what it would take to get where you want to go.

If all this seems like too much work, then simply pick an image of what you want and put it up where you can see it. Or write a mission statement for your life. This statement would include your means, motive, and opportunities, as well as your goal.

Another way to simplify the planning process is to go through magazines and catalogs and cut out pictures that represent the things you want. Then paste them to a board, making a collage. If you want to get fancy, cut out the pieces so they look like pieces of a puzzle, and as you achieve one you start putting the complete picture together. This way you see your progress, and it gives you something to shoot for.

You might make a meter with benchmarks written along the side. As you reach each level you color it in. For example, if your goal is to save $10,000, you would fill in a rung for each $100 you save. You could also make your plan look like a board game. Each square is a goal, and you move your game piece along as you go.

Or have a list of goals, and for each one indicate how many moves you can make. If you have cut your living costs by $200 a month, you move three spaces, and so forth.

Maybe you would be better off making a mind-map with your main goal in the middle of the page and sub-goals branching out from that. Let your imagination run wild, and start adding in how you will reach your main goal.

I carry around a deposit slip with the figure $1,000,000 written in. I laminated it and look at it all the time. This deposit is what I would like to be able to deposit from my writing. You could make up a fake bankbook or bank statement the way you would like it to be.

You could use index cards and write your goals on them and carry the stack with you in your purse. Pull them out, shuffle them around, and make sure you are doing something about one of them each day. Or just write what you want to make in a month or year and write it down in your planner and look at it every day.

Of course, you could just make a "wish list" of all the things you want to have happen and check them off as you go. Next to each thing you want, write down how much money you'll need to get it.

I am sure you can come up with even more creative ways to plan. The goal is to create something you will look at and stay with. Here are a few guidelines that may help you in the planning process. In the beginning don't worry about the "how the hell am I going to pull this off" part. Just focus on what you want if you could have anything and everything you desire. Then start to think about how you'll accomplish it. When it comes to dealing with dollars, it is better to be specific. "I want to make more money" is too vague. How much more do you want to make? Pick a number. Then you can break it down to how much you'll need to make in a month, week, and day. How much money do you want to accumulate, by when, and then work backward. Look at where this money may come from. If you want to make more than you are now, how do you plan to do it? Do your homework. It gets easier and easier to make educated guesses. Use previous sales for a benchmark. Look at someone you know as a model.

Once you break it down you may realize you have to downsize the dream just a little. (Or increase the number!) This happens when you look for ways to make the money. Will I want to work as hard as I'll have to work to make the big bucks? Will I have to sell out to make this much? Am I willing to do this or that? You can have all the money you want—you just may not have it as soon as you want. By breaking down your financial goals you can stretch it out, but by all means select a target date. Then ask yourself, "What can I do to reach that number right now?" Make a list of all the things you want to do when you have all the money you need. List all the things you think you need to make more. How much will they cost?

7

CREATIVE WAYS TO SAVE

*"Most bands don't make money—they just squander
it on producers and cocaine and lots of other bullshit,
and it's disgusting. There's so much idiotic excess."*
—Sting

In this chapter I'm going to use the "F-word" a lot. The "F-word," of course, is "frugal." Being frugal has gotten a bad rap. My wife said to me the other day that I was starting to become cheap. (This was after I dismantled the riser for my drums and used some of the wood for shelving.) I quickly corrected her and said, "I am not cheap, I'm smart with money." That said, I have to admit, the older I get the closer I am to becoming my father. He isn't cheap, he's smart with money. I can remember him making all kinds of crazy things with leftover parts from some project or other. He would turn old rusty engine parts into a wind chime or turn a block of wood jammed against the accelerator into instant cruise control. (I'm not kidding, either.) So when I find myself underwriting a recent trip to the tropics by cashing in some of my frequent-flier miles for myself and then trading the rest of them to my buddies in exchange for free room and car and almost making a profit from the trip, I have to smile. I know I am in danger of being called the "F-word." The goal, as I see it, is to live the good life for less (so you can get more of it).

People will pay top dollar for things they could have bought for less with just a little bit of effort. You don't have to wait for the "blue light" to start flashing to save a buck or two, either. There are plenty of ways to make your money last longer. Is that so bad? Take a twenty-dollar bill out of your wallet and tear it up into little pieces. How does that feel? (Can't do it, can you?) So how come we are so willing to waste twenty dollars on other things without thinking? Because we can't really see it. It's on a credit card. It's a hidden cost. We rationalize it by saying, "Yeah, but I had fun" or "It's a tax write-off" or "I needed it now and they had it, so . . ." Or it happens in such small increments we hardly notice the money being lifted out of our pocket. It's sneaky and leaky.

Overspending is a problem if you have debt, no savings, want to work less and have more life in your life, and are one bad month from bankruptcy. Ideally, you should be able to survive for six months or more without any income. With the up-and-down cycle of the creative life, it pays to be cost-conscious and reduce living expenses so that during the lean times it's not as much of a struggle. It can become a vicious cycle if you have to make a large amount of money just to keep up. It may mean you need a "real job" to pay the bills, which takes you away from what you really want to be doing—creating. (By the time you're done doing the day gig, you have nothing left for your art.) You may have more stuff, but you have less time to spend, practicing, performing, and so on, the basics that further a creative career. So let's look at how to get more of what we want for less.

 QUICK QUIZ

The number-one rule to financial freedom is: a.) Spend as much money as you can, b.) sell all your worldly possessions and live like a monk, or c.) spend less than you earn and invest the difference. As much as I want to say that "a" is the correct answer, it is "c," of course.

Until you can live on less you'll never be able to save, regardless of how much you make. And saving some money IS financial security. Maybe you think if you could make more money all your problems would be solved. It doesn't really work that way. It's never enough. People live from paycheck to paycheck no matter how big that paycheck may be, and many feel deprived no matter what they make. I would not call that success. Successful people are willing to give up nonessential items for essential ones. Maybe they passed on throwing a party or two and instead saved that money for a class that furthered their career. If you really want to be a full-time, financially secure artist with total creative freedom, you have to make some sacrifices. Nobody wants to hear this and it will probably fall on deaf ears, but I had to mention it. Otherwise you are wasting your money and your life on cars, clothes, and cocktails.

When did life get so complicated and expensive? When people decided they wanted to have it all. I have to ask, does it make them happy? Fulfilled? Usually the answer is "no." You could go nuts with things that should make you feel better—therapists, coaches, personal trainers, masseurs, decorators, Botox treatments, club dues, publicists, promotions, car payments, homes, vacation homes, personal shoppers, lavish parties, and so on. Then there is the cost and maintenance on all that stuff. The more stuff you have the more you have to worry about and the harder you have to work to pay for it. The good life is becoming a burden.

All of a sudden fear grips you and you realize you have to work or else it will all come crumbling down. You start to feel the pressure from such a big financial burden. It's a trap! You end up just treading water until you run out of energy and drown. You have to work yourself to death, and for what? You hate your job, co-workers, the commute, and even the clients. Your kids suffer, too, as they have to spend their youth in day care. There is no time for your dreams. The only time you can relax is when you take a vacation two weeks a year, and you are miserable the other fifty weeks a year. Freedom (financial and artistic) comes from a place of not having to worry and work (yourself to death). It isn't about accumulating things. Don't compromise your dream for a nice rig and sweet crib. Less stress means more creativity, and more creativity can mean more money. My advice is to slow down and get in touch with your creativity and your dreams.

How? Cutting costs means you don't have to earn as much, which means you don't have to work as much. You could cut day care, pass on difficult clients and boring projects, cut the commute by working one day less a week, find more work you love, and spend more time with your loved ones. Then you can tell your boss and co-workers to take this job and shove it. Success and richness is *your* definition of what that means to you. What *you* want. Go ahead, be a little selfish. What would bring you contentment, satisfaction, pure joy? Are material things or a way of life what you are looking for? Cut out or cut back on things that *don't* make you happy. I see friends moving into these huge homes. Then they have to fill them up with furniture, do the landscaping, and pay to maintain them. I don't want to work that hard. I call some of these people to ask if they want to go sailing or hang out at the beach. They can't. Why? Because they are always working (to afford these homes), or on the weekends they have to work around the house.

I say simplify. Just the word makes you pause, sigh, and say "aaaaaahhhhhh." Barbra Streisand sold five of the seven homes she owned and auctioned off many of her possessions in an effort to simplify and save. Maybe you have to simplify your life a little to cut your expenses so you can work on projects YOU really want. Maybe you live like a monk to survive the lean years and lower your monthly nut. The fact that you are independently wealthy means that you don't have to rely on anyone else to tell you what to do, when to do it, or even how to do it. You are in charge of your life because you have enough money saved to say, "See ya." Maybe you can't retire right now, but by reducing the amount you need to make to survive, you can enjoy your life now.

Make choices based on your heart and soul. But, but, but . . . I know, the mortgage, car payment, vacation, etc. It's your choice. Do you really need a maid, nanny, car detailing, and pedicures? If you worked less you could do some of that stuff yourself, thus saving money. "But I need all this stuff." Need? Hmmmm. People worry about money (and the lack of it) more than anything else. The irony is that the solutions to all their worries are sooooo simple. Earn more, spend less, invest and/or save the difference. You can even improve your life without making more money. Spend your money in a more meaningful way. Use your creativity and resourcefulness and find ways to live on less. It's actually "kinda" fun. Some people think there is no way they can reduce their spending. Shoot for a few bucks at first. How much do you want to cut back? According to several reports, at the height of the last booming economy Americans continued to spend as fast as their incomes grew (and even beyond their income) and even raided their savings to buy goods and services they said they "needed."

Successful people are frugal. They don't waste money or spend money they don't have. They don't obsess about every nickel, but they are aware. You don't have to deny yourself guilty pleasures. The goal is to get good stuff for less, and don't think people with money don't do it, too. That's how they hang on to their money. Kelly Preston, the actress who is married to John Travolta, is worth millions. Yet she was one of the bargain hunters at the Fred Segal store for the boutique's annual 50 percent off sale. I'm *not* saying you have to be cheap. Someone once said that being frugal is using a coupon to save money on a meal and being cheap is not leaving a tip. Speaking of which, I read in *Travel Holiday* magazine that the main reason people tip is for social approval and not necessarily for good service. Big tippers want the recipient to like them. Like you will ever see them again. Anyway.

This may be falling on deaf ears because a lot of creative types live off of "the big score" and can clean up overspending with one lucrative project or deal. You need to know how to survive (and thrive) on what you have now. Then when you do hit it big, you can stick some of that money away for a rainy day. If you can live on less you can make it through the tough times that always come when you least expect them. (A canceled contract, the closing of a show, the loss of a job, and so on.) Sarah Jessica Parker makes millions a year from her popular show *Sex and the City* ($100,000 per episode, I read somewhere) but knows that it won't last forever. "Every TV show I do gets great ratings, wins Emmys, and is canceled." Parker comes from a poor background. She and her seven siblings lived a bohemian lifestyle and lived off food stamps. This has had an effect on the way she deals with money. She tends to be superfrugal but has a weakness for shoes.

Something I've noticed is that as your income grows people expect more for you and from you. They think you should drive a nice car, buy a big house, and, of course, pick up the tab for dinners. There is some pressure to live up to *their* expectations.

More money doesn't have to mean more problems if you pace yourself. Think about this for a second. Once you have cool stuff it's harder to give it up than if you never had it in the first place. The few times I have flown first-class have ruined me. I almost wish I was never up there in the lap of luxury, because coach now seems so cramped, where before it was fine.

Most millionaires live beneath their means. Even people with less than millions do this. Dion DiMucci, as in Dion and the Belmonts and the singer of songs like "The Wanderer" and "Runaround Sue," is in the Rock and Roll Hall of Fame but lives in a modest suburban home in Boca Raton. Pierre Omidyar, the software developer who created eBay and became a billionaire, still drives a VW and shops at Target. He plans to donate most of his money to various causes. Linda Ronstadt lives in a modest home with a big garden where she grows fruits and vegetables. She does, however, invest in the stock market.

💰 FUN FACT

In 1987 American Airlines eliminated one olive from each salad served in first class and saved $40,000.

- **Two for the price of one.** As you can see by the examples above, even when creative people have a lot of money they are still smart about how they spend it. I read that Bridget Fonda and boyfriend Dwight Yoakam were shopping at a Los Angeles supermarket, and when Yoakam got to the register he realized he didn't have his discount card. He borrowed one from a fellow shopper and saved five dollars. You can still have and do much of what you want—just find ways to do it for less. Take your dream vacation but go during the off-season. Dine out but use a coupon. Go to the movies but take in a matinee. You don't have to give up the good life altogether—just shop smarter.
- **Make it last all night.** Being "smart with money" doesn't have to mean doing without. It could just mean you care for and treat your possessions a little better and hang on to them a little longer. Treat what you own with respect. You can clean up something old and make it feel like new. I often ride my bike on the beach, and it was starting to look like a real beach cruiser (rusted). So instead of buying and ruining another bike, I simply cleaned, painted, and then protected the bike. Looks good as new. You can still get new stuff if you so desire—just get good value for your dollar. Usually paying a tad bit more for a quality item will save money

down the road because it should last longer. I play the drums with really thin sticks, 7As, so they tend to break fairly easily. But it wasn't because I rock or that they were thin that they were breaking. It was because I bought "cheap" sticks. I switched to more expensive and better-made sticks that last ten times longer but cost only a buck more. It's always nice to buy things that will appreciate or hold their value, but that isn't always necessary. Believe it or not, a Rolex watch is a good investment, but a Mickey Mouse watch will also do the trick.

• **Start me up.** Creative people have some fairly quirky and costly and eccentric behavior when it comes to increasing their creativity. I have seen it all—everything from renting another home down the block (or by the beach) to find some solitude, to having to have a new laptop and all the latest software, to hiring help just to get going on a project. You have to ask yourself: Will buying this really help push the project along, or is it just another form of procrastination?

• **Screw the Joneses and the SUV they rode in on.** Stop trying to compare yourself to others and trying to keep up with them. If you really are flush with cash and begin to flaunt it, others will just resent you anyway. And if you don't have a great deal of money (or worse, you did but are now in dire straits), it is better to be honest with yourself and others that the game of "my stuff is bigger and better than your stuff" is too rich for your blood. Besides, I have noticed that lately there is more importance placed on the person and not on possessions. So impress them with your creativity and craftiness instead. Trying to solve problems with money actually kills creativity. I have also found that those who try to outdo each other with material things are as shallow as a lagoon at low tide. It's fascinating to watch people spend themselves into the ground. I'm appalled. Their "wealth" doesn't impress me. If anything, it has the opposite effect. I feel pity for them, or worse still, resent them and want them to fall on their face. I have heard it said that the bigger the boat the smaller a man's (fill in the blank). Like a lot of sayings, there is some truth to that. People who feel inadequate on the inside try to surround themselves with nice things on the outside to compensate. It doesn't work! The bottom line is this: *You* are still valuable even if you don't own a lot of valuables.

• **Frugal means freedom.** There is an old African proverb that says, "From contentment with little comes happiness." What really makes you content and happy? How much do you really need? It doesn't cost anything to enjoy simple things like gardening, walking, talking, painting, playing music, tinkering, or creating. You would probably prefer more time and less money. Right? Oh, you want both, huh? Anyway, when you slow down you'll have more insights, ideas, and intuition. More insights and ideas lead to more money. Break the cycle and slow down. To do that, buy less and live more. Why waste time and money today on things that don't make you happy and then be so busy working to afford them that you have no time to truly enjoy them? Before you buy, ask yourself: What will it cost me not only in money but also in time to buy this? Is it worth it? Do I really need this? You begin to focus your attention on what is most important—people. One day I decided to self-park down the street rather than valet park. The walk to the restaurant gave me a chance to have a nice chat with my brother. At least I thought so. All he could talk about was how much his expensive shoes were hurting his feet.

• **Comfort creatures?** The last time I was in Key West I met another writer at Mallory Square watching the sunset. We got to talking. He doesn't own a car, a home, or a boat. He bikes around town, rents a cool little place by the beach, and crews on someone else's boat when he feels the urge to go sailing. He has total artistic and financial freedom. He was once working two jobs, and owned a bunch of toys until his home burned and he lost everything. (He was *not* insured. He couldn't afford it!) After the fire he realized he didn't need all that stuff after all. He felt relieved, actually. He has become quite resourceful since, and his only extravagance is the iBook that he writes on. Every day he watches the sunset (free) and has more time now to work on his book. Before, he was so busy working he never had a moment to himself. Now he's happier than he has ever been.

It can be fun to find creative ways to cut back, and it almost becomes a game that you will always win. In many ways, all you are doing is trying to rearrange the way you spend your money so that you get more value for each dollar spent, to decide what is *most* important to you.

How to Live Like a Star on a Production Assistant's Salary

"The art of living easily as to money is to pitch your scale of living one degree below your means."

—Sir Henry Taylor

• **Stay the course.** Ask yourself: Will this purchase bring me closer or take me away from my financial goals? Set a target of how much you want to cut back on costs. Make it a game or a contest. Start small and trim the fat. Maybe you get rid of call waiting, cancel a subscription for a magazine you don't even read, or cut out one club membership you don't use. Know the difference between needs and wants. You may *need* strings, art supplies, a computer, health insurance, or more training. You *want* a studio overlooking a stream, a Porsche Boxter, high-speed Internet access, and a new laptop. Know the difference.

 ACTION ITEM

Make a list of all the things you would like in your life. Then separate them into wants and needs. For the needs look for ways to acquire each without spending a bundle. For the wants, organize them into a top-ten list. Reward yourself with one when you can afford it.

• **Don't wait until the last minute.** Don't buy on impulse. If you wander around the mall long enough, I'll bet you'll find something you want. You are also more likely to buy something when with friends, so shop alone. I watch my wife shop, and it's almost like she's in a trance. As she deftly works the rounders she seems so content. I tell her that shopping is NOT therapy, but she doesn't listen. I try to break the spell, but she is in another world. That's why there should be a five-day waiting period for large purchases. Serious shoppers need a "cooling off" period until the urge passes. Or carry a limited amount of cash and leave credit cards at home so you are more likely to stay within your means. Along those same lines, why not rent something first when the urge to own is strong and then see if still seems like something you must own later. How many hobbies have you started and got the gear? Then later, you move on to something else but still have the stuff. Snowboarding is a good example. Many people make it to the slopes only two or three times a year. Is it worth it to buy a board, boots, and all the other accessories for a few days a year of use?

• **I think it's a mind-set.** B.C. (before I was cutting back) I spent $600 for pond rocks for my backyard waterfall. One day while walking on the beach I noticed these same rocks that I could have had for FREE. I picked up the rocks, and I swear I couldn't tell the difference.

• **Don't buy, borrow.** Sometimes on a warm summer's day I have the urge to go for a motorcycle ride up the coast. One problem— I no longer own a motorcycle. I sold it some time ago. So I just go over to my buddy's house and borrow his. Same thrill, but a cheaper thrill than owning one.

• **Your time is valuable.** Don't spend four hours to save four bucks. But if you can spend four hours and save $400, that's different. A carpenter told me that he gets his best wood from people who are throwing it away. When he is on-site he takes the time to sift through some of the wood that is being tossed and many times finds things he can clean up and use again (and sell again).

• **You suck.** I have found that when you have been wronged it pays to complain, but it can be time-consuming to set things straight. You know the drill, "Sorry, all of our operators [all TWO of them!] are helping more worthy customers. Your call will be answered in . . . t-w-o . . . d-a-y-s." I have become the designated complainer for my family because I am good at it. Not because I freak out but because I am organized (I use photos, dates, receipts, warranties, and documentation to overwhelm the recipient) and I am goal-oriented. I go in with a plan and a goal of what would make a bad situation better and I ASK FOR IT and almost always get it. Get what's rightfully yours.

• **Almost everything is negotiable.** Someone said that if you take a cab from JFK Airport in New York to the city, it's a flat, non-negotiable fee of $30. However, if you are a foreign traveler who doesn't speak English, the price is $600. Ha, ha. Seriously, don't hesitate to ask for a discount or deal. If you are selling your home, Realtors many times will cut their commission, and as little as one percent off can save you tens of thousands of dollars. When you go into a music supply store they expect you to ask for a discount. If you don't it's your loss. The sticker price is there just for the suckers. This applies to services, too. I was making a new promotional video, and when I got the estimate from the producer, I asked if there was some way we could get the cost down. He said sure, if I was willing to write the copy and help with the editing, he'd knock off $1,000. Being the perfectionist I am, I would have done those things anyway! Sometimes the price is etched in stone, but maybe they can throw in something extra. It happens all the time. You just have to ask. I should note that it's all in the way you ask. When they say to you, "You're killin' me" or "Take a hike," you may have gone too far. Do it nicely. Many times you can also get a good deal if you pay cash. Ask if there is a sale coming up or a better time to do it or a used model sitting around. In Hawaii locals get a Kama'aina discount, which is 10 to 50 percent off what a tourist would pay, but you gotta ask, brah.

• **Know what prices are.** Keep a couple of catalogs handy so you can look up prices and have a benchmark to compare when searching for a deal. The Internet is both good and bad for cutting costs. It makes it soooo easy to get anything you want with a couple of clicks of a mouse. Not good. But it also gives us access to information that allows us to comparison-shop and shop smart. Some things are downright cheaper online, like airline tickets and books. Others are about the same as if you walked into a store (when you factor in shipping). Compare prices and go to the retailer you really want to buy from and ask them to match the price. Know what the right price is—otherwise you end up looking like an idiot and pay too much. Many creative people don't want to be bothered with details like checking *Consumer Reports* and reading reviews. "Saw it, wanted it, had a fit, got it." Watch out for the hidden costs that may be lurking if you don't look closely. Don't just say, "Whatever, wrap it up, let's go." Then later find out, "You mean this rate is per person?!" Or you get home and realize you also need cables, adapters, software, and a guru to help you install it. One guy bought a dresser without measuring, and it didn't fit where he wanted it. He then had to have it customized, which was very costly. Besides, the hunt for a good deal is part of the fun, isn't it?

• **Don't be "penny wise and pound foolish."** Why is it that we will work hard to save a few bucks here and there but when it comes to big-ticket items we all of a sudden get very generous? I think because we aren't usually paying cash so the amount of money doesn't seem real. Keep this in mind.

• **Being a bit organized can save you money.** If you can find a receipt and the warranty information, you may be able to return something or have it replaced when it breaks. (Don't be afraid to return things you don't need, either.) Being able to plan ahead and anticipating your needs can mean you can wait for a sale and stock up. If you wait till the last minute you may buy things you already have but can't find. Being organized keeps you from losing things or loaning things out and not recalling who has what when you need it. Another problem is having so much stuff you have to rent a storage unit to house it. You're never quite sure what's in there, and you have to pay the price for that—in more ways than one.

⑤ ACTION ITEM

How much do you need to make to support your current lifestyle? What could you live without? Look for five expenses you can cut from your life. Then look for five things you could cut back on.

Down and Out in Beverly Hills

"Status symbols are poor excuses for values."

—Merry Browne

Your biggest expense is likely your rent or mortgage. So this is an area where you can save a lot of money depending on your decisions. Make a poor choice and it could be a big burden for years to come. Consider this, with more than 85 million copies of her books in print, bestselling novelist Nora Roberts makes seven figures a year in income yet still lives in the same modest Maryland three-bedroom house that she moved into twenty-nine years ago as a young home-maker and mother. (She did have her closet remodeled to accommodate her hundreds of shoes. "My one weakness," she admits.) Jenna Elfman and her husband live in a modest home in the Hollywood hills that she describes as "very simple—like, 3,000 square feet of simple." The old rule of thumb was that you should spend less than

28 percent of your take-home pay to keep a roof over your head. Good luck. Still, anything you can do to cut that number down is a good thing.

• **Location, location, location.** Many NFL players want to live in Florida, for obvious reasons (warm weather, water sports, and a nice way of life) and some not-so-obvious reasons (lower cost of living and tax benefits). Where you choose to live can affect how much you have to shell out in monthly expenses. The median home price in Carmel, California, is almost $1 million. In Joshua Tree, California, the median price is $37,500. The average monthly cost of day care in Boston is $622, while in Tampa it is only $260. When I first moved to Maui I wondered why everyone worked two and three jobs until I started to notice how expensive it was to live there. Living in Hawaii can cost 40 percent more than the mainland. So you either have to cut back on costs, work more, or find creative (and legal, I would hope) ways to make more money just to live like you used to outside the islands. Commuting costs a small fortune when you consider how much you spend on gas, maintenance, parking, tolls, and—most of all—time. Moving closer to your place of work makes good fiscal sense. Better yet, working out of your home makes that commute a matter of making your way down the hall without spilling your coffee on the carpet.

• **Interior motives.** That's the popular show with Christopher Lowell, who redesigns and redecorates living spaces with his magic touch. If you feel that you need more room, try rearranging your current space first before you sign a lease for a bigger (and more expensive) place. Look at the garage. Are things stored as efficiently as possible? Could you add shelves, hang some things, or better yet, discard some junk to free up room? How about the attic to send stuff to its final resting place? Maybe you could rearrange your closets, cabinets, and crawl space to make room for your clutter and free up some space. (Warning: Having a spare room means the mother-in-law now has a place to stay when she's in town.) Hang your own art on the walls. Pamela Lee Anderson says, "My idea of relaxation is working on upholstery. I spend hours in junk shops buying furniture. I do all the upholstery work myself, and it's like therapy." There are a lot of things I could say about that quote, but I won't. The thing is, if you buy furniture new, much the same as a car, the minute you put your tush on it it's depreciated by 50 percent. But with antiques, the value stays the same or goes up. Plus, it's fun looking for hidden treasures at antique shops, and like Pamela says, fixing things up is like therapy. Rather than redecorate, clean the clutter. Move some things around, trade some stuff with friends, and make the most of what you have.

• **Three's company.** Don't be afraid to ask for a reduced rent. I did years ago, and lo and behold, they cut the rent by $100 a month. They felt I was a good tenant and that was worth something (little did they know) and so I saved $1,200 a year! I have also been a landlord. For the most part it was a joy (there was only one psycho out of ten renters), the renters became friends, and their rent money helped me make my mortgage payments. Three *is* company if you are looking for a place to rent yourself. You won't have Jack, Janet, and Chrissy living with you, but you can get more for your money if you pool your resources. Ask that your security deposit be put in an interest-bearing account and that YOU get that interest. When you leave, clean the place up like your mother-in-law was coming to town and get that deposit back. Protect what you have with surge protectors, locks, a fire extinguisher, and smoke detectors.

• **Home free.** Move back home. As an up-and-coming writer, wouldn't it be nice to have a famous, bestselling author to help you with your manuscript? Christopher Rice lives with his mom, Anne Rice (*Interview with a Vampire*), and father, Stan Rice (a poet). After completing his manuscript he gave it to his mom to read, who stayed up all night to finish it. She then slipped a note under his door. It said, "Your book is devastating as well as brave, and wrought with beautiful angst." Christopher admits, "That was very important to me." With nothing but $1,200 left on a credit card, entrepreneur Ron Perry moved back home while building his business. No freeloader, he made a deal with his folks. He said, "If this business takes off I'll pay off your house." He found that living at home was motivational—he wanted to make it *so he could move out.* His business took off and so did he, keeping his promise to his parents. Of men between the ages of 25 to 29, 20 percent still live with their parents. Only 8 percent of women ages 25 to 29 still live with their parents, according to a *USA Today* poll.

• **Light my fire.** Author Sebastian Junger, while working on *The Perfect Storm,* holed up in his parents' summer home on Cape Cod during the coldest winter on record. To force himself to work on the book he made a deal with himself. He would turn the heat on only if he was working on the book. Otherwise the house was freezing. "If I tracked snow into the kitchen, it would be there for weeks." He wore a hat and coat to bed. But the book got finished and turned out to be a big hit. See if there are any income-tax credits for installing energy efficient devices (like solar heating) in your home.

 FOR FUN
A license plate on a Lincoln Town Car read: "PD2MUCH."

Don't Love Something That Can't Love You Back
"Lots of people want to ride with you in the limo, but what you want is someone who will take the bus with you when the limo breaks down."

—Oprah Winfrey

Lee Iacocca said, "People want economy and they will pay any price to get it." After paying for your pad, the cost of getting around is usually your second biggest expense. Cars can be expensive—a hole in the ground into which you pour money. It's not just the cost of the car, either. There is registration, taxes, gas, and parking. A car is NOT a good investment. You spend about two to three months working just to pay for your car. Enzo Ferrari, the man behind the car that bears his name, lived in a little apartment over his warehouse but didn't have to have every car that he built. According to the book *The Millionaire Next Door,* most millionaires drive domestic cars they bought used. Don't confuse success with *symbols* of success.

• **Previously Loved.** The best thing to do is buy a used car. We all know that the car goes down in value the minute you release the brake and put it in gear. Trust me when I tell you that the new-car smell, warranty, and easy payment plans can be very seductive. I used to get a new car every two years. S-T-U-P-I-D! I have had the same car for the past ten years (my wife has a nice new one), and I couldn't be happier. The downside of used cars is that you may be buying someone else's problems. You can still get the car of your more recent dreams—just get one that was "previously loved" rather than new. Buy from a reputable dealer, not from a tent on wheels.

• **Classic Cars.** How would you like to drive a Ferrari or a Maserati or a Lamborghini? Surprise! You can get one of these classics for less than it would cost to buy an SUV. Plus, it should also appreciate in value! It's like driving a piece of art! If you choose the right car it can be both reliable and a real head-turner.

• **What's Worse Than a Used-Car Salesman?** A *new* car salesman. I can recall going in to buy a new car (I know, stupid, stupid, stupid), and it was such a stressful situation that I got a horrible nosebleed from the stress. But I did get a good deal on a demo model. If you insist on getting a new car, here are some ideas that can help you get the most car for the least money. If you buy smart, maintain the car, and keep it a long time, then buying new isn't that bad (especially if you paid cash and told them to shove it when they tried to sell you Teflon coating and an extended warranty). Step one is to do your homework. Know the dealer's cost, check on the reliability of the make and model you want, and know where the different dealers are (and not just in your area, because they can trade). Also, check the insurance rate on the car you are considering. Don't negotiate the trade-in until after you have a deal for the new car. Better yet, sell your car yourself. Think ahead. What kind of car will you need down the road? There are a lot of almost-new Miatas for sale by people who started a family and the two-seater sports car was the first thing to go. Pay cash if you can. (Just take a look at the price you pay after all the finance charges. Scary.) Finally, don't get emotionally attached to a car. You need to have walk-away power. Don't put yourself in a position where you *have* to have it today.

• **A New Lease on Life?** To lease or buy? That is the question. The answer is simple—buy. Like a guy you meet at a bar after four glasses of wine, he looks real good until you sober up and realize he's only after one thing (I'll let you finish the sentence). It's the same with leasing a car. You're lusting after it, and all it takes is a little sweet talk and the next thing you know you are in a long-term relationship that you just know is gonna end badly. With a lease, what draws you is the fact that you only have to put a little money down and your monthly payments are low. You rationalize it out. Leasing is like renting a car. For most people, buying is better and less expensive overall. But all my friends lease cars. "If they jump off a bridge . . ." Seriously, if you plan to keep the car more than three years, you don't drive more than 15,000 miles a year, or tend to trash your car—buy it.

• **Refinance.** Have you ever considered refinancing your car at a lower interest rate?

• **Grease Monkey.** Should you fix your car yourself? My buddy is a mechanic and he says "N-O." You should not mess with the major repairs yourself. You will wind up doing more damage, and it will cost you more time and money in the long run. I like working on cars. I used to rebuild cars when I was younger. I recently opened up the hood of a friend's new car, and I swear I wasn't even sure if it ran on gasoline. I was lost. Still, knowing the basics can keep you from getting ripped off. A friend of my wife's is clueless about cars and was taken for $1,000 in needless repairs because she thought a caliper was a small bug and that an engine block was the former Soviet Union. (My wife now knows to pull over when that cute little light that says "Engine Oil" comes on. Jeez!) Knowledge is power! Do maintain your car—rotate the tires, change the oil, replace the timing belt—but don't do it yourself unless you really know what you are doing. Get a good mechanic, one you can trust. Also, if you pay for repairs with your credit card you can dispute it. If you look in your junk mail, there are almost always coupons for repairs, car washes, and maintenance. It's not as embarrassing as using a two-for-oner at a restaurant.

• **Get into AA.** Oops, I meant AAA. The Automobile Club of America is a good deal (and not just because of the free maps, either). They will also run a diagnostic test on any potential used car you are thinking of purchasing. There is the free towing, too.

• **Please Step Away from the Vehicle.** "But Officer, I was just trying to get out of your way" just doesn't cut it. Right-brainers are known for being impatient thrill-seekers who are frequently running late. See where I am going with this? Right. We tend to get more tickets than the average Joe. The cost of the ticket is just the beginning. Your insurance goes up, or worse, they drop you. Fight your traffic tickets, pay your parking tickets. If you are a good driver with a clean record, make sure you are getting the good-driver discount.

• **Truck Stop.** My friend keeps an old truck around "just in case." This is in addition to two other cars. Not only does he have to insure and maintain it, he is always having to help people move. It would have been better to rent a truck if he needed it. Another friend of mine poured a ton of money into "tricking out" his truck. He got the lift kit, expensive rims and tires, roll bar, winch, lockers, and so on. All this so that when he goes off-roading (about once every two years), he can climb some hill. The rest of the time he struggles with the thing on real roads. The worst part is that when he went to sell it, he was unable to get back the $5,000 he spent in upgrades.

Lily's Limo

You can use your creativity instead of a car to get around in some cases. For example, when Lily Tomlin was performing on the New York coffeehouse circuit in the mid-'60s, wearing glamorous clothes bought at a thrift shop, she would take the subway from her apartment to the theater district and then rent a limo. "I knew you could get a limo since they were waiting for people in the theater, and I'd give him ten bucks and he'd drive me up to the Improv. I'd sweep in, in this big outfit, do ten minutes, sweep out, and get in that car and drive away."

Here Today, Gone to Maui

> *"The reason most of us don't live within our income is that we don't consider that living."*
>
> —John Moore

When I ask people in my workshop what they would do if they won a million dollars, travel is always on their wish list. You don't have to be wealthy to see the world. One couple I know (she's a writer) spent a year working their way around the world and even sold sponsorships to help finance their trip. (People paid the couple for weekly updates on their adventure.) To them, traveling was a high priority, so they sold all their worldly goods to go on this trip. When they got back they settled down and started a family. While they were away, they got the wanderlust out of their system and had time to reflect on the past and plan their future.

I have been able to travel a LOT by combining business with pleasure. I look for speaking opportunities in places I want to go see, or I try to get a writing assignment to cover a place for a paper or magazine. You can travel without the burden of having to pay off the trip long after your tan has faded.

If you can't get away physically, go somewhere mentally. Take a vacation in your mind. Go back to your favorite places in your head to escape from whatever is stressing you out. It's a cheap way to get away from what bugs you. Here's some more travel tips.

• **People overspend when going away.** Get only the gear you need.

• **The weather is here, wish you were beautiful.** Negotiate hard to get the best deal on hotels. There are some simple strategies that can save you a bundle. When you call to book a room always ask for the *best* rate. If you don't ask you get quoted the rack rate. Try calling the hotel's 800 number and then try calling the hotel directly. If you can stay flexible you can get the best deals. My rule is to travel either off-season or, better yet, just before or just after the peak season. (The weather is still nice.) It's always off-season somewhere. If you can get a group of ten or more, you may be entitled to a free trip; the others get the group rate.

• **Get away without going broke.** You could go on a vacation in your hometown.

• **Crew cut.** Volunteer to crew on a yacht. At my marina there are always captains looking for compatible people to help out on long trips, no experience necessary. Can you cook? Check marine-supply stores and classifieds under "Crew Wanted." You could also transport a rental car back to its original location. There are always ads looking for people to drive cross-country and return a rental car.

• **Do the bump.** Volunteer to be bumped and get extra airline miles, a free ticket, cash vouchers for hotel and food. How? Book your flight on one of the busier days of the week (where business-people HAVE to get where they are going) or before a big holiday. When you check in (early) volunteer to give up your seat if the plane is overbooked.

- **Warm towels, free drinks, super-comfy seats, and extra legroom.** Ask for a free upgrade. There are what are called discretionary upgrades that can be granted upon check-in. The secret to getting one? Kindness, creativity, and charity. You have to use all of your strength to stay calm and smile and ask politely if there is some way you could be upgraded today. One balloon artist makes elaborate balloon figures for gate agents and flight attendants. If you are tall, pregnant, or injured (two of which can be faked) you are more likely to get bumped up to first-class. If all else fails try donuts or chocolates.

💰 ACTION ITEM

To save on souvenirs, my wife and I made signs that we held up in photos that said, "Wish you were here" with their names and the beach in the background. People loved them. It let them know we were thinking about them. We also photographed little messages in the sand and sent them.

💰 SOMETHING TO THINK ABOUT

According to a recent survey 18 percent of the women polled regularly spend more than $50 on a haircut. In many ways, it's cheaper to be a man. This isn't a sexist statement so hold your threatening e-mails and hear me out. For women, a larger chunk of change goes out each month to maintenance items like manicures, shoes, dry cleaning, pedicures, shoes, dry cleaning, shoes, and more shoes. To cut back could you go longer between haircuts and nail appointments? Maybe go with a simple hairstyle rather than one that needs constant maintenance. Do you really need those highlights in your hair? (Some people who are obviously *not* blondes but want to be the ones "who have more fun" spend a lot of time and money making sure their roots don't clash with the rest of their hair.) In the winter do you really need a pedicure and waxings? Teeth whitening can cost hundreds of dollars. Maybe you can do just the uppers? With the money a boob job costs you could invest in the stock market or give your bank account a boost rather than your bust size.

Dollar "Stretchers"

"I tried Flintstones vitamins. I didn't feel any better, but I could stop the car with my feet."

—Joan St. Onge

Doctor to a patient: "I'm going to prescribe something that works like aspirin but costs much, much more." If you can't afford health care you have to really be careful about taking care of yourself. One accident or illness can wipe you out. When a freelancer goes down, not only is there no sick pay but you fall behind in your work, and marketing and business suffers along with you. Getting sick is costly. And not just *really* sick, either. Headaches, burnout, and minor injuries can slow us down enough to affect our income. So take preventative measures to keep from getting sick or hurt. Become a germaphobe. Look at how you do your work. Is it ergonomically correct? Do you exercise enough? (If you belong to a gym that you never go to, get rid of that expense and find fun ways to stay fit that cost less, like walking, swimming, hiking, biking, and so on.) Quit smoking and save BIG bucks. Sign up for a support group instead of seeing a shrink and save your sanity and your money.

Appearances Are Deceptive

"A bargain is something you can't use at a price you can't resist."

—Franklin Jones

Do clothes make the man (or woman)? Depending on which area of the arts you work in, yes. Some artists would benefit from wearing a nice new Armani suit to work; others would be shot if they showed up in something so extravagant. The goal is to dress to impress, and that doesn't necessarily mean you have to spend a lot of money to do it. If you need nice clothes to look and act the part, borrow from a friend. Fix old clothes that may just need a button or alteration. Same for your favorite shoes.

Simplify your color scheme so you need far fewer shoes, belts, and accessories to match. Discover your best color. Go for quality, not quantity. (Shop where you can get labels for less.) Buy classic styles and colors that are always in style, like black, for example. "In the first grade, they wanted to put me in a special learning program because my favorite color was black. They thought I was profoundly disturbed, but even in first grade, I knew that black was slimming," says Rob Lowe. Speaking of slimming, keeping the weight off is good for your health and your wallet. Having to have a wardrobe for your diet days and another for when you are carrying more weight is expensive.

Classy is always in style. Buy for fit and not for fashion. Narrow and deep and a simplified wardrobe is effective. Go through your closet and separate all the things that are quality, flattering, and fit, and then ditch the rest (or sell it).

I came across an interesting article in *Mademoiselle,* written by Nicole Beland, describing women getting together for what she calls a "Bitch 'n' Swap." What is it? It's a kind of party where you get to raid your friends' clothes closets. You swap clothes with your friends while sharing the tragic story behind the giveaways while sipping some whine—oops, I meant wine.

Some people always look more glamorous than others. How do they do it? Many times they find the funkiest outfits at thrift shops and prefer vintage to Versace. Actor Eddie Cahill (Rachel's assistant on *Friends*) says that despite his increasing income, he's still a sec-ondhand kinda guy. "There is something very Zen about sifting through thrift stores." I can't tell you how many times I've come across stories of struggling artists (who are now famous) who shopped at thrift shops before they made it big.

 FAST FACT

Here's a little useless fact that makes you go hmmmm. According to a survey in the book *Are You Normal About Money?* by Bernice Kanner, women with household incomes under $40,000 are eight times more likely to wear thong underwear.

ACTION ITEM

Name five things you can do for under ten dollars that will make you feel like a million bucks.

You Don't Have to Be a "Starving" Artist

"It's so beautifully arranged on the plate—you know someone's fingers have been all over it."

—Julia Childs

I read about one guy who was homeless by choice. By his own admission he was lazy. Lazy, yes, crazy, no. He found a little loophole for free food—gourmet food. Years ago he was able to sneak backstage before a Guns 'N' Roses concert and accidently ate Axl Rose's sub sandwich. He realized he'd hit the homeless jackpot. He now sneaks into concerts of all kinds (rock stars have the best buffets, he boasts) and gorges himself on food and then heads for the seats to look for lost loot and drugs. How does he get in? He won't say, but he hasn't been caught yet. There are better ways to save on food.

• **Coupons for Couples.** One mother sent her teenage son out to pick up a pizza and gave him money and a coupon. Later he returned with the pizza and the coupon. When the mother asked what happened he replied, "Mom, I had enough money. I didn't need the coupon." Go shopping on "double" days. Some items with a coupon and/or a rebate are almost free.

• **Never Shop on an Empty Stomach.** That way you're not tempted to steal those yogurt-covered pretzels. Don't bring your kids. Avoid convenience stores. Shop at stores you know so you're not tempted by end caps. Buy in bulk. Check expiration dates. Compare unit prices. Double-check your inventory before shopping.

• **"Dinner and a Movie."** I love that show on TNT where the hosts show you how to cook a different dish each week while they also show a movie. Learn to cook. One family eats out so much that when they sat down for a home-cooked meal and the mother handed her three-year-old a glass of milk and told her to drink it, the little girl frowned and said, "But I didn't order milk."

• **Free Handouts.** Stores with perishable inventory like Mrs. Field's often mark down their merchandise (cookies!) an hour before closing. Same thing with bagel shops, bakeries, and flower shops.

• **Lunchbox.** Bring lunch to work. According to a survey, nearly half of respondents eat a lunch they packed at home. Amazingly, 32 percent skip lunch.

• **Dinner Is Served.** I can't rattle off my agent's phone number nor do I remember my editor's, but I do know the number for the local pizza-delivery place. Sometimes you just don't feel like dealing with making a meal. So you either go out to eat (more on that in a minute) or order a pizza. I can't imagine paying full price for a pizza. There are so many coupons or specials that you would have to try hard *not* to find one. With a deal ("pizza, pizza!") you would be hard-pressed to make a meal for as little as it costs to have a piping hot pizza delivered to your door.

• **Drinks Are on Me.** I don't want you to think I'm a lush, but having a beer here and there is just the American way, and I like to sip the suds. But I have noticed that booze does boost the bill a great deal. When I started to track my spending, I looked for ways to cut down on my bar tab. For ideas I would ask people at the bar for their suggestions. When they weren't spitting and slobbering all over themselves, they gave me some good ideas. One woman says she makes a meal of happy-hour food and loads up on drinks during the time when they are half price and then nurses another when they are full price (and she's already lit). One couple told me that they don't leave a credit card with the waitress to run a tab when with a big group because whenever the bill comes and it is time to settle up, they always get stiffed by people who can't drink and add at the same time. Now they pay as they go. I have more notes from my bar research, but I can't read them.

• **Dining for Dollars.** It's a waiter's job to try to pad the bill, and it's your job to try and resist. Besides, we all need to drink more water. Think about getting a discount card that gives you a free meal when you buy one. I know, not on a first date. But some people are impressed that you are "smart with money." No more picking up the tab. Who do you think you are? People don't appreciate (enough) when you treat them. Sure, it's awkward when the bill arrives and you have to figure out what you owe. Guys will just throw in a coupla twenties, but the women will whip out their calculators. Lastly, there is the tip. When the waitress draws a little happy face and puts her name on the bill, it's proven, people will pay more in the way of a tip. Give good tips, but not extraordinary tips.

Chillin'

"Give me Books, fruit, French wine and fine weather and a little music out of doors, played by somebody I do not know."
—John Keats

Entertainment is a fairly large expense for most folks. "Entertainment" means different things to different people. For some it's going to parties (or throwing parties and entertaining people), and for others, it's renting a video and kicking it at home. Both cost money, so let's look at how we can cut some and still have fun.

• **Put People First.** For the new millennium my wife and I went to see Jimmy Buffett in Los Angeles. The cost for the New Year's concert and hotel came to about $1,500. For the next New Year's celebration we hung out with my grandfather and my wife's grandmother. We knew they would be alone and home, so we invited them over to ring in the new year. The cost for this was zero. To be honest, both New Year's celebrations were fun, but it was nice to lay low with people we care about and who care about us.

• **Losers.** The San Diego Chargers football team won one game and lost fifteen in 2000. I feel bad for people who paid to see that. Instead, I stayed home and watched a game or two before I gave up and put together some pickup games with friends. We had more fun playing football than watching it, and I saved $1,000.

• **Be Kind, Rewind.** Creatives are chronically late, and this can extend to video rentals. Late fees are one of Blockbuster's primary sources of income. One guy forgot to return a video before he went on vacation and owed thirty bucks in "extended viewing" charges. That guy was *me*. When it comes to going to the theater to catch a flick, a matinee is always cheaper, and for fun, see how much food you can sneak in.

• **Combine Business with Pleasure.** A drummer I know became an usher to get good seats to shows. Another works for a radio station part-time. Still another is a house roadie. Annette Bening was once a cook aboard a dive boat in exchange for free scuba diving.

- **How to Be More Crafty.** My friend made the ultimate Halloween costume. It's hard to describe, but it looks like an old lady is on his back. For the past few years he has entered costume contests and won a trip to Cabo San Lucas and cash prizes up to $500. I'm trying to teach my nephew that creative play is better than paying for play. I took him to a video arcade one afternoon and spent a hundred bucks. Then I took him hiking, climbing, snorkeling, and cliff-jumping (don't tell his mom), and we came up with all kinds of adventures. (We pretended to be Navy SEALs and hunted down some of my friends in a mock mission.) He talks more about the free stuff we did than the video arcade and laser tag I took him to.

- **Reading Is a Cheap Thrill.** Hey, you're reading this book, so there's no need to elaborate.

💰 FAST FACT

In a recent Gallup Poll, 78 percent of people earning more than $60,000 a year own a library card. Only 48 percent of people earning less than $20,000 do. This proves my theory that the more you learn, the more you earn.

Creative Dating

"I don't have a boyfriend right now. I'm looking for anyone with a job that I don't have to support."

—*Anna Nicole Smith*

Dating doesn't have to be a drain on your finances but can still be fun. It can be expensive when you are first hooking up with someone; that can cut both ways. You want to impress the person, and sometimes the easiest way to do that is to pay—for everything. Instead, use your creativity to come up with thoughtful, romantic, and free ways to show you care. That also includes finding fun things to do that don't cost a lot, or anything at all. Here are some suggestions to get you started.

You could watch a courtroom drama unfold at the county courthouse for free. Maybe you set up a tent in your backyard for a campinglike trip. Take a drive up the coast or around the lake. Take your date to a lookout spot and bring a thermos of hot chocolate to stay warm. Watch the sunset or sunrise together. Take a tour of the local TV station, newspaper, or an airport control tower (usually all you have to do is call). Attend a ball game but go watch Little Leaguers play the game. Go for a hike. Go to a park for a picnic and lay on the grass and watch clouds pass by. Go people-watching. Go for a bike ride. Take a hike or fly a kite. Wade in the tidepools. Visit a museum. Go window-shopping. Go up on the roof and set up a romantic dinner for two. Go house-hunting in a wealthy neighborhood (with no intention of buying but just for the thrill). Find out what their favorite things are and give them a night that includes their favorite food, video, and whatever else they want (wink, wink). Meet at midnight for a moonlit walk on the beach and maybe a little skinny-dipping. Do charity work together. Pass out cups of hot coffee to the homeless. Instead of going to an expensive restaurant for dinner, meet there for an appetizer, and then go to a inexpensive restaurant for the main course, and then yet another expensive one for dessert and coffee. Gaze at the stars. Go ice sliding (this is a "sport" where you race down grassy hills while sitting on a big block of ice). Ride bikes. Get a bucket of cutout hearts spread all over the house. Bake a heart-shaped cake. Make a heart in the snow. Cut the grass in a heart shape. Basically, show them you care and that you are creative (and smart with money). Not a cheap date, but a fun one.

It's the Thought

"I have enough money to last me the rest of my life, unless I buy something."

—Jackie Mason

When it comes to gift-giving, it truly is the thought that counts. Plus, gifts that come from the heart mean more and cost less. One of the best gifts you can give someone is the gift of time. Give someone you care about twenty minutes of your complete attention. Wash her car for her while she is at work. Offer to help her with her work.

Free or almost-free gift-giving ideas. Write a poem or song for someone. Do a painting. Take out a free classified ad. Request a song on the radio. Burn a CD of her favorite songs. Write a love letter.

Write a song. Paint a picture. Slip love notes in her lunch, glove box, briefcase. Call and leave a loving message on her answering machine. Make a wish book, and ask her to put all her hopes and dreams in it. Make a book called "A Few of My Favorite Things" and ask her to write down all her favorite things. Serenade her outside her window. Serve her breakfast in bed. Give a good massage. Make signs and post them in the grass. Send her on a treasure hunt in the house. (Make a tape, map, clues, or riddles that lead to a gift.) Give a coupon book of "things" you will do for her, like cook, clean, cuddle, or whatever. Make a scrapbook of your time together. Make a calendar on your computer with important dates mentioned. (You'll be there for her 365 days a year.) Decorate her car with love notes, flowers, or cut-out hearts. Make personal stationery for her using a computer. Decorate a tree outside her window with lights from Christmas. Have a bath waiting for her when she gets home. Pick flowers from a garden.

If you are getting married, the holidays are approaching, or it's your birthday, don't hesitate to let those around you know what YOU want. Otherwise you end up getting crap. Ask for things you need and can use. Gift certificates for a cab company, ad space, a class, software, a personal trainer, or a car service. It's smart to set a limit for what you will spend on others for gifts, but that doesn't mean there has to be a limit on what *you* will accept.

Up in Smoke

"I decided to give up cigarettes in two stages.
First I'm going to give up smoking my cigarettes—
and then I'll give up smoking other people's."

—Unknown

Ever been to a Denny's restaurant? They are open twenty-four hours, which means people come in plastered after having a few drinks earlier in the evening. That's why (I suspect) their menu is made up of pictures. This way people can just point to what they want. "Aaaalllllll'llll haffvvv thaaaaaaat!" By this time price is *not* an issue. "Need . . . food." Richard Lewis, an admitted alcoholic, said that during the height of his drinking days he tried to buy a palm-tree lamp from the Argyle, an expensive hotel on Sunset Boulevard in Los Angeles. It could have been his for a mere $25,000. Luckily, it wasn't for sale. I guess what I'm trying to say is that partying leads to poor and potentially costly decisions. Before you know it you and your buddies are throwing twenties at strippers—or worse. I heard a DUI can cost upward of $11,000 by the time you are done—and that's if you *don't* get into an accident. Doing drugs and other destructive habits can suck money out of your bank account faster than a big bong hit. Take a pack of cigarettes. A pack-a-day habit means you spent over $1,000 last year on smokes. If you drink a six-pack a day that equals almost $2,000 a year (and a big ole belly). According to the Hazelden Clinic, the main reason people can't quit smoking is stress (29 percent), and only 12 percent said because they enjoy it. Okay, that's the end of my sermon. Just something to think about.

Yada, Yada, Yada

"Mobile phones are the only subject on which men boast about who's got the smallest."

—Neil Kinnock

When I was a kid my father was a traveling salesman. To save money he and my mother had a system. My father would call collect and ask for "Mr. Yako" ("okay" spelled backward) and if everything was fine, my mother would say there was no "Mr. Yako" there and not accept the call. If she needed to talk to him she would say "Mr. Yako should be back soon," and my father would call back later. It's no wonder I had no problem writing this section on cutting costs—I've lived it since I was a child. But since my friends call me "The Rambler" because of my tendency to be verbose on the phone, I thought this might be a good place to save a buck or two (and I'm not talking about dialing 1-800-CALL-ATT).

• **Mr. Silber's Not Home.** Don't buy anything over the phone! When a telemarketer asked Bernadine Castle, who was recovering from surgery, if she would participate in a door-to-door fund-raising effort, she replied, "Sorry, but I've been incapacitated." This didn't deter the determined caller. So Bernadine interrupted and said, "I'm incapacitated. Do you know what that means?" The caller hesitated and then said, "It means your head was cut off?" I have a policy that I will not buy anything over the phone. Sometimes that doesn't get through to the person on the other end. I've tried hanging up, but they just call back. I've tried asking them to take me off their list, but they still call. I've used the line "I'm sorry, but I just filed for bankruptcy." Still, they call trying to sell me something. I have used the "I'm crazy" act, asking the telemarketer if the call is being recorded by the CIA and then start talking in code, continually asking the caller if they heard that clicking noise. No luck. I've asked telemarketers if they've accepted Jesus into their hearts and then asked them to pray with me. (This works only if they *aren't* religious.) I've played that kid's game and repeated everything they say. They hate that and always hang up, saying, "What's wrong with you, mister?" Create your own game. It's fun.

• **Step Away from the Phone.** To save on long-distance costs between an artist and her agent, the artist suggested that they use e-mail rather than the agent calling her on her cell phone (calls she had to pay for). Her request fell on deaf ears as her agent refused to e-mail instead of calling her cell phone. Finally, the agent thought she got it and sent a message via e-mail. It read: "Call me at 4 P.M." The only way e-mail isn't cheaper than phoning is when you have to pay a toll charge to dial-up your modem, and that should be avoided at all costs. Shop around for the best service providers and hosts. You want reliable service and FREE technical support.

• **Here's the "4-1-1."** Here are some more thoughts on how to save on your phone bill. Use the phone book or go to the online Yellow Pages, or if it's a company you want to reach you can call 1-800-555-1212 for free directory assistance on toll-free numbers. Switch partners. No, no, I mean switch long-distance carriers when one makes you an offer you can't refuse. Are they loyal to you? No way. So sleep around until you find the one that is most pleasing. If you threaten to leave them they will beg you to stay. Make long-distance calls during off-peak hours for the best rates. Better yet, get them to call you. Get rid of those stupid extras the phone company tries to add on. If you don't look at your phone bill closely, there may be things on there you didn't ask for. Check. Quick calls save money. Call when you know you'll get their answering machine, and then they can call you back.

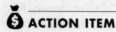

⬥ ACTION ITEM

List all the things you like to do in your free time. Prioritize them by which bring you the most joy. Make a top-ten list and drop the rest. Then look at how much each hobby costs you to enjoy. Choose hobbies that have a high cost/joy ratio.

Frugal to a Fault

*"If you want to say it with flowers, a single rose says:
'I'm cheap!'"*

—*Delta Burke*

My wife works for a department store famous for accepting returns (they even took back a tire even though they sell clothes). Of course, people take advantage of this policy. One of the biggest "scams" is buying an outfit, wearing it for a while, and then returning it for a refund. One day a worker found a discarded jacket hanging on the return rack. It had clearly been worn. She turned to her supervisor and said, "Can you believe this. People have no shame. This jacket is old, dirty, and hideous." The supervisor then scowled and said, "Hey, that's my jacket." The point is, there is a limit to how far you want to take the concept of cutting back. Anything illegal, immoral, or that in any way endangers you is not worth it. You don't have to live a life of deprivation just to save a few bucks. Gordon Elwood drank outdated milk, refused to turn on the heat in his house, and held up his secondhand pants with a bungee cord. He left an estate of $10 million when he died at 79. But did he ever really live?

YOU'VE GONE TOO FAR WHEN YOU . . .

__ Steal shot glasses, silverware, and condiments from restaurants.

__ Pretend you are having a wedding so you can sample cakes for free.

__ Serve Top Ramen at dinner parties.

__ Fake your birthday for the free dessert at a restaurant.

__ Can be found rummaging through the neighbor's trash.

__ Feel duct tape is your most important tool.

__ Steam off stamps that haven't been canceled.

__ Talk incessantly about how much you saved.

__ Don't adhere to the rule that when it's brown you to flush it down.

__ Go scuba diving in a wishing well for spare change.

__ Split two-ply toilet paper into two tubes.

__ Take anything not bolted down when you check out of a hotel (lightbulbs, towels, iron, Bible).

Perky

> "Made enough money to buy Miami but I pissed it
> away so fast."
>
> —Jimmy Buffett lyrics from "A Pirate Looks at Forty"

Wouldn't you like it if your company provided gourmet-to-go dinners that are free for you to take home (Valassis Communications) or a free BMW 323i or Z3 Roadster with insurance (Revenue Systems Inc.) or have your car serviced and detailed while you work (BMC Software) or a variety of other perks in addition to your pay? In an effort to make employees happier (and a happier employee is more productive), companies offer all kinds of extra benefits that can save time and money. How about an on-site laundry room, gym, concierge, a month-long sabbatical, days off if there is surf, a nail salon, college tuition, tennis lessons, tax preparation, airline tickets, free movie passes, yoga and art classes. At LucasArts Entertainment, creativity is encouraged. That's the best perk of all. (They also have a thirty-foot company sailboat that employees can use at will.)

Downsize This

> "I bought materials from junkyards where it didn't cost me as
> much. I found in a junkyard on Alameda Street years ago
> quite a bit of stainless steel, and I did a whole series of work
> with that metal."
>
> —John Outterbridge, artist

It's not how much you make that matters, it's how much you keep. The funny thing is that it's actually easier to spend money than it is to make it. Meaning, we can find all kinds of creative ways to blow bundles on our business—consultants, equipment, supplies, technology, advertising, and so on. Smart businesspeople are frugal when it comes to their companies. They may choose to do something themselves, but they also realize that it makes sense to hire help and have professional marketing materials. What they don't do is throw money at problems. They look for low-cost, creative solutions to the challenges. But business is booming, why should I care how much things cost? Hmmm, let's see. For one, you will be making more money for the same amount of effort. If you cut back costs, you can cut back on the amount you have to work. You can be choosier about the kind of work you accept.

When Anita Roddick founded the Body Shop she had no money, so she ran the business the way her mother ran her household—by being resourceful. She refilled, recycled, and reused everything.

When Rachel and Andy Berliner founded Amy's Kitchen, a company that produces healthy (vegetarian) frozen foods for health-food stores and supermarkets, they did so without a lot of cash. (Money wasn't their motivator to begin with.) To get up and running the couple sold their watches and cars and remortgaged their home. Because they couldn't afford to hire help, they did the work themselves and learned as they went. Today the couple are millionaires but still live a frugal lifestyle and run their business the same way.

Words like "efficiency," "productivity," and "profit" are not often used by the creative person when describing his work. But we need to learn how to reduce spending when times get tough (and even when things are going well). Use your creativity to cut costs. Two of the reasons Apple Computers bounced back from bad times after the return of co-founder Steve Jobs as the CEO were his focus on design and trimming costs by lowering inventories and outsourcing manufacturing. Many movies and television shows are shot in Canada to cut costs. It is possible to be profit-minded and creative at the same time. It all comes down to needs versus wants. We want more software, a bigger studio, or more gear, but we don't really need it. Let the business grow to the point where it can pay for itself, and even then ask yourself if you want to put some money in your pocket or plow it back into the business. I used to think I needed a new laptop every two years. Every time I'm tempted to get more equipment I remember that books have been written (and still are) in longhand and on typewriters. Work on improving your craft instead of buying things as a crutch.

Once you start to think like an artist who is in *business* and wants to stay in business, you start to see things in a different light. You'll look for ways to boost your bottom line, and one way is to cut costs. (The other is to make more.) Our overhead can include things like backup singers, a horn section, extra gear, lighting, wardrobe, stylists, managers, and so on. In my band when we get paid for performing and split it up six ways, it sometimes makes me wonder if I wouldn't be better off in a three-piece band. Could you renegotiate your lease or move to a cheaper location? I know of an artist who moved to out-of-the-way places to cut costs (and eliminate distractions). Need to get away from it all? Why don't you house-sit for someone who is out of town? Use a summer home in the winter. For $1.50 I can escape to a coffee shop overlooking the ocean. If you want to travel to Hawaii, set up a talk, exhibit, demonstration, visit vendors, go to some training or a retreat, and it's tax-deductible.

Buying low and selling high works for investing and as a principle for turning a profit in your business. Every dollar counts. I'm not saying you need to be all about the money and pinch pennies, becoming obsessed with the bottom line—the arts don't always work that way. But by increasing income and cutting costs you end up more profitable, and that is at least part of your goal, isn't it? To make some money so he could survive and continue to create, artist John Baldessari learned to recycle and reuse everything from his father's salvage business. Like myself, his father had him taking nails out of old lumber and straightening them out and taking broken items apart for spare parts. His father owned several old buildings, one of which was partially vacant. Even though he was teaching part-time to pay the bills, the free studio space was a blessing. Baldessari set up shop in the windowless room and started painting. He also incorporated materials he found in Dumpsters into his art.

Some people would sell their mothers (in-law) to get their work out into the world. I'm not saying you shouldn't explore any and all options (just get fair market value for your mother-in-law), but don't let the excitement cloud your judgment. For example, one author I know spent thousands on a lavish reception for her new book (which was self-published). For her it was all about the prestige. I gladly wolfed down the hors d'oeuvres, but I know she lost a lot of money. Until she realizes it is a business and she needs to run her creative career as such, she'll never make it.

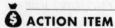

ACTION ITEM

Make a list of everything you spend money on and how much it costs. Look at each item and see if you can cut it down or cut it out of your budget. Make a list of monthly expenses and see where you can trim. Small stuff adds up when you multiply the expense by twelve months.

Do Sweat the Small Stuff

Maybe you can e-mail your newsletter rather than printing and mailing it. I started asking for my Zip disks back on design jobs. Hey, that's ten bucks. Disposable items (paper, pens, Post-it Notes) are things that are used and then discarded. This is an area where you can cut costs. For all the jokes about my father's frugality, he was a very smart businessman, and I learned a lot from working in his warehouse. He had me recycle boxes from incoming stock to use to ship orders. He saved the packing materials and reused them. He turned file folders inside out and relabeled them. I learned from the master. I've melted down old crayons to create a multicolored "crayon cookie." I still like new file folders, but I have become more aware of ways to recycle and save. In the past when I sent in manuscripts, I paid for the shipping. Then I simply asked for my publisher's FedEx number, and they said, "Sure." What an idiot I was. I was paying for something I didn't have to.

Seventy percent of small-business owners do not know where to find deals on items they buy regularly to run their business. Why wouldn't you try to get the best deal? This includes everything from insurance down to something as insignificant as inkjet cartridges. Cutting costs is in vogue again. According to a recent poll, 31 percent of chief financial officers say that cutting costs will be crucial to their businesses over the next two years. One entrepreneur who owns a craft company realized that by switching her packaging she could save $1.20 on each product she shipped. That ended up saving her thousands a year. Look at where you get your materials. When was the last time you shopped around? Are you sure you're getting the best prices? Have you ever asked your vendors for a break?

At several of my workshops I began asking people what they do to cut costs in their business, and here are some of the things they told me. Many felt that software upgrades are a waste of money. One attendee said she went through all her drawers to seek out and collect pens, pencils, paper clips, and anything else she could use. She realized that her disorganization meant she couldn't find things she needed (so she would buy more), which was getting costly. (I noticed she kept the pen the hotel provided each person.) A copywriter says he meets clients for coffee or breakfast rather than a fancy dinner, and if he is taking them out for lunch, he will be sure to choose a restaurant he can afford. A trainer says she looks for hotels that include breakfast because the clients pay for the room but not food, and this way she collects on at least one meal. Another artist says she stocks up on free boxes from the post office to ship her portfolio and samples. She also said she used to wait until the last minute to send something but quickly realized there was a big difference between overnight mail and regular mail. (Peeling off stamps that weren't canceled may be a little much.) Others began chiming in about "going postal." One said she uses the free postcards the post office provides. Everyone agreed that first-class mail is still a bargain and Priority Mail is a steal. Also, get a scale and know postal rates so you don't guess at the postage and waste stamps. Other comments included one freelance writer who reads the newspaper at the library or online for free. I told them that in addition to being paid to teach the class they attending at for the Learning Annex, it was also free for me to take any other class in the catalog I wanted. I chose the class "How to Strip for Your Lover." I'm kidding—please.

You should see if there is any co-op money available to you. Try to convince the gallery, bookstore, or venue to pay for as much promotion as possible. Ask vendors, if you pay on time could they do away with your COD status and switch to "net 365," or something like that? We talked about buying in bulk. The big plus is that because you buy ten years' worth of paper clips you get a better deal.

It means less time schlepping to the store, which saves money. The downside is that you have to store the stuff. Plus, when you make an impulse buy, it could mean you are now the proud owner of 144 pink pens. That and the fact that you have to save enough to at least pay for the membership. Just know your prices (warehouse clubs don't always have the best deals), and if possible, go in with a couple of other creatives to split the costs. Don't be too cheap. A recycled inkjet cartridge can do more harm than good.

Bargains on the Big Stuff

Salesman, "This copier will pay for itself in no time." Customer, "Good—when it does, send it to me." Businesses go broke buying the best of everything from four-color brochures to brand-new office furniture. Use your creativity instead of your credit card. One guitarist made big boxes for his tiny speakers for gigs. It looks like he has all kinds of good gear, and the sound is fine. When I decided to hold the first annual "Retreat for Right-Brainers," I looked into renting space and hiring other trainers for this event. Then it occurred to me: Shouldn't a retreat be outdoors? So I found the perfect place, a beautiful park complete with rolling hills, lots of grass, privacy, a gazebo, hiking trails, plenty of parking and (clean) bathrooms. It was free and better than any indoor venue we would have paid for.

💰 ACTION ITEM

Think before you buy. Ask yourself, "What if I didn't get this, what would happen? Do I really need it? How often will I use it? Is it worth it? Will it increase profits? Where else can I get/use it (free)? Is there a way I could borrow this? Do I need the top-of-the-line model? Is this the best deal? Can I get a used one for less?"

When it comes to office furniture and equipment, get used stuff at auctions or from going-out-of-business sales. If that seems too tacky, ask a retailer if you can purchase a floor model at a reduced price. Maybe you notice a nick or scratch—point it out before you purchase and ask for a deal. Ask for a deal from suppliers and vendors. Negotiate better terms. Talk to the printer for suggestions to make the project less expensive. If you are short on cash but need equipment to do a job, you can lease it. Construction companies rent equipment all the time as the job requires. The creative person could lease everything from copiers to computers. The monthly payments can be tax-deductible. When the thing becomes obsolete, you simply turn it in. There are times when buying an item makes sense. I used to run to Kinko's for copies before I bought my own copier, which saved time and money. But you should buy only things you need with money you've made. Geeks used to think that the best gear meant they were cool. Hello, you're still a geek. Our bass player has old stuff, but he shreds. I make do without a lot of the latest software and still do good design. No matter what you need to own, make it last. Cover up your gear and protect it from theft. Get an anti-virus program and back up your work.

💰 ASK A PRO

PAUL SCHMITT
CEO AND PRESIDENT OF (BELIEVE IT OR NOT)
A LOWLY APPRENTICE PRODUCTION (ALAP)

Many software-development companies like yours don't make a profit. I understand that ALAP does. How do you do it?
We have not tried to grow beyond what we could financially support. I think that success has made me more responsible. I realized I have an opportunity not everyone gets, and I should do my best to care for it and help it grow. I think gorging yourself in newfound success is a sure road to failure. I think like I will always be a lowly apprentice. I don't want to get too big-headed.

💰 ACTION ITEM

List everything you need for your business on index cards. Then prioritize them with most important on top to least important on bottom. On each card write the cost. Drop things that don't pay off, and look for less costly alternatives.

Let's Make a Deal

"To form new, frugal habits, develop an awareness about all the small actions you do every day."

—Amy Dacyczyn

When you have a lot in the way of talent and little in the way of money, you are in a pretty good position to get what you want and need. In the old days a skilled hunter could cruise into town and trade his hides and meat for supplies he needed to survive (and hopefully a bath) when out in the woods. Well, we can trade our skills and talents for stuff, too. Singer Jimmy Buffett travels with what he calls his "swag box," which includes "Parrotphernalia" (his own Margaritaville tequila, CDs, books, and T-shirts) and trades these valuables for everything from greasing the wheels in immigration to free drinks. Plus, by giving away gear with his name on it, he's marketing at the same time. Author Joyce Maynard makes a mean poppyseed cake. When she produced a soundtrack to go with one of her books, she sent a cake to each of the great musicians whose music she wanted to use. I understand she wasn't turned down once. You can have a "free trade agreement" with people you want something from, too. You can also offer to refer others in exchange for free services.

Free Help Is a Phone Call Away

Did you know that you can have your very own business consultant for free? The Service Corps of Retired Executives (SCORE) is only a phone call away. They'll send someone who has been there, done that, and kicked ass and now wants nothing more than to help you do it, too. You can also get a free Small Business Startup Kit from the U.S. Small Business Administration. You also may be able to get free helpers in the way of interns who want to learn more about what you do in exchange for helping you get things done. It's a nice trade-off and usually a big boost to your ego to have a protégé hanging on to your every word. Certain trade associations also offer free legal and tax advice.

Nice Bottom . . . Line

I am NOT a fan of big business. Those big retail chains that are gobbling up the mom-and-pop coffee shops and independent bookstores are like a virus spreading to a town near you. But there is a cure. If small businesses are to survive, they have to be smarter, more resourceful, and start to think like big businesses. What I mean is, they have to think about the bottom line. If they do that without losing their individuality and quirkiness, then there is hope. This is true of you, too. As much as we want to make decisions based on what we want to do, we must also look at how it affects our profits. So the next time you need to make a decision that involves spending money, make it with a clear understanding that every dollar that goes out must be replaced by two coming in if you are ever going to grow.

For example, the freelancer who has inventory must be concerned with "turns" (how fast you are able to sell through your stuff and thus make your money back and then some). If you overbuy, it takes longer to get your money back (if you ever do), and this can cost you. If you had done a small test run and found that you had a dud on your hands, you could have used the money left over to produce something that may sell better. Or if you have too many different products, you may also be in danger of being burdened with dead stock. Plus, if you start offering all kinds of products and services, you may need all kinds of equipment. The point is, your decisions should almost always be based on how it affects your bottom line. Maybe you can allow others to rent some of your excess studio space or equipment, or share a secretary. As an employee you may be thinking about joining a trade organization. Ask yourself if you will get your money's worth. Better yet, get your employer to pay.

Real-World Situations: Make-Over

"I realized one day that if I kept going down the path I was on I would never realize my dreams. I would end up being a bitter forty-year-old woman who was deeply in debt. So I made some changes."

—Joan, an aspiring comedienne

"Joan," a stand-up comic living in New York, worked two jobs (not related to her career aspirations) just to keep up with her extravagant lifestyle and mounting debt. She was frustrated because as each year passed, she was getting further and further away from her dream of being able to pursue her comedy career full-time. So on New Year's Day she decided to make some drastic (and much-needed) changes in her life. She realized that if she was ever going to make a go of it as a comedienne, she had to cut back on costs and spend more time on her craft. Here's what she did.

Her biggest expense was her rent. She gave up her expensive Manhattan apartment and moved in with her single sister. Her sister welcomed the idea of having her younger sibling move in and help with household expenses. Another mutual benefit was that the two sisters became closer and better friends. By not having to shell out thousands in rent, Joan was able to quit her coffee-shop job, which meant no more late nights and expensive cab fares home. (She didn't want to ride the subway at that hour.)

She also realized that her coffeehouse gig limited the nights she could perform at open-mike opportunities, something she really wanted and needed to do. (Although a lot of her material came from customers at the coffee shop, the trade-off wasn't worth it.) Her day job as a receptionist provides health care and other perks (plus steady income) so she is keeping it, switching to four ten-hour days instead of a five-day workweek (saving on commuting costs and clothing, and giving her Fridays to work on her comedic material). She now brings her lunch to work and walks in the nearby park.

For entertainment she sees other comics she knows (for free), and she and her sister have found that their favorite thing to do at night is talk and walk around the neighborhood. She began interviewing some of her neighbors and shop owners and discovered a lot of new material on these walks.

With her expenses next to nothing, Joan paid off her credit card debt, got some new headshots and tapes of her act, and began sending them out. Her whole mind-set changed, and she realized that her career was far more important to her than living larger than she really could afford.

 ASK A PRO

BARBARA KAUFMAN, FOUNDER OF CHAPTER 11 BOOKS

Do you have any words of wisdom about managing money?
I believe very strongly that the stock market is the best place to put your money for the long term. I believe you save for a rainy day. I

believe that you don't spend money on little junk. I also believe that you should save until you can afford to buy exactly what you want. I have no qualms about buying a $300 pair of shoes that I love versus three $100 pairs that I only sort of like. I believe in buying for quality over quantity. I will save until I can get a piece of furniture that will not lose its value versus something I will want to replace in a few years.

CONTACT INFORMATION

First, I want you to pat yourself on the back for reading this entire book. I know that when I finished reading several of the books I started while researching this book, I felt empowered because I now had a better understanding of how to make and manage my money. I hope you are filled with that same outlook and sense of optimism now that you have completed *this* book. But with any book, the best of intentions to act on what we have learned wanes as time passes. That's why it's so important we stay connected to support and encourage each other to continue on the path to creative and financial freedom. If I can help you in any way, please feel free to contact me.

For a complete and updated schedule of workshops for the creative person (many offered free in a bookstore near you), bookmark www.creativelee.com, or better yet, invite Lee to speak to your group by calling 858-792-5312.

FREE BONUS CHAPTER

Send a SASE for the free twenty-page booklet
I Did It My Way, filled with tips on
how to start and run your own business.

CreativeLee
SPEAKING™

www.creativelee.com

Lee Silber
c/o CreativeLee Speaking™
11224 Carmel Creek Rd.
San Diego, CA 92130

leesilber@earthlink.net
www.creativelee.com

BIBLIOGRAPHY

In the past when I would research a book I would buy anything and everything I could get my hands on. This became very costly. This time, however, I was able to save money by using the library and Internet to do my research. I did buy a book or two, but for the most part I was very careful about how I spent my research dollars. To save *you* time and expense, let me highlight the best books I read in case you want to continue learning about managing your money.

Amende, Coral. *Rock Confidential.* New York: Plume, 2000.

Bly, Robert W. *Secrets of a Freelance Writer.* New York: Henry Holt and Company, 1997.

Buzzell, Linda. *How to Make It in Hollywood.* New York: HarperCollins, 1996.

Cameron, Julia, and Mark Bryan. *Money Drunk, Money Sober.* New York: Ballantine Publishing Group, 1992.

Caplin, Lee. *The Business of Art.* Paramus, NJ: Prentice Hall Press, 1998.

Carlson, Richard. *Don't Worry, Make Money.* New York: Hyperion, 1997.

Dacyczyn, Amy. *The Tightwad Gazette.* New York: Villard Books, 1992.

Dominguez, Joe, and Vicki Robin. *Your Money or Your Life.* New York: Penguin, 1992. Wow! This is a life-altering book. I loved it.

Edelman, Ric. *The New Rules of Money.* New York: HarperCollins, 1998.

Edwards, Paul, and Sara Edwards. *Finding Your Perfect Work.* New York: Jeremy P. Tarcher/Putnam, 1996.

Fein, Art. *The Greatest Rock & Roll Stories.* Los Angeles: General Publishing Group, 1996.

Gallon, Mitch. *Stop Worrying About Money.* New York: Hatherleigh Press, 1997.

Getty, J. Paul. *How to Be Rich.* New York: Jove Books, 1965. The title says it all.

Grant, Daniel. *The Business of Being an Artist.* New York: Allworth Press, 1996.

Hopkins, Del, and Margaret Hopkins. *Careers as a Rock Musician.* New York: Rosen Publishing Group, 1993.

Isenberg, Barbara. *State of the Arts.* New York: HarperCollins, 2000.

Jamison, Kay R. *An Unquiet Mind.* New York: Vintage, 1995. A powerful and moving book that opened my eyes to what some creative people have to overcome to create.

Kelly, Jason. *The Neatest Little Guide to Personal Finance.* New York: Plume, 1999.

Koslow, Brian. *365 Ways to Become a Millionaire (Without Being Born One).* New York: Penguin Putnam, 1999.

Lathrop, Tad, and Jim Pettigrew Jr. *This Business of Music Marketing & Promotion.* New York: Billboard Books, 1999.

Lerner, Betsy. *The Forest for the Trees.* New York: Riverhead Books, 2000.

Lesonsky, Rieva, and Gayle Sato Stodder. *Young Millionaires.* Irvine, CA: Entrepreneur Media, 1998.

Levinson, Jay Conrad, and Kathryn Tyler. *Guerrilla Saving.* New York: John Wiley & Sons, 2000.

Lewis, M. K., and Rosemary Lewis. *Your Film Acting Career.* Santa Monica, CA: Gorham House, 1993.

Mariotti, Steve, and Mike Caslin, with Debra DeSalvo. *The Very, Very Rich.* Franklin Lakes, NJ: Career Press, 2000.

Maisel, Eric. *A Life in the Arts.* New York: Jeremy P. Tarcher/ Putnam, 1994.

McCormack, John. *Self-Made in America.* New York: Addison-Wesley Publishing, 1990.

Michels, Caroll. *How to Survive & Prosper as an Artist.* New York: Henry Holt and Company, 1997.

Monroe, Paula Ann. *Left-Brain Finance for Right-Brain People.* Naperville, IL: Sourcebooks, 1998. With a title like this . . . I learned a lot from this book.

Mundis, Jerrold. *How to Get Out of Debt, Stay Out of Debt & Live*

Prosperously. New York: Bantam Books, 1988. This is one of those books you are embarrassed to buy but really want to read. It was worth the raised eyebrow from the cashier at the bookstore.

O'Connor, Karen. *A Woman's Place Is in the Mall and Other Lies.* Nashville, TN: Thomas Nelson Publishers, 1995. This was a very good book.

Orman, Suze. *The 9 Steps to Financial Freedom.* New York: Crown, 1997.

Oseary, Guy. *Jews Who Rock.* New York: St. Martin's Press, 2001.

Perry, Joan, with Dolores Barclay. *A Girl Needs Cash.* New York: Times Books, 1997. We ALL need cash. I read this book while on vacation and because of the title (and the fact the cover is pink) I got a lot of curious looks from people who saw me reading it. I didn't care. This was an outstanding book—for everyone.

Pond, Jonathan. *1001 Ways to Cut Your Expenses.* New York: Dell Publishing, 1992.

Rosanoff, Nancy. *The Complete Idiot's Guide to Making Money Through Intuition.* New York: Alpha Books, 1999.

Rozakis, Laurie. *The Complete Idiot's Guide to Making Money in Freelancing.* New York: Alpha Books, 1998.

Schwartz, Daylle Deanna. *Start and Run Your Own Record Label.* New York: Billboard Press, 1998.

Silber, Lee. *Time Management for the Creative Person.* New York: Three Rivers Press, 1998.

__. *Career Management for the Creative Person.* New York: Three Rivers Press, 1999.

__. *Self-Promotion for the Creative Person.* New York: Three Rivers Press, 2001.

Spurge, Lorraine. *Money Clips.* New York: Hyperion, 2000.

Stanfield, Jana. *The Musician's Guide to Making & Selling Your Own CDs & Cassettes.* Cincinnati, OH: Writer's Digest Books, 1997. This book is required reading for every working musician and those who want to be.

Stanley, Thomas, and William Danko. *The Millionaire Next Door.* New York: Pocket Books, 1996. This really is a groundbreaking book and a must-read for anyone interested in financial security.

St. James, Elaine. *Living the Simple Life.* New York: Hyperion, 1996.

Stone, Clement W. *The Success System That Never Fails.* New York:

Pocket Books, 1962. This book has been on my bookshelf for
YEARS. I decided to dust it off and read it again. It was even better than I remembered. A classic book with timeless ideas.

Warren, Roz. *Women's Lip.* Naperville, IL: Hysteria Publications,
1998.

Wuorio, Jeff. *Got Money?* New York: AMA Publications, 1999. This
book is LOADED with phone numbers and websites that provide
financial advice. This book is a good investment.

Variety editors. *The Variety History of Show Business.* New York:
Harry N. Abrams, 1993.

INDEX

AAA (Automobile Club of America), 290

Accomplishments, journal of, 147–148, 153

Accountants, 182, 185

Adams, Scott, 18, 61–62

Advisers, *see* Financial advisers

Affirmations, 49–52, 62

Agents, 144–145, 151, 154, 155, 177, 182

Alexakis, Art, 65

Alexander, Daena Title, 22, 183

Alexander, Jason, 22, 183

Allure, 182

Alpert, Herb, 167–168

American Airlines, 279

American Express credit card, 112

American Pie (film), 10

A&M Records, 167–168

Anderson, Ian, 174

Anderson, Pamela Lee, 158, 286

Anderson, Sherwood, 32

Antin, Eleanor, 218–219

Apocalypse Now (film), 267

Apple Computers, 195, 306

Applegate, Jane, 20

Aragon Consulting Group, 214

Arc of a Diver (Winwood), 68

Are You Normal About Money? (Kanner), 295

Arnaz, Desi, 28, 153

Art industry, 22–26

Artwork, protection of, 213

Assets, protection of, 213

Association, success by, 137–138

ATMs, 208–210

Attitude, artistic, 136–137

Authors Guild, 178, 190

Automatic saving, 241

Automobile insurance, 214

Automobiles, 288–291

Awards, 138–139

Azoff, Irving, 150

Bach, Richard, 195

Bacon, Kevin, 166, 176

Bacon, Michael, 166

Bader, David M., 67

Bad habits, 5

Bailey, Pearl, 199

Baldessari, John, 306

Ball, Lucille, 28, 101, 153

Bam Bam, 267

Banking, 208–211

Bankruptcy, 111

Barnes & Noble, 178

Barter, 218

Bean, Leon, 57

Beautiful Losers (Cohen), 172

Beck, Jeff, 267

Beland, Nicole, 295

Bell, Catherine, 82

Benatar, Pat, 167

Bening, Annette, 298

Berger, Suzy, 143

Berle, Milton, 111, 146

Berliner, Andy, 306

Berliner, Rachel, 306

Berman, Gail, 164

Bernhard, Sandra, 167

Berryhill, Cindy Lee, 114, 165

Best, Pete, 177

Bialik, Mayim, 59

"Big Fix" mentality, 35–36

Biggs, Jason, 138

Big-picture thinking, 30–31

Billing, 205–207

Billings, Josh, 70

Bill-paying, 204, 207–208

Binoche, Juliette, 91
Body Shop, 306
Boiardi, Hector "Chef," 165–166
Bolton, John, 176
Bonds, 254
Bon Jovi, John, 174
Book-keeping, 199–204
Bowie, David, xi, 225
Brach, Emil, 157
Brand New Day (Sting), 263
Brandy, 255
Bravo, Manuel Alvarez, 61
Braxton, Toni, 111
Breathnach, Sarah Ban, 68
Brecht, Bertolt, 48
Brokerage accounts, 210
Brolin, James, 203
Brooks, Garth, 167
Brown, James, 217
Brown, Patty, 201
Brown, Rob, 164
Browne, Merry, 285
"B-skills," 169–170
Buckingham, Lindsey, 68
Budgeting, 228–233
Buffett, Jimmy, 112, 146, 162, 173, 174,
      186, 298, 305, 312
Buffett, Warren, 224, 247, 249
Burke, Delta, 304
Burpee, John, 164
Burroughs, William, 268
Business expenses, 202, 305–313
Business plans, 271
Business ventures, 255
Butler, Brett, 156
Byrne, Robert, 55

Cahill, Eddie, 295
Cahn, Elliot, 191
Caiati, Manny, 191
Cameron, James, 129
Cameron, Julia, 17, 74
Caporilli, Peter, 164
Capote, Truman, 145
Capshaw, Kate, 161
Career, investing in, 266–269
*Career Management for the Creative
      Person* (Silber), 108
Carelessness, 122–123

Carlisle, Belinda, 167
Carrey, Jim, 85
Carter, Judy, 208
Carter, Regina, 214
Cash-basis method, 202
Cashing in, 19
Castle, Bernadine, 302
Chandler, Raymond, 68
Change, 36, 89–90
Chapter 7 bankruptcy, 111
Chapter 11 bankruptcy, 111
Checking accounts, 204, 210
Cher, 226
Childs, Julia, 296
Chrematophobia, 77–78
Christian, Holly, 138
Churchill, Winston, 240
Cigarette smoking, 302
Clapton, Eric, 243
Classic cars, 289
Clooney, George, 167, 212
Clothes, 294–295
Clutter, 33
Cocker, Joe, 167
Coffee Will Make You Black (Sinclair), 67
Cohen, Leonard, 172
Cole, Natalie, 115–116
Coleman, Gary, 10, 188
Collectibles, investing in, 255
College costs, 236
Collins, Phil, 174
Commuting costs, 286
Comparison shopping, 284
Comparison with others, 83–84
*Complete Idiot's Guide to Making
      Money Through Intuition, The*
      (Rosanoff), 89
Compulsive spenders, 98
Confidence, 153
Consumer Reports, 284
Contracts, 191, 194–198
Cooke, Sam, 267
Coppola, Francis Ford, 267
Copyrights, 177, 193, 198–199, 215
Corcoran, Tom, 173
Cosby, John, 179–180
Costner, Kevin, 167
Covey, Stephen, 182
Creative accounting, 185
Creative financing, 153

Creative life, xv, 1–37
  artistic temperament and, 21
  arts as a business, 22–26
  bad habits and, 5
  big-picture thinking and, 30–31
  cashing in and, 19
  day jobs and, 18, 26
  debt and, 99–100
  decision-making and, 17–18
  dreams and, 6, 15–17
  factors preventing financial freedom, 26–28
  financial planning and, 13–14
  importance of money and, 2–3, 7, 21–22
  insurance and, 20
  investing and, *see* Investing
  luck and, 19–20
  marketing and, 11–12
  millionaire potential and, 15
  money mind-set and, 7–9
  multiple revenue streams and, 18–19
  passion and, 17
  respect for money and, 11
  right-brain thinking drawbacks, 32–37
  right-brain *vs.* left-brain thinking and, 1–2, 5, 16, 28–30
  risk-taking and, 20, 31–32
  self-starting and, 19
  size of income and, 20
  "starving artist" image and, 13–15
  traditional money management books and, 1
  trust and, 13
Creative vision, 139–140
Creativity, xvi
Credit cards, 94–95, 100–103, 106–108, 112, 202–204, 213, 225
Credit reports, 107, 203
Credit unions, 209
Creed, 268
Creedance Clearwater Revival, 194
Crime, 121
Cusack, John, 195–196

Dacyczyn, Amy, 312
Daltrey, Roger, 174

Dangerfield, Rodney, 120
Darwish, Tiffany, 239
Dating expenses, 299–300
David, Larry, 85
Day jobs, xvi, 18, 26, 40, 163–171
Debit cards, 204, 211
Debt, 94–114
  acceptable, 94
  bad, 94
  bankruptcy and, 111
  compulsive spenders and, 98
  consolidation of, 104
  creative life and, 99–100
  credit card, 94–95, 100–103, 106–108, 112, 225
  denial about, 104
  emotions and, 97
  income level and, 95
  prevention of, 112–113
  reduction of, 103–111
  self-esteem and, 96
  selfishness and, 97
  tracking, 96, 107, 109, 112
Decision-making, 17–18, 85–93
Denial, 26–27
Denton, Eric, 12
Destructive habits, 301–302
Details, dealing with, 33
Devine, Jeff, 61
De Vries, Peter, 217
DiCaprio, Leonardo, 189
Dido, 165
DiMucci, Dion, 279
Disability insurance, 214
Discounts, 283–284
Disorganization, 33
Divergent thinking, 36–37
Dividends, 252
Divorce, 116–117
Dr. Seuss, 28
Dolby Sound, 176
Dolphin, Johnny, 177
Dominguez, Joe, 114
Donahue, Heather, 213–214
Dorsey, Lee, 242
Dow Jones Industrial Average, 250
Downey, Michelle, 204
Down payments, 263, 264
"Drama queens," 33
Dream board, 52

Dreams, 6, 15–17, 38–40, 52
  See also Goals
Drinking alcohol, 301–302
Duchovny, David, 167
Duritz, Adam, 168
Dylan, Bob, 68
Dyson, Kat, 269

Earnings target, 127
East, Nathan, 137
Educational attainment, 139
Einstein, Albert, 28
Einstein, Elsa, 28
Electronic bill-paying, 207–208
Elfman, Jenna, 118, 270, 285
Elwood, Gordon, 304
Emergency money, 236–237
Emerson, Ralph Waldo, 257–258
Emotions, 34, 97
Engelbreit, Mary, 161
Entertainment expenses, 298–299
Entwistle, John, 243
Estimated taxes, 217
Ethics, code of, 91

Faithfull, Marianne, 175
Fame, xvi
Family Productions, 187
Fanning, Shawn, 193–194
Farley, Chris, 189
Farley, William, 147
Far Side, The (Larson), 176
Faulkner, William, 82
Favorite Game, The (Cohen), 172
Favreau, Jon, 157
Fear, 6, 53–54, 77–79, 82, 131
Fees, 129, 140–156, 179–180
Feist, Raymond, 161
Ferrari, Enzo, 288
Ferry, Brian, 166
Fields, Debbie, 185
Fields, W. C., 189, 225
Financial advisers, 4, 181–199
  choosing, 183, 188–189
  cost of, 186–187
  lawyers, 155, 177, 190–198
  learning from, 187
  level of success and, 186
  need for, 181–183
  problems with, 184–185, 187–190
  qualities of, 185–186, 188
  taxes and, 216
  trust and, 181
Financial insecurity, 24–25
Financial planning, 13–14, 269–273
Fisher, Carrie, 229
Fixed expenses, 233
Flea, 174, 188
Fleetwood, Mick, 111
Fleming, Peggy, 40
Fletcher, Cyril, 119
Fletch (film), 106
Flynn, P., 262
Fogerty, John, 194
Following the Equator (Twain), 112
Fonda, Bridget, 279
Food expenses, 296–297
Forbes, 228, 250
Forbes, Malcolm, 147
Ford, Diane, 116
Forest for the Trees, The (Lerner), 149
401(k) plans, 255–257
Foxx, Redd, 217
Frakes, Jonathan, 173
Franklin, Aretha, 192
Franklin, Ben, 172, 221
Franks, Michael, 179
Frantz, Chris, 165
Franz, Dennis, 167
Frasier (TV program), 252
Freak Out (Mothers of Invention), 268
Friends (TV program), 155, 232,
  238–239
Front end, 26
Frugality, 274–315
  borrowing *vs.* buying and, 283
  business expenses and, 305–313
  cars and, 288–291
  clothes and, 294–295
  comparison shopping and, 284
  dating and, 299–300
  destructive habits and, 301–302
  discounts and, 283–284
  entertainment and, 298–299
  food and, 296–297
  freedom and, 281
  gift-giving and, 300–301
  impressing others and, 280

impulse buying and, 282–283
limits on, 304–305
make-over example of, 313–314
needs *vs.* wants and, 282
organization and, 285
perks and, 305
preventive medicine and, 294
residence and, 285–288
resourcefulness and, 281
sacrifice and, 276
telemarketing and, 302–303
telephone expenses and, 303
travel and, 291–293
value and, 279–280
Fuchs, Jackie, 191

Gabriel, Peter, 154, 167
Gallon, Mitch, 225–226
Gallup Poll, 299
Gambling, 120–121
Gandhi, Mohandas, 22
Garcia, Jerry, 171
Gardner, David, 250
Garfunkel, Art, 248
Gates, Bill, 195
Giacchetto, Dana, 189
Gift-giving, 300–301
Gish, Lillian, 142
Giuliani, Rudolph, 212
Goals, 38–72
   affirmations and, 49–52
   financial freedom, 125
   financing of, 42–44
   hard work and, 61–66
   importance of, 39
   limitless thinking and, 53–54
   money biography and, 38
   passion and, 55–61
   perseverance and, 67–70
   planning and, 39–40, 269–273
   saving and, 241
   support and, 70–71
   time and, 66–67
   traditional careers and, 40–41
   visualization and, 39, 42
   zero debt, 107, 110
Goethe, Johann Wolfgang von, 85
Gogh, Vincent van, 68
Goldberg, Whoopi, 68

Goodman, John, 167
Gordon, Jim, 179
Gordy, Berry, 268, 269
Gosselin, Kim, 19
Grafton, Sue, 64, 165
Grant, Hugh, 86
Green, Brenda, 138
Griffith, Melanie, 17, 267
Groening, Matt, 55, 198, 219
Grove, Bob, 255

Haggard, Merle, 115
Hall, Daryl, 257
Hamilton, Virginia, 139
Hammer, MC, 119
Hampton, Lionel, 212
Hannah, Daryl, 121–122
Hansen, Beck, 69
Happiness, money and, 83
Hard Candy, 185
Hard work, 61–66
Harpo Productions, 174
Harris Poll, 207
Harvey Penick's Little Red Book, 149
Haskins, Ernest, 237
Hayek, Selma, 182
Hayes, Isaac, 111
Hays, Robert, 240–241
Health habits, 117
Health insurance, 213–214
Heat-Moon, William Least, 60–61
Heckerling, Amy, 59, 138
Henley, Don, 55, 90
Hepburn, Katherine, 42
Hidden costs, 141
Hill, Faith, 165
Hoag, Tami, 16
Hoffman, Alice, 202
Hoffman, Dustin, 199
Holland, Dave, 235
Home equity loans, 104, 107
Homeowner's insurance, 214–215
Honeymoon in Vegas (film), 120
Hooker, John Lee, 178
Hotels, 292
Hubbard, Frank, 243–244
Hunt, Mary, xv
Hunter, Evan, 162
Hynde, Chrissie, 167

Iacocca, Lee, 288
Impulse buying, 282–283
Indecent Proposal (film), 120
Indigo Girls, 162–163
Inflation, 140, 145
Insurance, 20, 212–215
Intellectual property, 122
Interest rates, 264
Internet, 251
Intuition, 89–92, 257–259
Investing, 12, 29, 243–269
  in business ventures, 255
  in career, 266–269
  in collectibles, 255
  in 401(k) plans, 255–257
  goal of, 243–244
  intuition and, 257–262
  learning, 247–248
  readiness for, 248
  in real estate, 244, 262–266
  risk and, 31–32, 245–247
  in stock, 249–255
  wealth accumulation and, 227
Investment brokers, 184
Iovine, Jimmy, 11
IRS audits, 218
It's a Wonderful Life (film), 208
Ivy, Percy, 177

Jackson, Valerie, 198
Jagger, Mick, 140
Jean, Wyclef, 165
Jett, Joan, 251
Jewel, 14, 133, 174
Jive Records, 163
Jobs, Steve, 306
Joel, Billy, 23, 187–188
Johnson, Samuel, 145
Jones, Franklin, 294
Jones, Rickie Lee, 68–69
Jong, Erica, 53
Judas Priest, 193
"Jump, Jive and Wail" (Setzer), 267
Junger, Sebastian, 20, 288

Kanarek, Lisa, 205
Kanner, Bernice, 295
Kaplan, Dave, 219–220

Kaplan, Gabe, 249
Karan, Donna, 257
Katz, Steve, 168
Kaufman, Barbara, 314–315
Kaye, Lenny, 168
Keats, John, 298
Kelley, Steve, 166
Kelly, Jason, 245
Kinnock, Neil, 302
Klainer, Pamela York, 38
Knopfler, Mark, 69
Koontz, Dean, 164
Kournikova, Anna, 80
Krall, Diana, 179
Kudrow, Lisa, 28

Lamas, Lorenzo, 167
Lamb, Jennifer, 41
Larson, Gary, 176
Lauper, Cyndi, 167
Lauren, Ralph, 176
Lawyers, 155, 177, 190–198
"Layla" (Clapton and Gordon), 179
Leasing *vs.* buying cars, 289–290
Leblond, Rich, 263
Lee, Spike, 173
Left-brain *vs.* right-brain thinking, 1–2,
    5, 16, 28–30, 91–92, 271
Lemmon, Jack, 55–56
Lennon, John, 222
Leo Burnett, 142–143
Leonardo da Vinci, 172
Lerner, Betsy, 133, 149
Leverage, 155
Lewis, Jerry Lee, 192
Lewis, Joe E., 234
Lewis, Richard, 301–302
Life expectancy, 233
Life in Hell (cartoon), 198
Life insurance, 214
Limitless thinking, 53–54, 76–80
Litigation, 191
Little Richard, 192
Living fast, 34
Lloyd, Charles, 195
Long Program, The (Fleming), 40
Lonstein, Shoshanna, 42
Love, Courtney, 167
Lowe, Rob, 295

Lowell, Christopher, 286
Loy, Myrna, 44
Lucas, George, 155
Lucas Arts Entertainment, 305
Luck, 19–20
Lumsden, Robert, 270
Lynne, Shelby, 121
Lynn Marie, 136

MacFarlane, Seth, 162
Mademoiselle, 295
Madonna, 199
Magnum P.I. (TV program), 97, 176
Mahoney, John, 54
Maisel, Eric, 171
Making of a Bestseller (Vanderbilt),
    58–59
Managers, 182, 185
Manheim, Camryn, 166
Manilow, Barry, 267
Mann, Barry, 178
"Margaritaville" (Buffett), 174
Marin, Cheech, 172
Marketability, xvii, 11–12, 133–140,
    144, 169
Mason, Jackie, 300
Math skills, 32–33
Maugham, W. Somerset, 257
Max, Peter, 217
Maynard, Joyce, 156–157, 312
McCartney, Paul, 124
McCormack, Ed, 260
McDonald, Judy, 87–88
McLaren, Malcolm, 149
Meat Loaf, 111
Medical bills, 214
Mellow Gold (Hansen), 69
Melton, Barry "The Fish," 191
"Memory" (Lloyd Webber and Nunn),
    177
Merrill Lynch, 240
Mesa-Bains, Amalia, 184
Messiness, 33
Michael, George, 167
Michelangelo, 8, 137
Michels, Caroll, 194
Millionaire Next Door, The, 288
Millionaire potential, 15
Mission Impossible (film), 24

Mitchell, Joni, 118
Mitchell-Smith, Ilan, 59
Moby, 179
Mohajer, Dineh, 185
Mohajer, Pooneh, 185
Mohammed, 8
Money:
    easy, 118–119
    importance of, 2–3, 7, 21–22
    lending, 119
    myths about, xv–xviii, 10–11
    power of, 128–129
    respect for, 11
    up-front, 205–206
Money biography, 38
Money generation, 124–180
    creative solutions for, 156–160
    day jobs, xvi, 18, 26, 40, 163–171
    discussing fees, 131–132
    earnings target and, 127
    marketability and, xvii, 11–12,
        133–140, 144, 169
    multiple streams of income, 171–175
    negotiating and, 129, 144–145,
        144–156
    power of money and, 128–129
    raising fees, 140–141, 144, 148
    royalties, 175–179
    setting fees, 142–144
    support and, 161–163
    valuing one's worth and, 130–133
    waiving fees and, 145–146
Money-market accounts, 244
Money mind-set, 7–9, 132
Monroe, Marilyn, 130
Monroes, The, 12
Monthly expenditures, 229–232
Mood swings, 34
Moore, Demi, 263
Moore, John, 291
Moore, Lorrie, 58
Morissette, Alanis, 174
Morris, Jim, 85
Morrison, Shana, 15
Morrison, Van, 15
Morrissey, 243
Morse, Samuel F. B., 172
Mortgage interest, 264, 265
Mortgage payments, 264
Moss, Jerry, 167

Mothers of Invention, 268
Motown Records, 268
Munoz, Sylvia, 157
Musicians, 114, 201, 219–220
Mutual funds, 245, 254–255
"My Eyes Adored You" (Valli), 267
My Own Prison (Creed), 268

Naisbitt, John, 190
Napster, 194
Needs *vs.* wants, 113–114, 282
Negotiating, 129, 144–156
Neil, Vince, 167
Nelson, Willie, 217
Net worth, 225–226
Newman, Paul, 179
Newman, Randy, 21
Newton, Wayne, 111
Niche markets, 136, 138
Nicks, Stevie, 68, 167
Nilsson, Harry, 4, 189
Norton, Edward, 84
Nunn, Trevor, 176–177

O'Donnell, Rosie, 174
Office furniture and equipment,
    310–311
"Old Man Down the Road, The"
    (Fogerty), 194
Omidyar, Pierre, 279
101 Home Office Success Secrets
    (Kanarek), 205
Online banking, 209
On-the-job training, 170
Orbison, Roy, 68
Orman, Suze, 21, 188
Outterbridge, John, 305
Owens, Peter, 53

Pace, Elizabeth, 58
Palm Pilot, 203
Parfitt, Rick, 49
Parker, Dorothy, 204
Parker, George, 17, 159
Parker, Sarah Jessica, 278
Parton, Dolly, 266
Partying, 117–118

Passion, 17, 55–61
Patents, 193, 199
Patience, 34–35
Peale, Norman Vincent, 89
Peanuts (cartoon), 162
Peart, Neil, 186
Penick, Harvey, 149
Penn, Sean, 166
Performance improvement, 136
Perkins, Stephen, 267
Perks, 148, 305
Perseverance, 67–70, 83, 85
Perspective, 81, 107, 114
Peters, Tom, 137
Petty, Tom, 111, 232
Pfeiffer, Michelle, 236
Philbin, Regis, 138
Picasso, Pablo, 172, 244
Pitfalls, 73–123
    bad health habits, 117
    bad relationships, 121–122
    carelessness, 122–123
    crime, 121
    debt, *see* Debt
    decision-making and, 85–93
    divorce, 116–117
    easy money, 118–119
    gambling, 120–121
    handling success badly, 118
    intellectual property and, 122
    lending money, 119
    musicians and, 114
    partying, 117–118
    perseverance and, 83, 85
    procrastination, 116
    recognition of, 73–74
    scams, 119–120
    self-esteem and, 74–85, 96, 115
Planet Hollywood, 255
Planning, 13–14, 39–40, 269–273
Plant, Robert, 1
"Popsicle Toes" (Franks), 179
Positive thinking, 27, 80–82
Poundstone, Paula, 207
Powell, Cozy, 139
Presley, Elvis, 207
Preston, Kelly, 278
Probst, Jeff, 78–79
Procrastination, 116
Publicists, 186–187

Purple Skirt (Purple Pants), 255
Puryear, Martin, 215

Quan, Dionne, 84
Quicken, 203
Quindlen, Anna, 85–86

Raises, 148
Raphael, 137
Rate card, 144
Rauschenberg, Robert, 10–11
Ray, Amy, 163
Real estate investments, 244, 262–266
Realsongs, 175
Red flags, 218
Refinancing cars, 290
Reliability, 137
Renter's insurance, 214–215
Renting, 265–266, 287
Report from Engine Co. 82 (Smith), 43
Reputation, 136–137, 156
Residence, 262–266, 285–288
Residuals, 176
Retirement, xvi, 235–236, 255–257
Revenue streams, multiple, 18–19
Revenue Systems Inc., 305
Reynolds, Nick, 178
Rhodes, Zandra, 138
Rice, Ann, 287
Rice, Christopher, 287
Rice, Stan, 287
Rich, Buddy, 34
Richards, Keith, 228–229
Right-brain thinking, 1–2, 5, 16, 28–30,
    32–37, 91–92, 271
Righteous Brothers, 194
Ringgold, Faith, 172–173
Ripp, Artie, 187
Risk-taking, xv, 20, 31–32, 245–247
River-Horse (Heat-Moon), 60
Rivers, Joan, 94
Roberts, Julia, 91
Roberts, Nora, 285
Robin, Vicki, 114
Roddick, Anita, 306
Rodriguez, Alex, 136
Rogers, Will, 215
Roland Users Group, 65

Rolling Stone, 99
Rolling Stones, 134
Rollins, Henry, 167, 174
Romano, Ray, 156
Ronstadt, Linda, 279
Rosanoff, Nancy, 89
Rosenberg, Flash, 61
Roth, David Lee, 154
Royalties, 175–179
Run for Your Life (TV program), 42
"Run Through the Jungle" (Fogerty), 194
Russell, Bertrand, 115
Ruthless People (film), 132

Safety deposit boxes, 213
St. Onge, Joan, 294
Sandler, Adam, 26
Saving, xvi, 5, 25, 31, 221–244
    automatic, 241
    budgeting and, 228–233
    career time lines and, 235
    college costs and, 236
    consistency in, 221–222
    emergency money and, 236–237
    excuses and, 237–240
    financial freedom and, 234–235
    frugality and, *see* Frugality
    income tracking and, 232–233
    investing and, *see* Investing
    for low-income cycles, 236
    net worth and, 225–226
    for retirement, 235–236
    security and, 235
    suggestions for, 240–243
    toward a goal, 241
    wealth and, 223–224, 226–228
Schmitt, Paul, 311
Segal Co., 139
Seger, Bob, 69, 102
Self-esteem, 74–85, 96, 115, 235
Self-sabotage, 115
Self-starting, 19
Selleck Tom, 176
Selling items for cash, 158
Sellman, Jane, 161
Service Corps of Retired Executives
    (SCORE), 312
Setzer, Brian, 267
Severson, John, 55

Seymour, Jane, 76
Shatner, William, 90
Shawshank Redemption, The (film), 38
Sheen, Charlie, 118
Sherak, Tom, 133
Simmons, Gene, 135, 149
Simon, Paul, 248
Simple Abundance (Breathnach), 68
Sinatra, Frank, 62–63
Sinclair, April, 67
Sixth Sense, The (film), 257
Slaughter, Mark, 69
Small-claims court, 207
Smith, Anna Nicole, 299
Smith, Dennis, 42–43
Smith, Margaret, 228
Smith, Sunshine, 161–162
Smith, Will, 102
Snell, David, 99
Snider, Dee, 168
Somers, Suzanne, 154
Soul Beat, 58
Spafford, Suzy, 174
Spears, Britney, 163
Spector, Phil, 194
Spectrum Group, 256
Spelling, Aaron, 222
Spending habits, 228–232, 242
Spending journal, 112
Spielberg, Steven, 161
Spike's Joint, 173
Stained Glass (Judas Priest), 193
"Starving artist" life, 13–15, 40, 130, 221
Steele, John Washington, 113
Stefani, Gwen, 45
Stein, Gertrude, 226
Stein, Jules, 185
Steinbeck, John, 163
Stevenson, Adlai, 5
Stewart, Jon, 163
Stifler, Steve, 10
Sting, 111, 174, 179, 181, 263, 274
Stock investing, 249–255
Stock options, 148, 253–254
Stone, Sharon, 123
Stone, Sly, 111, 116
Stop Worrying About Money! (Gallon), 225–226
Streisand, Barbra, 203, 277

Student loans, 102–103, 107
Subotnick, Morton, 173
Summers, Andy, 90
Support, 70–71, 161–163
"Suzanne" (Cohen), 172
Suzy's Zoo, 174

Taxes, 200, 215–220
Taylor, James, 10
Taylor, Lili, 91
Taylor, Sir Henry, 282
Technology stocks, 258
Telemarketing, 302–303
Telephone expenses, 303
Thakkar, Darshan, 203
Thomas, Seth, 155
Thoreau, Henry David, 12
Tidewater Workshop, 164
Tipping, 297–298
"Tom Dooley" (Kingston Trio), 178
Tomlin, Lily, 291
Tovey, Robin, 84
Track record, 155
Trademarks, 193, 199
Traffic tickets, 290–291
Travel, 291–293
Travel Holiday, 278
Travolta, John, 267
Trend-spotting, 90
Trump, Donald, 111
Trust, 13, 181, 197
Tull, Jethro, 174
Turk, Mike, 158
Turner, Ted, 42
Turner, Tina, 101
Turtle Bay Hilton, Oahu, 169
Twain, Mark, 112

Ullman, Tracy, 255
Umbrella insurance, 215
Unemployment insurance income, 158
Unity Marketing, 4
Updike, John, 228
Up-front money, 205–206
Upgrades, discretionary, 293
U.S. Small Business Administration, 312
USA Today polls, 220, 287
Used cars, 288–289

Valassis Communications, 305
Valli, Frankie, 267
Vanderbilt, Arthur T., II, 58–59
Van Halen, 154
Variable costs, 233
Velez, Eddie, 64
Velez, Lauren, 106
Visualization, 39, 42
Voigt, Deborah, 59–60

Wahlberg, Mark, 99–100
Waits, Tom, 199
Waiving fees, 145–146
Walkaway power, 154
Walken, Christopher, 232
Walker, Georgianne, 84
Walton, Sam, 138
Wants *vs.* needs, 113–114, 282
Warhol, Andy, 133, 171–172
Warren, Diane, 175
Washington, Walter "Wolfman,"
    242
Waters, Muddy, 178
Wayans, Keenen Ivory, 64
Wayne, John, 249
Wealth, 223–224, 226–228
Weil, Cynthia, 178
Weinstein, Joel, 145
Welnick, Vince, 179
West, Dottie, 217
West, Mae, 236

Weymouth, Tina, 165
"What if?" scenarios, 92
Where Love Goes (Maynard), 157
Wilkes, James, 147
Willis, Bruce, 257, 263
Wilson, Brian, 190
Winfrey, Oprah, 174, 288
Winwood, Steve, 68
Wise, Anita, 178
Wonder, Stevie, 193
Work-for-hire agreement, 198
Working Girl (film), 17
Wozniak, Steve, 139, 195
Writers Guild, 24
Wyle, Noah, 128

Yearwood, Trisha, 187
Yoakum, Dwight, 279
Young, Neil, 139
Your Money or Your Life (Dominguez
    and Robin), 114
You've Got Mail (film), 78
"You've Lost That Loving Feeling"
    (Spector, Mann, and
    Weil/Righteous Brothers), 194

Zappa, Frank, 117–118, 268
Zellweger, Renee, 80
Zeta-Jones, Catherine, 116
Ziglar, Zig, 266

ABOUT THE AUTHOR

Lee Silber understands better than anyone the challenges of making and managing money as a creative person. In addition to being the author of nine books, including *Self-Promotion for the Creative Person, Career Management for the Creative Person,* and *Time Management for the Creative Person,* Lee is an accomplished graphic artist, drummer, workshop leader, radio talk show host, and the founder of five companies. Lee resides with his wife in San Diego, California. For more about Lee Silber and his books visit www.creativelee.com.